Social Media Strategies for Tourism Interactivity

Célia M.Q. Ramos
University of Algarve, Portugal

Teresa Costa
Instituto Politécnico de Setúbal, Portugal

Filipe Segurado Severino
Estoril Higher Institute for Tourism and Hotel Studies, Portugal

Maria de Lurdes Calisto
Estoril Higher Institute for Tourism and Hotel Studies, Portugal

A volume in the Advances in Hospitality, Tourism, and the Services Industry (AHTSI) Book Series

IGI Global
PUBLISHER of TIMELY KNOWLEDGE

Published in the United States of America by
IGI Global
Business Science Reference (an imprint of IGI Global)
701 E. Chocolate Avenue
Hershey PA, USA 17033
Tel: 717-533-8845
Fax: 717-533-8661
E-mail: cust@igi-global.com
Web site: http://www.igi-global.com

Library of Congress Cataloging-in-Publication Data

Names: Ramos, Célia M. Q., editor. | Costa, Teresa Gomes da, 1964- editor. | Severino, Filipe Segurado, 1990- editor. | Calisto, Maria de Lurdes, 1965- editor.
Title: Social media strategies for tourism interactivity / Edited by Célia Ramos, Teresa Costa, Filipe Severino, Maria de Lurdes Calisto.
Description: Hershey, PA : Business Science Reference, 2024. | Includes bibliographical references and index. | Summary: "In an increasingly interconnected world, with the uncertainty related to new tourist behaviors, and the pressure towards a circular economy, coopetition between TMSEs might be the most effective way to respond (collaboratively) to the challenges ahead, using technological advances to their benefit, promoting digitalization, gaining scale, more efficient use of resources, and rapid adaptation of the tourism product to the new demand in balance with sustainable concerns"-- Provided by publisher.
Identifiers: LCCN 2023055030 (print) | LCCN 2023055031 (ebook) | ISBN 9798369309605 (hardcover) | ISBN 9798369309612 (ebook)
Subjects: LCSH: Tourism--Information technology. | Social media--Influence. | Tourism--Internet marketing. | Consumer behavior.
Classification: LCC G156.5.I5 S63 2024 (print) | LCC G156.5.I5 (ebook) | DDC 910.68/8--dc23/eng/20231228
LC record available at https://lccn.loc.gov/2023055030
LC ebook record available at https://lccn.loc.gov/2023055031

This book is published in the IGI Global book series Advances in Hospitality, Tourism, and the Services Industry (AHTSI) (ISSN: 2475-6547; eISSN: 2475-6555)

British Cataloguing in Publication Data
A Cataloguing in Publication record for this book is available from the British Library.
All work contributed to this book is new, previously-unpublished material.
The views expressed in this book are those of the authors, but not necessarily of the publisher.
For electronic access to this publication, please contact: eresources@igi-global.com.

Advances in Hospitality, Tourism, and the Services Industry (AHTSI) Book Series

ISSN:2475-6547
EISSN:2475-6555

Editor-in-Chief: Maximiliano Korstanje, University of Palermo, Argentina

MISSION

Globally, the hospitality, travel, tourism, and services industries generate a significant percentage of revenue and represent a large portion of the business world. Even in tough economic times, these industries thrive as individuals continue to spend on leisure and recreation activities as well as services.

The Advances in Hospitality, Tourism, and the Services Industry (AHTSI) book series offers diverse publications relating to the management, promotion, and profitability of the leisure, recreation, and services industries. Highlighting current research pertaining to various topics within the realm of hospitality, travel, tourism, and services management, the titles found within the AHTSI book series are pertinent to the research and professional needs of managers, business practitioners, researchers, and upper-level students studying in the field.

COVERAGE

- Destination Marketing and Management
- International Tourism
- Casino Management
- Sustainable Tourism
- Service Management
- Service Training
- Hotel Management
- Tourism and the Environment
- Leisure & Business Travel
- Service Design

IGI Global is currently accepting manuscripts for publication within this series. To submit a proposal for a volume in this series, please contact our Acquisition Editors at Acquisitions@igi-global.com or visit: http://www.igi-global.com/publish/.

The Advances in Hospitality, Tourism, and the Services Industry (AHTSI) Book Series (ISSN 2475-6547) is published by IGI Global, 701 E. Chocolate Avenue, Hershey, PA 17033-1240, USA, www.igi-global.com. This series is composed of titles available for purchase individually; each title is edited to be contextually exclusive from any other title within the series. For pricing and ordering information please visit http://www.igi-global.com/book-series/advances-hospitality-tourism-services-industry/121014. Postmaster: Send all address changes to above address.

Titles in this Series

For a list of additional titles in this series, please visit:
http://www.igi-global.com/book-series/advances-hospitality-tourism-services-industry/121014

Mountain Tourism and Ecological Impacts Himalayan Region and Beyond
Soumendra Nath Biswas (Assam University, Silchar, India) and Pradip Kumar (Assam University, Silchar, India)
Business Science Reference • © 2024 • 280pp • H/C (ISBN: 9798369308233) • US $250.00

Promoting Sustainable Gastronomy Tourism and Community Development
Andrea Edurne Jimenez Ruiz (Universidad Autonoma del Estado de Mexico, Mexico) Shivam Bhartiya (Jain University, India) and Vaibhav Bhatt (Central University of Tamil Nadu, India)
Business Science Reference • © 2024 • 287pp • H/C (ISBN: 9798369318140) • US $285.00

Impact of AI and Robotics on the Medical Tourism Industry
Viana Hassan (University of Malta, Malta) Ahmad Albattat (Management and Science University, Malaysia) and Shakeel Basheer (Lovely Professional University, India)
Business Science Reference • © 2024 • 361pp • H/C (ISBN: 9798369322482) • US $300.00

Service Innovations in Tourism Metaverse, Immersive Technologies, and Digital Twin
Surabhi Singh (G.L. Bajaj Institute of Management and Research, India)
Business Science Reference • © 2024 • 295pp • H/C (ISBN: 9798369311035) • US $275.00

Utilizing Smart Technology and AI in Hybrid Tourism and Hospitality
Sanjeev Kumar (Lovely Professional University, India) Mohammad Badruddoza Talukder (International University of Business Agriculture and Technology, Bangladesh) and Ana Pego (Nova University of Lisbon, Portugal)
Business Science Reference • © 2024 • 367pp • H/C (ISBN: 9798369319789) • US $290.00

Innovative Technologies for Increasing Service Productivity
Sridhar Manohar (Chitkara Business School, Chitkara University, India) Amit Mittal (Chitkara Business School, Chitkara University, India) Sekar Raju (Ivy College of Business, Iowa State University, USA) and Arjun J. Nair (Chitkara University, India)
Business Science Reference • © 2024 • 404pp • H/C (ISBN: 9798369320198) • US $290.00

For an entire list of titles in this series, please visit:
http://www.igi-global.com/book-series/advances-hospitality-tourism-services-industry/121014

IGI Global
PUBLISHER of TIMELY KNOWLEDGE

701 East Chocolate Avenue, Hershey, PA 17033, USA
Tel: 717-533-8845 x100 • Fax: 717-533-8661
E-Mail: cust@igi-global.com • www.igi-global.com

Editorial Advisory Board

Table of Contents

Detailed Table of Contents

This study delves into the multifaceted macro-environmental factors shaping the tourism sector, encompassing economic, political, socio-cultural, technological, and sustainability dimensions. To navigate the challenges and opportunities within this dynamic industry, a deep understanding of these elements is crucial. The research aims to uncover the significant relationship between these factors and tourism domains through a systematic literature review and bibliometric analysis. Bridging theory and practice, it provides real-world implications for industry professionals, policymakers, researchers, and practitioners. This study contributes substantially to scholarly discourse, comprehensively exploring how diverse macro-environmental factors converge to shape the trajectory of the tourism and hospitality industries. Beyond academia, the findings offer practical insights for strategic decision-making, policy formulation, and future research initiatives in this ever-evolving field.

This chapter will explore the transformative potential of "smart tourism using IoT" within the context of social media strategies for enhanced tourism interactivity. With the advent of the Internet of Things (IoT), the tourism industry is undergoing a profound revolution. In this chapter, we will delve into how IoT technologies are reshaping the tourism landscape and creating new avenues for tourist engagement, satisfaction, and sustainability. The chapter emphasizes the strategic importance of integrating IoT solutions with social media strategies to create a seamless and immersive travel experience. The discussion will encompass real-time tourist information, personalized travel assistance, resource management, safety and security, and data-driven decision-making, all underpinned by the broader theme of social media interactivity.

Recognizing the substantial impact of external environmental factors on the tourism industry, obtaining insights into potential scenarios that the sector may encounter in the near future, particularly within a limited timeframe, is of utmost importance. The primary objective of this study was to envisage scenarios for the tourism sector over the next five years, striving for a comprehensive understanding of potential developments and challenges that could shape the industry's trajectory. Employing a two-phase qualitative methodology involving semi-structured interviews, the research first engaged with non-tourism experts and subsequently with tourism experts. Building on the identified key mid-term events—climate change and digital transformation—and employing a CATWOE framework analysis, two distinct scenarios for tourism development were crafted for the upcoming five years. This approach ensures a nuanced exploration of the influential factors and expert perspectives that contribute to the formulation of strategic insights for the industry's future.

Social media has an important role in marketing a destination as it can assist in both demand and supply. Social media in tourism supports providing search information about a destination, and the decision-making among the stakeholders. Leverage of social media for marketing tourism products along with sustainability is stated to be an excellent strategy. The current study is conducted by obtaining data from social media sites about the reviews of the customer's thought process on the island tourist destination. The findings from the study will help policymakers make appropriate decisions while marketing an island tourism destination.

Cruise tourism has significantly increased in popularity in recent years, being among the most common forms of tourism. Oman is regarded as one of the distinguished destinations that has fundamental elements, capabilities, and ingredients of cruise tourism, such as infrastructures, superstructures, and other cruising facilities. The expansion of cruise tourism in the contemporary digital era offers different opportunities for destination management organizations and concerned entities to implement digital marketing strategies. However, some challenges to effectively adopt digital marketing strategies for cruise tourism should be considered. Consequently, the purpose of the current chapter is to provide a more thorough understanding of the cruise tourism business, particularly in the context of Oman. It also aims to highlight the key opportunities and challenges of adopting digital marketing strategies to advance cruise tourism in Oman. This chapter offers a range of contributions to academics and professionals. Directions for further research are also given.

Personalization allows customers to access customized information more efficiently at any time. The importance of applying personalization in smart technology expanded during the COVID-19 pandemic. This chapter aims to present how can use the data about the clients from customer relationship management (CRM) to use them on customer lifetime value (CLV) models to classify the potentialities of customers. In addition, the authors suggested using personalization to make promotions for specific clients. The motivation of this chapter is to increase the competitiveness of the hotels and offer attractive services to achieve the loyalty of current and new clients. Also, to offer exclusive products or services to increase user satisfaction.

Digital gastronomy has been a common topic of conversation while talking about robotic breakthroughs in the hospitality sector. Most notably by producing highly personalized and imaginative goods via 3D food printing. Nevertheless, several studies have revealed its frequent association with negative notions. This derogatory idea is frequently the consequence of consumers' neophobia stemming from ignorance. It has been proposed that positive advertising of the technology's key advantages be utilized to boost the hedonic perception of food goods; however, no one has correlated the use of multiple avenues to share the information. For this purpose, this study used both a hedonic analysis and a presentation. Most of inquiries were aware of 3D printed food and linked it to favorable words. The practical approach had a positive effect on perception, while the theoretical had no significant correlation. The study's findings support the investment in this technology for small-scale food producing facilities.

Chapter 8

Preface

In the dynamic landscape of global tourism, where innovation and adaptation are paramount, the need for comprehensive strategies to navigate this ever-evolving terrain becomes increasingly apparent. As editors of *Social Media Strategies for Tourism Interactivity*, we are pleased to present a compendium that delves into the multifaceted realm of tourism management in the digital age.

Tourism stands as a cornerstone of economic prosperity, fostering cultural exchange, bolstering local economies, and providing unparalleled experiences for travelers worldwide. However, the industry is not immune to challenges, from environmental concerns to shifting consumer behaviors and the relentless march of technological progress. In the face of such complexity, the imperative to rethink traditional approaches and embrace innovation has never been more pressing.

This edited volume serves as a beacon for stakeholders across the tourism spectrum, from policymakers and entrepreneurs to researchers and students, offering insights and strategies to navigate the intricate web of challenges and opportunities that define modern tourism.

We advocate for a paradigm shift towards sustainable tourism practices, leveraging the power of collaboration, technological advancements, and digitalization to not only meet the evolving needs of travelers but also to ensure the long-term viability of tourism destinations.

Across diverse chapters, contributors explore the intersection of social media, technology, sustainability, and consumer behavior, offering valuable insights and practical strategies for navigating the complexities of the tourism industry. From macro-environmental factors shaping the sector's trajectory to the transformative potential of smart technologies and IoT in enhancing tourist experiences, each chapter provides a nuanced perspective on key challenges and opportunities facing the industry. Through scenario planning, digital marketing strategies, and the integration of personalized services, this book equips industry professionals, policymakers, researchers, and practitioners with the knowledge and tools needed to thrive in an ever-evolving tourism landscape.

Chapter 1 provides a comprehensive exploration of the macro-environmental factors influencing the tourism sector. By analyzing economic, political, socio-cultural, technological, and sustainability dimensions, the research uncovers the intricate relationship between these factors and tourism domains. Through a systematic literature review and bibliometric analysis, the chapter bridges theory and practice, offering valuable insights for industry professionals, policymakers, researchers, and practitioners. It contributes significantly to scholarly discourse, shedding light on how diverse macro-environmental factors shape the trajectory of the tourism and hospitality industries, while also providing practical implications for strategic decision-making, policy formulation, and future research initiatives.

Delving into the transformative potential of "Smart Tourism using IoT," chapter 2 explores the intersection of IoT technologies and social media strategies within the tourism industry. It discusses how IoT is revolutionizing the tourism landscape, enhancing tourist engagement, satisfaction, and sustainability. The strategic integration of IoT solutions with social media strategies is emphasized, offering insights into real-time tourist information, personalized travel assistance, resource management, safety, security, and data-driven decision-making. By highlighting the symbiotic relationship between IoT and social media interactivity, this chapter provides a roadmap for creating seamless and immersive travel experiences.

Focusing on scenario planning for the tourism sector, chapter 3 aims to anticipate potential developments and challenges over the next five years. Through a qualitative methodology involving semi-structured interviews with non-tourism and tourism experts, the research crafts two distinct scenarios for tourism development. By analyzing key mid-term events and employing a CATWOE framework analysis, the chapter offers nuanced insights into the factors shaping the industry's trajectory. It provides strategic insights for industry stakeholders, policymakers, and researchers, facilitating informed decision-making and proactive planning in response to future challenges and opportunities.

In chapter 4, the role of social media in marketing island tourism destinations is examined. By analyzing customer reviews on social media platforms, the study provides insights into tourist decision-making processes and offers recommendations for policymakers to effectively market island destinations. The findings contribute to understanding the dynamics of destination marketing in the digital age, offering practical implications for enhancing the attractiveness and competitiveness of island tourism destinations.

Focusing on cruise tourism in Oman, chapter 5 explores the opportunities and challenges of adopting digital marketing strategies to advance cruise tourism. By examining Oman's capabilities and infrastructures in the context of cruise tourism, the chapter highlights the potential for leveraging digital marketing to enhance destination management and visitor experiences. It offers valuable insights for academics and professionals, with directions for further research to optimize digital marketing strategies in the cruise tourism sector.

Chapter 6 investigates the application of personalization in smart technology, particularly in the hotel industry. By leveraging customer relationship management (CRM) data, the study explores how personalization can enhance customer lifetime value (CLV) models and promote customer loyalty. The chapter provides practical strategies for hotels to increase competitiveness and customer satisfaction through personalized services, emphasizing the importance of adapting to evolving consumer preferences and technological advancements.

Exploring the concept of digital gastronomy, chapter 7 examines the perception of 3D food printing technology in the hospitality sector. By employing both hedonic analysis and presentation methods, the study evaluates consumer attitudes towards 3D printed food and suggests strategies to improve its acceptance. The findings highlight the potential of 3D food printing technology for small-scale food production facilities, advocating for positive advertising to enhance consumer perception and adoption.

Chapter 8 conducts an analysis of environmental and social factors impacting tourism development, proposing mitigation measures based on sustainable practices derived from a circular economy approach. By discussing the integration of social media strategies with sustainable tourism management, the chapter offers recommendations for fostering sustainable tourism interactivity through computational technologies. It concludes with insights for future research and practical implications for promoting sustainable tourism practices.

Examining the role of social media in fostering sustainable tourism, chapter 9 analyzes stakeholder engagement through platforms like Twitter. By studying the type of content disseminated and level of engagement, the research offers insights for protected area managers to improve their social media strategies and encourage stakeholder involvement. The findings provide valuable guidance for enhancing the preservation of natural areas through effective social media engagement.

Chapter 10 explores the rise of mindful customers in the Bangladesh restaurant business and the implications for marketing strategies. By emphasizing locally sourced products, sustainability, and social responsibility, the study offers recommendations for restaurant owners and marketers to attract and retain mindful consumers. It provides valuable insights into shifting consumer trends and practical strategies for adapting to the evolving marketplace.

Utilizing bibliometric analysis, this chapter synthesizes current knowledge on social media and tourist behavior, offering insights into past studies and future research directions. By analyzing research papers published between 2012 and 2023, chapter 11 identifies emerging themes and trends in the field, providing valuable insights for researchers and practitioners. It offers a comprehensive overview of the literature landscape and highlights areas for further exploration in the realm of social media and tourist behavior.

In an era characterized by rapid change and uncertainty, understanding the dynamics of tourist behavior, harnessing the potential of emerging technologies, and fostering a culture of innovation are indispensable pursuits. This book endeavors to equip readers with the knowledge and tools necessary to thrive in this dynamic landscape.

Our recommended topics span a wide array of disciplines, reflecting the interdisciplinary nature of contemporary tourism management. From artificial intelligence and business analytics to environmental sustainability and social media strategies, each chapter offers valuable insights and practical guidance for navigating the complexities of the modern tourism industry.

As editors, it is our sincere hope that this volume will serve as a catalyst for dialogue, innovation, and positive change within the tourism community. We extend our gratitude to the contributors whose expertise and dedication have enriched this collection, and we invite readers to embark on a journey of exploration and discovery within the pages of *Social Media Strategies for Tourism Interactivity*.

Célia M.Q. Ramos
University of Algarve, Portugal

Teresa Costa
Instituto Politécnico de Setúbal, Portugal

Filipe Segurado Severino
Estoril Higher Institute for Tourism and Hotel Studies, Portugal

Maria de Lurdes Calisto
Estoril Higher Institute for Tourism and Hotel Studies, Portugal

Acknowledgment

The editors would like to acknowledge the help of all the people involved in this project and, more specifically, the authors and the reviewers that took part in the review process. Without their support, this book would not have become a reality.

The editors thank each one of the authors for their contributions. Our sincere gratitude goes to the authors of the chapters who contributed with their time and expertise to this book.

The editors would also like to thank the Research Centre for Tourism, Sustainability and Wellbeing (CinTurs) - Portuguese Foundation for Science and Technology (FCT) (project UIDB/04020/2020), the Centre for Tourism Research, Development and Innovation (CiTUR) - Portuguese Foundation for Science and Technology (FCT) (project UIDB/04470/2020), RESILIENCE - Center for Regional Resilience and Sustainability and project SHIFT with reference PTDC/EGE-OGE/2146/2021.

Chapter 1
Macro-Environmental Dynamics Shaping Tourism and Hospitality

Ana Teresa Machado
Escola Superior de Comunicação Social, Instituto Politécnico de Lisboa, Portugal & CiTUR, Portugal

Filipe Segurado Severino
https://orcid.org/0000-0002-9865-4664
Escola Superior de Hotelaria e Turismo do Estoril, Portugal & CiTUR, Portugal

Teresa Costa
Escola Superior de Ciências Empresariais, Instituto Politécnico de Setúbal, Portugal & CiTUR, Portugal

Zelia Raposo Santos
https://orcid.org/0000-0003-3858-311X
Escola Superior de Comunicação Social, Instituto Politécnico de Lisboa, Portugal

Maria de Lurdes Calisto
https://orcid.org/0000-0003-1636-0150
Escola Superior de Hotelaria e Turismo do Estoril, Portugal & CiTUR, Portugal

ABSTRACT

This study delves into the multifaceted macro-environmental factors shaping the tourism sector, encompassing economic, political, socio-cultural, technological, and sustainability dimensions. To navigate the challenges and opportunities within this dynamic industry, a deep understanding of these elements is crucial. The research aims to uncover the significant relationship between these factors and tourism domains through a systematic literature review and bibliometric analysis. Bridging theory and practice, it provides real-world implications for industry professionals, policymakers, researchers, and practitioners. This study contributes substantially to

DOI: 10.4018/979-8-3693-0960-5.ch001

scholarly discourse, comprehensively exploring how diverse macro-environmental factors converge to shape the trajectory of the tourism and hospitality industries. Beyond academia, the findings offer practical insights for strategic decision-making, policy formulation, and future research initiatives in this ever-evolving field.

INTRODUCTION

Tourism and hospitality (T&H) are not just economic sectors; they are vibrant engines driving global economic prosperity, cultural enrichment, and social development. As integral components of the service industry, they play a crucial role in creating job opportunities, fueling economic growth, and fostering cross-cultural exchanges. The global significance of tourism in the economic landscape is underscored by its substantial contribution, constituting 10.3% of the Gross Domestic Product (GDP) and supporting nearly 10% of the global workforce in 2019, as reported by the World Travel and Tourism Council (2022).

Their impact extends beyond traditional economic measures. These sectors form complex networks of interconnected businesses and supply chains, encompassing airlines, hotels, restaurants, tour operators, and souvenir shops. Furthermore, they stimulate investments in infrastructure, urban renewal, and environmental conservation, thereby propelling socio-economic advancement across destinations worldwide (Thullah & Jalloh, 2021)

Additionally, T&H are vital channels for cultural exchange and mutual understanding among nations and communities. Travelers do not just visit new places but also immerse themselves in diverse cultures, traditions, and lifestyles. Through interactions with residents, participation in cultural events, and exploration of heritage sites, tourists cultivate tolerance, respect, and appreciation for cultural diversity (Amoiradis et al., 2021).

However, the sustainability and success of T&H enterprises depend on their ability to adapt to the ever-changing macro environment. Thus, industry stakeholders must remain vigilant and agile in navigating these dynamic forces.

The global economic downturn caused by the COVID-19 pandemic resulted in significant fluctuations in tourism demand and consumer spending patterns. Many businesses in the T&H sectors had to adapt their strategies to cope with reduced consumer confidence and changing financial circumstances (Gössling & Hall, 2020).

The recent cases of conflicts in Ukraine and Palestine are examples of how political instability adversely impacts tourism in affected regions, evidenced by declines in visitor numbers and disruptions to infrastructure. The ongoing conflicts create safety concerns and prompt travel advisories, deterring international tourists and impeding travel logistics. Imposed travel restrictions, security measures, and the perception of these regions as conflict zones further deter potential tourists (Pandey & Kumar, 2022).

The importance of adhering to legal and regulatory frameworks in the tourism industry cannot be overstated, emphasizing the need for businesses to stay abreast of evolving laws and regulations to maintain integrity, protect consumers, and avoid legal risks (Robinson et al., 2020). Recent examples include the implementation of the General Data Protection Regulation (GDPR) by the European Union in 2018, which imposes strict requirements on businesses handling personal data of EU citizens, prompting adjustments in data handling practices across the tourism sector (Tassikas, 2021). Additionally, ongoing adaptations to accessibility regulations, particularly in digital accessibility for websites and online booking platforms, highlight the sector's efforts to ensure inclusivity and compliance with evolving accessibility laws such as the Web Content Accessibility Guidelines (WCAG) (Darcy et al., 2020).

Demographic shifts in the tourism industry, such as the rise of millennials and Generation Z as influential travel demographics, alongside the growing importance of seniors (Bąk & Szczecińska, 2020), have led to notable changes in consumer preferences. These shifts underscore the need for businesses to adapt their offerings, emphasizing unique experiences, sustainability, authenticity, and accessibility.

Moreover, technological advancements present both opportunities and challenges for T&H businesses. The emergence of online travel agencies (OTAs) such as Booking.com and Expedia has revolutionized the booking process for travel accommodations, intensifying competition with traditional brick-and-mortar travel agencies and hotels. Additionally, the integration of innovative technologies like virtual reality (VR) and augmented reality (AR) is reshaping the travel experience, offering travelers immersive encounters with destinations and attractions (Pencarelli, 2019). However, recent incidents in 2020, like the data breach at Marriott International, where hackers gained unauthorized access to the personal information of over 5.2 million guests, and the ransomware attack on CWT (Carlson Wagonlit Travel), which disrupted its booking systems and operations, affecting travel plans for numerous clients, highlight the susceptibility of the tourism industry to cyber-attacks and underscore the importance of robust cybersecurity measures to safeguard sensitive data and ensure the continuity of operations in the sector (Chen & Jai, 2019).

Tourism faces significant challenges due to the increasing frequency and severity of natural disasters, including hurricanes, wildfires, and floods. Recent examples include wildfires in California, Australia, and Greece, which devastated landscapes and led to evacuations, as well as hurricanes such as Maria in Puerto Rico and Dorian in the Bahamas, causing extensive damage to tourism infrastructure (Estevão & Costa, 2020). Climate change-induced coastal erosion also threatens coastal destinations globally (Arabadzhyan et al., 2020). These challenges emphasize the necessity for sustainable practices and resilience measures in tourism.

In conclusion, while T&H offers vast potential for economic growth, cultural exchange, and social cohesion, its long-term success relies on its ability to adapt to the complexities of the macro environment. By embracing innovation, sustainability, resilience, and responsible stewardship, industry stakeholders can harness the transformative power of tourism to shape a more inclusive, equitable, and sustainable future for generations to come.

This research is driven by unraveling the intricate relationship between macro-environmental factors and the dynamics of the T&H sectors. While existing literature offers valuable insights into this area, it often suffers from fragmentation. Many studies focus solely on one macro-factor or specific regions or countries, providing a limited perspective. Moreover, some research may only examine a particular aspect of tourism, neglecting the holistic view of the sector.

This study endeavors to bridge this gap by adopting a comprehensive approach. Rather than isolating individual macro-factors or limiting the scope to specific regions or aspects of tourism, it seeks to examine the impact of all macro-factors on the T&H sector. By taking this holistic perspective, the study aims to offer a more nuanced understanding of the intricate dynamics at play within the industry.

The study aims to pinpoint and evaluate the critical macro-environmental elements that influence the sector by employing a rigorous methodology that involves a systematic literature review and bibliometric analysis. Furthermore, it endeavors to delve deeper into the nuances of these factors, shedding light on their role in shaping both the vulnerabilities and growth opportunities within the sector.

This study is a crucial bridge between academic theories and practical applications within the T&H sector, catering to various stakeholders, including industry professionals, policymakers, researchers, and practitioners. The research sheds light on impacts on the industry's trajectory by comprehensively examining various macro-environmental factors such as political, economic, socio-cultural, technological, and sustainability issues. Synthesizing diverse information sources offers valuable insights into the complex influences shaping the sector's evolution. Beyond academia, the research's implications extend to strategic decision-making, policy formulation, and future research initiatives to enhance sustainability, competitiveness, and innovation within the industry. Ultimately, the study aims to enrich scholarly understanding while providing practical guidance for steering the T&H sector towards a more resilient and prosperous future.

IMPACT OF MACRO-ENVIRONMENTAL FACTORS ON TOURISM AND HOSPITALITY

The resurgence of tourism following the COVID-19 pandemic underscores the sector's susceptibility to disruptive events and its resilience to recover (Aldao et al., 2022). Various significant events and the broader macro environment of tourism play crucial roles in shaping its trajectory, and a thorough analysis of these factors can improve the outlook for the tourism industry. Ha et al. (2022) emphasize the necessity of exploring the impact of the macro environment on the expansion of the tourism value chain, particularly in developing countries. The literature's most widely reported macro factors affecting tourism include economic fluctuations, political instability, technological disruptions, environmental challenges, regulatory shifts, and evolving consumer preferences (Page & Connell, 2020).

Bianchi (2018) emphasizes the importance of having open and stable political and legal institutions to effectively operate organizations and the overall economy. In this sense, Ghalia et al. (2019) emphasize that the tourism sector is susceptible to political stability (Can & Güler, 2022; Lee & Chen, 2020;) and to the institutional and regulatory frameworks (Derbisheva & Kyzy, 2022; Kosevich et al., 2020; Toirxonovna et al., 2020), which are molded by the distinct developmental trajectories and specific characteristics of each country such as legal frameworks, subsidiary legislation, specific policies, and administrative structures.

Furthermore, favorable public policies (Afrisal, 2022; Collazos et al., 2023; Robinson et al., 2020), positive international relations (Chitadze, 2023; Máthé, 2018; Mckercher & Prideaux, 2020), and crisis management (Raykova, 2021) are pivotal political factors shaping the tourism sector's environment and growth trajectory. These elements collectively influence investment confidence, destination attractiveness, regulatory compliance, visitor flow, and resilience in crises, underlining their critical role in shaping the industry's prospects and performance (Aguinis et al.,2023).

The scholarly dialogue surrounding the correlation between tourism and economic growth has been dynamic, often examining the intricate relationship between these two phenomena. While initial discussions highlighted tourism's role in driving economic growth, recent studies have expanded their focus to explore the reciprocal influence, investigating how economic variables impact tourism (Pulido-Fernández & Cárdenas-García, 2020). Following the conventional tourism decision theories, travel decisions are defined as a function of tourist's disposable incomes, costs of travel, time preferences, and personal interests (Eugenio-Martin, 2003; Otero-Giráldez et al., 2012; Perles-Ribes et al., 2016). In their study, Martins et al. (2017) show that increases in the world's gross domestic product (GDP) per capita significantly boost tourism demands in 218 countries over the 1995–2012 period. The economic turbulence experienced in late 2008 and 2009 marked an unprecedented global decline in international tourist arrivals. During economic uncertainty, tourist demand decreases or adjusts due to cautious spending, job insecurity, and rising travel costs. This decline leads to fewer visitors and reduced revenue for tourism businesses, forcing them to adjust by offering discounts or cutting back on services. The resulting financial strain may hinder investment and expansion, contributing to job losses and instability within the tourism sector (Nguyen et al.,2022). More recently, the COVID-19 pandemic initially impacted travel due to compulsory lockdowns, resulting in drastic consequences for all businesses associated with the tourism sector. Subsequently, as the pandemic persisted and an economic crisis ensued, the sector again faced the pressure of economic uncertainty (Naseer et al., 2023).

The tourism sector must continually adapt its offerings to respond to social and cultural influences that shape tourist decisions about destinations, activities, and travel experiences (Ooi et al., 2015; Zhuang et al., 2019). Cultural norms and values play a crucial role in shaping preferences for travel destinations and activities, as tourists may seek experiences that resonate with their cultural background or offer opportunities to explore new cultures (e.g., Artal-Tur et al., 2018; Correia et al., 2011; Lee et al., 2021). Additionally, generational factors such as the preferences and priorities of different age groups, like millennials or baby boomers, can influence travel decisions (e.g., Huber et al., 2019; Kim & Park, 2020; Pérez-Tapia et al., 2022; Vancia et al., 2023). Social trends and peer influences also impact travel choices, with the popularity of specific destinations or travel experiences often influenced by friends or social media influencers (Liu et al., 2020; Pop et al., 2021). Moreover, family dynamics and social status can further shape travel behavior, with family-oriented tourists seeking destinations suitable for all ages and individuals focused on prestige opting for luxury travel experiences (e.g., Kuncharia, 2019; Priya et al., 2019).

Technological factors encompass the broader technological landscape, including communication, information technology, and digital infrastructure advancements, significantly impacting tourism (Cheng et al., 2023; Pencarelli, 2019). From a supplier standpoint, embracing digital transformation is crucial to remaining competitive and meeting evolving consumer expectations. Leveraging technology allows these entities to enhance customer experiences, streamline operations, and optimize efficiency (Nikolskaya et al.,2021). For instance, hotels are implementing mobile check-in/out processes and keyless entry systems (Flinta, N. (2022)., while airlines are using data analytics to personalize services and improve flight operations (Tian et al.,2021). Moreover, tour operators are adopting virtual reality (VR) and augmented reality (AR) technologies to offer immersive travel experiences (Ercan, 2020). From a demand perspective, travelers increasingly rely on digital channels for planning, booking accommodations, and accessing destination information. Consumers expect seamless online booking platforms (Masiero et al., 2020), mobile-friendly interfaces (Kim & Kim, 2020), and personalized recommendations based on their preferences (Cao et al., 2021; Gu et al., 2020). This shift towards digitalization has led to greater convenience, flexibility, and customization in travel experiences (Nuenen & Scarles, 2021).

Environmental challenges pose significant threats to the tourism industry, affecting both natural resources and the communities dependent on them. Many tourism destinations rely on favorable weather conditions for their appeal, making them susceptible to the impacts of climate change. Changes in average temperatures and precipitation patterns directly affect the attractiveness of these destinations, influencing tourism visitation rates (Amelung et al.,2007; Soontiens-Olsen et al., 2023). Additionally, climate change has led to more significant variability and increased extreme weather events, posing risks to both natural and human systems. This situation exposes human-natural systems to increased risk of hazardous events and trends, highlighting the vulnerability of many natural and human systems and the tourism industries that operate within them (Ooi et al., 2018). Moreover, environmental challenges such as water scarcity and waste management issues strain local infrastructure and resources, affecting the quality of tourist experiences and posing long-term sustainability concerns for the industry (Delgado et al., 2023; Gretzel et al., 2019; Muñoz & Navia, 2015). Addressing these challenges requires concerted efforts from stakeholders to implement sustainable practices, promote environmental conservation, and mitigate the impacts of tourism on fragile ecosystems (Abdullaeva & Oripova, 2023. Giurea et al., 2018; Gomes & Lopes,2023; Pan et al., 2018).

METHOD

This study involves a systematic literature review and bibliometric analysis that aims to identify and comprehend the primary macro-environmental factors that influence the context of T&H. The methodological approach adheres to established guidelines; specifically those suggested by Templier and Paré (2015), guaranteeing systematicity and transparency in the process. The study follows a systematic six-step procedure, which includes problem formulation, literature search, inclusion screening, quality assessment, data extraction, and data analysis and synthesis.

To commence the evaluation, a systematic and detailed approach utilizing structured search methods, as recommended by Paré et al. (2016), was employed. The search strategy entailed conducting an automated search in the Scopus and Web of Science databases, using a combination of keywords including (Challeng* OR trend* OR opportunit* OR threat* OR driver*) AND (hospitality OR touris* OR hotel*). The decision to expand the scope of the study was considered essential to include a wide range of topics of interest. This wide range will thoroughly examine the challenges, opportunities, and threats encountered by the T&H sectors.

The search process was guided by specific criteria, which included a defined time frame (starting from 2008), document types (journal articles and reviews), subject areas (covering all academic knowledge fields), and language (English). After an initial search, a total of 1801 articles were obtained. These articles were carefully examined and filtered, resulting in 1436 primary studies after eliminating duplicates.

To effectively handle the large quantity of articles, a quality criterion was implemented to choose studies for further analysis. This approach entailed exclusively considering top-tier journals and studies with high citation scores, per the recommendations by Menon et al. (2021). Two criteria were employed: scientific articles published in journals ranked in the top 50% and top 25% by Scimago Rankings and the implementation of thresholds based on publication year and average citation count. As a result of this process, 842 articles were chosen for thorough analysis.

The subsequent screening phase, conducted under the guidance of specific inclusion and exclusion criteria, entailed the participation of five marketing and tourism researchers who carefully reviewed abstracts to identify articles pertinent to the research objective. A total of 385 studies were kept for further examination. These studies were divided into six categories based on their impact factors: political-legal, economic, sociocultural, technological, sustainability, and trends. The exclusion criteria were strictly enforced, eliminating articles that did not primarily focus on tourism or hospitality, those with a limited contextual scope, and those that discussed the impact of the tourism sector on other areas.

Pertinent information was recorded and extracted from the 50 eligible articles in the final analysis phase. These records included details such as the article's title, year of publication, authors, journal, number of citations, and the characteristics of the factors based on predefined categories. This rigorous and systematic approach guarantees the excellence and pertinence of the chosen research, thereby enhancing our comprehensive comprehension of the macro-environmental factors that impact T&H.

BIBLIOMETRIC ANALYSIS OF LITERATURE: FINDINGS AND DISCUSSION

The results of this review are presented in two sections: (1) descriptive quantitative analysis and (2) qualitative analysis.

First, a descriptive analysis of the following aspects was carried out: the distribution of publications by macro-factor, the distribution over time; the distribution by the geographical context where the study was conducted, the distribution per journal, the distribution by the type of study conducted, and the frequency of key words.

Subsequently, the content of the selected articles was analyzed to identify the key themes discussed for each macro factor.

Quantitative Analysis

Five macro factors were identified: politico-legal, economic, sociocultural, technological, and sustainability. These factors are commonly recognized as components of the macro-environment context in the tourism industry (e.g., Khan et al.,2020; Sofronov, 2018)

Based on the data presented in Table 1, sociocultural factors comprise 30.00% of the overall distribution of articles, political-legal factors comprise 28.00%, and technological factors comprise 22.00%. It is worth noting, however, that many studies on economic and sustainability aspects, which were often tied to specific events and cases, made them ineligible for inclusion in this analysis.

Table 1. Articles distribution by macro-factor

Macro environmental factors	Number of articles	Percentage
Political-Legal	14	28.00%
Economic	4	8.00%
Sociocultural	15	30.00%
Technology	11	22.00%
Sustainability	6	12.00%
Total	50	100%

As shown in Figure 1, the distribution of articles based on their publication years demonstrates a steady upward trend from 2011 to 2022, with a significant surge in 2020 and 2021. It is essential to emphasize that this research was conducted in early 2022, acknowledging the apparent decrease in publications observed during that specific year. Nonetheless, the overall trend indicates a growing interest in exploring the influence of the macro-environmental context on the hospitality and tourism industry.

Figure 1. Articles distribution by publication year

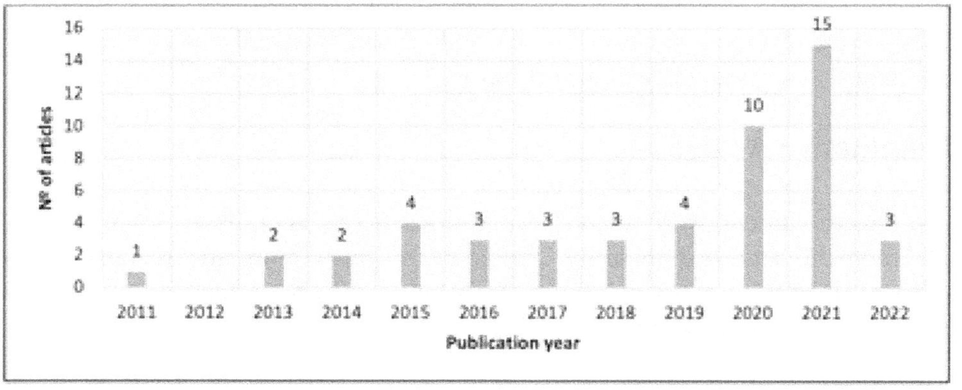

As depicted in Figure 2, the continuous upward trend observed from 2011 to 2022 and the surge in publications in 2021 and 2022 is attributed to all macro factors except for the economic factor. The data reveals that the economic factor experienced intermittent publications, specifically in 2013, 2016, 2019, and 2021. This situation suggests a fluctuating or periodic interest in studying the economic aspects within the context of T&H. It could indicate certain events, trends, or developments in those years that drew researchers' attention to the economic factor's impact on the industry. Such as the economic crisis of 2007 and the most recent economic crisis of 2020 caused by the Covid-19 pandemic (e.g., Khalid et al., 2020; Papatheodorou et al., 2010; Smeral, 2009)

Figure 2. Articles distribution by factor and year

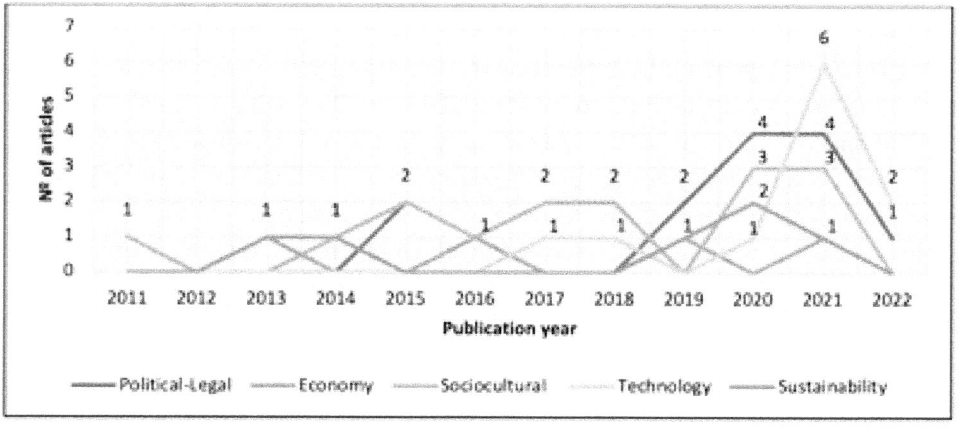

Figure 3 reveals the spatial distribution of the published work. Most of the analyzed studies were conducted internationally (13). Additionally, two studies were conducted in Europe, two in the European Union and one in Greenland. Five studies were conducted in the USA, while China had two studies. The remaining eight studies were conducted in eight different countries. It is interesting to note that a limited number of studies use a cross-regional or multi-regional approach.

Figure 3. Articles distribution by geographic regions

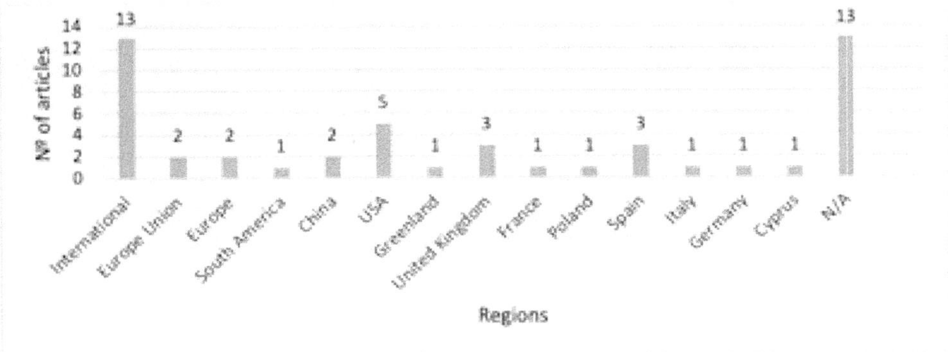

Examining the geographical distribution of articles across macro factors reveals that studies investigating the influence of each factor on the H&T sector have been conducted in both international and national contexts, as depicted in Figure 4, albeit with different numbers of papers.

Figure 4. Articles distribution by macro-factor and geographic region

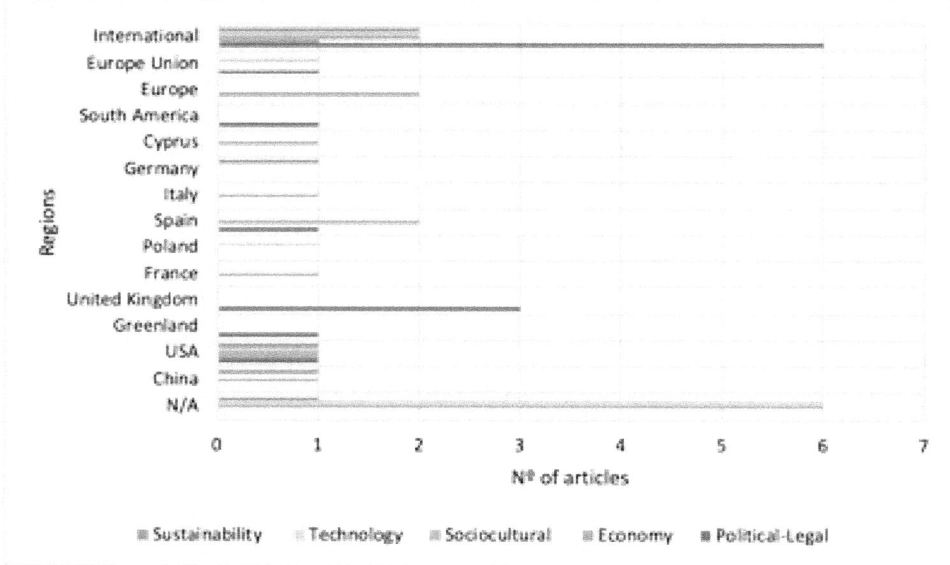

The list of journals where selected studies have been published, along with the frequency of papers published in each journal, is presented in Table 2 below. The articles were found to be published in various multidisciplinary journals, indicating the relevance and breadth of this topic to different fields. Out of 34 other journals, a high prevalence (44.00%) of journals belong to the "tourism, leisure, and hospitality management" field. The top journals in this category were "Current issues in Tourism" (3) and "Tourism Management Perspectives" (3), followed by "Journal of Tourism Futures" (2), "Worldwide Hospitality" (2), and "Tourism Themes" (2). The journal 'Sustainability' recorded the highest number of publications (5).

Apart from the economic factor, whose publications were all in journals in the field of tourism, for the remaining macro factors, most articles are published in journals from other areas, differing between factors. This diversity in publication venues across various areas may reflect the interdisciplinary nature of those factors and their relevance to multiple fields of study.

Table 2. Articles distribution by factor and publication

Political-legal area		
Journal	**Absolute frequency**	**Percentage**
Arctic Anthropology	1	7.14%
Current Issues in Tourism	1	7.14%
Journal of Tourism Futures	2	14.30%
Journal of Travel Research	3	21.44%
Land	1	7.14%
Marine pollution bulletin	1	7.14%
Ocean & Coastal Management	1	7.14%
Sustainability	1	7.14%
Tourism Economics	1	7.14%
Tourism Management Perspectives	1	7.14%
Tourism Planning & Development	1	7.14%
Total	14	100%
Economic area		
Journal	**Absolute frequency**	**Percentage**
Annals of Tourism Research	1	25.00%
Journal of Hospitality Marketing & Management	1	25.00%
Tourism Economics	1	25.00%
Tourism Planning & Development	1	25.00%
Total	4	100%
Sociocultural area		
Journal	**Absolute frequency**	**Percentage**
Annals of Tourism Research	1	6.66%
Buildings	1	6.66%
Current issues in Tourism	1	6.66%
Journal of Cleaner Production	1	6.66%
Journal of Destination Marketing & Management	1	6.66%
Journal of Sustainable Tourism	2	13.32%
Journal of Tourism Futures	2	13.32%
Psychology & Marketing	1	6.66%
Cornell Hospitality Quarterly	1	6.66%
Service Business	1	6.66%
Sustainability	1	6.66%
Worldwide Hospitality and Tourism Themes	2	13.32%
Total	15	100%

Table 2. Distribution of articles by fact and publication (cont.)

Technology area		
Journal	**Absolute frequency**	**Percentage**
Asia Pacific Journal of Tourism Research	1	9.09%
Electronics (Switzerland)	1	9.09%
Emerald Publishing Limited	1	9.09%
International Journal of Hospitality Management	1	9.09%
African Journal of Hospitality, Tourism and Leisure	1	9.09%
Information Technology & Tourism	1	9.09%
Sustainability	1	9.09%
Technological Forecasting and Social Change	1	9.09%
Tourism Management Perspectives	1	9.09%
Worldwide Hospitality and Tourism Themes	2	18.18%
Total	11	100%
Sustainability area		
Journal	**Absolute frequency**	**Percentage**
Climatic Change	1	16.66%
Current Issues in Tourism	1	16.66%
European Journal of Tourism Research	1	16.66%
Polar Science	1	16.66%
Sustainability	1	16.66%
Tourism Management Perspectives	1	16.66%
Total	6	100%

Regarding the research methodologies employed, most studies (25) adopted a quantitative approach, followed by literature review (15) and qualitative studies (7). However, there is a shortage in qualitative and quantitative research (2), as depicted in Figure 5.

Figure 5. Distribution of articles by type of study

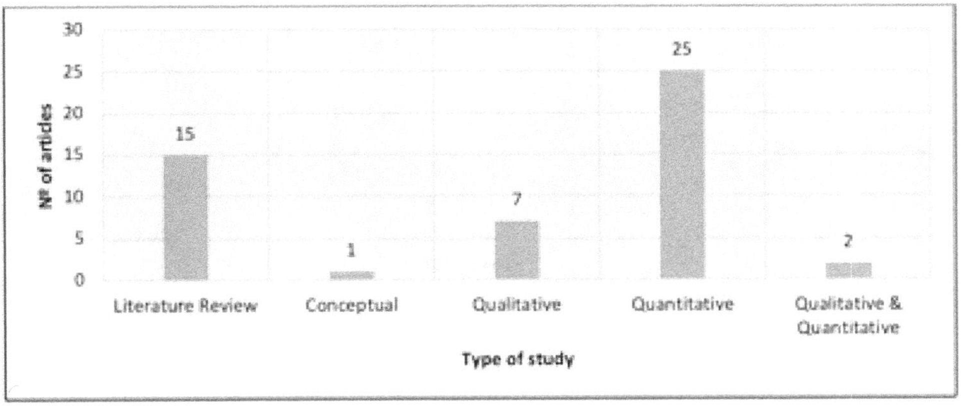

In Figure 6, the analysis of types of study by macro factor reveals distinctive patterns in the utilization of research methodologies across them.

The body of articles on the macro-political-legal factor showcases a rich tapestry of research methodologies, employing literature reviews, quantitative analyses, qualitative investigations, and mixed-methods approaches.

The socio-cultural macro factor, diverging from the macro-political-legal factor, takes a distinctive approach by employing a comprehensive array of study types, except the mixed approach. Notably, it stands out as the sole macro factor to conduct a conceptual study. This is the factor with the most significant number of quantitative studies (10).

The technological macro factor mirrors the study methodology observed in the social factor, except for conceptual studies.

Like the political-legal macro factor, the sustainability macro factor employs a mixed-methods approach featuring a singular study. However, it diverges in methodology by exclusively incorporating literature reviews and quantitative analyses.

Finally, the economic factor stands out in the methodological approach for solely employing quantitative studies.

In essence, this methodological diversity across macro factors reflects the intricacies of the subject matter and underscores the comprehensive and thoughtful approach taken in unraveling the complexities within each facet.

Figure 6. Distribution of articles by macro-factor and type of study

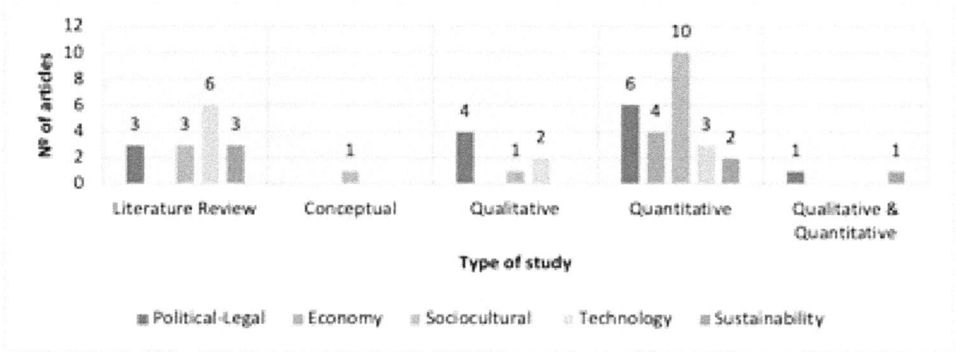

Individual word clouds were generated using the Nvivo software, 12th version, incorporating word frequency data from titles, keywords, and abstracts to uncover the most frequently used terms in the selected articles for each macro factor; Figure 7 illustrates the outcomes.

In examining the sociocultural factor, the 15 most frequently occurring terms, listed in descending order of frequency, encompass significant terms such as "travel" (1.39%), "environmental" (1.08%), "hotel" (0.87%), "tourist" (0.87%), and "millennials" (0.82%). The prominence of these terms reflects researchers' evident focus on unraveling the complex relationships among travel dynamics, environmental factors, the hospitality industry, and the impact of distinct generations—especially millennials—within the broader socio-cultural landscape.

Upon inspecting the word cloud within the political-legal factor, it becomes apparent that "development" holds the highest frequency (1.33%), trailed by "sustainable" (1.09%), "tourist" (1.03%), and "management" (0.79%). Additionally, terms like "cities" (0.73%), "economy" (0.73%), and "country" (0.67%) are notable. These findings may suggest a robust emphasis within the political-legal factor on the interplay between political and legal dynamics and their impact on development, sustainability, tourism management, and economic aspects at urban and country levels.

Analyzing the technological factor's word cloud, "data" emerges as the most prominent term (2.09%), followed by "hospitality" (1.61%), "mobile" and "trends" (1.37%), and "hotel" (1.01%). These results indicate a heightened interest among researchers in exploring the role of technology, especially within the hospitality industry context. The focus on mobile technology and emerging trends suggests a dynamic exploration of how technology shapes various facets within this macro factor.

In the sustainability factor, dominant terms in descending order include "climate" (2.59%), "change" (2.30%), "sustainable" (1.58%), "international" (1.29%), "polar"

(1.01%), and "protection" (0.86%). These results suggest a keen research interest in the environmental dimensions of sustainability, encompassing climate change, sustainable practices, international perspectives, polar regions, and protective measures. The prevalence of these terms indicates a comprehensive exploration of sustainability issues from diverse angles within the selected articles.

Lastly, the economic factor's word cloud highlights prevailing terms, with "crisis" (2.65%) at the forefront, followed by "demand" (1.59%), "cutback" (1.33%), and "hotel" (1.33%) in descending order. These results imply a specific research emphasis on economic crises, the dynamics of demand, and economic considerations explicitly about the hotel industry.

Figure 7. Word clouds represent word frequency according to abstracts, titles, and keywords

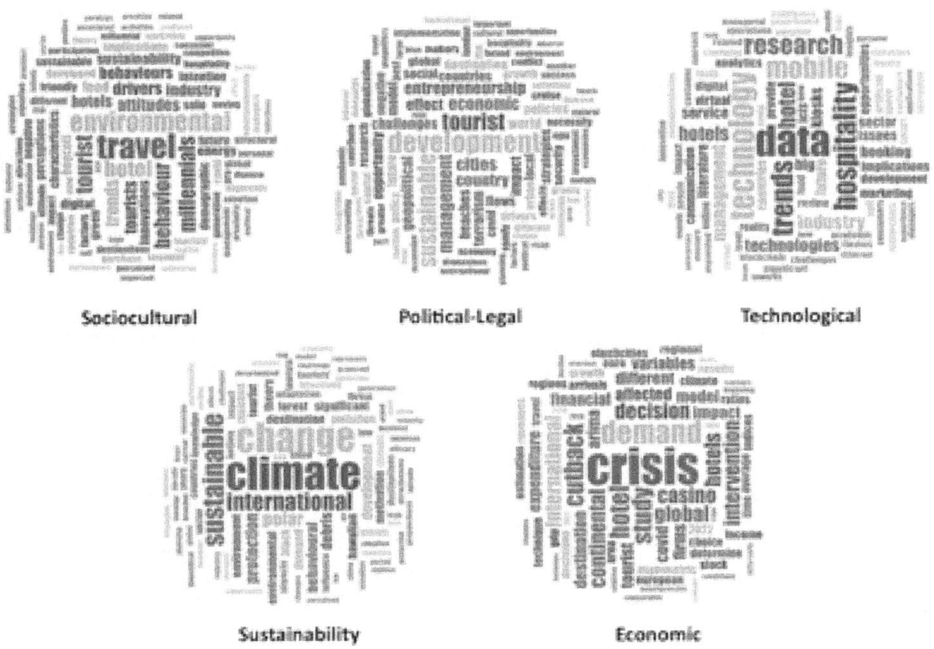

Qualitative Analysis

The chosen articles were carefully reviewed and analyzed to uncover the main themes for each macro factor. The results are shown in Figure 8. Interestingly, the sociocultural factor stands out with the most diverse topics (5), followed by the political-legal factor (4). The technological and sustainability factors share an equal number of topics (2), while the economic factor concentrates on a single theme.

In comparing topics across macro factors, "digital technologies" stands out as the predominant theme (9), followed by "sustainability threats," "sustainable tourism policy," and "Geopolitical risk," with six occurrences each. Themes with minimal representation, each featuring in only one article, include "demographic changes," "entrepreneurship policy," and "economic policy."

This analysis highlights the richness and diversity of research within each macro factor, with specific themes emerging as dominant and shared across factors, such as "sustainability." The findings provide insights into the current literature landscape, suggesting well-explored and less-explored avenues within the research scope.

Figure 8. Distribution of articles by macro factor/key topics

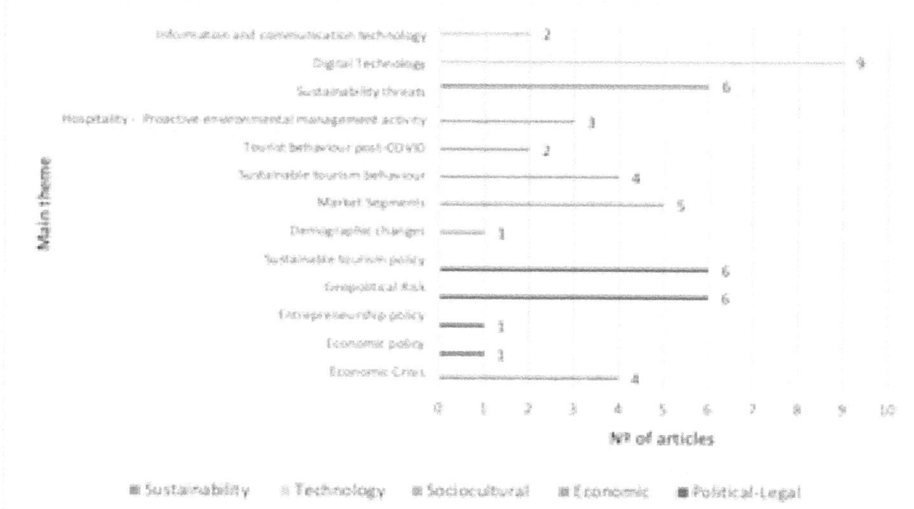

Sociocultural Factor

The articles were examined and classified into different thematic categories, here presented in decrescent order: "market segments" (5); "sustainable tourism behavior" (4); "hospitality – proactive management activity (3); "tourist behavior post-COVID19; demographic changes (1).

While globalization has contributed to shared trends like an increased focus on ecological behavior, health and well-being, and a desire for authentic experiences, societal shifts have given rise to novel categories of tourists. The evolving demographic landscape and exploring diverse generations have brought attention to Millennials and older adults.

Millennials acknowledged their dedication to sustainability, technological expertise, preference for experiential activities, and prudent financial management, which present challenges and opportunities for the T&H sector. This underscores the significance of delivering personalized, sustainable, and socially responsible travel experiences (Ketter, 2020; Mandić & Vuković, 2022; Santos et al., 2016; Veiga et al., 2017). On the other hand, seniors, a diverse demographic characterized by growing numbers, ample time, financial resources, good health, and an active lifestyle, represent a substantial target audience for the tourism sector (Santos et al., 2016).

The surge in solo travel emerges as a contemporary and increasingly popular trend, shedding light on a crucial yet insufficiently studied aspect of the tourism industry. Understanding solo travelers' needs, living conditions, and motivations is imperative for implementing necessary adaptations (Yang, 2021; Yang et al., 2019; Leith, 2020).

Research on sustainable tourism behavior explores the factors that influence environmentally friendly actions, such as activism, ethical consumerism, moral obligations, psychological factors, and sociodemographic factors (Juvan & Dolnicar, 2017; Leonidou et al., 2015; Seyfi et al., 2021; Wang et al., 2021).

The COVID-19 pandemic has revealed shifts in tourist behavior and consumption patterns (Abdullah et al., 2020; Li et al., 2020; Rasoolimanesh et al., 2021). Studies conducted post-COVID-19 underscore the importance of factors such as risk attitudes and demographic and generational disparities in influencing decision-making regarding tourist and travel activities (Lebrun et al., 2022; Zhang et al., 2020).

Demographic changes and hospitality behavior are acknowledged as crucial factors on the supply side. The increasing proportion of elderly individuals presents difficulties for the tourism and hospitality industry, requiring the implementation of strategies such as automation (Nagarajan et al., 2019; Webster & Ivanov, 2020).

In today's T&H sector, there is a pronounced emphasis on environmental sustainability, driven by the acknowledgment of the substantial impact that tourism activities have on environmental degradation (Han et al., 2021). This recognition is a response to consumers' growing environmental awareness and concerns, which have prompted a thorough exploration of environmentally sustainable practices within the industry (Dong et al., 2020; Garvey & Bolton, 2017). Research emphasizes the importance of environmental commitment in the hospitality industry, illustrating how eco-friendly services and sustainable strategies contribute to positive behavioral intentions (Cozzio et al., 2018; López-Gamero et al., 2011; Razumova et al., 2015).

Political-Legal Factor

Political-legal factors exert a notable influence, bringing up important topics like sustainable tourism policies (6), geopolitical risk (6), economic policy (1), and entrepreneurship policy (1).

Research emphasizes the importance of implementing public policies to ensure the sustainable development of tourism across environmental, cultural, and economic dimensions (Brendehaug et al., 2017; Guo et al., 2019; Neto, 2003). In this context, effective government leadership and stakeholder collaboration are critical in implementing sustainable tourism policies. The active engagement of stakeholders is crucial for the effective implementation of regulations (Begum et al., 2014; Moyle et al., 2014; Sobhanifard & Vaeysi, 2020), particularly vital for addressing issues like overtourism, especially in popular destinations (Andrade et al., 2021; Buzzi et al., 2022; Heikkinen et al., 2020; Maxim, 2015, 2019; Merino & Prats, 2020).

Tourism is significantly affected by geopolitical risks, which include wars, terrorist acts, and state tensions. Some studies examine these risks, emphasizing their impact on the movement of tourists and their choices. Geopolitical risks impede capital investment in travel and tourism, particularly in developing nations grappling with significant security crises (Gozgor et al., 2022). Nevertheless, policies targeted at revitalizing tourist destinations that have been affected by conflicts yet remain popular can effectively stimulate economic activity (Mestanza-Ramón & Jiménez-Caballero, 2021).

Events such as the 9/11 attacks, the Iraq invasion in 2003, and the 2022 Russia-Ukraine crisis have an impact on tourists' travel choices because of concerns about personal safety (Demir et al., 2019; Ghaderi et al., 2017; Song et al., 2019). Persistent conflicts and political instability harm long-term investment opportunities and damage the reputation of a particular location (Demiralay & Kilincarslan, 2019; Wernick & von Glinow, 2012).

In times of global economic uncertainty, government monetary policies pose additional challenges that affect tourism demand, extending beyond the typical factors (Akadiri et al., 2020; Işık et al., 2020). Economic policy uncertainty makes consumers hesitant to make significant travel-related decisions (Khan et al., 2021).

Public sector actors have a crucial role in promoting an entrepreneurial environment in the T&H sector, as they acknowledge the importance of entrepreneurship for employment and innovation (Dias et al., 2022; Fu et al., 2019).

Technological Factor

The technological factor was split into two key topics: digital technologies (9) and information and communication technology (ITC) (2), both of which hold vital importance in today's technological environment. Digital technologies are reshaping how businesses function, while ITC is crucial in facilitating communication and sharing information.

Historically viewed as a labor-intensive sector, implementing digital technologies, recognized as critical drivers of efficiency and competitive edge, has significantly transformed hotel operations and outcomes (Iranmanesh et al., 2022). The analyzed articles primarily focus on the following digital technologies: social media virtual reality (VR) and augmented reality (AR), artificial intelligence (AI) and robotics, big data, blockchain technology, self-service technology, and mobile apps.

From a business perspective, the acknowledged impacts of digital technologies on tourism and hospitality include improved efficiency and cost reduction through self-service technology, mobile apps, and intelligent automation (Gupta & Sharma, 2021; Chamboko-Mpotaringa & Tichaawa, 2021; Bowen & Whalen, 2017; Knani et al., 2022). Furthermore, there is a potential for increased revenue by attracting new customers and generating more bookings using digital marketing tools, VR, and AR (Chamboko-Mpotaringa & Tichaawa, 2021; Roman et al., 2022). Moreover, these technologies enable valuable insights into customer behavior and preferences, facilitating data-driven decision-making (Bowen & Whalen, 2017; Chamboko-Mpotaringa & Tichaawa, 2021; Yallop & Seraphin, 2020). Additionally, they enhance the security, transparency, and efficiency of transactions and interactions (Nam et al., 2021).

Customers can expect a more tailored and individualized experience thanks to big data analytics, mobile apps, and social media. An enhanced customer experience is achieved through increased convenience and flexibility, improved transparency via recommendation and review systems, and simplified access to tourist activities aided by VR and AR technologies (Bowen & Whalen, 2017; Gupta & Sharma, 2021; Knani et al., 2022; Tao et al., 2018; Yallop & Seraphin, 2020; Roman et al., 2022).

ITC plays a crucial role in fostering the expansion of the hospitality industry and contributes positively to the financial well-being of enterprises. Utilizing ICT, hospitality businesses can streamline operations and cut costs, positively influencing their economic conditions (Kozłowski et al., 2021).

The advent of 5G technology, with its enhanced speeds and lower latency, holds the potential to revolutionize the travel and hospitality experience. This technology could facilitate real-time translation services, augmented reality experiences, and quicker mobile payments, transforming how people engage with the hospitality industry (Chen et al., 2021).

Sustainability Factor

The primary focus of the reviewed articles (6) is the influence of the natural environment on tourism, with particular attention given to environmental hazards. Long-term systemic climate changes, such as increased temperatures, modified precipitation patterns, and more frequent extreme weather events, have impacted tourism destinations that depend on specific climates (Ooi et al., 2018). Climate change presents a substantial peril to the T&H sector, affecting the level of demand and modifying the appeal of different destinations (Pulido-Fernández et al., 2019).

According to Scott (2021), global climate change is a significant obstacle that affects investment, planning, operations, and demand in the tourism industry. According to Rosselló and Santana-Gallego (2014), the increase in global temperatures is predicted to change the patterns of international tourism. This means that typically warm destinations may become less appealing, while countries in high-latitude regions may become more attractive. Thimm et al. (2019) raise concerns regarding the potential impact of climate-induced restrictions on traditional sports and recreational activities on mountain tourism. Additionally, Shijin et al. (2020) highlight Polar Tourism's high vulnerability to climate change due to its location in high-latitude regions.

The perception of a nation as a desirable place to visit plays a pivotal role in tourists' decision-making process. The empirical evidence presented by Ruan et al. (2020) shows that pollution and environmental disasters, such as severe smog, can damage the reputation of a destination and discourage tourists from visiting. Natural calamities, such as the wreckage caused by the Japanese tsunami in 2011, have the potential to disrupt the stability of affected regions, hindering the progress of sustainable tourism development and the smooth operation of the tourism industry (Ghaderi & Henderson, 2013; Rosselló et al., 2020). Debris can instill fear and uncertainty, causing once-appealing destinations to become unappealing.

Economic Factor

The reviewed articles concentrate on the "economic crisis" (4), covering the economic downturn of 2007 and the more recent 2020 crisis instigated by the COVID-19 pandemic.

The studies by Eugenio-Martin and Campos-Soria (2014) and Jiménez-Guerrero et al. (2021) highlight the significant decrease in global tourism in 2009, specifically in revenue. When analyzing specific areas, Zheng et al. (2016) observed that casino hotel companies faced a rapid decrease in performance during the 2007 recession. In contrast, the effect on traditional hotel companies became apparent nine months later.

Campos-Soriaa et al. (2015) examine the intricate effects of economic crises on travel behavior and find that tourists display various patterns of response in reaction to reduced income and economic instability. Possible alternatives include reducing travel frequency, selecting domestic trips instead of international holidays, shortening the duration of stays, or opting for more cost-effective and nearby destinations.

Differently, the reduction in tourist demand during the COVID-19 pandemic was initially attributed to mandatory lockdown measures and subsequently stemmed from the decline in household income due to the ongoing economic crisis, as highlighted by Plzáková and Smeral (2022).

CONCLUSION

This study comprehensively explores macro-environmental factors influencing the tourism industry through a systematic literature review and bibliometric analysis of 50 articles. The research underscores the pivotal roles played by sociocultural, political-legal, technological, sustainability, and economic factors in shaping the macroenvironment of T&H.

The sociocultural factor analysis provides a nuanced understanding of the industry's complexities, encompassing market dynamics, demographic shifts, responses to global events like the COVID-19 pandemic, and alignment with the escalating focus on environmental sustainability.

Essentially, political-legal factors significantly impact sustainability practices, respond to geopolitical risks, address global event repercussions, navigate economic policy uncertainties, and foster an entrepreneurial environment. These insights highlight the intricate connections between governmental policies, geopolitical dynamics, and economic uncertainties in shaping the trajectory of the T&H sector.

Furthermore, the technological factor emerges as a driving force shaping the contemporary landscape of T&H. It introduces innovative solutions, enhances operational efficiency, and redefines customer experiences, signifying the industry's ongoing evolution in response to rapid advancements in digital and ICT technologies.

The reviewed articles emphasize the intricate interplay between climate change, environmental hazards, and tourism. This underscores the imperative for sustainable practices and strategic planning to mitigate adverse impacts and ensure the long-term resilience of tourism destinations.

Finally, the study highlights economic crises' profound and multifaceted impacts on the tourism industry. These crises significantly affect revenue, alter travel behavior, and influence demand patterns. The findings underscore the adaptability of tourists in response to economic challenges and stress the importance of understanding the nuanced factors contributing to reduced travel during periods of economic uncertainty.

This study makes significant contributions to the field by comprehensively analyzing macro-environmental factors influencing the T&H sector. It systematically explores sociocultural, political-legal, technological, sustainability, and economic dimensions, offering a holistic perspective. The synthesis of insights from a diverse array of articles contributes to an understanding of the intricate relationships between different macro factors. Additionally, the study categorizes and identifies key themes within each macro factor, providing a structured overview that facilitates a deeper comprehension of the macroenvironment shaping the industry.

The study's practical contributions lie in providing industry professionals with a more subtle understanding of the macro-environmental factors shaping the T&H sector, facilitating informed decision-making and strategic planning.

Although systematic reviews have inherent limitations in being retrospective and selective, this study is a groundbreaking attempt to systematically examine the complex role of macro-environmental factors in tourism. Its findings contribute valuable insights to the current understanding and establish a robust foundation for future academic research endeavors in this evolving field.

Based on the significant contributions of this study, future research in tourism and hospitality should consider several key directions. Firstly, there is a need for longitudinal studies to track the evolving impact of macro-environmental factors on the T&H over time, providing insights into trends and patterns. Additionally, exploring the intersectionality of macro factors and their combined effects on the industry could offer a more nuanced understanding of their influence. Furthermore, investigating the role of emerging technologies, such as artificial intelligence and blockchain, in addressing sustainability challenges and enhancing the guest experience warrants attention. Moreover, comparative studies across different regions and countries can shed light on the contextual variations in the impact of macro factors on the tourism industry, informing more targeted strategies and policies. Lastly, research focusing on the resilience and adaptive capacity of T&H businesses in response to macro-environmental challenges can provide valuable insights for building a more robust and sustainable industry.

FUNDING AND ACKNOWLEDGEMENTS

This research was supported by "Fundação para a Ciência e Tecnologia" (FCT), Portugal, through the SHIFT project (Sustainability-oriented, Highly interactive, and Innovation-based Framework for Tourism marketing), reference number PTDC/EDE-OGE/2146/2021.

REFERENCES

Abdullaeva, S., & Oripova, D. (2023). Development of Main Directions for Achieving Sustainability in Tourism. *International Journal of Social Science Research and Review*, *6*(6), 154–159. doi:10.47814/ijssrr.v6i6.1358

Abdullah, M., Dias, C., Muley, D., & Shahin, M. (2020). Exploring the impacts of COVID-19 on travel behavior and mode preferences. *Transportation Research Interdisciplinary Perspectives*, *8*, 100255. doi:10.1016/j.trip.2020.100255 PMID:34173481

Afrisal, A. (2022). Collaborative Governance in Tourism Development Policy. *Journal of Social Sciences*, *3*(6), 1266–1270. doi:10.46799/jss.v3i6.478

Aguinis, H., Kraus, S., Poček, J., Meyer, N., & Jensen, S. H. (2023). The why, how, and what of public policy implications of tourism and hospitality research. *Tourism Management*, *97*, 104720. doi:10.1016/j.tourman.2023.104720

Ahmad, N., Harun, A., Khizar, H. M. U., Khalid, J., & Khan, S. (2022). Drivers and barriers of travel behaviors during and post COVID-19 pandemic: a systematic literature review and future agenda. *Journal of Tourism Futures*, 1-23. doi:10.1108/JTF-01-2022-0023

Akadiri, S. saint, Alola, A. A., & Uzuner, G. (2020). Economic policy uncertainty and tourism: evidence from the heterogeneous panel. In Current Issues in Tourism, 23(20), 2507–2514). Routledge. doi:10.1080/13683500.2019.1687662

Aldao, C., Blasco, D., & Espallargas, M. P. (2022). Lessons from COVID-19 for the future: destination crisis management, tourist behavior and tourism industry trends. *Journal of Tourism Futures*, 1-15. doi:10.1108/JTF-02-2022-0059

Amelung, B., Nicholls, S., & Viner, D. (2007). Implications of Global Climate Change for Tourism Flows and Seasonality. *Journal of Travel Research*, *45*(3), 285–296. doi:10.1177/0047287506295937

Amoiradis, C., Velissariou, E., & Stankova, M. (2021). Tourism as a Socio-Cultural Phenomenon: A Critical Analysis. *The Social Science Journal*, *4*(2), 10–21. doi:10.31014/aior.1991.04.02.271

Andrade, M. J., Costa, J. P., & Jiménez-Morales, E. (2021). Challenges for European tourist-city-ports: Strategies for a sustainable coexistence in the cruise post-COVID context. *Land (Basel)*, *10*(11), 1269. doi:10.3390/land10111269

Arabadzhyan, A., Figini, P., García, C., González, M., Lam-González, Y., & León, C. (2020). Climate change, coastal tourism, and impact chains – a literature review. *Current Issues in Tourism, 24*(16), 2233–2268. doi:10.1080/13683500.2020.1825351

Artal-Tur, A., Villena-Navarro, M., & Alamá-Sabater, L. (2018). The relationship between cultural tourist behaviour and destination sustainability. *Anatolia, 29*(2), 237–251. doi:10.1080/13032917.2017.1414444

Awedyk, M., & Niezgoda, A. (2016). New opportunities for future tourism after 25 years of political and socioeconomic transformation – foresight in Poland's tourism planning. *Journal of Tourism Futures, 2*(2), 137–154. doi:10.1108/JTF-05-2015-0031

Bąk, I., & Szczecińska, B. (2020). Global Demographic Trends and Effects on Tourism. *European Research Studies, 4*(4), 571–585. doi:10.35808/ersj/1701

Begum, H., Er, A. C., Alam, A. S. A. F., & Sahazali, N. (2014). Tourist's Perceptions towards the Role of Stakeholders in Sustainable Tourism. *Procedia: Social and Behavioral Sciences, 144*, 313–321. doi:10.1016/j.sbspro.2014.07.301

Bianchi, R. (2018). The political economy of tourism development: A critical review. *Annals of Tourism Research, 70*, 88–102. doi:10.1016/j.annals.2017.08.005

Bowen, J., & Whalen, E. (2017). Trends that are changing travel and tourism. *Worldwide Hospitality and Tourism Themes, 9*(6), 592–602. doi:10.1108/WHATT-09-2017-0045

Brendehaug, E., Aall, C., & Dodds, R. (2017). Environmental policy integration as a strategy for sustainable tourism planning: Issues in implementation. *Journal of Sustainable Tourism, 25*(9), 1257–1274. doi:10.1080/09669582.2016.1259319

Buckley, R., Guitart, D., & Shakeela, A. (2017). Contested surf tourism resources in the Maldives. *Annals of Tourism Research, 64*, 185–199. doi:10.1016/j.annals.2017.03.005

Buhalis, D. (2019). Technology in tourism-from information communication technologies to eTourism and smart tourism towards ambient intelligence tourism: A perspective article. *Tourism Review, 75*(1), 267–272. doi:10.1108/TR-06-2019-0258

Buzzi, N. S., Menéndez, M. C., Truchet, D. M., Delgado, A. L., & Severini, M. D. F. (2022). An overview on metal pollution on touristic sandy beaches: Is the COVID-19 pandemic an opportunity to improve coastal management? *Marine Pollution Bulletin, 174*, 113275. doi:10.1016/j.marpolbul.2021.113275 PMID:35090269

Campos-Soriaa, J. A., Inchausti-Sintes, F., & Eugenio-Martin, J. L. (2015). Understanding tourists' economizing strategies during the global economic crisis. *Tourism Management*, *48*, 164–173. doi:10.1016/j.tourman.2014.10.019

Can, Y., Gaberli̇, Ü., & Güler, M. (2022). Impact of Political Stability and Absence of Violence/Terrorism on Tourism: A Panel Co-Integration Analysis. *Yönetim ve Ekonomi Araştırmaları Dergisi*, *20*(4), 387–400. doi:10.11611/yead.1168124

Cao, B., Zhao, J., Lv, Z., & Yang, P. (2021). Diversified Personalized Recommendation Optimization Based on Mobile Data. *IEEE Transactions on Intelligent Transportation Systems*, *22*(4), 2133–2139. doi:10.1109/TITS.2020.3040909

Chamboko-Mpotaringa, M., & Tichaawa, T. M. (2021). Tourism Digital Marketing Tools and Views on Future Trends: A Systematic Review of Literature. *African Journal of Hospitality, Tourism and Leisure*, *10*(2), 712–726. doi:10.46222/ajhtl.19770720-128

Chen, H., & Jai, T. (2019). Cyber alarm: Determining the impacts of hotel's data breach messages. *International Journal of Hospitality Management*, *82*, 326–334. doi:10.1016/j.ijhm.2018.10.002

Chen, S., Law, R., Zhang, M., & Si, Y. (2021). Mobile communications for tourism and hospitality: A review of historical evolution, present status, and future trends. *Electronics (Basel)*, *10*(15), 1804. doi:10.3390/electronics10151804

Cheng, X., Xue, T., Yang, B., & Ma, B. (2023). A digital transformation approach in hospitality and tourism research. *International Journal of Contemporary Hospitality Management*, *35*(8), 2944–2967. doi:10.1108/IJCHM-06-2022-0679

Chitadze, N. (2023). International Tourism and its Impact on World Politics and World Economy. *Journal of Social Sciences*, *8*(2). doi:10.31578/jss.v8i2.146

Collazos, A., Obando, J., López, J., & García, L. (2023). Public policy and its impact on innovation, competitiveness, and performance in the tourism sector. *Cogent Social Sciences*, *9*(2), 2249692. Advance online publication. doi:10.1080/23311886.2023.2249692

Correia, A., Kozak, M., & Ferradeira, J. (2011). Impact of culture on tourist decision-making styles. *International Journal of Tourism Research*, *13*(5), 433–446. doi:10.1002/jtr.817

Cozzio, C., Orlandi, L. B., & Zardini, A. (2018). Food sustainability as a strategic value driver in the hotel industry. *Sustainability (Basel)*, *10*(10), 3404. doi:10.3390/su10103404

Croce, V. (2018). With growth comes accountability: Could a leisure activity turn into a driver for sustainable growth? *Journal of Tourism Futures*, *4*(3), 218–232. doi:10.1108/JTF-04-2018-0020

Darcy, S., Mckercher, B., & Schweinsberg, S. (2020). From tourism and disability to accessible tourism: A perspective article. *Tourism Review*, *75*(1), 140–144. doi:10.1108/TR-07-2019-0323

Delgado, A., Rodriguez, R., & Staszewska, A. (2023). Tackling Food Waste in the Tourism Sector: Towards a Responsible Consumption Trend. *Sustainability (Basel)*, *15*(17), 13226. doi:10.3390/su151713226

Demir, E., Gozgor, G., & Paramati, S. R. (2019). Do geopolitical risks matter for inbound tourism? *Eurasian Business Review*, *9*(2), 183–191. doi:10.1007/s40821-019-00118-9

Demiralay, S., & Kilincarslan, E. (2019). The impact of geopolitical risks on travel and leisure stocks. *Tourism Management*, *75*, 460–476. doi:10.1016/j.tourman.2019.06.013

Derbisheva, E., & Kyzy, E. (2022). Regulatory Regulation of Construction of Tourist Facilities. *The herald of KSUCTA n a N Isanov*. . doi:10.35803/1694-5298.2022.2.769-776

Dias, Á., González-Rodríguez, M. R., & Hallak, R. (2022). Nascent entrepreneurship: A critical perspective and research agenda in tourism and hospitality. *International Journal of Contemporary Hospitality Management*. doi:10.1108/IJCHM-07-2022-0853

Dong, X., Liu, S., Li, H., Yang, Z., Liang, S., & Deng, N. (2020). Love of nature as a mediator between connectedness to nature and sustainable consumption behavior. *Journal of Cleaner Production*, *242*, 118451. doi:10.1016/j.jclepro.2019.118451

Ercan, F. (2020). An examination on the use of immersive reality technologies in the travel and tourism industry. *Business & Management Studies: An International Journal*, *8*(2), 2348–2383. doi:10.15295/bmij.v8i2.1510

Estevão, C., & Costa, C. (2020). Natural disaster management in tourist destinations: A systematic literature review. *European Journal of Tourism Research*, *25*, 2502. doi:10.54055/ejtr.v25i.417

Eugenio-Martin, J. (2003). Modelling Determinants of Tourism Demand as a Five-Stage Process: A Discrete Choice Methodological Approach. *Tourism and Hospitality Research*, *4*(4), 341–354. doi:10.1177/146735840300400407

Eugenio-Martin, J. L., & Campos-Soria, J. A. (2014). Economic crisis and tourism expenditure cutback decision. *Annals of Tourism Research*, *44*(1), 53–73. doi:10.1016/j.annals.2013.08.013

Flinta, N. (2022). Modern electronic booking and reservation systems in the hotel business. *Scientific Herald of Chernivtsi University. Geography (Sheffield, England)*, *839*(839), 40–49. doi:10.31861/geo.2022.839.40-49

Fossgard, K., & Stensland, S. (2021). Broadening the scope of resources in nature: An explorative study of nature-based tourism firms. *Journal of Ecotourism*, *20*(1), 35–50. doi:10.1080/14724049.2020.1751650

Fu, H., Okumus, F., Wu, K., & Köseoglu, M. A. (2019). The entrepreneurship research in hospitality and tourism. *International Journal of Hospitality Management*, *78*, 1–12. doi:10.1016/j.ijhm.2018.10.005

Garvey, A. M., & Bolton, L. E. (2017). Eco-product choice cuts both ways: How pro-environmental licensing versus reinforcement is contingent on environmental consciousness. *Journal of Public Policy & Marketing*, *36*(2), 284–298. doi:10.1509/jppm.16.096

Ghaderi, Z., & Henderson, J. C. (2013). Japanese tsunami debris and the threat to sustainable tourism in the Hawaiian Islands. *Tourism Management Perspectives*, *8*, 98–105. doi:10.1016/j.tmp.2013.09.001

Ghaderi, Z., Saboori, B., & Khoshkam, M. (2017). Does security matter in tourism demand? *Current Issues in Tourism*, *20*(6), 552–565. doi:10.1080/13683500.2016.1161603

Ghalia, T., Fidrmuc, J., Samargandi, N., & Sohag, K. (2019). Institutional quality, political risk, and tourism. *Tourism Management Perspectives*, *32*, 100576. doi:10.1016/j.tmp.2019.100576

Giurea, R., Precazzini, I., Ragazzi, M., Achim, M., Cioca, L., Conti, F., Torretta, V., & Rada, E. (2018). Good Practices and Actions for Sustainable Municipal Solid Waste Management in the Tourist Sector. *Resources*, *7*(3), 51. doi:10.3390/resources7030051

Gomes, S., & Lopes, J. (2023). Insights for Pro-Sustainable Tourist Behavior: The Role of Sustainable Destination Information and Pro-Sustainable Tourist Habits. *Sustainability (Basel)*, *15*(11), 8856. doi:10.3390/su15118856

Gössling, S., Scott, D., & Hall, C. (2020). Pandemics, tourism, and global change: A rapid assessment of COVID-19. *Journal of Sustainable Tourism*, *29*(1), 1–20. doi:10.1080/09669582.2020.1758708

Gozgor, G., Lau, M. C. K., Zeng, Y., Yan, C., & Lin, Z. (2022). The Impact of Geopolitical Risks on Tourism Supply in Developing Economies: The Moderating Role of Social Globalization. *Journal of Travel Research*, *61*(4), 872–886. doi:10.1177/00472875211004760

Gretzel, U., Murphy, J., Pesonen, J., & Blanton, C. (2019). Food waste in tourist households: A perspective article. *Tourism Review*, *75*(1), 235–238. doi:10.1108/TR-05-2019-0170

Gu, J., Song, C., Jiang, W., Wang, X., & Liu, M. (2020). Enhancing Personalized Trip Recommendation with Attractive Routes. *Proceedings of the AAAI Conference on Artificial Intelligence*. IEEE. 10.1609/aaai.v34i01.5407

Guo, Y., Jiang, J., & Li, S. (2019). A sustainable tourism policy research review. *Sustainability (Basel)*, *11*(11), 3187. Advance online publication. doi:10.3390/su11113187

Gupta, K., & Sharma, S. (2021). Kiosks as self-service technology in hotels: Opportunities and challenges. *Worldwide Hospitality and Tourism Themes*, *13*(2), 236–251. doi:10.1108/WHATT-10-2020-0125

Ha, T. K. D., Nguyen, T. K., Pham, T. M. N., Nguyen, D. Q., Truong, B. T., Le, V. S., & Nguyen, H. T. (2022). Influence of Macro Environment on Tourism Value Chain in Vietnam. *Geo Journal of Tourism and Geosites*, *41*(2), 400–407. doi:10.30892/gtg.41209-843

Han, S. H., Lee, J., Edvardsson, B., & Verma, R. (2021). Mobile technology adoption among hotels: Managerial issues and opportunities. *Tourism Management Perspectives*, *38*, 100811. doi:10.1016/j.tmp.2021.100811

Heikkinen, H. I., Bjørst, R., Pashkevich, A., & Fi, H. I. H. (2020). Challenging Tourism Landscapes of Southwest Greenland: Identifying Social and Cultural Capital for Sustainable Tourism Development. *Arctic Anthropology*, *57*(2), 212–228. doi:10.3368/aa.57.2.212

Huber, D., Milne, S., & Hyde, K. (2019). Conceptualizing Senior Tourism Behaviour: A Life Events Approach. *Tourist Studies*, *19*(4), 407–433. doi:10.1177/1468797619832318

Iranmanesh, M., Ghobakhloo, M., Nilashi, M., Tseng, M. L., Yadegaridehkordi, E., & Leung, N. (2022). Applications of disruptive digital technologies in hotel industry: A systematic review. *International Journal of Hospitality Management, 107*, 103304. doi:10.1016/j.ijhm.2022.103304

Işık, C., Sirakaya-Turk, E., & Ongan, S. (2020). Testing the efficacy of the economic policy uncertainty index on tourism demand in USMCA: Theory and evidence. *Tourism Economics*, *26*(8), 1344–1357. doi:10.1177/1354816619888346

Jena, R. K., & Dwivedi, Y. (2021). Prioritizing the barriers to tourism growth in rural India: an integrated multi-criteria decision making (MCDM) approach. *Journal of Tourism Futures*, 1-24. doi:10.1108/JTF-10-2020-0171

Jiménez-Guerrero, J. F., Piedra-Muñoz, L., Galdeano-Gómez, E., & Pérez-Mesa, J. C. (2021). The Global Economic Crisis and International Tourism: A Sub-Continental Analysis. *Tourism Planning & Development, 18*(1), 1–24. doi:10.1080/21568316.2019.1683887

Juvan, E., & Dolnicar, S. (2017). Drivers of pro-environmental tourist behaviours are not universal. *Journal of Cleaner Production, 166*, 879–890. doi:10.1016/j.jclepro.2017.08.087

Ketter, E. (2020). Millennial travel: Tourism micro-trends of European Generation Y. *Journal of Tourism Futures*, *7*(2), 192–196. doi:10.1108/JTF-10-2019-0106

Khalid, U., Okafor, L. E., & Shafiullah, M. (2020). The Effects of Economic and Financial Crises on International Tourist Flows: A Cross-Country Analysis. *Journal of Travel Research*, *59*(2), 315–334. doi:10.1177/0047287519834360

Khan, K., Su, C. W., Xiao, Y. D., Zhu, H., & Zhang, X. (2021). Trends in tourism under economic uncertainty. *Tourism Economics*, *27*(4), 841–858. doi:10.1177/1354816620909608

KhanN.HassanA. U.FahadS.NaushadM. (2020). Factors affecting the tourism industry and its impacts on the global economy of the world. SSRN. https://ssrn.com/abstract=3559353 or doi:10.2139/ssrn.3559353

Kim, D., & Park, S. (2020). Rethinking millennials: How are they shaping the tourism industry? *Asia Pacific Journal of Tourism Research*, *25*(1), 1–2. doi:10.1080/10941665.2019.1667607

Kim, Y., & Kim, H. (2020). Usability Evaluation and Improvements of Mobile Travel Apps. *International Journal of Internet. Broadcasting and Communication*, *12*, 27–36. doi:10.7236/IJIBC.2020.12.1.27

Knani, M., Echchakoui, S., & Ladhari, R. (2022). Artificial intelligence in tourism and hospitality: Bibliometric analysis and research agenda. *International Journal of Hospitality Management*, *107*, 103317. doi:10.1016/j.ijhm.2022.103317

Kosevich, A., Novikova, N., Gladkikh, V., Sharonin, P., & Smirnov, M. (2020). Improving Economic and Legal Regulation in the Tourism Sector. *Journal of Environmental Management and Tourism*, *11*(4), 979–984. doi:10.14505//jemt.v11.4(44).23

Kozłowski, M., Brzozowska-Rup, K., & Piotrowska-Piątek, A. (2021). Information and Communication Technologies in Food and accommodation sector in EU Countries: Sticker or Challenge for tourism development? *Technological Forecasting and Social Change*, *171*, 120941. doi:10.1016/j.techfore.2021.120941

Kuncharia, K. (2019). Influence of family and culture on youth consumers. *Asian Journal of Development Matters*, *13*, 79–85.

Lebrun, A. M., Corbel, R., & Bouchet, P. (2022). Impacts of Covid-19 on travel intention for summer 2020: A trend in proximity tourism mediated by an attitude towards Covid-19. *Service Business*, *16*(3), 469–501. doi:10.1007/s11628-021-00450-z

Lee, C., & Chen, M. (2020). Do Country Risks Matter for Tourism Development? International Evidence. *Journal of Travel Research*, *60*(7), 1445–1468. doi:10.1177/0047287520954539

Lee, C., Kang, S., Ahmad, M., Park, Y., Park, E., & Kang, C. (2021). Role of cultural worldview in predicting heritage tourists' behavioural intention. *Leisure Studies*, *40*(5), 645–657. doi:10.1080/02614367.2021.1890804

Leith, C. (2020). Tourism trends: Lifestyle developments and the links to solo tourism. *Journal of Tourism Futures*, *6*(3), 251–255. doi:10.1108/JTF-11-2019-0126

Leonidou, L. C., Coudounaris, D. N., Kvasova, O., & Christodoulides, P. (2015). Drivers and Outcomes of Green Tourist Attitudes and Behavior: Sociodemographic Moderating Effects. *Psychology and Marketing*, *32*(6), 635–650. doi:10.1002/mar.20806

Li, Y., Huang, S. S., & Song, L. (2020). Opportunity and necessity entrepreneurship in the hospitality sector: Examining the institutional environment influences. *Tourism Management Perspectives*, *34*, 100665. doi:10.1016/j.tmp.2020.100665

Liu, X., Mehraliyev, F., Liu, C., & Schuckert, M. (2020). The roles of social media in tourists' choices of travel components. *Tourist Studies*, *20*(1), 27–48. doi:10.1177/1468797619873107

López-Gamero, M. D., Claver-Cortés, E., & Molina-Azorín, J. F. (2011). Environmental perception, management, and competitive opportunity in Spanish hotels. *Cornell Hospitality Quarterly*, *52*(4), 480–500. doi:10.1177/1938965511420694

MacNeill, T., & Wozniak, D. (2018). The economic, social, and environmental impacts of cruise tourism. *Tourism Management*, *66*, 387–404. doi:10.1016/j.tourman.2017.11.002

Mandić, A., & Vuković, M. (2022). Millennials attitudes, choices and behaviour - integrative analysis. *Journal of Ecotourism*, *21*(1), 87–97. doi:10.1080/14724049.2021.1932925

Marin, D. (2015). Study on the economic impact of tourism and of agrotourism on local communities. *Research Journal of Agricultural Science*, *47*, 160–163.

Martins, L., Gan, Y., & Ferreira-Lopes, A. (2017). An empirical analysis of the influence of macroeconomic determinants on World tourism demand. *Tourism Management*, *61*, 248–260. doi:10.1016/j.tourman.2017.01.008

Masiero, L., Viglia, G., & Nieto-García, M. (2020). Strategic consumer behavior in online hotel booking. *Annals of Tourism Research*, *83*, 102947. doi:10.1016/j.annals.2020.102947

Máthé, I. (2018). Multiculturality and Interculturality in Tourism. *Valahian Journal of Economic Studies*, *9*(1), 39–46. doi:10.2478/vjes-2018-0004

Maxim, C. (2015). Drivers of Success in Implementing Sustainable Tourism Policies in Urban Areas. *Tourism Planning & Development*, *12*(1), 37–47. doi:10.1080/21568316.2014.960599

Maxim, C. (2019). Challenges faced by world tourism cities–London's perspective. *Current Issues in Tourism*, *22*(9), 1006–1024. doi:10.1080/13683500.2017.1347609

Mckercher, B., & Prideaux, B. (2020). *Tourism Theories*. Concepts and Models., doi:10.23912/9781911635352-4280

Menon, D., Gunasekar, S., Dixit, S. K., Das, P., & Mandal, S. (2021). Present and prospective research themes for tourism and hospitality education post-COVID19: A bibliometric analysis. *Journal of Hospitality, Leisure, Sport and Tourism Education*, *100360*. doi:10.1016/j.jhlste.2021.100360 PMID:34840528

Merino, F., & Prats, M. A. (2020). Sustainable beach management and promotion of the local tourist industry: Can blue flags be a good driver of this balance? *Ocean and Coastal Management*, *198*, 105359. doi:10.1016/j.ocecoaman.2020.105359

Mestanza-Ramón, C., & Jiménez-Caballero, J. L. (2021). Nature tourism on the Colombian—Ecuadorian Amazonian border: History, current situation, and challenges. *Sustainability (Basel)*, *13*(8), 4432. doi:10.3390/su13084432

Moyle, B. D., McLennan, C. J., Ruhanen, L., & Weiler, B. (2014). Terrorist incidents and tourism demand: Evidence from Greece. *Journal of Sustainable Tourism*, *22*(7), 1037–1051. doi:10.1080/09669582.2013.839694

Muñoz, E., & Navia, R. (2015). Waste management in touristic regions. *Waste Management & Research*, *33*(7), 593–594. doi:10.1177/0734242X15594982 PMID:26185162

Nagarajan, N. R., Wada, M., Fang, M. L., & Sixsmith, A. (2019). Defining organizational contributions to sustaining an aging workforce: a bibliometric review. In European Journal of Ageing, 16(3). Springer Verlag. doi:10.1007/s10433-019-00499-w

Nam, K., Dutt, C. S., Chathoth, P., & Khan, M. S. (2021). Blockchain technology for smart city and smart tourism: Latest trends and challenges. *Asia Pacific Journal of Tourism Research*, *26*(4), 454–468. doi:10.1080/10941665.2019.1585376

Naseer, S., Khalid, S., Parveen, S., Abbass, K., Song, H., & Achim, M. (2023). COVID-19 outbreak: Impact on global economy. *Frontiers in Public Health*, *10*, 1009393. doi:10.3389/fpubh.2022.1009393 PMID:36793360

Neto, F. (2003). A new approach to sustainable tourism development: Moving beyond environmental protection. *Natural Resources Forum*, *27*(3), 212–222. doi:10.1111/1477-8947.00056

Nguyen, C. P., Thanh, S. D., & Nguyen, B. (2022). Economic uncertainty and tourism consumption. *Tourism Economics*, *28*(4), 920–941. doi:10.1177/1354816620981519

Nikolskaya, E., Zakharova, E., Galkin, D., Kovaleva, N., & Panova, N. (2021). *The Impact of Digital Technologies on the Transformation of the Tourism and Hospitality Industry*. Revista Gestão Inovação e Tecnologias. doi:10.47059/revistageintec.v11i4.2133

Nuenen, T., & Scarles, C. (2021). Advancements in technology and digital media in tourism. *Tourist Studies*, *21*(1), 119–132. doi:10.1177/1468797621990410

Ooi, N., Duke, E., & O'Leary, J. (2018). Tourism in changing natural environments. *Tourism Geographies*, *20*(2), 193–201. doi:10.1080/14616688.2018.1440418

Ooi, N., Laing, J., & Mair, J. (2015). Sociocultural change facing ranchers in the Rocky Mountain West as a result of mountain resort tourism and amenity migration. *Journal of Rural Studies*, *41*(October), 59–71. doi:10.1016/j.jrurstud.2015.07.005

Otero-Giráldez, M., Álvarez-Díaz, M., & González-Gómez, M. (2012). Estimating the long-run effects of socioeconomic and meteorological factors on the domestic tourism demand for Galicia (Spain). *Tourism Management*, *33*(6), 1301–1308. doi:10.1016/j.tourman.2012.04.005

Page, S. J., & Connell, J. (2020). *Tourism: A modern synthesis*. Routledge. doi:10.4324/9781003005520

Pan, S., Gao, M., Kim, H., Shah, K., Pei, S., & Chiang, P. (2018). Advances and challenges in sustainable tourism toward a green economy. *The Science of the Total Environment*, *635*, 452–469. doi:10.1016/j.scitotenv.2018.04.134 PMID:29677671

Pandey, D., & Kumar, R. (2022). Russia-Ukraine War and the global tourism sector: A 13-day tale. *Current Issues in Tourism*, *26*(5), 692–700. doi:10.1080/13683500.2022.2081789

Papatheodorou, A., Rosselló, J., & Xiao, H. (2010). Global economic crisis and tourism: Consequences and perspectives. *Journal of Travel Research*, *49*(1), 39–45. doi:10.1177/0047287509355327

Paré, G., Tate, M., Johnstone, D., & Kitsiou, S. (2016). Contextualizing the twin concepts of systematicity and transparency in information systems literature reviews. *European Journal of Information Systems*, *25*(6), 493–508. doi:10.1057/s41303-016-0020-3

Pencarelli, T. (2019). The digital revolution in the travel and tourism industry. *Information Technology & Tourism*, *22*(3), 455–476. doi:10.1007/s40558-019-00160-3

Pérez-Tapia, G., Mercadé-Melé, P., Yeong-Hyeon, H., & Almeida-García, F. (2022). Cultural Context or Generational Cohort: Which Influences Tourist Behavior More? *Frontiers in Psychology*, *13*, 767035. doi:10.3389/fpsyg.2022.767035 PMID:35282202

Perles-Ribes, J., Ramón-Rodríguez, A., Sevilla-Jiménez, M., & Moreno-Izquierdo, L. (2016). Unemployment effects of economic crises on hotel and residential tourism destinations: The case of Spain. *Tourism Management*, *54*, 356–368. doi:10.1016/j.tourman.2015.12.002

Plzáková, L., & Smeral, E. (2022). Impact of the COVID-19 crisis on European tourism. *Tourism Economics*, *28*(1), 91–109. doi:10.1177/13548166211031113

Pop, R., Saplacan, Z., Dabija, D., & Alt, M. (2021). The impact of social media influencers on travel decisions: The role of trust in consumer decision journey. *Current Issues in Tourism*, *25*(5), 823–843. doi:10.1080/13683500.2021.1895729

Priya, G., Mathew, S., & Subbaiyan, G. (2019). Household Structure and the Travel Pattern of Senior Citizens for Leisure Trips. *Transportation Research*, *45*, 325–340. doi:10.1007/978-981-32-9042-6_26

Pulido-Fernández, J., & Cárdenas-García, P. (2020). Analyzing the Bidirectional Relationship between Tourism Growth and Economic Development. *Journal of Travel Research*, *60*(3), 583–602. doi:10.1177/0047287520922316

Pulido-Fernández, J. I., Cárdenas-García, P. J., & Espinosa-Pulido, J. A. (2019). Does environmental sustainability contribute to tourism growth? An analysis at the country level. *Journal of Cleaner Production*, *213*, 309–319. doi:10.1016/j.jclepro.2018.12.151

Rasoolimanesh, S. M., Seyfi, S., Rastegar, R., & Hall, C. M. (2021). Destination image during the COVID-19 pandemic and future travel behavior: The moderating role of past experience. *Journal of Destination Marketing & Management*, *21*, 100620. doi:10.1016/j.jdmm.2021.100620

Raykova, M. (2021). Crisis Management in Tourism. *Socio-Economic Analyses*, *13*(1), 86–91. doi:10.54664/OYZN2909

Razumova, M., Ibáñez, J. L., & Palmer, J. R. M. (2015). Drivers of environmental innovation in Majorcan hotels. *Journal of Sustainable Tourism*, *23*(10), 1529–1549. doi:10.1080/09669582.2015.1062016

Robinson, P., Lück, M., & Smith, S. (2020). Tourism policy and planning. *Tourism (Zagreb)*. doi:10.1079/9781780642970.0391

Roman, M., Kosiński, R., Bhatta, K., Niedziółka, A., & Krasnodębski, A. (2022). Virtual and Space Tourism as New Trends in Travelling at the Time of the COVID-19 Pandemic. *Sustainability (Basel)*, *14*(2), 628. doi:10.3390/su14020628

Rosselló, J., Becken, S., & Santana-Gallego, M. (2020). The effects of natural disasters on international tourism: A global analysis. *Tourism Management*, *79*, 104080. doi:10.1016/j.tourman.2020.104080 PMID:32287755

Rosselló, J., & Santana-Gallego, M. (2014). Recent trends in international tourist climate preferences: A revised picture for climatic change scenarios. *Climatic Change*, *124*(1–2), 119–132. doi:10.1007/s10584-014-1086-3

Ruan, W., Kang, S., & Song, H. J. (2020). Applying protection motivation theory to understand international tourists' behavioural intentions under the threat of air pollution: A case of Beijing, China. *Current Issues in Tourism*, *23*(16), 2027–2041. doi:10.1080/13683500.2020.1743242

Santos, M. C., Veiga, C., & Águas, P. (2016). Tourism services: Facing the challenge of new tourist profiles. *Worldwide Hospitality and Tourism Themes*, *8*(6), 654–669. doi:10.1108/WHATT-09-2016-0048

Scott, D. (2021). Sustainable tourism and the grand challenge of climate change. *Sustainability (Basel)*, *13*(4), 1–17. doi:10.3390/su13041966

Seyfi, S., Hall, C. M., Saarinen, J., & Vo-Thanh, T. (2021). Understanding drivers and barriers affecting tourists' engagement in digitally mediated pro-sustainability boycotts. *Journal of Sustainable Tourism*. Advance online publication. doi:10.1080/09669582.2021.2013489

Shijin, W., Yaqiong, M., Xueyan, Z., & Jia, X. (2020). Polar tourism and environment change: Opportunity, impact and adaptation. *Polar Science*, *25*, 100544. doi:10.1016/j.polar.2020.100544

Siddiqui, S., & Imran, M. (2019). Impact of Climate Change on Tourism. *Environmental Impacts of Tourism in Developing Nations,* 68-83. doi:10.4018/978-1-5225-5843-9.ch004

Smeral, E. (2009). The impact of the financial and economic crisis on European tourism. *Journal of Travel Research*, *48*(1), 3–13. doi:10.1177/0047287509336332

Sobhanifard, Y., & Vaeysi, M. (2020). Mixed modeling of the social network mechanisms for the sustainable development of tourism: The case of Iranian Kurdistan. *Sustainable Development (Bradford)*, *28*(1), 187–196. doi:10.1002/sd.1981

Sofronov, B. (2018). The development of the travel and tourism industry in the world. Annals of Spiru Haret University. *Economic Series*, *18*(4), 123–137. doi:10.26458/1848

Song, H., Livat, F., & Ye, S. (2019). Effects of terrorist attacks on tourist flows to France: Is wine tourism a substitute for urban tourism? *Journal of Destination Marketing & Management*, *14*, 100385. doi:10.1016/j.jdmm.2019.100385

Soontiens-Olsen, A., Genge, L., Medeiros, A., Klein, G., Lin, S., & Sheehan, L. (2023). Coastal Adaptation and Vulnerability Assessment in a Warming Future: A Systematic Review of the Tourism Sector. *SAGE Open*, *13*(2), 21582440231179215. doi:10.1177/21582440231179215

Tao, M., Nawaz, M. Z., Nawaz, S., Butt, A. H., & Ahmad, H. (2018). Users' acceptance of innovative mobile hotel booking trends: UK vs. PRC. *Information Technology & Tourism*, *20*(1–4), 9–36. doi:10.1007/s40558-018-0123-x

Tassikas, A. (2021). Data Processing and Legal Protection in Contracts in the Technologically Innovative Tourism Sector. *European Journal ofTourism. Hospitality and Recreation*, *11*(1), 77–90. doi:10.2478/ejthr-2021-0008

Templier, M., & Paré, G. (2015). A Framework for Guiding and Evaluating Literature Reviews. *Communications of the Association for Information Systems*, *37*(August), 2–28. doi:10.17705/1CAIS.03706

Thimm, T., Bild, C., & Kalff, M. (2019). Climate change in low mountain ranges: Opportunities in sustainable Black Forest tourism. *European Journal of Tourism Research*, *23*, 63–70. doi:10.54055/ejtr.v23i.389

Thullah, A., & Jalloh, S. (2021). A Review of the Economic, Social, and Environmental Impacts of Tourism Development. *American Journal of Theoretical and Applied Business*, *7*(2), 39–46. doi:10.11648/j.ajtab.20210702.12

Tian, H., Presa-Reyes, M., Tao, Y., Wang, T., Pouyanfar, S., Miguel, A., Luis, S., Shyu, M., Chen, S., & Iyengar, S. (2021). Data Analytics for Air Travel Data: A Survey and New Perspectives. *ACM Computing Surveys*, *54*(8), 1–35. doi:10.1145/3469028

Tohmo, T. (2018). The economic impact of tourism in Central Finland: A regional input–output study. *Tourism Review*, *73*(4), 521–547. doi:10.1108/TR-04-2017-0080

Toirxonovna, A., Obloqulovich, U., & Tuychiev, I. (2020). Institutional Framework for the Development of the Tourism Market. *Tourism Management*, *8*. doi:10.21070/ijler.2020.V8.687

Tolkach, D., & Pratt, S. (2019). Globalisation and cultural change in Pacific Island countries: The role of tourism. *Tourism Geographies*, *23*(3), 371–396. doi:10.1080/14616688.2019.1625071

Vancia, A., Băltescu, C., Brătucu, G., Tecău, A., Chițu, I., & Duguleană, L. (2023). Examining the Disruptive Potential of Generation Z Tourists on the Travel Industry in the Digital Age. *Sustainability (Basel), 15*(11), 8756. doi:10.3390/su15118756

Veiga, C., Santos, M. C., Águas, P., & Santos, J. A. C. (2017). Are millennials transforming global tourism? Challenges for destinations and companies. *Worldwide Hospitality and Tourism Themes, 9*(6), 603–616. doi:10.1108/WHATT-09-2017-0047

Wang, Q. C., Xie, K. X., Liu, X., Shen, G. Q. P., Wei, H. H., & Liu, T. Y. (2021). Psychological drivers of hotel guests' energy-saving behaviors—Empirical research based on the extended theory of planned behaviour. *Buildings, 11*(9), 401. doi:10.3390/buildings11090401

Webster, C., & Ivanov, S. (2020). Demographic change as a driver for tourism automation. *Journal of Tourism Futures, 6*(3), 263–270. doi:10.1108/JTF-10-2019-0109

Wernick, D. A., & von Glinow, M. A. (2012). Reflections on the Evolving Terrorist Threat to Luxury Hotels: A Case Study on Marriott International. *Thunderbird International Business Review, 54*(5), 729–746. doi:10.1002/tie.21496

World Travel and Tourism Council. (2022, November 14). *Travel & Tourism Economic Impact 2022*. WTTC. https://wttc.org/Portals/0/Documents/Reports/2022/EIR2022-Global%20Trends.pdf

Yallop, A., & Seraphin, H. (2020). Big data and analytics in tourism and hospitality: Opportunities and risks. *Journal of Tourism Futures, 6*(3), 257–262. doi:10.1108/JTF-10-2019-0108

Yang, E. C. L. (2021). What motivates and hinders people from traveling alone? A study of solo and non-solo travelers. *Current Issues in Tourism, 24*(17), 2458–2471. doi:10.1080/13683500.2020.1839025

Yang, E. C. L., Yang, M. J. H., & Khoo-Lattimore, C. (2019). The meanings of solo travel for Asian women. *Tourism Review, 74*(5), 1047-1047–1057. doi:10.1108/TR-10-2018-0150

Zhang, K., Hou, Y., & Li, G. (2020). Threat of infectious disease during an outbreak: Influence on tourists' emotional responses to disadvantaged price inequality. *Annals of Tourism Research, 84*, 102993. doi:10.1016/j.annals.2020.102993 PMID:32834227

Zheng, T., Farrish, J., & Kitterlin, M. (2016). Performance Trends of Hotels and Casino Hotels Through the Recession: An ARIMA With Intervention Analysis of Stock Indices. *Journal of Hospitality Marketing & Management, 25*(1), 49–68. doi:10.1080/19368623.2015.970725

Zhuang, X., Yao, Y., & Li, J. J. (2019). Sociocultural impacts of tourism on residents of world cultural heritage sites in China. *Sustainability (Basel)*, *11*(3), 840. doi:10.3390/su11030840

Chapter 2
Interacting With the Future:
Smart Tourism Evolution Through IoT and Social Media Strategies

C. V. Suresh Babu
https://orcid.org/0000-0002-8474-2882
Hindustan Institute of Technolgy and Science

C. S. Akkash Anniyappa
Sri Sivasubramaniya Nadar College of Engineering, India

Sunil Kumar Jampani
Hindustan Institute of Technology and Science, India

Podishetti Sai Santhosh
Hindustan Institute of Technology and Science, India

Inavolu Mohith Nithin
Hindustan Institute of Technology and Science, India

Popuri Janaki Raam
Hindustan Institute of Technology and Science, India

ABSTRACT

This chapter will explore the transformative potential of "smart tourism using IoT" within the context of social media strategies for enhanced tourism interactivity. With the advent of the Internet of Things (IoT), the tourism industry is undergoing a profound revolution. In this chapter, we will delve into how IoT technologies are reshaping the tourism landscape and creating new avenues for tourist engagement, satisfaction, and sustainability. The chapter emphasizes the strategic importance of integrating IoT solutions with social media strategies to create a seamless and immersive travel experience. The discussion will encompass real-time tourist information, personalized travel assistance, resource management, safety and security, and data-driven decision-making, all underpinned by the broader theme of social media interactivity.

DOI: 10.4018/979-8-3693-0960-5.ch002

INTRODUCTION

Overview of the "Smart Tourism using IoT" Concept

Smart Tourism is a contemporary paradigm that leverages technology to enhance the overall tourist experience. At its core, Smart Tourism involves the integration of Internet of Things (IoT) devices to collect and process data, creating an intelligent ecosystem within the tourism industry. The use of IoT in tourism allows for real-time data analysis, personalized services, and improved operational efficiency. This section delves into the nuances of Smart Tourism, emphasizing the role of IoT in reshaping the tourism landscape.

Importance of Integrating IoT with Social Media Strategies

The integration of IoT with social media strategies marks a crucial evolution in the tourism sector. Social media platforms serve as powerful tools for communication and information dissemination. When combined with the capabilities of IoT, a symbiotic relationship emerges. Real-time data from IoT devices enriches social media content, providing tourists with dynamic and up-to-date information. Conversely, social media platforms amplify the reach of IoT-generated insights, fostering engagement and interaction. This section explores the synergies between IoT and social media, emphasizing the transformative impact on smart tourism experiences.

Objectives and Structure of the Chapter

The primary objectives of this chapter are twofold: first, to elucidate the fundamental concepts underpinning Smart Tourism using IoT, and second, to explore the strategic integration of IoT with social media to enhance the overall tourist experience. The chapter unfolds in a structured manner, beginning with an in-depth exploration of the Smart Tourism landscape. Subsequently, it delves into the pivotal role of IoT in transforming tourism experiences. The latter part of the chapter scrutinizes the strategic fusion of IoT and social media, providing insights into effective implementation strategies.

Review of Literature

The contribution of Marine-Roig et al. (2015) is to underscore the significance of big data analytics in supporting smart destinations. This is achieved through an examination of the online portrayal of Barcelona—a leading smart city and tourist destination—extracted from social media. The study analyzes over 100,000 pertinent travel blogs and online travel reviews (OTRs) written in English by tourists who visited the city in the last decade. The findings reinforce the capacity of cities like Barcelona to formulate a smart city and destination concept, along with a strategic framework. In this social context, smart tourism is integral to the smart city strategy.

Gautam et al. (2016) endeavor to merge the Internet of Things (IoT) with smart tourism by establishing an IoT information technology public platform for regional revitalization. IoT big data tourism applications necessitate the integration of social media, content marketing, and wearable IoT devices. Building on conceptual insights into the IoT and its potential for smart cities, Wise et al. (2019) furnish practical foundations for destination organizers and stakeholders within the emerging smart tourism paradigm.

The period from 2013 to 2018 witnessed the emergence of trends like "big data," "e-tourism," "green experience," and "smart tourism." In contrast, Nusair (2020) aims to unveil the rapid progress in social media research from 2002 to 2018, addressing the expansion in the breadth and depth of thematic areas.

The crux of smart cities lies in developing automated methods to support smart applications. Liu et al. (2020) propose an automatic method to extract entity relations using deep learning techniques in a two-level neural network named Bi-CLSTM. Mardhiyani (2020) investigates the marketing strategy employed by the Semarang City Government in tourism promotion through digital media.

From smart cities to smart homes, industry monitoring to product evolution, smartwatches to smart health monitoring systems, there are numerous aspects where IoT plays a pivotal role. Singh et al. (2020) focus on the strategies adopted and potential attack scenarios on IoT.

Montero et al. (2021) adopt a formal and structured approach to review the intersection of data science and smart tourism destinations. Data science technologies underpinning current research in smart destinations encompass big data, smart data, data analytics, social media, cloud computing, the Internet of Things (IoT), smart card data, geographic information system (GIS) technologies, open data, artificial intelligence, and machine learning.

Dewantara et al. (2022) propose a travel vlog ecosystem involving three actors: the vlogger, the viewer, and the destination marketer. Recognizing the growing importance of social media in destination marketing, the paper provides valuable insights for practitioners to inform strategic marketing activities using vlogs.

Looking ahead, leading technologies for various complex applications include metaverse, digital twin, and autonomous vehicle applications. These technologies were previously inaccessible in areas such as health and life sciences, smart home, smart agriculture, smart city, smart car and logistics, Industry 4.0, entertainment (video game), and social media applications. Recent developments in process modeling, supercomputing, cloud data analytics (deep learning, etc.), communication networks, and AIoT/IIoT/IoT technologies have paved the way for these advancements. Hou et al. (2023) analyze and highlight the trends and challenges of the AIoT technology ecosystem, encompassing core hardware (MCU, MEMS/NEMS sensors, and wireless access medium), core software (operating system and protocol communication stack), and middleware (deep learning on a microcontroller: TinyML).

Smart Tourism: A Technological Odyssey

Smart Tourism, characterized by the infusion of cutting-edge technologies, redefines how tourists engage with destinations. Traditional tourism paradigms are giving way to intelligent ecosystems where IoT devices seamlessly interact, generating a wealth of data to enhance various facets of the tourist experience.

The objective is to seamlessly integrate and deeply develop tourism physical and information resources, catering to the needs of tourists, tourism enterprises, and government management departments in a forward-looking manner. This concept extends beyond traditional tourism services, encompassing smart tourism government affairs.

The Internet of Things (IoT) stands out as a revolutionary technology gaining momentum in today's wireless telecommunications landscape. Its profound impact on various facets of daily life and user behavior is a key strength (Atzori et al., 2010). Within the tourism industry, IoT plays a crucial role, emerging as one of the primary drivers of internet usage in the economy (Hjalager, 2002).

Smart tourism services (STS), emerging from "smart system" initiatives, specifically target the tourism sector or destinations (Suresh Babu, C. V. Rubajini, et. al. 2013 and Xiang et al., 2021). The overarching goal of an STS system is to seamlessly blend convenience with precision through an easily accessible platform, driven by technological advancements (Gretzel et al., 2015b). Examples of such platforms include smart travel mobile apps or websites that provide a unified environment for tourists to integrate service proposals. This enhances the user experience by offering travel information related to routes and their status (Choe and Fesenmaier, 2017). The platform facilitates trip planning for tourists, serving as decision support, and for practitioners, it extends to managing rental and booking services relevant to tourism. Essentially, this platform integrates tourist-oriented services and management, underscoring the importance of delivering information to tourists through technological applications (Li et al., 2017).

The Pivotal Role of IoT in Tourism Transformation

Real-Time Data Analytics for Personalized Experiences

One of the key contributions of IoT to Smart Tourism lies in its ability to facilitate real-time data analytics. IoT devices, such as sensors and beacons, gather data on tourist behavior, preferences, and movement patterns. This data forms the basis for personalized experiences, allowing service providers to tailor offerings to individual preferences. *(Johnson, 2018; Smith et al., 2020)*

Enhanced Operational Efficiency and Resource Management

IoT-enabled devices streamline operations within the tourism industry. From smart transportation systems optimizing traffic flow to connected hotel rooms adjusting settings based on guest preferences, IoT enhances operational efficiency. This not only improves resource management but also contributes to a more sustainable and eco-friendly tourism sector. *(Chen & Zhang, 2019; Li et al., 2021)*

Integrating IoT With Social Media: A Synergistic Approach

Enriching Social Media Content With Real-time Insights

The amalgamation of IoT-generated data with social media platforms results in enriched and dynamic content. Tourists can access real-time information on crowd density, weather conditions, and local events, enhancing their decision-making process. For instance, an Instagram post from a tourist can be complemented with real-time data on the popularity of the location. *(Wang & Xie, 2017; Buhalis & Sinarta, 2022)*

Fostering Engagement through Social Media Amplification

Social media serves as a catalyst for amplifying the impact of IoT-generated insights. Platforms like Twitter, Facebook, and Instagram enable tourists to share their experiences, creating a virtual community. This not only fosters engagement but also provides destination marketers with valuable user-generated content to promote the locale. *(Xiang et al., 2015; Neuhofer et al., 2019)*

Implementation Strategies and Challenges

Strategies for Seamless Integration

Effective integration of IoT and social media requires a strategic approach. Tourism stakeholders need to establish robust infrastructures, ensure data security, and create seamless interfaces between devices and platforms. Additionally, collaboration among industry players is crucial for the success of integrated Smart Tourism initiatives. *(Li & Wang, 2018; Gretzel & Yoo, 2021)*

Addressing Ethical and Privacy Concerns

As Smart Tourism evolves, ethical and privacy concerns come to the forefront. The chapter discusses the importance of implementing ethical frameworks and privacy measures to address potential challenges associated with the collection and use of personal data in the IoT and social media nexus. *(Li et al., 2019; Tussyadiah & Park, 2018)*

Conclusion

In conclusion, the integration of IoT with social media strategies heralds a new era for Smart Tourism. The dynamic interplay between these two technological pillars enhances the tourist experience, offering personalization, real-time insights, and a sense of community. However, to fully realize the potential of this symbiotic relationship, industry stakeholders must navigate challenges, embracing ethical considerations and ensuring a seamless integration of technologies.

The key findings from the discussed literature are as follows:

1. **Big Data Analytics in Smart Destinations:** Marine-Roig et al. (2015) emphasize the role of big data analytics in supporting smart destinations, using the online image of Barcelona as a case study.
2. **IoT and Smart Tourism:** Gautam et al. (2016) integrate IoT and smart tourism, providing a public platform for regional revival. Wise et al. (2019) contribute practical foundations for smart tourism, focusing on IoT applications.
3. **Emerging Trends (2013-2018):** The period witnesses trends like "big data," "e-tourism," "green experience," and "smart tourism."
4. **Social Media Research:** Nusair (2020) uncovers rapid progress in social media research from 2002 to 2018, addressing the growth in thematic areas.

5. **Automated Methods in Smart Cities:** Liu et al. (2020) propose an automatic method for extracting entity relations in smart cities using deep learning techniques.
6. **Marketing Strategy through Digital Media:** Mardhiyani (2020) investigates the marketing strategy of Semarang City Government in tourism promotion through digital media.
7. **IoT Applications:** Singh et al. (2020) focus on IoT strategies and potential attack scenarios across various domains.
8. **Data Science and Smart Tourism:** Montero et al. (2021) review the intersection of data science and smart tourism destinations, highlighting key technologies such as big data, IoT, AI, and machine learning.
9. **Travel Vlog Ecosystem:** Dewantara et al. (2022) propose a travel vlog ecosystem involving vloggers, viewers, and destination marketers, providing insights for strategic marketing activities.
10. **Future Technologies:** Hou et al. (2023) analyze trends and challenges in the AIoT technology ecosystem, covering core hardware, software, and middleware, with a focus on TinyML.

These findings collectively contribute to a better understanding of the role of technology, data, and digital strategies in shaping smart destinations and cities.

THE EVOLUTION OF TOURISM IN THE DIGITAL AGE

Historical Perspective on Tourism and its Transformation by Digital Technologies

Tourism, as a socio-cultural phenomenon, has undergone significant evolution over the years. Historically, travel was influenced by factors such as economic prosperity, political stability, and cultural exchange. The digital age, marked by the widespread adoption of digital technologies, has revolutionized the tourism landscape.

In the late 20th century, the advent of the internet transformed the way people plan and experience travel (Gursoy et al., 2019). Online booking platforms and travel websites democratized access to information, allowing travelers to research destinations, compare prices, and make reservations with ease (Xiang et al., 2015). The digitalization of travel agencies and the emergence of e-commerce reshaped the entire tourism value chain, from planning to post-trip reflections.

Emergence of IoT as a Game-Changer in the Tourism Industry

In recent years, the tourism industry has witnessed a paradigm shift with the emergence of the Internet of Things (IoT). IoT, characterized by interconnected devices that communicate and share data, has introduced a new dimension to the tourism experience. From smart hotels and connected transportation to wearable devices that track health and provide personalized recommendations, IoT has become a game-changer.

The integration of IoT devices in the tourism sector has streamlined operations, enhanced safety, and improved overall customer satisfaction (Sigala, 2020). For example, smart luggage with built-in GPS trackers ensures that travelers' belongings are easily traceable, reducing the stress associated with lost luggage. Additionally, smart destination management systems utilize IoT to monitor and manage tourist flows, optimizing the allocation of resources and minimizing environmental impact (Al-Fuqaha et al., 2015).

Integration of Social Media into the Tourism Landscape

As digital technologies evolved, social media platforms emerged as influential tools in shaping travel behaviors and perceptions. Social media serves as a dynamic space where travelers share experiences, seek recommendations, and engage with destinations. The integration of social media into the tourism landscape has transformed how destinations market themselves and how tourists gather information.

Social media platforms, including Instagram, Facebook, and Twitter, have become integral to the travel experience. Tourists share real-time updates, photos, and reviews, influencing the choices of their peers (Gretzel & Yoo, 2019). Destination marketing organizations leverage social media to showcase the unique aspects of their locales, creating virtual communities of travelers (Hays et al., 2019). User-generated content on social media platforms has become a powerful marketing tool, shaping perceptions and driving tourism trends.

Illustrative Examples

Example One: IoT-Enabled Smart Hotels

Imagine a tourist checking into a smart hotel equipped with IoT devices. The room adjusts its temperature based on the guest's preferences stored in the hotel's system. IoT sensors in the room detect when the guest leaves, automatically adjusting lighting and climate control to conserve energy. Such smart hotel experiences not only enhance guest comfort but also contribute to sustainable tourism practices. (Suresh Babu, C. V., Akshayah N. S., 2023).

Example Two: Social Media Influencers Shaping Travel Trends

Consider a scenario where a travel influencer shares a video on social media showcasing an off-the-beaten-path destination. The video goes viral, and soon, the destination experiences a surge in tourist interest. Social media influencers, through their curated content, play a pivotal role in shaping travel trends and influencing the choices of a vast audience.

Conclusion

The evolution of tourism in the digital age reflects a dynamic interplay between historical travel trends and the transformative impact of digital technologies. From the early days of online bookings to the current era of IoT-driven smart tourism, the industry continues to adapt to technological advancements. Social media, as a catalyst for information dissemination and community building, has become an inseparable part of the contemporary travel experience. As we delve deeper into the realms of Smart Tourism, understanding the historical context and the role of digital technologies is crucial for appreciating the full spectrum of this transformative journey.

SMART IOT APPLICATIONS IN TOURISM

IoT-Enabled Tourist Information Services

Tourist information services have undergone a significant transformation with the integration of Internet of Things (IoT) technologies. IoT enables the creation of dynamic, real-time information systems that enhance the tourist experience.

In cities around the world, IoT-powered information kiosks and mobile applications provide tourists with instant access to relevant information. These systems utilize sensors and data analytics to offer details on local attractions, events, transportation options, and real-time updates, ensuring that tourists have the most current and personalized information at their fingertips (Li et al., 2018). For example, a tourist exploring a city can use a mobile app to receive notifications about nearby points of interest, current weather conditions, and local events. (Li, X., Wang, D., Liang, Y., & Huang, D., 2019)

Personalized Travel Assistance Through IoT

The personalization of travel experiences has become a focal point in the tourism industry, and IoT plays a pivotal role in delivering tailored services to individual preferences.

IoT devices, such as wearables and smartphones, enable personalized travel assistance. For instance, a smart wristband worn by a tourist can provide location-based recommendations, personalized itineraries, and even health-related insights. These devices can also facilitate seamless interactions with smart infrastructure, such as automated check-ins at hotels or personalized greetings at tourist attractions (Neuhofer et al., 2019). This level of personalization enhances the overall travel experience, making it more engaging and satisfying for the tourist. (Neuhofer, B., Buhalis, D., & Ladkin, A., 2019)

Resource Management and Sustainability Initiatives

Smart tourism initiatives leveraging IoT extend beyond enhancing the visitor experience to addressing broader concerns such as resource management and sustainability.

IoT-enabled resource management systems monitor and optimize the utilization of resources in tourist destinations. For instance, smart transportation systems use real-time data to manage traffic flow, reducing congestion and environmental impact. Energy-efficient solutions in hotels and attractions, driven by IoT, contribute to sustainable practices. These initiatives not only enhance the environmental footprint of tourism but also improve the overall quality of life for local communities (Chen & Zhang, 2019).

Enhanced Safety and Security Measures

Safety and security are paramount concerns for tourists, and IoT technologies provide innovative solutions to address these issues.

Smart surveillance systems, equipped with IoT sensors, enhance security in tourist destinations. These systems can detect unusual activities, monitor crowd density, and provide real-time alerts to authorities. Wearable devices with panic buttons and location tracking capabilities offer an additional layer of safety for tourists. In the event of an emergency, these devices enable swift response and assistance (Li

& Wang, 2018). This integration of IoT into safety measures contributes to creating a secure environment for tourists.

Data-Driven Decision-Making for Improved Tourist Experiences

The wealth of data generated by IoT devices empowers tourism stakeholders to make informed decisions, ultimately enhancing the overall tourist experience.

Data analytics derived from IoT devices offer insights into tourist behavior, preferences, and trends. Tourism businesses can leverage this information to tailor services, optimize operations, and create targeted marketing campaigns. For example, a hotel can use data on guest preferences to customize room amenities, and a destination management organization can use analytics to understand peak tourist times and plan accordingly. This data-driven approach ensures that resources are allocated efficiently and that tourists receive personalized and timely services (Wang & Xie, 2017).

Illustrative Examples

Example One: IoT-Enhanced City Information System

Imagine a tourist arriving in a smart city equipped with an IoT-enabled information system. The tourist, armed with a mobile app, receives real-time updates on available transportation options, recommendations for nearby attractions based on personal preferences, and alerts about local events. This dynamic system not only enhances the tourist's exploration but also contributes to the efficient utilization of city resources. (Suresh Babu, C. V., Monika, R., et. al. 2023).

Example Two: Wearable Devices for Enhanced Safety

Consider a scenario where a group of tourists explores a natural park. Each member wears a smart wristband that not only provides location-based information about the park's flora and fauna but also acts as a safety device. In case of an emergency or if someone deviates from the designated path, the wearable device sends an alert to park authorities, enabling a quick and coordinated response.

Conclusion

The infusion of IoT applications into the tourism sector represents a paradigm shift, providing innovative solutions to longstanding challenges while enhancing the overall tourist experience. From personalized travel assistance to sustainability initiatives, IoT-driven smart tourism initiatives redefine how destinations interact with visitors. As we delve into the future, the integration of IoT in tourism is poised to shape a more connected, efficient, and sustainable industry.

SYNERGY BETWEEN IOT AND SOCIAL MEDIA STRATEGIES

Exploring the Interplay Between IoT Technologies and Social Media Platforms

The integration of Internet of Things (IoT) technologies with social media platforms creates a dynamic synergy, reshaping the way tourists interact with destinations. The interplay between IoT and social media introduces new dimensions of real-time engagement and information dissemination.

IoT devices generate a vast amount of real-time data, ranging from environmental conditions to user preferences. Social media platforms act as conduits for sharing this data with a global audience. For instance, a tourist exploring a smart city equipped with IoT sensors can instantly share experiences on platforms like Instagram or Twitter. This real-time sharing not only enhances the immediacy of travel narratives but also provides valuable insights for fellow travelers and destination marketers (Buhalis & Sinarta, 2022). The integration of IoT and social media thus transforms tourists into active contributors to a dynamic, global tourism conversation.

Leveraging Social Media for Real-Time Tourist Engagement

Social media platforms serve as powerful tools for real-time engagement, allowing tourists to share, discover, and interact with content instantaneously. When coupled with IoT, this engagement becomes richer and more contextually relevant.

Imagine a tourist visiting a smart museum equipped with IoT-enabled exhibits. As the tourist interacts with exhibits, IoT sensors capture data on preferences and engagement. This data can be seamlessly integrated into social media platforms, creating immersive and personalized content in real time. A tourist, for example, might share a live video of an interactive exhibit on Facebook, triggering a cascade of comments and likes. The integration of IoT data into social media amplifies the immediacy and impact of the tourist experience, fostering a sense of connection and community (Neuhofer et al., 2019).

Case Studies of Successful IoT and Social Media Integration in Tourism

Case Study One: Disney's MagicBand System

Disney's MagicBand system exemplifies successful integration of IoT and social media in the tourism industry. MagicBands, worn by visitors to Disney parks, serve as multifunctional devices incorporating IoT technology. These bands link to social media accounts, allowing visitors to share their experiences in real time. The bands also collect data on visitor preferences, enabling Disney to personalize services, from character interactions to ride suggestions (Rihova et al., 2018). The synergy between MagicBands and social media creates a seamless and interactive theme park experience.

Case Study Two: Amsterdam's Smart City Initiatives

Amsterdam's smart city initiatives showcase the integration of IoT and social media for sustainable tourism. The city employs IoT sensors to monitor air quality, traffic flow, and energy usage. Social media platforms are utilized to disseminate real-time information on sustainable practices, encouraging tourists to participate in eco-friendly activities. Tourists can share their sustainable experiences, creating a community-driven movement toward responsible tourism. This integration not only enhances the tourist experience but also contributes to the city's commitment to sustainability (Gretzel & Yoo, 2019).

Illustrative Examples

Example One: Smart Wearables at a Tourist Attraction

Consider a tourist visiting a historical site equipped with smart wearables. As the tourist explores, the wearables capture data on historical points of interest, engagement levels, and preferences. This data is seamlessly integrated into social media platforms, allowing the tourist to share a real-time narrative of the visit. Friends and followers can engage with the content, and the destination gains exposure as a dynamic and technologically advanced attraction.

Example Two: IoT-Enhanced Food Experiences Shared on Social Media

Imagine a tourist attending a smart food festival where IoT devices capture data on taste preferences, popular dishes, and crowd flow. This data is shared on social media platforms, enabling real-time updates on the best culinary experiences. Tourists, in turn, share their food adventures, creating a digital foodie community and influencing others to explore the event.

Conclusion

The synergy between IoT technologies and social media platforms represents a transformative force in the tourism industry. The real-time engagement facilitated by social media, enriched by the data generated by IoT devices, reshapes how tourists experience and share their journeys. Successful case studies demonstrate that the integration of IoT and social media goes beyond technological collaboration; it fosters a new era of connected, immersive, and community-driven smart tourism.

CHALLENGES AND OPPORTUNITIES

Addressing Challenges in Implementing IoT Solutions for Tourism

As the tourism industry embraces the evolution towards Smart Tourism through the integration of IoT and social media, several challenges need careful consideration for successful implementation.

Challenges

- **Data Security and Privacy Concerns:** The extensive collection of personal and location-based data by IoT devices raises significant privacy concerns. Tourists may be apprehensive about the potential misuse of their data, necessitating robust security measures and transparent data usage policies (Li et al., 2019).
- **Interoperability Issues:** The heterogeneity of IoT devices and platforms may lead to interoperability challenges. Ensuring seamless communication and data exchange between various devices and systems is crucial for a cohesive and effective Smart Tourism ecosystem (Gretzel & Yoo, 2021).

- **Infrastructure Development:** Many destinations may lack the necessary infrastructure for widespread IoT deployment. The implementation of IoT solutions requires substantial investment in technology infrastructure, including sensors, communication networks, and data processing capabilities (Sigala, 2020).

Addressing Challenges

- **Privacy by Design:** Implementing a "Privacy by Design" approach involves integrating privacy considerations into the development of IoT solutions from the outset. This includes anonymizing data, providing transparent opt-in mechanisms for data collection, and ensuring compliance with data protection regulations (Tussyadiah & Park, 2018).
- **Standardization Efforts:** Industry-wide standardization efforts can address interoperability challenges. Establishing common protocols and communication standards can facilitate seamless integration and collaboration between different IoT devices and platforms (Li et al., 2018).
- **Public-Private Partnerships:** Governments and private sector entities can collaborate to invest in the development of necessary infrastructure. Public-private partnerships can expedite the deployment of IoT technologies in tourism destinations, ensuring a more widespread and sustainable implementation (Gretzel & Yoo, 2021).

Identifying Opportunities for Collaboration Between IoT Providers and Social Media Platforms

The convergence of IoT and social media presents unique opportunities for collaboration that can amplify the impact of Smart Tourism initiatives.

Opportunities

- **Enhanced User Engagement:** Combining the real-time data generated by IoT devices with the interactive nature of social media platforms can create engaging and dynamic content. Tourists become active contributors to the tourism narrative, sharing experiences, recommendations, and insights with a global audience (Buhalis & Sinarta, 2022).
- **Targeted Marketing Campaigns:** Social media platforms provide a rich source of user-generated content and insights. Analyzing this data, combined with information from IoT devices, enables destination marketers to tailor

targeted campaigns. For example, a destination can promote specific attractions based on real-time popularity and user preferences (Xiang et al., 2015).

- **Community Building:** Social media platforms foster communities of like-minded individuals. Integrating IoT-generated data into these communities creates a sense of shared experience. For instance, tourists exploring a smart city can connect with others who share similar preferences, fostering a community-driven approach to tourism (Neuhofer et al., 2019).

Collaboration Strategies

- **API Integration:** Establishing Application Programming Interface (API) integrations between IoT platforms and social media networks allows seamless data sharing. This integration enables the automatic sharing of real-time data on social media platforms, enhancing the visibility and reach of IoT-generated insights (Wang & Xie, 2017).
- **Coordinated Marketing Campaigns:** Collaborative efforts between IoT providers and social media platforms can result in coordinated marketing campaigns. For instance, a destination could launch a campaign encouraging tourists to share their IoT-enhanced experiences on a specific social media hashtag, creating a viral and interactive marketing strategy (Buhalis & Sinarta, 2022).
- **User-Generated Content Platforms:** Developing platforms that combine user-generated content from both IoT and social media sources can create a comprehensive repository of tourism-related information. Tourists can contribute, discover, and engage with a diverse range of content, fostering a collaborative and dynamic tourism community (Xiang et al., 2015).

Regulatory and Ethical Considerations

The integration of IoT and social media in tourism necessitates careful consideration of regulatory frameworks and ethical standards.

Regulatory Considerations

- **Data Protection Regulations:** Adherence to data protection regulations, such as the General Data Protection Regulation (GDPR), is paramount. IoT and social media solutions must comply with these regulations to ensure the lawful and ethical use of tourist data (Tussyadiah & Park, 2018).

- **Cross-Border Data Transfer:** As tourism is inherently international, navigating the complexities of cross-border data transfer regulations is crucial. Clear guidelines on data transfer, storage, and access ensure legal and ethical use of tourist data across different jurisdictions (Li et al., 2019).

Ethical Considerations

- **Informed Consent:** Tourists must provide informed consent for the collection and use of their data. Transparent communication about the purpose and scope of data collection ensures that tourists are aware of and comfortable with the information being gathered (Tussyadiah & Park, 2018).
- **Digital Inclusion:** As Smart Tourism evolves, efforts should be made to avoid digital exclusion. Ensuring that all tourists, regardless of technological proficiency, can benefit from IoT and social media initiatives is essential for ethical tourism practices (Sigala, 2020).
- **Sustainable Practices:** Ethical considerations should extend to sustainability. The implementation of IoT and social media in tourism should prioritize environmentally sustainable practices to minimize the ecological impact of technology-driven initiatives (Gretzel & Yoo, 2021).

Illustrative Examples

Example One: Privacy-Aware Social Media Integration

Consider a scenario where a tourist visiting a smart city opts to share their experiences on social media. Before sharing, the social media platform prompts the user to review and approve specific data points from IoT devices, such as location or preferences. This privacy-aware integration ensures that tourists have control over the information shared while still contributing to the dynamic tourism narrative.

Example Two: Collaborative Campaign for Sustainable Tourism

Imagine a collaborative campaign between a destination's IoT providers and a social media platform to promote sustainable tourism. Tourists using eco-friendly transportation options equipped with IoT sensors receive badges or rewards that they can share on social media, contributing to a shared commitment to sustainable practices. This collaborative campaign not only engages tourists but also promotes ethical and environmentally conscious tourism.

Conclusion

The challenges and opportunities in the integration of IoT and social media in Smart Tourism underscore the need for a thoughtful and strategic approach. By addressing privacy concerns, fostering collaboration, and navigating regulatory landscapes, the tourism industry can unlock the full potential of these technologies. Ethical considerations should guide the implementation, ensuring that Smart Tourism initiatives enhance the tourist experience while respecting individual rights and contributing to sustainable and inclusive tourism practices.

THE FUTURE OF SMART TOURISM AND IOT INTEGRATION

Projections for the Future of IoT in Tourism

The future of Smart Tourism promises to be even more intricately intertwined with the evolution of the Internet of Things (IoT). As technology continues to advance, several projections offer insights into the potential trajectory of IoT in the tourism industry.

Projections

- **Ubiquitous Connectivity:** The proliferation of IoT devices is expected to lead to a state of ubiquitous connectivity. Tourist destinations, accommodations, transportation systems, and attractions will be seamlessly connected, creating a holistic and integrated Smart Tourism ecosystem (Buhalis & Sinarta, 2022).
- **Hyper-Personalization:** The integration of IoT technologies will enable hyper-personalization of tourist experiences. From personalized travel recommendations to adaptive environmental controls in smart accommodations, tourists can expect highly tailored and context-aware services (Neuhofer et al., 2019).
- **Predictive Analytics:** The vast amount of data generated by IoT devices will fuel the development of sophisticated predictive analytics models. Tourism businesses can leverage these models to anticipate tourist preferences, optimize resource allocation, and enhance overall operational efficiency (Sigala, 2020).

Potential Innovations and Emerging Technologies

The future of Smart Tourism will witness the emergence of innovative technologies and applications that further augment the integration of IoT in the tourism experience.

Innovations

- **Blockchain for Secure Transactions:** Blockchain technology has the potential to enhance security and transparency in tourism transactions. From secure and transparent booking processes to the creation of tamper-proof traveler profiles, blockchain can revolutionize the financial aspects of Smart Tourism (Gretzel & Yoo, 2021).
- **Augmented Reality (AR) Experiences:** The combination of IoT and AR can result in immersive and interactive tourism experiences. Tourists equipped with AR-enabled devices can receive real-time information, translations, and contextual overlays, enriching their understanding of destinations (Buhalis & Sinarta, 2022).
- **5G Connectivity for Enhanced Speed and Capacity:** The widespread adoption of 5G technology will facilitate faster and more reliable connectivity. This will enable real-time communication between IoT devices, ensuring swift data transfer and seamless interactions in Smart Tourism environments (Xiang et al., 2015).

Implications for Stakeholders in the Tourism Industry

The integration of IoT in Smart Tourism has profound implications for various stakeholders in the tourism industry, influencing business models, customer interactions, and destination management.

Implications

- **Transformation of Business Models:** Businesses in the tourism sector will need to adapt their models to leverage the capabilities of IoT. From data-driven decision-making to the provision of personalized services, the successful integration of IoT will redefine the competitive landscape (Wang & Xie, 2017).
- **Enhanced Customer Experiences:** Tourists can expect highly immersive and personalized experiences. The ability to receive real-time recommendations, personalized services, and interactive content will significantly enhance the overall satisfaction of tourists (Neuhofer et al., 2019).

- **Sustainable Tourism Practices:** The use of IoT for resource management and sustainability initiatives will play a crucial role in promoting environmentally conscious tourism practices. Stakeholders will need to align their strategies with sustainable development goals to meet the growing demand for responsible tourism (Chen & Zhang, 2019).

Illustrative Examples

Example One: Hyper-Personalized Smart Destinations

In the future, a tourist arriving at a Smart Destination equipped with IoT devices could experience hyper-personalization. The destination's smart infrastructure, recognizing the tourist's preferences stored in a secure traveler profile, could provide real-time suggestions for activities, dining options, and cultural experiences. The tourist might receive notifications about personalized promotions or events tailored to their interests.

Example Two: Blockchain-Enabled Secure Travel Transactions

Consider a scenario where a tourist books accommodations, transportation, and activities seamlessly through a blockchain-enabled platform. The decentralized and secure nature of blockchain ensures that transactions are transparent, tamper-proof, and secure. This innovation not only enhances the security of financial transactions but also builds trust among tourists and service providers.

Conclusion

The future of Smart Tourism integrated with IoT holds immense promise for transforming the tourism industry. Projections suggest a landscape where connectivity, personalization, and predictive analytics redefine how tourists experience and interact with destinations. Emerging technologies, such as blockchain and augmented reality, will further contribute to the evolution of Smart Tourism. As stakeholders navigate these developments, embracing innovation and sustainability will be key to unlocking the full potential of IoT in shaping the future of tourism.

CONCLUSION

Summarizing Key Takeaways From the Chapter

This chapter explores into the evolution of Smart Tourism through the integration of Internet of Things (IoT) and social media strategies. The exploration covered various facets, from the historical perspective of tourism's digital transformation to the synergies between IoT and social media. It further explores into the applications of IoT in tourism, addressing challenges, identifying opportunities, and projecting the future landscape. Throughout, illustrative examples and case studies were presented to contextualize the theoretical concepts.

Reinforcing the Significance of "Smart Tourism using IoT" for Tourism Interactivity

The significance of Smart Tourism using IoT lies in its transformative potential for the tourism industry. This integration redefines how tourists experience destinations and how businesses operate. The chapter highlighted the enhanced interactivity facilitated by IoT, from personalized travel assistance and resource management to real-time engagement through social media. As destinations become smarter, the tourism experience becomes more dynamic, connected, and tailored to individual preferences.

Call to Action for Tourism Industry Professionals and Researchers

As the tourism industry hurtles towards a more technologically advanced future, a call to action emerges for both industry professionals and researchers:

- **Adaptation and Integration:** Industry professionals are encouraged to embrace Smart Tourism using IoT as an opportunity for innovation. The integration of IoT technologies should be seen as a strategic imperative to enhance customer experiences, streamline operations, and contribute to sustainable practices.
- **Collaboration and Knowledge Sharing:** Given the interdisciplinary nature of Smart Tourism, collaboration is key. Tourism professionals, technologists, and policymakers should collaborate to share knowledge, best practices, and insights. This collaborative approach will accelerate the development and adoption of Smart Tourism solutions.

- **Investment in Research:** Researchers are urged to explore the multifaceted aspects of Smart Tourism using IoT. Further research is needed to understand the nuanced implications, identify emerging trends, and address potential challenges. This research will contribute to the development of frameworks, guidelines, and solutions that benefit the entire tourism ecosystem.
- **Ethical and Sustainable Implementation:** A call is made for ethical considerations in the implementation of Smart Tourism. Stakeholders should prioritize privacy, security, and sustainability to ensure that technological advancements contribute positively to the tourism industry and society at large.

Conclusion Illustration

Imagine a tourist arriving at a Smart Destination of the future. Equipped with IoT devices, the tourist seamlessly navigates the city, receiving personalized recommendations, engaging with real-time information, and contributing to the global tourism narrative through social media. The destination, in turn, leverages this interconnected web of data to optimize services, manage resources sustainably, and create a truly immersive and unforgettable experience.

REFERENCES

Al-Fuqaha, A., Guizani, M., Mohammadi, M., Aledhari, M., & Ayyash, M. (2015). Internet of Things: A Survey on Enabling Technologies, Protocols, and Applications. *IEEE Communications Surveys and Tutorials*, *17*(4), 2347–2376. doi:10.1109/COMST.2015.2444095

Buhalis, D., & Sinarta, Y. (2022). Tourism marketing in the smart era. In The Routledge Handbook of Tourism Experience Management and Marketing. Routledge.

Chen, Y., & Zhang, C. (2019). A survey on the internet of things security. *Journal of Network and Computer Applications*, *126*, 46–70.

Dewantara, M., Gardiner, S., & Jin, X. (2022). Travel Vlog Ecosystem in Tourism Digital Marketing Evolution: A Narrative Literature Review. *. *Current Issues in Tourism*, 2022.

Gautam, B. P., Asami, H., Batajoo, A., & Fujisaki, T. (2016). Regional Revival Through IoT Enabled Smart Tourism Process Framework (STPF): A Proposal. *2016 Joint 8th International Conference on Soft Computing*.

Gretzel, U., & Yoo, K. H. (2019). The Transformation of Consumer Behavior. In *Information and Communication Technologies in Tourism 2020* (pp. 12–25). Springer.

Gretzel, U., & Yoo, K. H. (2021). The future of robots in the hospitality industry: A Delphi study. *Tourism Management*, *82*, 104209.

Gursoy, D., Chi, C. G., & Lu, L. (2019). Antecedents and outcomes of travelers' information-seeking behavior: A meta-analysis. *Tourism Management*, *70*, 230–243.

Hays, S., Page, S. J., & Buhalis, D. (2019). Social media as a destination marketing tool: Its use by national tourism organisations. *Current Issues in Tourism*, *22*(9), 1052–1069.

Hou, K. M., Diao, X., Shi, H., Ding, H., Zhou, H., & de Vaulx, C. (2023). Trends and Challenges in AIoT/IIoT/IoT Implementation. *. *Sensors (Basel)*, *23*(11), 2023. doi:10.3390/s23115074 PMID:37299800

Johnson, A. (2018). The impact of the Internet of Things on tourism. *Information and Communication Technologies in Tourism*, *2018*, 63–74.

Li, X., Wang, D., Liang, Y., & Huang, D. (2019). An empirical examination of tourists' adoption of smart tourism destinations. *Journal of Travel Research*, •••, 0047287519896017.

Liu, Z., & Chen, X. (2020). Research on Relation Extraction of Named Entity on Social Media in Smart Cities. *. *Soft Computing*, *24*(15), 2020. doi:10.1007/s00500-020-04742-w

Mardhiyani, N. L. (2020). Tourism 4.0: Strategi Komunikasi Pemasaran Pariwisata Kota Semarang, 2020.

Marine-Roig, E., & Clavé, S. A. (2015). Tourism Analytics with Massive User-generated Content: A Case Study of Barcelona. *Journal of Destination Marketing and Management*, 5. (IF: 5)

Montero, A. A., & López-Sánchez, J. A. (2021). Intersection of Data Science and Smart Destinations: A Systematic Review. *. *Frontiers in Psychology*, 2021. PMID:34393952

Neuhofer, B., Buhalis, D., & Ladkin, A. (2019). Technology as a catalyst of change: Enablers and barriers of the tourist experience and their consequences. The Routledge Handbook of Transport Economics, 112-132. Routledge.

Nusair, K. (2020). Developing A Comprehensive Life Cycle Framework for Social Media Research in Hospitality and Tourism. *International Journal of Contemporary Hospitality Management, 3* (IF: 3)

Rihova, I., Buhalis, D., Moital, M., & Gouthro, M. B. (2018). Visitor attractions and events: From insourcing to crowdsourcing of the visitor experience. *Tourism Management, 66*, 308–321.

Sigala, M. (2020). Tourism and COVID-19: Impacts and implications for advancing and resetting industry and research. *Journal of Business Research, 117*, 312–321. doi:10.1016/j.jbusres.2020.06.015 PMID:32546875

Singh, M., Kumari, M., Deogam, M., Gupta, L., Behra, L., Bharti, K. M., & Karmakar, S. (2020). *A Study on Layered Security Threats and Counter-Measures in Internet of Things: International Conference on Recent Trends in Artificial Intelligence, IOT, Smart Cities & Applications (ICAISC-2020).* CompScirn: Software Network (Topic).

Smith, S., Bergner, N., Ross, C., Tjernström, O., & Weinberg, C. (2020). The internet of things and new business models in tourism: A case study from Sweden. *Journal of Tourism Futures, 6*(2), 133–144.

Suresh Babu, C. V. Rubajini, R. P., & Devi, K. (2013) An Integrated smart system for accident - avoidance in four wheelers by using GSM and GPS Module. *Fifth International Conference On Advanced Computing (Icoac).* IEEE.

Suresh Babu, C. V., Akshayah, N. S., Maclin Vinola, P., & Janapriyan, R. (2023). IoT-Based Smart Accident Detection and Alert System. In P. Swarnalatha & S. Prabu (Eds.), *Handbook of Research on Deep Learning Techniques for Cloud-Based Industrial IoT* (pp. 322–337). IGI Global., doi:10.4018/978-1-6684-8098-4.ch019

Suresh Babu, C. V., Monika, R., Dhanusha, T., Vishnuvaradhanan, K., & Harish, A. (2023). Smart Street Lighting System for Smart Cities Using IoT (LoRa). In R. Kumar, A. Abdul Hamid, & N. Binti Ya'akub (Eds.), *Effective AI, Blockchain, and E-Governance Applications for Knowledge Discovery and Management* (pp. 78–96). IGI Global. doi:10.4018/978-1-6684-9151-5.ch006

Tussyadiah, I. P., & Park, S. (2018). Consumer evaluation of hotel service robots. In Information and Communication Technologies in Tourism 2018, 135-148.

Wang, D., & Xie, C. (2017). The roles of IT in the hospitality industry: A review of the literature. *Journal of Hospitality and Tourism Technology*, *8*(1), 6–33.

Wise, N., & Heidari, H. (2019). Developing Smart Tourism Destinations with The Internet of Things. *Big Data and Innovation in Tourism, Travel, and Hospitality, 3*(IF: 3)

Xiang, Z., Du, Q., Ma, Y., & Fan, W. (2015). A comparative analysis of major online review platforms: Implications for social media analytics in hospitality and tourism. *Tourism Management*, *58*, 51–65. doi:10.1016/j.tourman.2016.10.001

Chapter 3
Exploring Future Scenarios in Tourism:
Climate and Digital Transformation

João Ferreira do Rosário
https://orcid.org/0000-0003-2524-8523
Escola Superior de Comunicação Social, Instituto Politécnico de Lisboa, Portugal & CiTUR, Portugal

Ana Teresa Machado
Escola Superior de Comunicação Social, Instituto Politécnico de Lisboa, Portugal & CiTUR, Portugal

Miguel Belo
https://orcid.org/0000-0002-7840-5994
Escola Superior de Hotelaria e Turismo do Estoril, Portugal & CiTUR, Portugal

Filipe Segurado Severino
https://orcid.org/0000-0002-9865-4664
Escola Superior de Hotelaria e Turismo do Estoril, Portugal & CiTUR, Portugal

Célia M.Q. Ramos
https://orcid.org/0000-0002-3413-4897
ESGHT, CinTurs, Universidade do Algarve, Portugal

Maria de Lurdes Calisto
https://orcid.org/0000-0003-1636-0150
Escola Superior de Hotelaria e Turismo do Estoril, Portugal & CiTUR, Portugal

Teresa Costa
Escola Superior de Ciências Empresariais, Instituto Politécnico de Setúbal, Portugal & CiTUR, Portugal

DOI: 10.4018/979-8-3693-0960-5.ch003

ABSTRACT

Recognizing the substantial impact of external environmental factors on the tourism industry, obtaining insights into potential scenarios that the sector may encounter in the near future, particularly within a limited timeframe, is of utmost importance. The primary objective of this study was to envisage scenarios for the tourism sector over the next five years, striving for a comprehensive understanding of potential developments and challenges that could shape the industry's trajectory. Employing a two-phase qualitative methodology involving semi-structured interviews, the research first engaged with non-tourism experts and subsequently with tourism experts. Building on the identified key mid-term events—climate change and digital transformation—and employing a CATWOE framework analysis, two distinct scenarios for tourism development were crafted for the upcoming five years. This approach ensures a nuanced exploration of the influential factors and expert perspectives that contribute to the formulation of strategic insights for the industry's future.

INTRODUCTION

Considering the profound influence of external environmental factors on the tourism and hospitality (T&H) sector, gaining insights into potential scenarios the sector might confront in the near future, especially within a constrained timeframe, is paramount (Ha et al., 2022). In the ever-evolving landscape of the T&H sector, maintaining a proactive awareness of impending scenarios becomes imperative (Rodrigues et al., 2023), even more so when the reality of recent years showed how negative impacts on the T&H sector can easily suffer considering all kinds of worldwide events like the recent pandemic (Aldao et al., 2022) but also natural disasters, financial crisis or wars. As the sector remains susceptible to diverse influences, understanding and anticipating potential developments is essential for strategic planning and adaptability, ensuring stakeholders are well-prepared to handle the dynamic challenges that may arise in the rapidly changing tourism environment. This proactive approach serves as a cornerstone for resilience and agility in addressing the uncertainties inherent in the sector's external environment (e.g., Khosravi & Jha-Thakur, 2019; Postma & Yeoman, 2021; Schwarz et al., 2019).

This study set out to envision scenarios for the T&H sector over the next five years, aiming for a comprehensive grasp of potential developments and challenges that could steer the sector's course. It will focus on two of the more impactful events that can be considered external and not possibly influenced by the T&H managers' decisions (Climate change) and the internal that can be influenced and managed by the T&H managers (Digital transformation). Considering climate change, while it can bring new tourist destinations that before were not attractive, like warmer regions in northern countries, it can also destroy other locations due to regular and severe natural disasters, affecting the tourism demand (Scott, 2021). Considering the digital transformation, it will allow not only new management practices based on new technologies but also new ways of reaching tourists digitally, as a new way of showing the tourism offer more interactively, also to allow virtual experiences or reality-augmented experiences in all kinds of locations (Gupta & Sharma, 2021; Iranmanesh et al., 2022).

The study employed a two-phase qualitative methodology. Initially, insights were gathered from non-tourism experts through semi-structured interviews with thirteen specialists across various fields. A unanimous consensus surfaced through discussions with experts outside the tourism domain, emphasizing climate change and digital transformation as pivotal events anticipated for the next five years. Subsequently, the CATWOE analysis framework guided semi-structured interviews with stakeholders from the T&H sector. These interviews included destination managers, events organizations, tourist information, restaurants, travel agencies, tourist entertainment, and hospitality.

Two distinct scenarios emerged from these insights, offering valuable perspectives for both academic and professional spheres. Academically, the research enriches the theoretical understanding of how transformative forces impact the T&H sector, incorporating diverse expert viewpoints and employing the CATWOE framework for methodological depth. On a professional level, the scenarios provide practical insights for strategic planning and decision-making within the T&H sector, serving as a valuable tool for anticipating challenges, identifying opportunities, and fostering adaptability in the face of a dynamic landscape shaped by climate change and digital transformation.

BUSINESS SCENARIO PLANNING

Bridging Toward Tourism Perspective

The identification of future trends and the anticipation of market changes have become crucial to the competitiveness of organizations.

Other than common environmental threats (e.g., changing consumer demands, stakeholder issues, competitors' actions), there are also exogenous shocks such as abnormal weather events, unpredictable supply chain interruptions, major global economic disruptions, cyber security failures, biosecurity risks that may harm firms (Ribeiro & Pereira, 2022). The recent COVID-19 pandemic showed the disruptive side of exogenous crises for various industries (Ghobadian et al.,2022).

One of the major challenges of globalization is that it can make the future more unpredictable. As the world becomes more interconnected, events and crises in one part of the world can have far-reaching effects on other parts (Grinin et al., 2022).

For example, economic downturns in one region can have a cascading effect on other areas, leading to uncertainty and volatility in global markets. The 2007-2008 financial crisis had a profound and widespread impact on the global economy, leading to a domino effect across various sectors. Furthermore, globalization has facilitated the rapid spread of diseases such as the COVID-19 pandemic or influenza A, natural disasters, and other threats, increasing the potential for global crises and uncertainties (Etemad, 2020).

Overall, globalization has both positive and negative impacts on the future, and individuals and organizations need to be prepared to adapt to a rapidly changing and uncertain world. Developing scenarios and other strategic planning tools can be an effective way to prepare for the future in a globalized world (Wu et al.,2021).

Scenarios portray the likely future based on some assumptions or conditions. Since they determine the crucial factors of uncertainties, scenarios can be used to explore different outcomes and prepare for various contingencies. Scenarios are often used in business and strategic planning, and other fields help organizations and individuals anticipate and prepare for potential challenges and opportunities (Seyitoğlu & Costa, 2022a).

In the management literature, the scenario is consensually considered an important instrument because it is a valid tool to deal with uncertainties and changes (e.g., Bouhalleb & Smida, 2020; Khosravi & Jha-Thakur, 2019; Tiberius et al., 2020)

Developing scenarios can help uncover potential risks and opportunities and provide a framework for responding to different events. This can be particularly important in uncertain times when it is difficult to predict what will happen, and traditional decision-making approaches may be less effective. Scenarios can also provide a way to test different assumptions and evaluate the potential impact of various actions, helping organizations to make more effective and strategic decisions (Gudz, 2020; Jashari et al., 2022; Tiberius, 2019).

Scenarios in the Tourism Activity

The T&H sector, marked by its intricate structure involving various actors and stakeholders, faces heightened vulnerability due to numerous external factors such as economic conditions, political instability, global health crises, and climate change. These elements contribute to the sector's inherent uncertainty and volatility, making it challenging to predict their evolution (Duan et al., 2021; Filippo et al., 2017).

In response to this dynamic environment, scenario planning emerges as a crucial tool for businesses within the T&H sector. By systematically exploring diverse scenarios, organizations can identify and assess potential risks and uncertainties, enabling them to formulate proactive strategies and enhance resilience in the face of unforeseen events (Ramírez et al., 2017; Ural, 2016).

Scenario planning also plays a vital role in assisting decision-makers within the T&H sector. By envisioning different possible futures, organizations can align their strategies with the most likely and impactful scenarios, increasing their chances of success.

To address the challenges of an uncertain future, the T&H sector must prioritize flexibility and adaptability, fostering adaptive behaviors and addressing long-term uncertainties (Postma et al., 2017). Specifically, developing scenarios that explore different economic conditions and their potential impact on travel demand allows businesses to anticipate market changes and adjust operations and marketing strategies accordingly.

Scenario planning is a proactive tool for strategic formulation and proves crucial in crisis management. The COVID-19 pandemic underscored the sector's lack of preparedness for significant crises (Seyitoğlu & Costa, 2022b; Fisher & Wilder-Smith, 2020).

A systematic review of scenario planning studies in T&H research emphasizes an ongoing need for such studies. Furthermore, there is a notable gap in research concerning the scenario development approach as a tool for crisis management. This calls for further exploration and integration of scenario planning within the strategic framework of the T&H sector (Seyitoğlu & Costa, 2022a).

METHOD

This study aims to build scenarios for the T&H sector over five years, offering a nuanced understanding of potential developments and challenges that could shape the sector's trajectory. The research methodology is designed in two distinctive phases to address this objective comprehensively.

Methodological Approach

Interviews With Non-Tourism Experts

In the first phase, the research sought to unravel influential events and comprehend evolving trends within the T&H sector. This was achieved through semi-structured interviews with non-tourism experts, employing a non-probabilistic sampling technique that prioritized diversity, relevance, and a snowball approach to solicit expert opinions. Thirteen participants were engaged, each specializing in demography, generations, economy, technology, sustainability, security, public health, or public policies. These interviews, conducted via the "Zoom" platform between May and September 2022, yielded many insights. The thematic analysis of responses uncovered key future events that would shape the subsequent scenario-building process.

Interviews With Tourism Experts

Building on the insights gleaned from the initial interviews, the second phase employed the CATWOE analysis framework - where CATWOE stands for Client, Actor, Transformation, Worldview, Owner, and Environment (Checkland & Scholes, 1990).

The study employed semi-structured interviews guided by a meticulously constructed interview guide based on the CATWOE dimensions. Participants included stakeholders from crucial business sectors within the T&H sector, such as destination management, events organization, tourist information, restaurant sector, travel agencies, tourist entertainment, and hospitality. The interview process, conducted in person between June and July 2023, involved a designated researcher with expertise in tourism. Confidentiality and permission were prioritized, and the interviews had an average duration of 31 minutes, allowing for a thorough exploration of participant insights.

After gathering the data, the interviews underwent transcription using "Microsoft Word" software, guaranteeing the precise preservation of participants' dialogues. Following this, the interviews underwent content analysis employing the "NVivo" software. In the initial round of interviews, an analysis grid was meticulously constructed through a blend of inductive and deductive processes. This involved a thoughtful synthesis of inductive reasoning, allowing for insights to emerge organically from the data, and deductive reasoning, incorporating predefined categories or themes based on existing knowledge or frameworks. The resulting analysis grid was a structured tool to systematically organize, categorize, and interpret the diverse information obtained during the interviews, ensuring a comprehensive and systematic approach to data analysis.

The content of the second round of interviews was analyzed using the CATWOE framework, chosen for its effectiveness in scenario-building. This approach provides a structured and comprehensive examination, offering a holistic perspective on various stakeholders' roles and perspectives. The method enhances the robustness of scenario development by ensuring a nuanced exploration of critical factors and their interconnections within the dynamic context of the T&H sector.

FINDINGS

Interviews With Non-Tourism Specialists

Thirteen interviews were conducted to ascertain non-tourism experts' perspectives regarding future trends across eight thematic areas: demography, generations, economy, technology, sustainability, security, public health, and public policies.

One of the subjects is particularly pertinent to the environment, specifically centering on climate change and its consequences. Climate change is exacerbating the occurrence of natural calamities, such as floods, wildfires, and the escalation of sea levels, leading to environmental displacements. Nevertheless, the absence of political determination, the economic framework, and the ability to carry out actions prevent the prompt resolution of these problems, leading to forthcoming difficulties concerning human security and food chain disruption. It is imperative to contemplate values such as sustainability, adequacy of resources, political movements' accountability, and the appreciation of ecosystem services to ensure the transmission of high quality of life to both present and future generations.

"There is an upcoming event. To be more precise, it is not imminent, but it is already here: climate change. Things are happening right now regarding natural disasters, which everyone knows are caused by climate change and human activity on the planet. Even though they have already been much discussed and are the focus of major political concerns, they have minimal capacity for execution and realization. This can be serious if they are not seriously mitigated (which I believe will not be the case). Moreover, it is not just a matter of not getting there on time. There will eventually be no political will." (Generation Specialist)

Another mentioned topic pertains to cybersecurity, specifically computer crime and the evolving security requirements of information technology. Computer crime poses a threat to human security by exposing personal data, potentially endangering biological life. It also undermines organizational security, leading to commercial conflicts, and poses a risk to national security through cyber warfare. Consequently, the significance of focusing on security is growing. Organizations should employ experts and prioritize the development of a customized security system specifically designed to meet their requirements (security by design). Additionally, they should allocate resources towards harnessing the untapped capabilities of cloud-based systems.

"There is a measure that accentuates this increased activity and intensity in information systems; it also opens the door to those who intend to cause damage,

damage that can have several objectives, such as illicit enrichment by people who practice fraud, but also by cyber-attacks aimed at weakening nations or companies within them for various reasons, namely with cyber warfare objectives." (Security Specialist)

Noteworthy within the field of economics are the short and medium-term economic cycles, characterized by events in Europe such as stagflation, the imminent risk of economic recession in the short term, and subsequent economic recovery in the medium term. Projections indicate three years of economic recovery, with the possibility of stagflation being eliminated.

"The expectation is that things will be more normalized and lower inflation. Thus, we are talking about 2025, when things will be smoother, with lower interest rates, growth around the trend, and unemployment to remain close to current levels." (Economics Specialist)

Significant importance is also given to the economic model within the economic sector. Given certain failures of globalization and recent events highlighting the dangers of interdependence, there seems to be a decline in the extent of globalization, with regional globalization being more justifiable than ever. Moreover, the main factors driving the economic model in the near to medium future are digital transformation, mutually reinforcing energy transition processes, and the utilization of the circular economy, which is emerging as the new standard for economic development. Similarly, achieving sustainability requires a fundamental change in the economic system and individual behavior. Introducing changes gradually to minimize adverse consequences and maximize beneficial effects is essential.

"Because of the energy problem, it is believed that globalization, as we have known it in the last twenty years, will have some limitations, as there will be regional integration, i.e., regionalized globalization." (Sustainability Specialist)

"In the coming years, we will witness positive and fantastic ruptures in technological resources and the path towards a digital society in which a great deal of knowledge, information, and telecommunication will intervene significantly with the real economy and how we organize society." (Sustainability Specialist)

"That is why companies are investing heavily in decarbonization, digitization, energy efficiency, and the circular economy so that they can respond and become more sustainable, reduce the risk of their business collapsing and, consequently, continue to deserve investors' preference" (Sustainability Specialist)

The notable trends in demography include the rise in life expectancy and the growth of population resulting from migrations. The reason for this uncertainty is that although the population will likely experience an increase in lifespan, the impact of migration on demographics remains unpredictable. Nevertheless, due to the declining birth rate and the progressive aging of the European population, it is improbable that migrations alone will alter the demographic trajectory.

"Within the demographic events, the ones that can surprise more are the migrations." (Demography Specialist)

"Again, we should not be surprised from a demographic standpoint, as we will continue to live longer and longer lives." (Demography Specialist)

A rise in population displacement can be attributed to deteriorating living conditions and climate change linked to migration. This may further strain the national health systems of the recipient nations and incite social unrest.

"The idea that large migrations of people will occur in the coming years in response to climate change and living conditions is not so far-fetched. We will see more situations than we are used to, as much as we do not want to. As we have seen, drought in South Africa has pushed populations into cities. Now, when that becomes unaffordable for the cities of South Africa, they will begin to move up and immigrate to other places. Then there is all the migration from the Middle East and the living conditions of the people there, which will strain the healthcare systems." (Public Health Specialist)

When discussing innovation, one can focus on current advancements in health and technology. The first case highlights the challenge of accessing health-related innovations and advancements in new robotics applications, disease treatments, and an Innovative approach to health-related research and development. Regarding technology, there has been a rise in the utilization of biometric applications, the development of novel robotics and blockchain applications, and the exploration of the potential of the metaverse, virtual reality, and augmented reality. Undoubtedly, the primary advancements that will shape the future at a societal level are directly linked to health research. Robotics will progressively supplant human workers at the organizational level, even in crucial roles for emotions or empathy.

"Another area that could see rapid growth is everything related to "metaverse" technologies such as augmented reality and virtual reality. These technologies are not new; they have been around for many years, and while they have yet to materialize

in the real world in terms of use, I do not doubt that the investment that the major technological players are making in these areas will have a significant impact in general." (Technology Specialist)

Pandemics, outbreaks, and diseases are also considered potential events, presenting urgent health challenges that lack immediate or medium-term solutions. Examples include the emergence of antibiotic-resistant bacteria in hospitals and the human health issues associated with using antibiotics in agriculture and livestock. Therefore, it is inevitable that pandemics will arise as a result of food production and environmental factors, such as heat waves and floods.

"Multidrug-resistant bacteria are on the rise and are becoming a growing problem in the hospital setting, for which we have no cure. At the moment, they are gaining resistance. They will soon be a problem severe enough to require, in more extreme cases, the closure of health units because they are too susceptible for a person to catch a relatively serious bacterial infection within that health unit." (Public Health Specialist)

Finally, the effects of the 2030 financial framework, European environmental policy (particularly the European Ecological Pact and new legislation on sustainability reports), and new European energy and health policies are highlighted in terms of public policy. Sustainability and environmental policy policies are designated by their consequences, including their influence on corporate management and society. Regarding financial support, the sectors that have benefited the most from public policies are rail and urban transportation. Therefore, the emphasis on human security is predominantly determined by security policies, including those enforced at the health system level. Nevertheless, these processes must be executed incrementally in a constantly evolving society.

"The European Ecological Deal, with climate change incorporated and appropriately emphasized, as well as resource use having a significant influence here (the circular economy issue), will be the most critical and determining aspects of what are decisions related to a more sustainable future." (Sustainability Specialist)

To summarize, non-tourism experts have emphasized various forthcoming occurrences encompassing the environment, cybersecurity, short and medium-term economic fluctuations, the economic framework, demography, migrations, innovation, pandemics, outbreaks, diseases, and public policies. Nevertheless, after considering the frequency of references, the range of responses, and the pertinence to the addressed subject, two events emerge as the most probable to transpire in the future: (1) the ramifications of climate change and (2) the novel prospects brought about by the digital transformation. The first trend is characterized by the occurrence of natural disasters, disruptions in the food system, and population movements. On the other hand, digital transformation will result in the rise of global competition, better consumer market access, a more customized offer, and societal changes.

Interviews With Tourism Specialists

The interviews with tourism specialists centered on the two critical potential events identified by the non-tourism specialists: (1) climate change and (2) digital transformation.

Climate Change

Table 1 presents the key perspectives of tourism experts on climate change and its anticipated impacts on the sector, organized according to the CATWOE framework dimensions.

Table 1. Expert perspectives on climate change's impact on tourism: Categorized by CATWOE dimensions

Costumers	Actors	Transformation	Worldview	Owners	Environment
Change for destination selection	New energy sources	Supply-side adaptation	Supply-side adaptation		Seasonality adaptation of supply
Supply-side adaptation	Operation low cost		180º world change		Seasonality adaptation of demand
	Contingency plans		No mid-term changes		Global warming
	Supply-side adaptation		Change of high and low seasons		Supply-side adaptation
			Air travel reduction		Change for destination selection
			Last Chance Destination		Long-term problem solution

The T&H sector is confronted with a considerable challenge posed by climate change, with evident trends and projections indicating an escalating impact over the next five years. Effectively managing these fluctuations becomes imperative for the sector's supply and demand facets, necessitating adaptive strategies to cope with seasonality. The looming threat of global warming significantly affects renowned tourist destinations, prompting extensive efforts to mitigate and adapt to its consequences. Adapting to evolving climate conditions requires tourism enterprises to embrace sustainable practices from the supply side. Additionally, governmental intervention is crucial, necessitating the implementation of policies, such as regulations governing bathing seasons. Concurrently, changing tourist preferences, influenced by climate factors, reshape the tourism landscape. To ensure long-term viability, proactively devising constructive strategies becomes imperative, acknowledging the time required for their effects to manifest.

"Tourism is expected to be significantly impacted by climate change, particularly in summer-heavy cities in Southern Europe. People visit here, particularly from Northern Europe, due to our more agreeable climate; however, at the moment, we are perpetually in a state of flux characterized by periods of heavy rainfall, extreme cold, prolonged heat, droughts, and more. While no fires have occurred in Portugal this year, this unfortunate occurrence affects us each year". (Restaurant Sector Specialist)

"The impact of climate change is already evident in Portugal, as evidenced by the early start of the bathing season. This has resulted in additional costs for tourists visiting the beaches, serving as a clear example of the effects of climate change. The management model commences in June and concludes in mid-September. We are experiencing a delayed summer, as evidenced by the absence of snow in Serra da Estrela, which is unusual for our Portuguese region. The expected snowfall is occurring at irregular intervals. Consequently, hotels can no longer generate revenue from the product as they did in the past. Hence, I believe that changes are indeed present, and they are a reality. How can we do it? We must assess the existing resources and determine how to profit from them. It may be necessary to start the bathing season earlier to break the tradition of students determining the holiday schedule and to allow for an earlier opening of the bathing season". (Hospitality Specialist)

Moreover, incorporating novel energy sources is not solely a reaction to environmental issues; it also corresponds to the increasing desire for sustainable tourism experiences. Tourists increasingly favor destinations and services prioritizing sustainability, prompting the sector to allocate resources towards cleaner and more efficient energy alternatives. Implementing cost-effective strategies helps businesses reduce operational expenses, improve competitiveness, and provide environmental benefits. Simultaneously, it is essential to create thorough contingency plans to guarantee the uninterrupted operation of businesses in the event of climate-induced disruptions, such as severe weather occurrences or unexpected environmental obstacles. Adopting a multifaceted strategy to adapt the supply side demonstrates the sector's dedication to reducing its environmental footprint and actively tackling the intricate difficulties that climate change presents to the T&H sector in the future.

"When it comes to events organization, it is becoming increasingly imperative to have contingency plans, such as plan B or even plan C, to mitigate the impact of adverse weather conditions. Last year, the Sintra mountain range was frequently closed due to political issues rather than climate issues while we were organizing events in the Sintra area. The scheduled events had to occur in some manner but did not occur at that location; instead, they took place elsewhere. Consequently, the implementation of plan B will become more necessary. There is a strong inclination to abandon plan A when alternative plans are considered. This results in presenting plan B as the primary option from the beginning and avoiding certain objectives. This could pose greater challenges concerning weather or climate volatility". (Events Specialist)

Moreover, a significant transformation in the T&H sector is occurring due to consumers' evolving preferences regarding destination choices. Customers increasingly select travel destinations based on traditional attractions and their preferred climate conditions. This shift not only demands businesses to reassess their marketing strategies but also underscores the need for a comprehensive adjustment on the supply side to meet customers' evolving expectations. Tourism providers must actively explore innovative approaches to enhance customer experience by integrating sustainable practices into their operations.

"Climate change and extreme events often drive people away from places." (Destination Management Specialist)

"In terms of the environment, previously overlooked destinations with milder temperatures will become desirable, while exotic destinations that were popular in the past due to their extreme temperatures (either very cold or very hot) may no longer be considered primary destinations and instead be relegated to secondary status." (Events Specialist)

Amidst the profound transformation of our world, the T&H sector faces a pressing need for adjustments in its practices. This calls for active recalibrations by businesses on the supply side to navigate the evolving landscape effectively. Recognizing the necessity for significant changes, the sector acknowledges that relying on conventional mid-term modifications is inadequate, necessitating a comprehensive restructuring. The traditional distinction between high and low seasons has become obsolete due to climate-induced fluctuations, disrupting established patterns and compelling businesses to implement adaptable strategies. The decrease in air travel, driven by environmental considerations, prompts a reevaluation of transportation methods and a renewed focus on local and regional tourism. The concept of "Last Chance Destinations" underscores the urgent and transient nature of climate-induced changes, compelling both the T&H sector and tourists to consider the broader ecological consequences of their decisions.

"It is imperative to confront and mitigate these challenges in the upcoming years. However, Portugal must reduce its reliance on beach tourism and actively pursue diversification in this sector. It is even shifting the peak season to a different time of year. In Portugal, the peak season occurs during the summer, while in recent years, the winter has been characterized by a scarcity of rainfall and elevated temperatures. Consequently, seeking refuge in these off-peak seasons would serve as an effective strategy to counteract these climatic alterations. In Northern Europe, we can expect relatively colder winters compared to previous years, along with hotter summers. Hence, I anticipate that the events unfolding in Portugal, Spain, and Italy will be replicated". (Restaurant Sector Specialist)

"The events that occurred during this period, considering the changes in climate in specific regions of the world, can be likened to a game of chess. The individual strongly prefers relocating to a place that offers better opportunities regarding food, housing, security, climate, and other factors that are currently lacking. The need for a significant change drives this decision, as the world undergoes a transformative evolution that necessitates a complete reversal of circumstances". (Tourism Information Specialist)

Drawing insights from expert perspectives on climate change's impact on T&H, categorized by CATWOE dimensions, a discernible scenario begins to take shape that can be formalized as follows:

Considered a complex problem to address over the long term, climate change was deemed increasingly unpredictable and prone to exacerbate global warming.

On the side of the tourist offer, an adaptation to the change in seasons considered usual in each destination is anticipated, requiring an adaptation of the offer by tourism agents, providing experiences adapted to the new climatic conditions. Additionally, investments will be made in novel energy sources and the development of contingency plans.

On the demand side, there will be an adaptation to the new seasons and a change in preferred destinations, including the search for destinations that may disappear or become less attractive.

Due to new public policies and regulations, there will be a trend toward less air travel.

Digital Transformation

Table 2 outlines the primary viewpoints of tourism experts regarding digital transformation and its expected effects on the sector, categorized based on the dimensions of the CATWOE framework.

Table 2. Expert perspectives on digital transformation's impact on tourism: Categorized by CATWOE dimensions

Costumers	Actors	Transformation	Worldview	Owners	Environment
Digital and physical (demand side)	Increased of connectivity	Process efficiency	Physical and digital (supply and demand side)	AI (Artificial Intelligence) investments	No adoption of process automation
Supply-side customization	Management tools	Supply-side partnerships	Augmented Reality (AR)+Virtual Reality (VR) investment		No adoption of virtual tourism
Digital platforms	Robotic & AI benefits (supply side process simplification)		Easier forecasting		Business travel reduction
Real-time digital interaction	Media communication				Predominance of AI (customization, new experiences, supply side process simplification)
AI applications (demand process simplification)					Virtual reality + metaverse (promotion)
More access to information					

Over the next five years, the T&H sector is on the brink of a substantial digital transformation. Embracing technology introduces a nuanced perspective as the sector grapples with the balance between adopting process automation and preserving the personalized touch in customer interactions. Despite the potential of virtual tourism experiences, their adoption remains limited, overshadowed by the enduring preference for authentic travel encounters. The integration of virtual collaboration tools and a growing emphasis on environmental responsibility is expected to contribute to a decline in business travel. Artificial Intelligence (AI) emerges as a pivotal force across various domains, promising tailored experiences, innovative products, and optimized supply chain operations. The synergy of Virtual Reality and the Metaverse emerges as a powerful tool for promotional efforts, providing immersive and participatory experiences for prospective tourists. To ensure enduring growth and relevance, the sector must meticulously navigate the dynamics between technological advancements, environmental consciousness, and user-centered experiences in its adaptation to the digital landscape.

"Regarding digital transformation, I anticipate that artificial intelligence will primarily dominate various sectors in the future, including tourism, education, and restaurants." (Restaurant Specialist)

"We offer a variety of hotels to cater to different needs; however, virtual tourism cannot fully substitute the authentic tourist experience, as our focus lies primarily on providing genuine experiences and personal interactions. If we were to examine an object we could physically interact with and perceive its scent, such an object does not exist. When embarking on a journey to a foreign nation such as China, one experiences a significant disparity in cultural norms and practices. And that does not occur with 3D glasses. Possibly, 3D glasses could be provided to individuals lacking the financial means to travel elsewhere, thereby enhancing the available options. However, this does not strictly qualify as tourism. Television enables individuals to virtually traverse the globe without physical presence solely by watching television programs. However, can this be classified as tourism?". (Hospitality Specialist)

In bolstering the resilience and responsiveness of the tourism ecosystem, enhanced interconnectivity, advanced management tools, and the integration of robotics and AI (Artificial Intelligence) on the supply side play a crucial role. Improved connectivity allows businesses to streamline operations, optimize resource allocation, and foster stronger collaborations within the sector. Implementing sophisticated management tools equips stakeholders with data-driven decision-making capabilities, ensuring adaptability in a dynamic environment. The synergy between robotics and AI simplifies operations, enabling enterprises to deliver personalized and efficient services, ultimately elevating customer satisfaction. Digital technology advancement within media communication empowers tourism providers to connect with a global audience. This comprehensive integration of technologies contributes to a more robust and flexible tourism infrastructure.

"Technologically speaking, it has transformed, and I believe it will persist in altering the lives of individuals engaged. Previously, I used to communicate with my partners through fax or computer. However, nowadays, individuals who possess a smartphone already receive a significant amount of the information that was previously accessible. Individuals are no longer constrained to a fixed location. They can now embrace the lifestyle of a digital nomad, allowing them to work remotely in various fields without being tied to a specific location. Despite the presence of digital events, I found it fascinating that a team of approximately 20 employees participated in the event from the comfort of their own homes. I believe this problem has arisen due to advancements in technology, and depending on the nature of the event, it may persist in the future". (Events Specialist)

"I believe it will serve as an additional instrument at our disposal, but I do not anticipate it to be a replacement. It can be a valuable instrument; if it benefits us, that is excellent. Regardless, we cannot impede the advancement of life, the forthcoming events, and growth. It is advisable to make an effort to derive maximum benefit from it rather than expressing dislike, as it is not worth dismissing it entirely". (Travel Agency Specialist)

"The machine's capacity for reasoning is remarkable, as humans possess the ability to reason but cannot simultaneously store and contemplate multiple concepts. An automated device is capable of performing the task. Rather than convening a meeting with clients who possess extensive knowledge on a specific topic, a machine can effortlessly transcribe the crucial information from the speeches of these individuals spanning the past two decades. The magnitude of this phenomenon is inconceivable, and its occurrence is imminent rather than distant in time". (Destination Management Specialist)

The evolving interplay between digital and physical dimensions in travel is poised to reshape the experience. As the demand for unique and tailored journeys increases among travelers, a more robust partnership is expected to emerge between travel providers and suppliers. This collaborative effort is set to yield a more personalized and customized approach to tourism offerings. Digital platforms will serve as comprehensive hubs for travelers, facilitating the organization and reservation processes and fostering an immediate connection with their chosen destinations. Integrating AI applications on the demand side will simplify processes, allowing travelers to navigate vast amounts of information effortlessly and seamlessly incorporate their preferences into their travel experiences. With readily available and abundant information, travelers will make informed decisions and actively contribute to shaping the dynamic evolution of the T&H sector.

"I believe the preference likely stems from the velocity of the proposal. The preference for simplicity, ease of use, personalization, and similarity are the primary factors influencing the accommodation choice. For instance, if tourists seek a straightforward experience where they can sleep and cook their meals, they are likely to book an Airbnb through the platform, as it offers a quicker and more convenient process compared to the variety of hotel options. We have observed a significant change in the reservation patterns at our Tourist Office over the past five years. In the past, we handled many reservations directly at the destination. However, since the onset of the pandemic, we have noticed a shift towards people feeling safer making reservations through online platforms rather than in-person inquiries. They prefer making reservations through the platform and, if needed, seek validation or endorsement from local tourism authorities. In addition, there is a significant increase in the number of online platforms dedicated to booking accommodations or activities, and this trend is expected to continue due to the convenience it offers: users can access these platforms with a single click". (Tourism Information Specialist)

"At the digital level, along with innovation, the focus is on improving search functionality, stimulating demand, and offering adaptable solutions to attract tourists. By "players," I am referring to companies operating globally. Hence, starting from the entity responsible for promoting the destination to those involved in promoting specific events or experiences, regardless of their nature, all stakeholders will strive to enhance sustainability, enabling customers to make informed choices". (Travel Agency Specialist)

In anticipation of the forthcoming years, owners in the T&H sector are poised to harness the potential offered by emerging AI technology. This strategic orientation integrates predictive analytics, automation, and chatbots to enhance operational efficiency and elevate customer interactions. The primary objective for owners is to sustain adaptability in response to market fluctuations, ensuring streamlined operations. Furthermore, they aim to deliver customized services that resonate with the evolving preferences of digitally savvy travelers, achieved through the effective utilization of AI technologies.

"One aspect pertains to acquiring knowledge, which necessitates...knowledge facilitates our decision-making, correct? Hence, possessing more knowledge enables us to make more informed and astute decisions. The process of digitization or digital transition will enable this. Acquiring more information and understanding. This technological problem pertains to the growing need and usefulness of real-time interaction when implemented practically". (Destination Management Specialist)

The travel experience undergoes a transformative shift with the advancements in AR (Augmented Reality) and VR (Virtual Reality) investments, seamlessly blending physical and digital elements. This integration signals the T&H sector's potential entry into a remarkable era of innovation. Adopting advanced technologies facilitates more accurate forecasting, enabling businesses to respond proactively to travelers' evolving demands. A pervasive commitment to optimizing operational efficiency streamlines processes and elevates the sector's sustainability and resilience. The interconnected nature of this digital transformation emphasizes the increasing importance of collaborations with suppliers. It's crucial to recognize that these technologies are not intended to replace the presence of on-site professionals; instead, they enhance and complement existing services. Embracing these trends positions the T&H sector not only for adaptation to the digital age but also for laying the groundwork for a more dynamic, interconnected, and customer-centric future.

"There will be designated areas catering to various forms of tourism, such as those focused on digital or robotic experiences. When we no longer require human assistance, we tend to be more amicable towards these services. In the future, we will be able to enjoy highly customized services, such as having a personal chef who can prepare dinner in the comfort of our room or hiring a babysitter who can attend to various tasks while caring for the children. I am willing to pay for these services but not for the current state of affairs in the aviation sector or any other unrelated matters. In my opinion, this is the anticipated outcome. Technology will be employed as necessary, and the service will persist in the locations where it is required. This phenomenon is already evident in countries such as Dubai, where there is remarkable technological advancement in certain areas while maintaining a strong adherence to conservative values in other aspects. Consequently, the two worlds will coexist without overlapping, operating simultaneously". (Hospitality Specialist)

"In my opinion, there will also be a shift towards investments in digital tourism. Regarding augmented realities and virtual realities, it is worth noting that they are becoming more accessible. For instance, a virtual reality helmet can now be purchased for €300 or €400, although this price may still be relatively high for most individuals. However, those who can do so are willing to pay for the opportunity to engage in digital tourism and utilize this tool to a greater extent. In addition, I anticipate a growing influx of investments in these domains. A greater range of diversity will enable us to attract and standardize this technology among a larger population". (Restaurant Sector Specialist)

Much like climate change, tourism experts have a consensus regarding the substantial impact of digital transformation in tourism.

Drawing insights from Expert Perspectives on Digital Transformation's Impact on Tourism, categorized by CATWOE dimensions, a discernible scenario begins to take shape that can be formalized as follows:

Artificial intelligence is expected to play a dominant role in digital transformation. However, other significant technologies such as virtual reality, augmented reality, metaverse, and robotization also have importance.

Regarding the side of the tourist offer, tourism activity already uses digital media as a supplementary tool to enhance the existing on-site and physical resources. This trend will grow with a significant investment focus on artificial intelligence, virtual reality, and augmented reality technologies. Future possibilities include streamlining procedures and enhancing decision-making abilities. In addition, it will ease the customization of products, the creation of novel experiences, and the virtual promotion of tourist destinations.

Using digital tools also eases the ability of tourism agents to forecast future situations and establish cooperation partnerships among various agents.

Regarding tourist demand, there is expected to be a prevailing tendency towards digital media platforms that offer real-time connection and enhanced information accessibility. However, tourists will continue showing sustained interest in face-to-face service and physical experiences. Artificial intelligence has the potential to simplify the various operations related to tourist demand, including in the creation of a tourism offer better adapted to the tourist profile.

Due to the convenience of virtual meetings, there is expected to be a decrease in business travel.

The prevalence of digital nomads is expected to rise because of the increasing level of interconnection, allowing them to work far from the company.

CONCLUSION

This study aimed to construct scenarios for the T&H sector over five years, seeking to develop a nuanced understanding of potential developments and challenges that may shape the sector's trajectory.

A two-phase methodology approach based on qualitative studies was followed. In the initial phase, the research sought insights from non-tourism experts, conducting semi-structured interviews with thirteen specialists in diverse fields. In the second phase, the study applied the CATWOE analysis framework. Semi-structured interviews were conducted with stakeholders from the T&H sector, including destination management, events organization, tourist information, restaurant sector, travel agencies, tourist entertainment, and hospitality.

Amidst discussions on diverse subjects with experts beyond the tourism domain, a unanimous consensus emerged, highlighting climate change and digital transformation as the pivotal events expected to unfold over the next five years. These overarching trends transcend various layers of societal and economic structures with profound implications. In the societal realm, these shifts can alter behavior, lifestyles, and cultural patterns, while economically, they carry the potential to reshape markets, trade dynamics, and job landscapes. The T&H sector, being particularly susceptible, faces pronounced effects. Climate change and digital transformation redefine how travelers engage with destinations, necessitating a fundamental rethink of sector strategies to align with evolving preferences and expectations. The convergence of opinions among non-tourism experts on these significant issues underscores the widespread recognition of their profound influence on the sector's future. This recognition emphasizes the vulnerability and centrality of the T&H sector in navigating and adapting to the complexities introduced by the tandem forces of climate change and digital transformation.

As the imminent challenges of climate change and digital transformation cast a shadow, experts from varied roles within the T&H sector contribute their insights on potential implications. This collaborative perspective, crucial for building scenarios, provides a nuanced understanding of challenges and opportunities that may shape the future trajectory of the sector. Here, the significance of the CATWOE approach becomes evident, as it allows for a systematic and comprehensive analysis. The scenario-building process gains strategic depth by integrating diverse viewpoints through CATWOE—considering Client, Actor, Transformation, Worldview, Owner, and Environment. This approach ensures that the scenarios developed capture the multifaceted nature of challenges and encompass a holistic range of considerations. As a result, applying the CATWOE approach facilitates a well-rounded evaluation of the potential future landscape of the T&H sector, enhancing the sector's ability to respond proactively to the intricate interplay of climate change and digital transformation.

Derived from these findings, two distinct scenarios materialize. In response to climate challenges, adaptations in the T&H sector are foreseen. On the supply side, tourism agents are expected to adjust offerings to accommodate changing seasons, providing experiences tailored to evolving climatic conditions. This adaptation involves investments in alternative energy sources and formulating contingency plans. On the demand side, there is an anticipation of adjustments to new seasons and a shift in preferred destinations. Travelers may seek destinations that align with changing climatic patterns or explore areas at risk of disappearing or losing appeal. The overall response to climate change involves comprehensively revaluating supply and demand aspects within the T&H sector.

According to this scenario, the T&H sector is expected to adapt on both the supply and demand sides. Supply-side adaptations include adjusting offerings to changing seasons, investing in alternative energy sources, and formulating contingency plans. On the demand side, travelers are anticipated to adapt to new seasons and reconsider preferred destinations, possibly seeking areas aligned with changing climatic patterns. Overall, the scenario highlights a comprehensive revaluation of the T&H sector, emphasizing the importance of sustainable practices and resilience to navigate the challenges posed by climate change.

AI is anticipated to lead in digital transformation, accompanied by VR, AR, metaverse, and robotization. In the tourist offer, digital media supplements on-site resources with significant investments in AI, virtual, and augmented reality. This facilitates streamlined procedures, better decision-making, customized products, novel experiences, and virtual destination promotion. Digital tools aid forecasting and collaboration among tourism agents. In tourist demand, there's a preference for real-time connection through digital platforms, alongside sustained interest in face-to-face service and physical experiences. AI simplifies operations related to tourist demand, adapting offers to tourist profiles. Virtual meetings may reduce business travel, and the prevalence of digital nomads is expected to rise due to increased interconnectivity allowing remote work. The evolving landscape of technology in tourism highlights a shift towards digitalization, influencing both the supply and demand sides of the sector.

Based on this scenario, it is expected that on the supply side, investments in AI, virtual reality, and augmented reality will streamline processes, aid decision-making, and allow personalized experiences. Digital tools will enhance forecasting and collaboration among tourism agents. Demand-wise, a preference for real-time connectivity through digital platforms and continued interest in face-to-face services is expected. AI will simplify operations related to tourist demand and adapt offerings to individual preferences. Virtual meetings may reduce business travel, and increased interconnectivity could foster a rise in digital nomadism. This tech evolution signifies a broader shift toward digitalization in tourism.

This study and formulating scenarios on climate change and digital transformation are highly academically and professionally relevant. Academically, the research contributes to the theoretical understanding of how these transformative forces impact the T&H sector. It provides a nuanced analysis, incorporating diverse expert perspectives and employing the CATWOE framework, which adds methodological depth. The scenarios offer practical insights for professionals, guiding strategic planning and decision-making within the T&H sector. They serve as a valuable tool for anticipating challenges, identifying opportunities, and fostering adaptability in an ever-evolving landscape shaped by climate change and digital transformation.

As with any research endeavor, the qualitative study conducted in this research has inherent limitations that warrant consideration. One notable limitation is the potential for sampling bias within the expert panel, which may impact the scenarios' comprehensiveness. The subjective nature of qualitative research introduces an element of interpretation, raising concerns about the generalizability of the scenarios derived from expert insights.

The CATWOE approach, while systematic, is not without its constraints. It may oversimplify the intricate complexity of the T&H sector, potentially missing crucial nuances. The efficacy of CATWOE relies heavily on the accuracy and inclusivity of expert opinions, and any oversight in this regard could compromise the holistic nature of the scenarios.

Moreover, splitting the scenarios into two may inadvertently oversimplify the range of potential future states. Given the dynamic nature of the T&H sector and its susceptibility to multifaceted influences, limiting scenarios to two might not adequately capture the diversity of possible outcomes.

Recognizing the macro factors' vulnerability in the T&H sector poses its challenges. The unpredictability of these factors, coupled with the potential for unforeseen global events or policy shifts, adds an element of uncertainty to scenario planning. Despite these limitations, the research aims to contribute valuable insights to academic discourse and professional practices within the T&H sector, acknowledging the complexities and uncertainties inherent in envisioning its future landscape.

FUNDING AND ACKNOWLEDGEMENTS

This research was supported by "Fundação para a Ciência e Tecnologia" (FCT), Portugal, through the SHIFT project (Sustainability-oriented, Highly interactive, and Innovation-based Framework for Tourism marketing), reference number PTDC/EDE-OGE/2146/2021.

REFERENCES

Aldao, C., Blasco, D., & Espallargas, M. P. (2022). Lessons from COVID-19 for the future: destination crisis management, tourist behavior and tourism industry trends. *Journal of Tourism Futures*, 1-15. doi:10.1108/JTF-02-2022-0059

Bouhalleb, A., & Smida, A. (2020). *Exploring the relationship between scenario planning and strategic flexibility and complexity*. European J. of International Management., doi:10.1504/EJIM.2020.107033

Checkland, P. B., & Scholes, J. (1990). *Soft systems methodology in action*. John Wiley & Sons.

Duan, J., Xie, C., & Morrison, A. M. (2021). Tourism Crises and Impacts on Destinations: A Systematic Review of the Tourism and Hospitality Literature. *Journal of Hospitality & Tourism Research (Washington, D.C.)*, *46*(4), 667–695. doi:10.1177/1096348021994194

Etemad, H. (2020). Managing uncertain consequences of a global crisis: SMEs encountering adversities, losses, and new opportunities. *Journal of International Entrepreneurship*, *18*(2), 125–144. doi:10.1007/s10843-020-00279-z

Filippo, M., Colangelo, D., & Farnia, L. (2017). *Innovation and new business models in tourism*, 149-168. doi:10.3280/RISS2017-001010

Fisher, D., & Wilder-Smith, A. (2020). The global community needs to swiftly ramp up the response to contain COVID-19. *Lancet*, *395*(10230), 1109–1110. doi:10.1016/S0140-6736(20)30679-6 PMID:32199470

Ghobadian, A., Han, T., Zhang, X., O'Regan, N., Troise, C., Bresciani, S., & Narayanan, V. (2022). COVID-19 pandemic: The interplay between firm disruption and managerial attention focus. *British Journal of Management*, *33*(1), 390–409. doi:10.1111/1467-8551.12556

Gudz, O. (2020). *Organizational and information aspects of management of modern enterprise developm*ent., 31. Taylor & Francis. . doi:10.31673/2415-8089.2020.010510

Gupta, K., & Sharma, S. (2021). Kiosks as self-service technology in hotels: Opportunities and challenges. *Worldwide Hospitality and Tourism Themes*, *13*(2), 236–251. doi:10.1108/WHATT-10-2020-0125

Ha, T. K. D., Nguyen, T. K., Pham, T. M. N., Nguyen, D. Q., Truong, B. T., Le, V. S., & Nguyen, H. T. (2022). Influence of Macro Environment on Tourism Value Chain in Vietnam: Case of Daklak Province. *Geo Journal of Tourism and Geosites*, *41*(2), 400–407. doi:10.30892/gtg.41209-843

Iranmanesh, M., Ghobakhloo, M., Nilashi, M., Tseng, M. L., Yadegaridehkordi, E., & Leung, N. (2022). Applications of disruptive digital technologies in hotel industry: A systematic review. *International Journal of Hospitality Management*, *107*, 103304. doi:10.1016/j.ijhm.2022.103304

Jashari, A., Tiberius, V., & Dabić, M. (2022). Tracing the progress of scenario research in business and management. *Futures & Foresight Science*, *4*(2), e109. doi:10.1002/ffo2.109

Khosravi, F., & Jha-Thakur, U. (2019). Managing uncertainties through scenario analysis in strategic environmental assessment. *Journal of Environmental Planning and Management*, *62*(6), 1000–1979. doi:10.1080/09640568.2018.1456913

Postma, A., Cavagnaro, E., & Spruyt, E. (2017). Sustainable tourism 2040. *Journal of Tourism Futures*, *3*(1), 13–22. doi:10.1108/JTF-10-2015-0046

Postma, A., & Yeoman, I. (2021). A systems perspective as a tool to understand disruption in travel and tourism. *Journal of Tourism Futures*. . doi:10.1108/JTF-04-2020-0052

Ramírez, R., Churchhouse, S., Palermo, A., & Hoffmann, J. (2017). Using scenario planning to reshape strategy. *MIT Sloan Management Review*, 58.

Ribeiro, H. N. R., & Pereira, B. R. (2022). The Age of Uncertainty: Prospects for Challenging Times. *IJTM International Journal of Trade and Management*, *1*(1), 148–161. doi:10.5281/zenodo.6564192

Rodrigues, V., Eusébio, C., & Breda, Z. (2023). Enhancing sustainable development through tourism digitalization: A systematic literature review. *Information Technology & Tourism*, *25*(1), 13–45. doi:10.1007/s40558-022-00241-w

Schwarz, J., Ram, C., & Rohrbeck, R. (2019). Combining scenario planning and business wargaming to better anticipate future competitive dynamics. *Futures*, *105*, 133–142. Advance online publication. doi:10.1016/j.futures.2018.10.001

Scott, D. (2021). Sustainable tourism and the grand challenge of climate change. *Sustainability (Basel)*, *13*(4), 1–17. doi:10.3390/su13041966

Seyitoğlu, F., & Costa, C. (2022a). A systematic review of scenario planning studies in tourism and hospitality research. *Journal of Policy Research in Tourism, Leisure & Events*, 1–18. doi:10.1080/19407963.2022.2032108

Seyitoğlu, F., & Costa, C. (2022b). A scenario planning framework for (post-) pandemic tourism in European destinations. *European Planning Studies*, *30*(12), 2554–2574. doi:10.1080/09654313.2022.2045571

Tiberius, V. (2019). Scenarios in the strategy process: A framework of affordances and constraints. *European Journal of Futures Research*, *7*(1), 1–14. doi:10.1186/s40309-019-0160-5

Tiberius, V., Siglow, C., & Sendra-García, J. (2020). Scenarios in business and management: The current stock and research opportunities. *Journal of Business Research*, *121*, 235–242. doi:10.1016/j.jbusres.2020.08.037 PMID:32895583

Ural, M. (2016). Risk management for sustainable tourism. European Journal of Tourism. *Hospitality and Recreation*, *7*(1), 63–71. doi:10.1515/ejthr-2016-0007

Wu, D. C., Cao, Z., Wen, L., & Song, H. (2021). Scenario Forecasting for Global Tourism. *Journal of Hospitality & Tourism Research (Washington, D.C.)*, *45*(1), 28–51. doi:10.1177/1096348020919990

Chapter 4
Social Media Platforms in Promoting Island Tourism Destination:
A Netnography Approach

Partho Pratim Seal
https://orcid.org/0000-0001-6867-8713
Manipal Academy of Higher Education, India

ABSTRACT

Social media has an important role in marketing a destination as it can assist in both demand and supply. Social media in tourism supports providing search information about a destination, and the decision-making among the stakeholders. Leverage of social media for marketing tourism products along with sustainability is stated to be an excellent strategy. The current study is conducted by obtaining data from social media sites about the reviews of the customer's thought process on the island tourist destination. The findings from the study will help policymakers make appropriate decisions while marketing an island tourism destination.

INTRODUCTION

A tourism destination has a natural entity that displays unique conditions and properties. Tourists before visiting a destination develop an image either through previous experience, word of mouth, press reports, or advertisement (Baloglu & Brinberg, 1997) and form a mental picture of the destination (Kavoura & Bitsani, 2013). A consumer has a large selection of destinations to choose from but less time

DOI: 10.4018/979-8-3693-0960-5.ch004

to make a buying decision. With the development of information and communication technology and social media, the relationship between destinations and tourists has changed radically to make the destination open to an international market and attract foreign direct investment and economic growth (Sukunesan et al., 2020).

With the growth of digital communication channels currently social media has become a powerful tool for marketing and broadcasting information about tourist destinations. An island destination does have a unique natural beauty that provides cultural richness and is attractive to travelers who seek diverse experiences. For the global tourism industry island tourism has a significant role in the economic development of host regions along with cultural exchange between visitors and local communities. With the increasing dependence on digital media platforms for information social media currently has developed as a key for destination marketing.

The marketing of tourism destinations has been revolutionized by social media platforms which provide a dynamic space for sharing visual content including videos of locations, reviews, and recommendations that influence the perceptions and decisions. Past studies have stated that social media platforms like Instagram, Facebook, and Twitter have considerably influenced travel preferences (Gretzel et al., 2015; Neuhofer et al., 2019). Low-cost marketing efforts have currently become a challenging task to make a destination attractive (Naciye & Adam, 2020) and sustainability is vital for a destination's overall image (Pahrudin, et al., 2022). The tourists contribute by promoting and making a destination sustainable through their behavior and the posts they put on social media (Pasquinelli, et al., 2021). Currently, social media platforms have an important role in destination marketing as they provide travelers with the prospect of sharing their experiences in real time (Khan, et al., 2022).

With the presence of social media, there is a revolution in destination marketing which offers a dynamic platform to engage travelers by showcasing unique offerings at a destination. The advent and accessibility of the Internet have brought about fundamental shifts in how travelers seek information, plan and book their trips, and share their travel experiences (Buhalis & Law, 2008; Senecal & Nantel, 2004; Xiang & Gretzel, 2010). A significant development in the Internet's evolution is the growing prevalence of social media platforms, which allow users to collaborate, communicate, and create original content like blogs, videos, wikis, reviews, or photos (Boyd and Ellison, 2008). Social media sites, which facilitate consumer-generated content (CGC), are widely utilized by online travelers (Gretzel, 2006). CGC and review platforms such as Tripadvisor.com are widespread and may even challenge the authority of traditional destination marketing organizations (DMOs) or conventional advertising methods (Gretzel, 2006; Gretzel et al., 2000). This research aims to investigate the extent to which marketing organizations for top international tourism destinations make use of social media.

To understand the role of social media platforms in promoting an island destination the chapter aims to analyze and present the role of social media platform in promoting Andamans as an island destination. The main objective of the study was to ascertain the various image components and attributes as they are reflected in social media. As the study involves a qualitative approach the same will be very useful for both the scholars and the practitioners. The study with the range of comments on TripAdvisor does support the significance of the destination products and overall atmosphere (Kladou & Mavaragani, 2015). Although tourists may comment on the cognitive and affective aspects the review comments do include a variety of characteristics and a positive attitude towards a destination is linked with more than one attribute (Kladou & Kehagias, 2014).

LITERATURE REVIEW

Social media platforms have significantly changed how society used to consume and contribute information. Technology advancement has enabled individuals to share their thoughts, opinions, and creations on the Internet thereby transforming the process of creating and spreading information (Buhalis & Law, 2018; Senecal & Nantel, 2004; Xiang & Gretzel, 2010). Initially Internet before the emergence of Web 2.0 operated in a one-way manner (Borges, 2009), static with minimal interaction with other Internet users. With Web 2.0 user-generated content through social media and social network sites changed into dynamic (Safko & Brake,2009; Buhalis & Law, 2008) content where the shift was towards the users rather than organizations taking charge of the Internet. Social media has a significant role in meeting the demand and supply of tourism which allows tourists to interact through various Internet platforms and react to visitors' opinions. It also states the characteristics of social media and its implications on destination marketing. The study states that the strategies aligned with social media can make the destinations to be competitive. In the context of tourism, marketers, and institutions no longer have complete control over how their destination or product is portrayed. Web 2.0 enables the incorporation of five key functional aspects: information representation, collaboration, communication, interactivity, and transactions (Gretzel, et al.,2006, p. 147). Social media represent an ongoing and continually evolving phenomenon involving user-generated content shared online (Kaplan & Haenlein, 2009; Stankov, Lazic, & Dragicevic, 2010; Xiang & Gretzel, 2010).

There is a preference for tourists to view social media sites as social media is used for experience-sharing before, during, and after visiting the destination (Xiang & Gretzel, 2010). Sometimes it is also observed that social media content is more trustworthy than the official website (Fortis, Buhalis, & Rossides, 2012). Stating about social media include, all online platforms and websites where the customers share their experience (Xiang & Gretzel, 2010). The customers share their experiences on social media through posts, stories, comments, and evaluations with pictures and videos. The sharing of travelers' views about the destination on social media just does not only influence friends and family but also potential travelers globally. There is an increase in acceptance of electronic word-of-mouth, as social media content is often stated as more dependable than the official tourism website of a destination (Fotis et al., 2012).

The concept of destination image has evolved over the years. The initial definition of destination image was stated as a summation of beliefs, ideas, and an impression an individual has of a destination (Crompton, 1979). A positive destination image influences the tourist and improves the business and investment at the destination. The destination image is considered to be formed by two interrelated components: cognitive (perceptual) obtained by individual knowledge and assessment of the perceived attributes of the destination, while the affective (emotional) is the individual feeling of a destination (Beerli & Martin, 2004). It is believed by researchers that the cognitive component influences beliefs while affective components drive customers' travel intention (Elliot et al.2011). Some past studies are based on how social media is used to promote destinations and enhance destination image as also tourists co-create the image of the destination through social media platforms (Iglesias- Sánchez et al., 2020).

In a tourism destination change is continuous and in an island destination, the development is more intense considering the geographical limitations (Rodríguez et al., 2008) so sustainability is of concern. The concept of sustainable tourism is about tourists visiting a place and how it has a positive impact on the environment, society, and economy. Tourism includes transportation to the destination, local transportation, accommodation, recreation, and sightseeing as there is no tourism without travel. Sustainable tourism practices are considered to conserve resources for future generations. To achieve sustainability developing countries and small islands should maximize the economic benefits for the local community and minimize environmental and social costs. Andamans and Nicobar Islands is a Union territory of India, a developing nation where sustainability is a concern. Andamans is also recognized as one of the most remote and sensitive tourism destinations in the world (Reddy, 2008). To achieve sustainable tourism continuous monitoring of the impact of tourism on the environment and local community must be observed so is it true for an island destination like Andaman. Andaman and Nicobar Islands are a group of 572 islets and islands that are found in the juncture of Andaman and Nicobar Islands. Of the total number of 550, only about 28 islands are inhabited by humans. The Andaman Islands encompass North, Middle, and South Andaman collectively known as Great Andaman. The original inhabitants of the islands are the Sentinalese, the Jarawa, and the Onge who are collectively known as Great Andamese. The island also has historically significant landmarks of freedom fighting like Cellular Jail, Netaji Subhash Bose Island, and Viper Island Port Blair is the current capital city of Andaman and Nicobar Islands; however, Ross Island was once the capital city during British rule. It was from here the British people lived and ruled the islands. In the South of Andaman, there is a territory known as Little Andaman which includes islands of Ritchie's Archipelago that encompasses world-famous Havelock and Neil islands. North -East of Ritchie's Archipelago has two islands the Narcondam and Barren Islands the latter being the only active volcano of India. Andaman & Nicobar Islands is also declared as the endemic bird area of the world with more than 200 species and subspecies of birds existing on the island. Andamans could be reached in two ways by airways or seaways. Andamans depicts the beauty of Mother Nature with silver sand beaches, tropical forests, and crystal blue sea along the brilliant coral reef which draws tourists from across the globe.

METHODOLOGY

Netnography-'A research methodology that adapts ethnographic research techniques to study the culture and communities that are influenced through computer-mediated communication' (Kozinets, 2002, p .62). It is an ethnographic study that focuses on observing and interpreting online communities' behavior and interactions (Kozinets, 2010). The netnography methodology has evolved from ethnography though it has some differences. Netnography and ethnography approaches are both naturalistic and not manipulative and help to know about online/ offline culture (Kozinets et al., 2010). Netnography provides researchers access to respondents who may be difficult to reach for their responses.

Netnography allows us to obtain downloadable internet-based secondary data which is cheaper and faster to obtain (Seal, 2023). With this method, the researchers have the advantage of understanding and interpreting individuals in a naturalistic environment leading to a deeper meaning to data collection. With the increasing usage of netnography, the same is becoming popular in business studies, especially in understanding consumer behavior (Tavakoli & Mura, 2018). The emphasis of netnography is on how communication is made within online communities and social media (Costello et al., 2017). Netnography is also adopted by tourism researchers (Podoshen, 2013) and is stated as a powerful method for causing natural and detailed descriptions of various activities. It is also believed that netnography can also be used to discover findings of new phenomena where less is known about the market and the tourism experience.

ANALYSIS

The influence of social media has affected the stakeholders of tourism. Although in social media platforms, Facebook is the market leader (Zeng & Gerritsen, 2014) for tourism TripAdvisor is considered the most popular social media website on tourism content. So the destination image as reflected by the TripAdvisor reviews generates the perception of probable tourists. The data analysis used two different methods narrative and content analysis. The narrative analysis is the stories that influence and create a perceived image of their followers at a destination. The study analyzed the review comments posted by the customers thereby allowing social media sources to collect the data and analyze it (Zeng & Gerritsen, 2014). The study considers a holistic approach that looks into initially identifying categories, searching for patterns and links that begin with narratives shared by groups of people (Lieblich et al.1998). The qualitative content analysis allows netnographers to comprehend the information stated on various social media platforms (Heinonen & Medberg, 2018). The review comments texts are the source of data collection for content analysis. Analyzing comments posted on TripAdvisor will offer an understanding of the importance of destination image. For the study, social media reviews posted on TripAdvisor were used as the primary source of data rather than opting for an alternative research tool. The information obtained from the reviews is limited as many review comments are anonymous without information on gender, age, and income. Therefore, profiling the TripAdvisor users of online experience is limited as compared to quantitative studies (lp et al., 2012). Later studies so can enhance the method by following a mixed-method approach in which the details of online reviewers are obtained by online questionnaire after they have shared their reviews on TripAdvisor.

An important step in promoting a tourist destination is to identify both the strengths and weaknesses of the destination in an individual's mind. The keen way currently to brand a destination is to portray organic images put by the customers in social media. So it is important to recognize both the positive and the negative images shared by the customers so that the destinations can suitable highlight the positive and negatives images of the destination. It was necessary to differentiate between negative and positive comments as specific words or expressions were either positive or negative in nature. For example, the negative codes that are stated to as negative image traits include *costly living* and *poor infrastructure*. The positive codes refer to image traits like a *great experience,* awesome, *memorable trip,* and *sustainability*. In some review comments the customers- did not use words that were negative or positive but the sentence expressed either positive or negative intuitions. Aligning with the literature a qualitative assessment of data through reviewers' comments was obtained. The comments received were classified as positive or negative for the destination. The findings state that 93.2% (340 of 365 of the total review comments) were positive about the destination. In detail 221 of the positive comments were cognitive while 119 were affective.

Table 1 portrays the various attributes frequencies of the two components of the destination image which are stated by the reviewers as the affective (A) and cognitive (C) of the destination image. The top three attributes are a great experience, a mesmerizing place, and the beaches followed by landscape and activity at sea. The cognitive and affective attributes have a significant role in destination marketing as they allow tourists to perceive and choose travel destinations. The cognitive attributes allow us to ascertain factual information about a destination including historical significance, activities, and infrastructure. It also considers the perceived quality including factors like safety, accessibility, and the infrastructure creates an impression of a destination. The destination image is the cognitive attribute that creates the mental image of a destination

The affective attributes are mostly feelings and emotions that are associated with a destination. It includes the atmosphere, ambiance, and experience that provoke positive emotions of excitement and adventure. The cognitive and affective attributes help to deliver the information that states specifically about the destination. The affective attributes do create an emotional resonance by conducting marketing campaigns that arouse aspirations and desire for travel experiences. The accurate cognitive information along with positive affective experience builds trust and credibility amongst the tourists.

Table 1. Destination image attributes of Andamans

Initial attributes	Categorized	Percentage
Dream Destination	Great Experience (a)	38
Great Experience		
Lovely destination		
Cool & Amazing	Mesmerizing place (a)	39
Mesmerizing place		
Charming place		
Exploratory	Exploratory (a)	15
Cruise Trips		
Authentic culture	Local food & culture (a)	8
Local food & culture Interactions with locals		
Total (Affective)		100
Beautiful beaches & clear water	Beaches (c)	28
Turtles and Coral reefs		
Admirable landscape	Admirable landscape (c)	18
Natural rock formation		
Activity in sea	Activity in sea (c)	17
Scuba diving, snorkel, jet ski ride		
History of island	History (c)	12
Cellular jail		
Viper island		
Netaji Subash Bose Island		
Costly	Expensive(c)	2
Expensive		
Conserving natural resources	Sustainability (c)	23
Preserving traditions & culture		
Total (Cognitive)		100

The comments obtained from the tourists as per the affective attributes can be classified as *Great experience*- The comments describe the tourists having a wonderful experience at the island destination. Some review comments stated that Andamans were their dream destination and the same was true being there as if their dreams had come true. Many reviews also state that the overall experience at Andamans was fabulous which included destination, travel, beaches, and the visit to the historical places. *Mesmerizing*- A cool and mesmerizing destination states how the attribute brings in the positivity of a destination based upon overall perception. The overall excitement at the destination is arousing with the natural habitat being the precursor to it. The comments of the tourists state about the location and how it touches the hearts of people by providing a pleasant experience to the tourist. *Exploratory-* The exploration mentions various sightseeing of wild nature, hiking in the mountains, and some cruises in the sea. Considering the food and the culture there are places where the local food of Andamans is served though most food for the tourist is either South Indian or Bengali. There are interactions between some of the local tribes of the Andaman as commented sharing of their lifestyle of hunting and foraging. *Local food and culture* -The authentic culture of the locals and their lifestyle can be observed in some of the model villages which shows their culture. Some tribal of Andamans who started interacting with tourists discussed how they are continuing with their food culture and trying to balance their lifestyle. The effective attribute that is most quoted is mesmerizing a little higher than the great experience which includes the place that is enthralling to the tourist. The attribute exploratory and local food and culture attributes are less stated by the tourists.

Amongst the cognitive attributes that the tourists comments stated included *Sustainability-* Among the attributes the experience at the destination was what attracted people to the Andamans the overall experience of the destination which includes the archipelago covered with mountains, wild nature and jungles, and some islands without human habitation. Sustainability in the Andaman Islands is through the conservation and preservation of natural resources, local culture, traditions, and heritage. Sustainable tourism takes into consideration long-term cooperation among the stakeholders to protect the ecosystem along with promoting tourism. Sustainability is observed by the review comment as the tourist could state how natural resources, local culture, and heritage are retained on the island. *Admirable landscape-* Natural rock formation on the island also includes various landscapes and seascapes including beaches, forests, and other natural attractions. The bright colour of the sea, the pristine beaches, and sunset at sea make the landscape wonderful. Many of the review comments state how they feel excited in viewing the dense forest, the sea, the hills, and the cliffs of mountains. *Activity in sea* -The sea and water activities include visiting beaches to view turtles and being involved in water activities like scuba diving, snorkeling, and jet ski riding the comments state the excitement of these activities. Some commented that we did not know that we would be able to see the leatherback turtles one of the largest sea turtles in the world. *History and Culture* -The not-so-beautiful history of Andamans is the Cellular jail where during colonial days prisoners were kept and convicts were hanged. The other historical location is Ross Island which was the seat of British administration during World War II and also was captured by the Japanese for a period during the war and has some constructions of that era. A comment by a reviewer was "enthralling sound and

Light Show at Cellular Jail - where the heroic saga of the Indian freedom struggle is brought alive by the enacting of freedom fighters and their struggle for India's Independence. *Expensive*- One of the last-mentioned categories was costly which was the least mentioned by the reviewers and was considerably negligible. *Beaches* -The beaches are covered by tropical wilderness on all sides and provide a panoramic view to the tourists. Some review comments also stated that the scenic beauty is enchanting and you feel joyful while you roam on the beach which is hugged by the tropical forest. The cognitive attributes of beaches are most preferred followed by sustainability. The attribute admirable landscape and activity in the sea come third and fourth followed by history. The attribute costly is the least stated by the tourists.

CONCLUSION

This study could be a foundation for the researchers about how tourists' experiences influence destination marketing in the future. The study also measured the perceived destination image by the attributes of the tourists which makes the findings more reliable and applicable in the future. The tourist destination is attributed to great experience and mesmerizing place. It also examines how the destination image is influenced by the netnographic approach by using the reviews of the tourist in the study. Although the adaptation of netnography is popular in marketing studies (Heinonen & Medberg, 2018) the approach of using the same for destination images is not that frequent(Kladou & Mavragani, 2015).

With the usage of both narrative and content analysis the study explores the influential process of destination image formation by the tourist review. Majorly tourism is the source of revenue for a destination but many budgetary cuts along with changes in media and technology require a change in destination communication strategy. Social media as a marketing tool is used more to convince destination marketers so that they can include it as an integral part of marketing campaigns. The tourists or consumer at a destination requires creativity, interactive communication empathy, and emotions. For a destination to be competitive social media can be useful by presenting interesting content, creativity and interactive communication. For promoting a tourist destination it is best to recognize both the strengths and the weaknesses as per individuals' viewpoints (Bosque & Martin,2008). For a destination to be branded smartly, it considers including images that are portrayed by the tourists in social media. Social media data need to capture and understand both the positive and the negative images shared by tourists about a destination.

Future research on social media in tourism may also include other facets like community engagement, differentiated destination marketing, and other ethical issues arising from social media in tourism. The same research methodology should be applied to other tourist destination studies so that the findings are been generalized. In the future, the research studies should focus on social media other than TripAdvisor so that generalization of findings does not happen.

REFERENCES

Baloglu, S., & Brinberg, D. (1997). Affective Images of Tourism Destinations. *Journal of Travel Research, 35*(4), 11–15. doi:10.1177/004728759703500402

Beerli, A., & Martín, J. D. (2004). Factors influencing destination image. *Annals of Tourism Research, 31*(3), 657–681. doi:10.1016/j.annals.2004.01.010

Borges, B. (2009). *Marketing 2.0: Bridging the gap between seller and buyer through social media marketing*. Wheatmark.

Bosque, I. R., & Martin, H. S. (2008). Tourist Satisfaction a Cognitive-Affective Model. *Annals of Tourism Research, 35*(2), 551–573. doi:10.1016/j.annals.2008.02.006

Boyd, D., & Ellison, N. (2008). Social Network Sites: Definition, History, and Scholarship. *Journal of Computer-Mediated Communication, 13*(1), 210–230. doi:10.1111/j.1083-6101.2007.00393.x

Buhalis, D., & Law, R. (2008). Progress in information technology and tourism management; 20 years on and 10 years after the Internet the state of eTourism research. *Tourism Management, 29*(4), 606–623. doi:10.1016/j.tourman.2008.01.005

Costello, L., McDermott, M.-L., & Wallace, R. (2017). Netnography: Range of practices, misperception. *International Journal of Qualitative Methods, 16*(1), 1–1. doi:10.1177/1609406917700647

Crompton, J. (1979). Motivations for Pleasure Vacation. *Annals of Tourism Research, 6*(4), 408–424. doi:10.1016/0160-7383(79)90004-5

Elliot, S., Papadopoulos, N., & Kim, S. S. (2011). An Integrative Model of Place Image: Exploring Relationships Between Destination, Product, and Country Images. *Journal of Travel Research, 50*(5), 520–534. doi:10.1177/0047287510379161

Fotis, J., Buhalis, D., & Rossides, N. (2012). Social media use and impact during the holiday travel planning process. In M. Fuchs, F. Ricci, & L. Cantoni (Eds.), *Information and Communication Technologies in Tourism* (pp. 13–24). Springer. doi:10.1007/978-3-7091-1142-0_

Gretzel, G., Fesenmaier, D. R., Formica, S., & O'Leary, J. T. (2006). Searching for the Future: Challenges Faced by Destination Marketing Organizations. *Journal of Travel Research*, *45*(2), 116–126. doi:10.1177/0047287506291598

Gretzel, U. (2006). Consumer generated content – trends and implications for branding. *e-Review of Tourism Research*, *4*(3), 9–11

Gretzel, U., Werthner, H., Koo, C., & Lamsfus, C. (2015). Conceptual foundations for understanding smart tourism ecosystems. *Computers in Human Behavior*, *50*, 558–563. doi:10.1016/j.chb.2015.03.043

Gretzel, U., Yuan, Y. L., & Fesenmaier, D. R. (2000). Preparing for the New Economy: Advertising Strategies and Change in Destination Marketing Organizations. *Journal of Travel Research*, *39*(2), 146–156. doi:10.1177/004728750003900204

Heinonen, K., & Medberg, G. (2018). Netnography as a tool for understanding customers: Implications for service research and practice. *Journal of Services Marketing*, *32*(6), 657–679. doi:10.1108/JSM-08-2017-0294

Iglesias-Sánchez, P. P., López-Delgado, P., Correia, M. B., & Jambrino-Maldonado, C. (2020). How do external openness and R&D activity influence open innovation management and the potential contribution of social media in the tourism and hospitality industry? *Information Technology & Tourism*, *22*(2), 1–27. doi:10.1007/s40558-019-00165-y

Ip, C., Lee, H., & Law, R. (2012). Profiling the Users of Travel Websites for Planning and Online Experience Sharing. *Journal of Hospitality & Tourism Research (Washington, D.C.)*, *36*(3), 418–426. doi:10.1177/1096348010388663

Kaplan, A., & Haenlein, M. (2009). Consumer Use and Business Potential of Virtual Worlds: The Case of "Second Life". *International Journal on Media Management*, *11*(3-4), 93–101. doi:10.1080/14241270903047008

Kavoura, A., & Bitsani, E. (2013). Managing the World Heritage Site of the Acropolis, Greece. *International Journal of Culture, Tourism and Hospitality Research*, *7*(1), 58–67. doi:10.1108/17506181311301363

Khan, M., Siddique, M., Yasir, M., Qureshi, M. I., Khan, N., & Safdar, M. Z. (2022). The Significance of Digital Marketing in Shaping Ecotourism Behaviour through Destination Image. *Sustainability (Basel)*, *14*(12), 14. doi:10.3390/su14127395

Kladou, S., & Kehagias, J. (2014). Assessing destination brand equity: An integrated approach. *Journal of Destination Marketing & Management*, *3*(1), 2–10. doi:10.1016/j.jdmm.2013.11.002

Kladou, S., & Mavragani, E. (2015). Assessing destination image: An online marketing approach and the case of TripAdvisor. *Journal of Destination Marketing & Management*, *4*(3), 187–193. doi:10.1016/j.jdmm.2015.04.003

Kozinets, R. (2002). The field behind the screen: Using netnography for marketing research in online communities. *JMR, Journal of Marketing Research*, *39*(1), 61–72. doi:10.1509/jmkr.39.1.61.18935

Kozinets, R. V. (2010). *Netnography: Doing ethnographic research online*. Sage Publications.

Kozinets, R. V., Valck, K., Wojnicki, A., & Wilner, S. (2010). narratives: Understanding Word-of-Mouth marketing in online communities'. *Journal of Marketing*, *74*(2), 74. doi:10.1509/jm.74.2.71

Naciye, G., & Adem, A. (2020). Impacts of COVID -19 on global tourism industry: A cross-regional comparison. *Journal of Tourism Management Perspective*, *36*

Neuhofer, B., Buhalis, D., & Ladkin, A. (2019). Technology as a catalyst of change: Enablers and barriers of the tourist experience and their consequences. The Routledge Handbook of Transport Economics, 247

Oreja Rodríguez, J. R., Parra-López, E., & Yanes-Estévez, V. (2008). The sustainability of island destinations: Tourism area life cycle and teleological perspectives. The case of Tenerife. *Tourism Management*, *29*(1), 53–65. doi:10.1016/j.tourman.2007.04.007

Pahrudin, P., Li- Wei, L., Shao-Yu, L. (2022). What is Role of Tourism Management and Marketing toward Sustainable Tourism? A Biblometric Analysis Approach. *Sustainability*, 14.

Pasquinelli, C., Trunfio, M., Bellini, N., & Rossi, S. (2021). Sustainability in Overtourisified Cities? A Social Media Insight into Italian Branding Responses to Covid -19 Crisis. *Sustainability*, 13.

Podoshen, J. S. (2013). Dark tourism motivations: Simulation, emotional contagion and topographic comparison. *Tourism Management*, *35*, 263–271. doi:10.1016/j.tourman.2012.08.002

Reddy, M. V. (2008). Sustainable Tourism Rapid Indicators for Less- developed Islands: An Economic Perspective. *International Journal of Tourism Research*, *10*(6), 557–576. doi:10.1002/jtr.700

Safko, L., & Brake, D. (2009). *The social media bible tactics tools and strategies for business success*. John Wiley & Sons.

Seal, P. P. (2023). Robots in the Hotel Kitchen: The Future Chef in Ed, Impactful Technologies Transforming the Food Industry. IGI -Global.

Senecal, S., & Nantel, J. (2004). The Influence of Online Product Recommendations on Consumers' Online Choices. *Journal of Retailing*, *80*(2), 159–169. doi:10.1016/j.jretai.2004.04.001

Stankov, U., Lazić, L., & Dragicevic, V. (2010). The Extent of Use of Basic Facebook User-Generated Content by the National Tourism Organizations in Europe. *European Journal of Tourism Research*, *3*(2), 105–113. doi:10.54055/ejtr.v3i2.51

Sukunesan, S., Selvarajah, C., & Mellström, Z. (2020). Internationalization Via Instagram: An Exploratory Study of Small and Medium Enterprises. *Contemporary Management Research*, *16*(2), 77–121. doi:10.7903/cmr.19811

Tavakoli, R., & Mura, P. (2018). Netnography in Tourism – Beyond Web 2.0. *Annals of Tourism Research*, *73*, 190–192. doi:10.1016/j.annals.2018.06.002

Xiang, Z., & Gretzel, U. (2010). Role of social media in online travel information search. *Tourism Management*, *31*(2), 179–188. doi:10.1016/j.tourman.2009.02.016

Zeng, B., & Gerritsen, R. (2014). What Do We Know about Social Media in Tourism? A Review. *Tourism Management Perspectives*, *10*, 27–36. doi:10.1016/j.tmp.2014.01.001

Chapter 5
Digital Marketing for Cruise Tourism in Oman:
Opportunities and Challenges

Mohammad Soliman
https://orcid.org/0000-0002-9359-763X
Research and Consultation Department, University of Technology and Applied Sciences, Salalah, Oman

Maha Khamis Al Balushi
https://orcid.org/0000-0002-5897-9800
Sultan Qaboos University, Oman

Rowan Kennedy
https://orcid.org/0000-0001-7551-9067
Sultan Qaboos University, Oman

ABSTRACT

Cruise tourism has significantly increased in popularity in recent years, being among the most common forms of tourism. Oman is regarded as one of the distinguished destinations that has fundamental elements, capabilities, and ingredients of cruise tourism, such as infrastructures, superstructures, and other cruising facilities. The expansion of cruise tourism in the contemporary digital era offers different opportunities for destination management organizations and concerned entities to implement digital marketing strategies. However, some challenges to effectively adopt digital marketing strategies for cruise tourism should be considered. Consequently, the purpose of the current chapter is to provide a more thorough understanding of the cruise tourism business, particularly in the context of Oman. It also aims to highlight the key opportunities and challenges of adopting digital marketing strategies to advance cruise tourism in Oman. This chapter offers a range of contributions to academics and professionals. Directions for further research are also given.

DOI: 10.4018/979-8-3693-0960-5.ch005

INTRODUCTION

As a sub-category of tourism (Papathanassis & Beckmann, 2011), cruise tourism emerged in the 1960s (Atef & Al Balushi, 2017; Jiao et al., 2021) when affordable air travel largely replaced ocean passenger transport (Aziz et al., 2020), and has rapidly expanded due to high standard offerings, attractive price offerings and a diverse range of on-board activities (Manthiou et al., 2017). The industry is dominated by three major cruise lines headquartered in Florida, USA (Carnival Corporation, plc., Norwegian Cruise Line Corporation, Ltd., and Royal Caribbean Group) who, collectively, account for 82% of the total market share (Chang et al., 2017) and control the majority of North American leisure cruising (Li & Kwortnik, 2017). Despite combined losses of USD$39 billion for the 'big three' resulting from the COVID-19 pandemic, industry estimates suggest that recovery will be fuelled by more than 31 million people taking a cruise in 2023 with that figure to exceed 36 million in 2024: industry rebound is further reflected in anticipated travel spending reaching USD$1.15 trillion that year (Cruise Market Watch, 2023). The most popular destinations remain the Caribbean, the Mediterranean, and Northern Europe (Cruise Lines International Association, 2022), however, Carnival Lines and Royal Caribbean are increasingly bringing tourists to Oman who are seeking natural and cultural exploration opportunities (Jiao et al., 2021).

Oman's need for economic diversification has driven an increased focus on tourism and, over the last two decades, there has been a steady increase in cruise ship traffic to the country's three key ports: Salalah Port in the south, Sultan Qaboos Port in Muscat and Khasab Port at the northern-most tip (Atef & Al Balushi, 2017) increasing from 24 visiting cruise vessels in 2005 to 135 cruise liners within the following seven years (Gutberlet, 2016). As Oman progresses towards economic diversity, tourism is acknowledged as a strategic and priority sector in the government's National Strategy for Tourism development and is predicted to develop a reputation for its tourist facilities. Cruise tourism in Oman is limited to the cooler months of October to April when temperatures average between 25C-35C daily, aligning well with the needs of the cruise industry for destinations offering escape from northern hemisphere winters. Consumers currently show a preference for travelling to less crowded and more unfamiliar destinations indicating an interest in secondary and nature-based travel experiences (World Travel & Tourism Council, 2022). Fitting flawlessly into this category, Oman has become a strategic emerging destination for the global cruise industry. Another change to the cruise tourism industry travelling alongside the expansion of destinations is the profile of cruise tourists themselves. The image of the 'luxury floating building' of the past (Brida & Zapata, 2010) has evolved to become less focused on luxury and to target a wider market including Generation X and Millennials (Jiao et al., 2021). According to Atef and Al Balushi

(2017, p. 4), millennials are now cruising for the first time: a younger and more demanding cohort with high expectations of entertainment and communication. Most recent Omani cruise tourist satisfaction research (Aziz et al., 2020) reveals that the senior market is still a critical segment, however, with the largest group of their survey participants (22.4%) aged over 60 years. This reflects the findings of Casado-Díaz et al. (2021) who found that the age group >63 years accounted for only 18% of the sample, confirming that younger people are becoming more attracted to this form of vacation. Han and Hyun (2019) similarly found that approximately one-third of their sample were between 18 and 34 years old.

Engaging with and building long-term relationships with these cohorts presents specific issues. Despite cruise travelling having become a preferred vacation form, an increasing challenge to cruise line operators is ongoing switching behaviour (Brida et al., 2015; Chua et al., 2015). Han and Hyun (2019) note that the rapid expansion of the sector has accelerated the competitive behaviour among cruise line operators. Consequently, the customer loyalty sought by all marketing firms is fundamental to the success of each company in this industry. Loyalty has been shown to be linked with satisfaction, and satisfaction with (un)met expectations. Customers form expectations about service during the search and decision-making process (Wirtz & Lovelock, 2022, p. 50). They subsequently evaluate their experiences (during and) following interactions with the service provider (Oliver, 1980). Satisfaction is related to the extent to which expectations are met – or not. Dissatisfaction results in the search for a future alternative service provider and consequent switching behaviour. Cruise line operators can shape and manage expectations through their communications and changes to their service and technologies (Wirtz & Lovelock, 2022, p. 50) which must include innovative and non-traditional methods of marketing such as digital marketing. It is not sufficient to rely on traditional methods of communication such as TVCs, brochures and positive in-person word-of-mouth (although still important), but cruise tourists today expect to be communicated with through digital methods such as travel blogs, vloggers, and web pages. Tourists have been shown to consider online word-of-mouth to have more credibility than other sources of information (Ďaďová & Soviar, 2021). This fastest-growing tourist segment requires the fastest-growing marketing communications methods; hence the need to promote the features and benefits of cruise travel through modern information networks and communication channels.

Direct and digital marketing provide immediate interaction and high dynamism, having a profound impact on the manner in which organisations engage and build relationships with customers (Sundaram et al., 2020). The targeted and personal nature of social networking sites (known as social media) appeals particularly to the growing millennial cohort (Kim & Ieng Lei, 2024) who expect to communicate on an array of social media platforms. Accordingly, social media is an indispensable tool for this, and other, generations of passengers expecting innovative and digitised communications from cruise operators (Buhalis et al., 2022), allowing relationships to grow with potential customers and the creation of a positive image for the destination and brand. The interactive nature of social media tools such as Instagram, YouTube, Facebook, X and LinkedIn, positions them as an ideal partner in the ongoing customer conversation and a critical tool for feedback. Tsai and Bui (2021) note that many tourism companies are using smart devices to integrate social media as a search engine for pre-travel information, and as a medium for sharing post-travel information with potential travellers. This preferred method of communication by millennials provides cruise operators with the ability to interact with timely and immediate marketing information and provides an opportunity to influence the decision-making process from the tourism marketing perspective (Pop et al., 2022).

Customers' engagement with brands has been significantly impacted by digital marketing (Magano & Cunha, 2020; Surucu-Balci & Balci, 2023) and in many cases begins prior to making a booking by tourists. Once passengers are on board, many cruise lines are using apps to communicate with passengers, to enable passengers to message others on board, make dining reservations, and find directions for navigating between the decks (Cruise Lines International Association, 2022). Following their return home, many cruise tourists use online review sites such as Trip Adviser or post videos on YouTube to share their experiences with others (Ďaďová & Soviar, 2021) and express satisfaction or dissatisfaction with their experience.

The research by Ružić et al. (2018) of a small number of river cruise operators in Europe found that a communications mix, including both traditional and non-traditional methods, was used to communicate with both loyal and potential passengers. Color-coded brochures distributed by travel agents were found to be heavily relied upon to convey messages through attractive illustrations of both on- and off-ship activities. Cruise operators use websites to promote and advertise their offers and events and to engage with loyal and potential passengers. Photo galleries and testimonies from satisfied passengers are valuable communication tools to persuade online bookings and electronic check-ins. These newer communication formats enable companies to engage consumers in virtual brand communities resulting in emotional bonds being formed not only between company and consumer but also consumer-consumer thus establishing stronger identification with the brand (Coelho et al., 2018). Digital marketing offers the opportunity for dialogue with (potential) consumers that allows for the development of relationship building and the development of competitive advantage.

Digital marketing is a valuable tool for the business-to-business as well as the business-to-consumer market. In Oman, the Ministry of Heritage and Tourism is responsible for preparing and implementing plans related to the development of the cruise ship sector, yacht tourism, and charter voyages in Oman (Ministry of Heritage

& Tourism, 2023). The Ministry prepares and implements all marketing advertising campaigns on behalf of the Sultanate through traditional and electronic channels with the aim of encouraging local tourism, attracting regional and international tourism, and highlighting tourism driving brand awareness through several channels.

Based on the preceding discussion, the current endeavor aims to offer a further comprehensive understanding of the cruise tourism industry, particularly in the context of Oman. Additionally, it attempts to unveil the most crucial advantages and major challenges of using digital marketing strategies to promote cruise tourism in Oman. The rest of this chapter will be structured as follows. The next section discusses the connection between digital marketing and tourism. The third section represents digital marketing for cruise tourism in Oman by highlighting the key features of cruise tourism in Oman and explaining the opportunities and challenges of digital marketing for cruise tourism in Oman. The last section demonstrates conclusions by providing theoretical and managerial implications and directions for further work as well.

DIGITAL MARKETING AND TOURISM

Digital marketing is a way of using online channels to promote tourism products and services to potential customers and get them interested in interacting with the product. Digital marketing refers to the promotion of products and services via electronic media with the sole aim of inducing customers to interact with the brand through digital media (Yasmin et al., 2015). It is a relative newcomer to the traditional integrated marketing communication models of the twentieth century and represents a disruptor in the value chain of the tourism industry (Damnjanović et al., 2020) in that it has transformed communications between organisations and their partners and customers. Digital tools allow organisations to reach large numbers of customers very cost effectively and are considered one of the most successful and capable mechanisms (Jaas, 2022). Hakkarainen (2016) credits Rowley (2001) as one of the pioneers in adapting traditional marketing communications to the internet environment and perceives it as a 'rescue' for marketers from demanding customers who have become more critical and more powerful. It has not only changed organisational behaviour, but it has shaped the behaviour of consumers and changed their expectations. This mobile technology strongly influences how consumers seek information and engage with brands and fellow consumers (Mathew & Soliman, 2021). Mathew and Soliman (2021) describe digital content as "an electronic space for reaching customers" (p. 61), providing consumers with a weapon with which to inflict damage on a brand and its reputation via review sites and social media platforms; and a sanctuary in terms of a virtual brand community created online by the company to build customer-to-customer relationships as well as customer-to-brand interactions (Brodie et al., 2013). Yasmin et al. (2015) identified seven key elements of digital marketing: social media marketing, text messaging, affiliate marketing, search engine optimisation, online advertising, email marketing, and pay-per-click. Digital marketing can be used to reach and engage consumers through a variety of digital platforms, such as company websites, blogs, social networks, virtual groups, and mobile applications (Mathew & Soliman, 2021, p. 3).

Organisations are vulnerable to the online power of consumer reviews and opinions which, when positive and supportive, can make substantial contributions to companies but, when negative and critical have the power to devastate the brand and its reputation. Virtual brand communities are used increasingly to build reliable relationships with target markets (Brodie et al., 2013) and this engagement of customers and the opportunity to develop strong and robust relationships between company-customer, and customer-to-customer is becoming an increasingly prevalent strategy shown to have positive outcomes for the company (Ahn & Back, 2020). Constructive and enduring relationships with target customers can provide significant rewards in times of brand crisis, resulting in increased tolerance and a decrease in negative responses to problems experienced by customers.

In terms of a marketing communications tool, digital marketing is cost-effective and allows content to be quickly updated, unlike traditional forms requiring long lead times for print vehicles, and filming and scheduling of television commercials. Selecting and applying appropriate digital solutions that satisfy customers improves the brand's relationship with customers and is used in collaborating with partners (suppliers and intermediaries) and employees. Digital marketing offers the opportunity for dialogue with (actual and potential) consumers that allows for the development of relationship building and the development of competitive advantage. It brings customers closer to the company and, in doing so, allows for better understanding between company and customer. It adds value to products and increases distribution which, in turn, has an impact on pricing strategy. It increases sales through digital marketing campaigns (Chaffey & Smith, 2022).

Digitalising Tourist's Experience

Digital communication tools have been shown to boost tourism (de Amorim et al., 2022) partly due to the constant connectivity through smartphones which allow daily sharing of online content (Mathew & Soliman, 2021). Today's tourist using technology in this way has been described as "an individual with a personal digital device connected to a myriad of information sources, allowing for interactions with a global social network" (Magano & Cunha, 2020, p. 2). Travel is a process of planning, experiencing, and reflecting. Wang et al. (2014) adapted the model of Gretzel et al.

(2006) to suggest those three stages of tourist experience thus: pre-consumption, consumption, and post-consumption. During the (pre-consumption) planning phase decisions are made, and expectations are formed (leading to subsequent (dis) satisfaction). Younger tourists in particular use computers and mobile technologies extensively during this period, accessing company websites for information and online platforms such as TripAdvisor and YouTube to review the experiences and recommendations of other travellers. The second, experiential phase, comprises the relatively short-term experience of the travel activity. During this phase, tourists access digital marketing from host country cultural and heritage sites and for local recommendations for food options and shopping. Should the travel experience involve an organised tour such as a bus tour or cruise, the operator will provide digital information relating to daily activities. During the third, (post-consumption) phase tourists reflect on their experience, documenting their memories and re-experience as they share the journey with others (Wang et al., 2014). During this final phase, consumers become digital marketers themselves as they provide reviews to future travellers and engage in online communities to share their experiences and to make recommendations. Clearly, understanding digital marketing and harnessing the power of digital media and mobile technology is critical to success in the tourism industry (Magano & Cunha, 2020).

Cruise Tourism and Digital Marketing

Cruise tourism is a socio-economic system generated by the interaction between human, organisational, and geographical entities, aimed at producing maritime transportation-enabled leisure experiences (Papathanassis & Beckmann, 2011). With the growth of leisure cruising (both river and ocean) and its accessibility to a wider group of people, the competition for bookings has resulted in not only affordable prices but forced innovation and continual evolution: new destinations/ports, new and different services and on-board entertainment, and new and different onboard activities have created a competitive environment demanding the use of innovative, technology-led marketing communication tools. Ružić et al. (2018) found that a communications mix was typically used to communicate with both loyal and potential customers. Cruise operators use websites to promote and advertise their offers and events and to engage with loyal and potential passengers. Photo galleries and testimonies in the post-purchase phase encourage potential customers to act as a call to action for potential and returning customers.

In addition to websites, cruise operators also employ social media marketing to include forums and blogs on platforms such as "Facebook, Twitter, Instagram, YouTube, Google+ and Pinterest" (Ružić et al., 2018, p. 6). These newer communication formats enable companies to engage consumers in virtual brand communities resulting in emotional bonds being formed not only between company and consumer, but also consumer-consumer thus establishing stronger identification with the brand (Coelho et al., 2018).

Cruise operators maintain relationships with three primary target groups: cruise tourists/passengers (seeking an optimal experience), partners (suppliers in both home country and visited ports and other intermediaries such as travel agents), and employees (information sharing). A digital strategy is necessary to manage the myriad marketing communications messages with each group. As a floating business, digital communications are mandatory and only electronic means can offer the fast response times demanded by each of the three target groups. Consequently, cruise line operators need to maintain a clear understanding of modern trends in the cruise industry, digitalisation, innovative business models, and, most importantly, how to respond with competitive offers to the wants and needs of stakeholders.

DIGITAL MARKETING FOR CRUISE TOURISM IN OMAN

Cruise Tourism in Oman

Travelling by watercraft typically involves an extended period aboard a ship for personal and leisure purposes. It commonly encompasses trips lasting several days or more, including the possibility of orbiting the globe. The cruise liner industry has experienced rapid growth in recent times, emerging as the fastest-growing sector in global tourism. The industry for cruise tourism is expected to expand because of rising disposable income and the growth of amenities and services offered onboard cruise ships. In addition, having coastal regions around the world as popular tourist destinations contributed to faster growth of the cruise ship industry sector in global tourism. The United States stands at the forefront of global cruise revenue due to its vast coastlines and convenient proximity to many neighbouring ports within the inviting Caribbean Sea. Cruise tourism offers consumers distinctive holiday experiences by fusing aspects of travel, leisure, refreshment, outdoor activities, and entertainment through cruise lines, cruise providers, and companies engaged in the production of cruise ships. These cruise passengers have the opportunity to experience a variety of ports in a short period of time and consequently identify places that they would like to return to for a longer stay. According to Buhalis et al. (2022), cruise passengers may be more likely to return to a port city for a longer vacation after having visited it on a cruise.

The cruise market is categorised based on geographical regions, including Latin America, North America, Asia Pacific, Europe, Africa, and the Middle East. Regarding the Sultanate of Oman, there is substantial untapped potential for developing the cruise industry. Sand beaches, rugged cliffs, and various intertidal species make up Oman's 1700 km of coastline. Furthermore, the exclusive passage into the Persian Gulf from either the Indian Ocean or the Arabian Sea is via the Gulf of Oman. This means that Oman's exceptional location holds significant potential as a valuable economic asset for the country. The cruise industry will bring about several positive transformations in the country. The 1990s witnessed the start of cruise travel to Oman's three main ports, Salalah Port in the Dhofar Governorate, Sultan Qaboos Port in Muscat, and Khasab Port in the Musandam Peninsula (Atef & Al-Balushi, 2017). The large-scale cruise business in Muscat, which began in 2004, has expanded in size over the previous few years. More specifically, during Oman's peak cruising season, which runs from October to May, the Port of Sultan Qaboos at Muscat sees the greatest influx of ship and cruise travellers. In 2005, 24 cruise ships carrying about 7600 people landed in Muscat. Seven years later, Muscat welcomed 135 cruise ships carrying 257,000 tourists (Gutberlet, 2017). In February 2010, Oman launched its first specialised cruise terminal. By the end of 2019, Oman welcomed 283,844 cruise tourists, with that number expected to reach 300,000 in 2020 (Arabian Business).

Oman cruise tourism has been seen as a strategy to rapidly augment visitor numbers in partnership with other destinations, notably Dubai, Abu Dhabi, and Bahrain, mirroring the development of international airports and the construction of hotels. The governments of these countries collaborated on Cruise Arabia Alliance with the ultimate objective to establish the entire Gulf region as a leading global cruise destination. With its primary aim set on enticing a youthful generation of travellers to explore the Middle East and the Sea of Oman, Oman has emerged as one of the emerging and promising cruise hotspots in the Middle Eastern region. Between 2020 and 2030, it is expected to attract 1.6 million and 2.1 million cruise tourists annually. The cruise industry is still growing, especially in Asia (Buhalis et al., 2022). In Oman, there are a few reasons for the growth of the cruise industry. First, the middle class in Oman is growing rapidly, and people have more disposable income to spend on leisure activities. Second, there is a growing interest in cruising among Omani travellers. Third, cruise lines are increasingly offering itineraries that appeal to Omani travellers, such as cruises that visit multiple countries in Europe and America.

Opportunities of Digital Marketing for Cruise Tourism in Oman

The cruise industry is facing a radically changed regulatory, demand, and operational landscape, demanding an accelerated adoption of smart technologies that are essential to the industry's business continuity (Papathanassis, 2017, p. 115). In general, the ongoing shift towards digitalisation in the travel industry compels the global cruise sector to greatly embrace the digital technologies. In this line of thought, the key to a leading online cruise tourism experience for cruise tourism intermediaries and suppliers, cruise tourists, and cruise destination promoters is the use of digital technology for creating, promoting, and delivering online tourism experiences. This includes the combined use of mobile phones, internet websites, social media platforms, and augmented reality experiences to have things like a well-designed website, social media to connect with potential cruise tourists, and online booking and payment options. Digital marketing tools and strategies are crucial for new cruise service providers and businesses to succeed online. By using digital marketing technology effectively, new cruise businesses can reach more potential customers, build stronger relationships with them, and generate more bookings. The utilisation of digital marketing effectively helps businesses build stronger relationships with customers, increase the value of their products and services, reach new customers, and boost sales using digital media channels, such as marketing research, online advertising, and affiliate marketing (Chaffey & Smith, 2022). In Oman, the national priorities to diversify the economy and encourage export to boost foreign exchange earnings reveal the revenue potential of digitalisation in cruise tourism. In many countries including Oman, small and medium-sized enterprises (SMEs) account for a majority of tourism businesses. SMEs in the tourism industry including cruise tourism must be at the forefront of adopting new technologies, including digital marketing technologies. These technologies can help SMEs in cruise-related businesses to reach an unlimited audience efficiently, market their products and services more effectively and without geographical obstacles, compete with larger businesses in a cost-effective manner, and increase their sales. Therefore, collaborations between cruise companies and local SMEs can enhance tourism offerings, benefit local development in port communities, and promote the industry collectively. For example, citizens can promote their small businesses, such as restaurants, hotels, lodgings, taxi drivers, coaches, coffee shops, supermarkets, tour guides or souvenir shops using digital marketing while also promoting the cruise trips.

Digital marketing in tourism "arouses the interest of individuals to travel and experience different cultures and places, and at the same time allows them to search and buy all the services and products that are needed to make the trip" (Leite & Azevedo, 2017, p. 89). These technologies allow cruise businesses to reach and engage with potential cruise customers and tourists in new and exciting ways. For example, mobile phones allow cruise tourists to book and pay for travel products on-the-go, while internet websites provide them with a wealth of information about different cruise destinations and products. With Oman's internet penetration rate at 96% in 2023 (Kemp, 2023), the groundwork for digital marketing campaigns is well-laid. This high connectivity allows for innovative engagement strategies, such as using mobile phones for on-the-go bookings and providing a wealth of information through internet websites. In a similar perspective, digital marketing tools and strategies are crucial for sustainable initiatives. In 2022, over 80% of global travellers said in a survey that "sustainable tourism was important for them" and they were willing to adopt "sustainable travel incentives." The global market size of the sustainable industry, also called ecotourism, was 172.4 billion USD (Statistica Research Department, 2024). The rising demand for sustainable tourism, presents a significant opportunity for Oman as it was ranked first among the GCC countries in the sustainable travel index 2020 by Euromonitor (Muscat Daily, 2021). Highlighting on various social media platforms Oman's sustainable practices such as laws prohibiting the hunting of animals and birds and eco-friendly cruise options for environmentally conscious travellers, reflects the synergy between digital marketing and sustainable tourism initiatives.

Social media allows building relationships with potential customers and creating a positive destination or brand image while augmented reality experiences can be used to give potential tourists a virtual tour of a cruise destination or product, which can help them to make a more informed decision about whether to book. As noted by Abdullahi et al. (2021), digital marketing technology is essential for new digital tourism businesses to maintain their competitive advantage. The rich cultural and natural heritage of Oman presents unique opportunities for digital marketing to arouse the interest of potential cruise travellers in Oman. Oman's 1,700 km long shoreline, home to unique marine biodiversity, offers compelling content for digital marketing campaigns. Highlighting destinations like the Daymaniyat Islands, known for its coral reefs, sea turtles, and diverse marine life, and Ras Al Jinz, known for sea turtles nesting on the beaches and the Dhofar Coast, which attracts a variety of marine species during the Khareef season, through short videos, virtual tours and engaging narratives that communicate a compelling story can help attract potential customers. The use of these media across multiple platforms can help cruise lines expand their target markets in different countries (Tiago et al., 2018). In addition, data analytics tools can be used by businesses to develop a detailed profile of their customers, such as their age, gender, location, interests as well as the platforms they use most frequently (Tiago et al.). Deeply understanding the interests and motives of potential cruise passengers can help the companies to tailor on-land activities that are sought by those customers. Using data analytics to develop customer profiles can also help companies to personalise their marketing messages to resonate with the target audience. It can further help them attract travellers of the similar profile from all over the world through targeted ads, leveraging platforms where potential tourists spend most of their time which can help increase conversion rates. For example, cultural packages such as visits to castles, forts, museums, and local markets (souqs) where they have the opportunity to interact with locals would appeal more to culturally-oriented travellers. Alternately, resorts and spas would appeal more to those seeking relaxation.

Digital technologies are essential for the cruise tourism industry in Oman to communicate with international tourists in the digital age. More people are using digital technologies to learn about and plan their travel. By using digital technologies, the tourism industry in Oman can reach potential tourists in general and cruise tourists specifically from all over the world and tell them about the amazing things that Oman has to offer. Given the seasonal nature of cruise tourism, digital marketing in tourism promotion strategies allows cruise service providers to reach potential tourists with relevant and timely messages, communicate with cruise tourists and potential tourists in a more targeted and personalised way, differentiate themselves from the competition, and attract tourists during the off-season. The role of digital marketing in building brand ambassadors through user generated content is invaluable. Encouraging tourists to share their experiences online, supported by cruise staff offering photography tips, suggesting picturesque locations, and offering to take pictures, can foster a community of loyal customers. Thus, having cruise tourists as brand ambassadors for the cruise tourism market, the use of digital marketing tools to share reviews, experiences, blogs, and impressions of a nation would enhance the allocation and identification of national cruise ambassadors or evangelists. The ability of consumers to communicate with companies and with each other worldwide through digital marketing creates new possibilities for marketing, such as the ability to exchange opinions and experiences (de Amorim et al., 2022). Kannan and Li (2017) assert that digital media gives consumers a platform to share their thoughts and experiences with other consumers and with businesses themselves about products, services, brands, and companies on companies' websites, social networks, and blogs.

Just as cruises offer avenues of "social interactions in a specific physical space", social networking sites offer digital spaces of tourism experiences, where cruise travellers can share past experiences and potential travellers can search for information regarding others' experiences (Tiago et al., 2018). Cruise companies as well as the Ministry of Heritage and Tourism in Oman can foster brand communities of loyal customers, tapping into the power of social proof, leveraging positive customer reviews and shared experiences to attract a wider audience. Since 62.7% of Oman's population is younger than 34 years (Kemp, 2023) who are more active on social media and prefer digital products and services, such communities can significantly enhance engagement and brand loyalty. Create social media platforms, such as YouTube, Instagram, Facebook, TikTok, LinkedIn, X, Snapchat, Pinterest, and WeChat, as advised by Hussain et al. (2024), in order to disseminate information about tourism and provide interesting content. Incorporating these insights into Oman's digital marketing strategies for cruise tourism not only addresses the need for technological adoption but also capitalises on the unique opportunities presented by Oman's rich heritage and natural beauty. Weaving together the on-ground experience, strategic digital marketing tools, and a focus on sustainable tourism can help create a compelling narrative for Oman's cruise tourism sector poised to attract a global audience in the digital age. Table 1 summarises opportunities for Oman's cruise tourism industry.

Table 1. Utilising opportunities of digital marketing for cruise tourism

Opportunities	Focus area	Strategies to leverage the opportunity	Metrics for success
Engage potential customers	Omni-channel strategy	▪ Offer 360-degree videos, live virtual tours virtual tours, and ensure customer service is readily available on digital platforms such as social media, email, and instant messaging. ▪ Utilise different platforms for different audiences e.g. LinkedIn for B2B engagements. ▪ Collaborate with influencers to highlight positive reviews and feedback about Oman's cruise tourism offerings and sustainable initiatives.	Engagement rates, customer satisfaction scores
Competitive differentiation	Promote authentic experiences	▪ Develop and share content that showcases Oman's unique cultural and natural heritage. ▪ Engage with audiences through storytelling and interactive media. Leverage influencers to enhance credibility and broaden reach. ▪ Foster brand communities of loyal customers. ▪ Help customers generate content and promote it through various marketing channels.	Brand awareness, social media reach
Competitive differentiation	Product offering	▪ Curate and promote itineraries that offer immersive local cultural experiences, capitalising on Oman's diverse attractions to differentiate from competitors.	Customer satisfaction scores
Building and maintaining brand presence	Social media and branding	▪ Regularly monitor and adapt to online trends relevant to Oman's culture and tourism offerings. ▪ Regularly analyse social media activity to identify patterns of user behaviour. ▪ Consistently engage with the audience to build a loyal following.	Growth in followers, engagement rates, and share of voice on social media.
Encouraging exports	Communicating with international tourists	▪ Utilise brand ambassadors to authentically communicate unique aspects of Oman's cruise tourism to international audiences, aiming to convert interest into bookings.	Increase in inquiries from international markets and conversion rates from these inquiries.
Enhancing SMEs	Cross-partner collaborations	▪ Foster collaborations between cruise companies and local SMEs for package offerings and cross-marketing campaigns, enhancing visibility and market reach for local businesses.	Increase in SMEs' sales; Increase in tourist footfall to SME locations
Enhancing SMEs	Support for local businesses	▪ Conduct training for local operators. ▪ Partner with other countries to learn from their good practices	Number of SMEs participating in training programmes, growth in digital presence of SMEs

Challenges of Digital Marketing for Cruise Tourism in Oman

Digital marketing practitioners have identified various challenges pertaining to the tourism and hospitality industry. Some consumers prefer face-to-face marketing, or personal interaction, with cruise service providers because they believe it allows them to communicate directly with cruise service personnel and physically examine the cruise-related products, all of which contribute towards developing trust with the cruise service providers. The expensive and luxurious nature of the cruise tourism business may require potential consumers to ask questions promptly, get advice, and see and feel the cruise-related products before they buy them. This helps them to feel more confident in their purchase. To address this challenge, an omni-channel strategy that combines digital and personal interactions can be used. Virtual tours of the cruise ship and key facilities, complemented by detailed information and accessible customer service representatives (Tiago et al., 2018), across platforms like email, social media, and WhatsApp can stimulate some benefits of face-to-face interaction. Omani influencers and brand ambassadors can further provide authentic feedback and personal interaction digitally. For premium offerings, a blend of in-person and digital strategies can ensure that valued customers receive the tailored experience they expect.

In today's increasingly digital world, it is important for digital marketing to be conducted with the utmost privacy. Overall, some specific examples of privacy concerns in digital marketing include data breaches, unauthorised data sharing, tracking consumer online activity, and phishing. Digital marketers in the cruise industry need to be careful about how they collect and use customer data. They should obtain explicit permission from customers before sharing their data with other companies and implement strong security measures to protect customer data from theft and unauthorised access.

Due to the infancy of the cruise market in Oman, cruise service providers and marketers are struggling to build and maintain a strong brand presence on social media, measure the success of their digital marketing efforts, and ensure existing and potential cruise consumers learn about and engage with their brands. To overcome this challenge, the Ministry of Heritage and Tourism could support local operators by arrange training workshops and facilitating learning from their counterparts in the GCC region who have successfully utilised digital media. As recommended by Hussain et al. (2024) to Oman's Ministry of Heritage and Tourism, form alliances with social media influencers, travel vloggers, or content creators to develop tourism-related content that highlights Oman's attractions. The global competition in cruise tourism necessitates a standout strategy for Oman. By analysing online trends, adopting a proactive online presence, and creating content that showcases a unique narrative highlighting Oman's unique landscapes and cultural heritage, digital marketers can differentiate Oman's offerings. They can ensure that their posts are being enhanced with personal content and shared by individuals with strong network connections. It is also important to consistently analyse data to monitor social media and web-driven strategies and make changes as required (Tiago et al., 2018).

Another challenge in digital marketing of cruise tourism is that tourists are increasingly demanding more authentic experiences since they want to feel that they are getting a real taste of the local culture and environment. Today, cruise companies are recognising that tourists want more than just to hear about different places; they want to experience them firsthand. This has prompted cruise companies to offer itineraries that include activities such as visiting local markets, trying local cuisine, and participating in cultural events. Cruise companies are moving away from simply telling tourists about different places towards offering them opportunities to experience these places for themselves by offering itineraries that include authentic experiences that are deeply rooted in the local culture and environment (Buhalis et al., 2022).Therefore, the shift to individual discovery is a positive development for both cruise operators in Oman and tourists, ensuring genuine insights into local culture and environments.

Cruise companies are facing competition from other types of travel experiences, such as Airbnb and adventure travel companies, which are offering tourists opportunities to experience new places in a more immersive way. Cruise companies can circumvent this challenge by partnering with companies for 'fly and cruise' packages. By collaborating, they can showcase Oman's diverse attractions beyond Muscat such as Jebel Akhdar mountains, Wahiba Sands and the Bahla Fort, which has been recognised as a UNESCO World Heritage site. This could help Oman realise larger financial gains, enhance Oman's appeal and encourage repeat visits. Table 2 summarises the strategies to overcome the challenges of utilising digital marketing for cruise tourism in Oman.

Table 2. Overcoming challenges of digital marketing for cruise tourism

Challenge	Focus area	Strategies to overcome the challenge	Risk management
Addressing privacy concerns	Trust and integrity	■ Manage customer data with care, focusing on explicit permissions and strong security measures.	Implement regular security audits, General Data Protection Regulation (GDPR) compliance
Overcoming market infancy	Market penetration and awareness	■ Employ targeted digital marketing and customer profiling to identify potential market. ■ Use a strong content strategy employing storytelling and emphasising Oman's unique offerings.	Diversify marketing channels to avoid over-reliance on a single platform
Customers' preference for face-to-face interactions	Customer experience	■ Implement omnichannel strategies that blend digital and personal customer service to mimic the benefits of face-to-face interaction.	Monitor and adapt customer service strategies based on feedback
Navigating global competition	Strategic positioning and partnerships	■ Highlight Oman's unique tourism attractions and cultural heritage through specialised digital marketing campaigns. ■ Partner with global platforms to increase visibility.	Competitive analysis and adaptability to market trends
Ensuring content authenticity	Content strategy	■ Develop content that promotes authentic experiences, supported by local stories and testimonials to enhance credibility and engagement.	Content freshness, relevance, and user engagement monitoring

CONCLUSION

Discussion

Cruise tourism has witnessed substantial growth in the last decades since it encompasses all aspects of tourism and hospitality-related activities, including transport, lodging, sightseeing, entertainment, etc. Consequently, cruising has become a preferred multi-activity pastime for tourists, making it a significant source of travellers to tourist destinations (Casado-Díaz et al., 2021; Sun et al., 2014). The Sultanate of Oman is regarded as one of the distinguished cruise tourism destinations that has solid infrastructure, several cultural and nature-based attractions, world heritage sites, diverse adventures, distinct climate and weather patterns, archaeological sites, museums, castles, forts, and other attractions. These elements render the country an exceptional cruise tourism destination, particularly in the Middle East region (Atef & Al-Balushi, 2017; Gutberlet, 2016). On the other side, given the current digital era, the growth of tourism, including cruise tourism, opens various prospects for destination management organisations and tourism businesses to deploy marketing strategies involving digital marketing (Mathew & Soliman, 2021; Mkwizu, 2019). However, the challenges of tourism marketing due to market diversity and changing consumer needs call for advanced and innovative marketing-related approaches to provide particular tourism experiences (Alves et al., 2020). Indeed, this applies to the case of cruise tourism in Oman, which still needs more effort to be put into adopting various and innovative marketing strategies, such as digital marketing, to achieve multiple gains.

Digital marketing is one of the cutting-edge marketing strategies that has recently gained more attention from both academics and practitioners in the tourism field due to its crucial role in affecting consumer behaviour and developing destinations (Mathew & Soliman, 2021; Mkwizu, 2019). It is regarded as the future evolution of marketing, and is altering how travellers engage with destinations (Magano & Cunha, 2020). The tourism and hospitality sectors as well as tourists (e.g., cruise visitors) can benefit greatly from digital marketing, revolutionising the way cruise companies attract and engage with their target audience. These include having the ability to assess digital content, providing a seamless and convenient experience for customers, reinforcing the perception of message source independence, fostering a sense of excitement and anticipation among potential travellers, offering better customer service, raising the awareness of brand and authority, and fostering greater customer loyalty and positive word-of-mouth recommendations (Mathew & Soliman, 2021).

Implications

The current chapter holds significant theoretical implications. First, it supports the extant body of knowledge related to digital marketing in tourism by investigating the drivers that influence digital marketing strategies within the cruise tourism industry. In other words, this work contributes to the evolving field of digital marketing theory, emphasising the industry-specific nuances that impact the strategies and effectiveness of digital marketing campaigns in the cruise sector.

Second, this paper expands the existing literature on the cruise tourism realm by highlighting the opportunities and challenges to adopt digital marketing strategies for cruise tourism in one of the Middle East countries, namely Oman. In this vein, earlier studies have focused on cruise tourism and outlined its significance, impacts, key issues, and challenges. For instance, Klein (2011) demonstrated the effects of cruise tourism on local economies, coastal and marine habitats, and the sociocultural makeup of port communities which have grown along with the industry's growth. London and Lohmann (2014) discussed certain challenges stemming from the substantial investments needed for cruise tourism infrastructure development in both emerging and established destinations. Casado-Díaz et al. (2021) pointed out that the high volume of cruise visitors is overwhelming some of the most widely recognised cruise tourism destinations. Pino and Peluso (2018) also examined the contextual factors that either support or impede cruise tourism development (e.g., infrastructural, organisational, and socioeconomic factors). However, little research has been done to outline the drivers influencing the development of the cruise tourism industry. This includes the dearth of studies examining the contribution of digital marketing strategies to the growth of cruise tourism. Furthermore, Blas and Carvajal-Trujillo (2014) argued that the majority of studies on cruise tourism have concentrated on a small geographic area (e.g., the Caribbean) due to its popularity. Hence, the present chapter adds to the limited attempts that have been made to investigate cruise tourism in Oman. More specifically, to the best of our knowledge, there is no known work that has been undertaken to explore the connection between digital marketing and cruise tourism in the Middle East region and in Oman in particular. Moreover, the opportunities and challenges of adopting digital marketing in cruise tourism have not been studied yet.

Third, it contributes to a deeper understanding of how digital technologies and online platforms are reshaping the marketing landscape within a specific niche of tourism, shedding light on the unique challenges and opportunities faced by cruise operators. Fourth, the present chapter highlights the dynamic nature of digital marketing in the context of the travel and tourism industry, showcasing how factors such as technological advancements, consumer behaviour, and competitive forces intersect to shape marketing strategies. Thus, this research can also extend our knowledge of consumer behaviour in the digital era, as it explores how travellers engage with cruise-related content and make booking decisions.

In addition, by highlighting the efficiency and potential of digital marketing strategies in the context of cruise tourism, the current chapter could bridge the gap between theory and practice by providing countless managerial contributions to concerned stakeholders and policymakers in the Omani tourism industry. Additionally, it might offer practical advice and best practices for cruise operators looking to enhance their utilisation of digital marketing channels. In addition, this work outlines the critical need for cruise marketers to find ways to overcome the challenges related to the utilisation of digital marketing in their operations to be successful. In an effort to address these challenges, the Omani cruise service providers and promotors need to create engaging and informative high-quality content on social media and other online platforms, respond to comments and messages from followers in a timely manner, use social media analytics to track users' progress and identify areas for improvement, set clear goals for campaigns and run paid advertising campaigns to target potential cruise customers, partner with other brands, destinations, websites, and influencers to reach a wider audience. By uncovering the key drivers in this realm, the paper equips industry professionals with valuable insights for crafting more effective and tailored digital marketing strategies to enhance customer engagement and competitiveness in an increasingly digitalised world.

Destination management organisations are requested to collaborate with local partners and government organisations (such as educational institutes and universities) to provide SMEs with the necessary opportunities for training and development in digital marketing to develop a strong cruise sector as Oman's tourism industry continues to grow. In addition, they are required to encourage cruise companies to offer "Fly and Cruise" packages beyond Muscat through digital publicity media could be a positive move in realising the financial advantages that cruising can bring. In this line of thought, cities need to invest in and coordinate with agents and tour operators to promote their tourist attractions and activities to the public (de Amorim et al., 2022).

Today, tourists are more likely to be loyal to brands that work with them to create value, and digital technologies such as mobile apps, online portals, gamification, and data-based innovations can help brands do this. Since digital marketing is used to inspire people to travel and experience new cultures and plays a major role in helping people plan and book their trips, utilising the digital technologies by Oman's Ministry of Tourism and Heritage to disseminate information about international cruise tourist arrivals in Oman becomes paramount. For example, the ministry can utilise its websites and social media platforms to create and share informative content, such as blog posts, articles, and videos, cruise tourist arrivals in Oman including statistics, trends, and forecasts. Also, it can partner with other businesses' websites and social media platforms in the cruise tourism industry to promote each other's products and services through affiliate marketing. Adding to that, it can optimise its website and content so that it ranks higher in search engine results pages. Moreover, it can utilise online advertising by running paid ads about Oman's cruise tourism experience on search engines and other websites to reach potential customers. In this line of suggestion, utilising pay-per-click advertising would be advantageous. In addition, targeted online advertising campaigns to specific demographics, interests, and locations can be run to reach potential cruise tourists from all over the world. By the same token, it can utilise email marketing by collecting email addresses from potential cruise tourists and sending them regular email newsletters with information about cruise tourist arrivals and departures, deals, and events.

Avenues for Future Research

Further, this conceptual research provides valuable directions for future research. Firstly, future research is recommended to conduct an empirical investigation to assess the factors affecting the adoption of digital marketing strategies for cruise tourism. Future research may expand some theoretical frameworks, such as the theory of planned behavior (TPB) (see, for example, Soliman, 2021), in order to determine how cruise tourists perceive the use of digital marketing tools. Future studies may also shed light on the link between intelligent customer experience (ICE) and destination loyalty (see, Gam et al., 2023) related to cruise tourism. In addition, this paper can serve as a starting point for future studies and the improvement of theoretical models in the field of digital marketing for travel and tourism. In this vein, technology and innovation based theories can be applied as underpinning theories by further research to explore the perspective of cruise managers toward the adoption of digital marketing. Also, it is recommended to conduct a systematised study in which it would be easier to understand the current state of digital marketing in the region by responding to certain parameters, dimensions, or metrics. Moreover, a thorough bibliometric analysis employing different measures (see, for instance,de Bruyn et al., 2023; Soliman et al., 2021; Soliman et al., 2023) to examine and visually map the scientific output on digital marketing and cruise tourism is another outstanding direction for future research. Furthermore, future studies are advised to determine the factors influencing of destination evangelism (see, Soliman & Al Balushi, 2023) of visitors who have past experience with cruise tourism.

REFERENCES

Abdullahi, M., Kilili, R., & Günay, T. (2021). E-tourism and digital marketing in africa: Opportunities and challenges. *Linguistica Antverpiensia*, *21*(1), 244–261.

Ahn, J., & Back, K. J. (2020). The structural effects of affective and cognitive elaboration in formation of customer–brand relationship. *Service Industries Journal*, *40*(3-4), 226–242. doi:10.1080/02642069.2018.1460358

Alves, G. M., Sousa, B. M., & Machado, A. (2020). The role of digital marketing and online relationship quality in social tourism: A tourism for all case study. In *Digital marketing strategies for tourism, hospitality, and airline industries* (pp. 49–70). IGI Global. doi:10.4018/978-1-5225-9783-4.ch003

Atef, T., & Al Balushi, M. (2017). Omani tourism and hospitality students' employment intentions and job preferences: Ramifications on Omanization plans. *Quality Assurance in Education*, *25*(4), 440–461. doi:10.1108/QAE-04-2016-0022

Atef, T. M., & Al-Balushi, M. (2017). Cruising Market in Oman: Current trends and future perspectives. *Journal of Tourism and Hospitality Management*, *5*(1), 1–14. doi:10.15640/jthm.v5n1a1

Aziz, H., El-Said, O., & Bontenbal, M. (2020). An analytical approach to cruise tourism as an option for development: A case study of the Sultanate of Oman. *Tourism in Marine Environments*, *15*(2), 95–109. doi:10.3727/154427320X15828792518754

Blas, S. S., & Carvajal-Trujillo, E. (2014). Cruise passengers' experiences in a Mediterranean port of call. The case study of Valencia. *Ocean and Coastal Management*, *102*, 307–316. doi:10.1016/j.ocecoaman.2014.10.011

Brida, J. G., Bukstein, D., & Tealde, E. (2015). Exploring cruise ship passenger spending patterns in two Uruguayan ports of call. *Current Issues in Tourism*, *18*(7), 684–700. doi:10.1080/13683500.2013.861391

Brida, J. G., & Zapata, S. (2010). Cruise tourism: Economic, socio-cultural and environmental impacts. *International Journal of Leisure and Tourism Marketing*, *1*(3), 205–226. doi:10.1504/IJLTM.2010.029585

Brodie, R. J., Ilic, A., Juric, B., & Hollebeek, L. (2013). Consumer engagement in a virtual brand community: An exploratory analysis. *Journal of Business Research*, *66*(1), 105–114. doi:10.1016/j.jbusres.2011.07.029

Buhalis, D., Papathanassis, A., & Vafeidou, M. (2022). Smart cruising: Smart technology applications and their diffusion in cruise tourism. *Journal of Hospitality and Tourism Technology*, *13*(4), 626–649. doi:10.1108/JHTT-05-2021-0155

Casado-Díaz, A. B., Navarro-Ruiz, S., Nicolau, J. L., & Ivars-Baidal, J. (2021). Expanding our understanding of cruise visitors' expenditure at destinations: The role of spatial patterns, onshore visit choice and cruise category. *Tourism Management*, *83*, 104199. doi:10.1016/j.tourman.2020.104199

Chaffey, D., & Smith, P. R. (2022). *Digital marketing excellence: planning, optimizing and integrating online marketing*. Taylor & Francis. doi:10.4324/9781003009498

Chang, Y.-T., Lee, S., & Park, H. K. (2017). Efficiency analysis of major cruise lines. *Tourism Management*, *58*, 78–88. doi:10.1016/j.tourman.2016.10.012 PMID:32287747

Chua, B.-L., Lee, S., Goh, B., & Han, H. (2015). Impacts of cruise service quality and price on vacationers' cruise experience: Moderating role of price sensitivity. *International Journal of Hospitality Management*, *44*, 131–145. doi:10.1016/j.ijhm.2014.10.012

Coelho, P. S., Rita, P., & Santos, Z. R. (2018). On the relationship between consumer-brand identification, brand community, and brand loyalty. *Journal of Retailing and Consumer Services*, *43*, 101–110. doi:10.1016/j.jretconser.2018.03.011

Cruise Lines International Association. (2022). *2022 Global Market Report*. CLIA. https://cruising.org/-/media/clia-media/research/2023/2022-1r-clia-001-overview-global-final.ashx

Cruise Market Watch. (2023). *Cruise travel is back but economic uncertainty may cool future demand*. Market Watch. https://www.marketwatch.com/video/sectorwatch/cruise-travel-is-back-but-economic-uncertainty-may-cool-future-demand/C979F72A-DF95-48FC-8C94-34E658E96C3C.html

Ďaďová, I., & Soviar, J. (2021). The application of online marketing tools in marketing communication of the entities with the tourism offer in 2020 in Slovakia. *Transportation Research Procedia*, *55*, 1791–1799. doi:10.1016/j.trpro.2021.07.170

Damnjanović, V., Lončarić, D., & Dlačić, J. (2020). Digital marketing strategy of Accor Hotels: Shaping the future of hospitality. *Tourism and Hospitality Management*, *26*(1), 233–244.

de Amorim, L. A., Sousa, B. B., Dias, A. L., & Santos, V. R. (2022). Exploring the outcomes of digital marketing on historic sites' visitor behaviour. *Journal of Cultural Heritage Management and Sustainable Development*. doi:10.1108/JCHMSD-11-2021-0202

de Bruyn, C., Said, F. B., Meyer, N., & Soliman, M. (2023). Research in tourism sustainability: A comprehensive bibliometric analysis from 1990 to 2022. *Heliyon*, *9*(8), e18874. doi:10.1016/j.heliyon.2023.e18874 PMID:37636413

Gam, A., Bahri-Ammari, N., & Soliman, M. (2023). Intelligent customer experience and behavioral brand loyalty: Empirical evidence from the commerce environment. *International Journal of Human-Computer Interaction*, *39*(10), 2090–2101. doi:10.1080/10447318.2022.2074120

Gretzel, U., Fesenmaier, D. R., & O'Leary, J. T. (2006). The transformation of consumer behaviour. *Tourism Business Frontiers: Consumers. Products and Industry*, *9*, 18.

Gutberlet, M. (2016). Socio-cultural impacts of large-scale cruise tourism in Souq Mutrah, Sultanate of Oman. *Fennia-International Journal of Geography*, *194*(1), 46–63. doi:10.11143/46532

Gutberlet, M. (2017). *Searching for an oriental paradise?: Imaginaries, tourist experiences and socio-cultural impacts of mega-cruise tourism in the sultanate of Oman* [Dissertation, Rheinisch-Westfälische Technische Hochschule Aachen, 2017].

Hakkarainen, T. (2016). *Opportunities and challenges of content marketing as a way of digital marketing communications.*

Han, H., & Hyun, S. S. (2019). Cruise travel motivations and repeat cruising behaviour: Impact of relationship investment. *Current Issues in Tourism, 22*(7), 786–805. doi:10.1080/13683500.2017.1313204

Hussain, K., Alam, M. M. D., Malik, A., & Al Balushi, M. K. (2024). Capitalizing social media content for attracting tourists: Implications for digital transformation of Oman's tourism sector. *2nd International Conference on Strategies for Empowering Oman as a Competitive Economy*, Arab University Oman Faculty of Business Studies, Muscat, Oman.

Jaas, A. (2022). E-Marketing and its strategies: Digital opportunities and challenges. *Open Journal of Business and Management, 10*(2), 822–845. doi:10.4236/ojbm.2022.102046

Jiao, Y., Hou, Y., & Lau, Y.-y. (2021). Segmenting cruise consumers by motivation for an emerging market: A case of China. *Frontiers in Psychology, 12*, 606785. doi:10.3389/fpsyg.2021.606785 PMID:33790831

Kannan, P., & Li, H. A. (2017). Digital marketing: A framework, review and research agenda. *International Journal of Research in Marketing, 34*(1), 22–45. doi:10.1016/j.ijresmar.2016.11.006

Kemp, B. S. (2023). *Digital 2023: Oman - DataReportal – Global Digital Insights.* Data Portal.

Kim, B., & Ieng Lei, S. (2024). Millennials' interactions with social media content on cruise tourism. *Tourism Review.* doi:10.1108/TR-08-2023-0582

Klein, R. A. (2011). Responsible cruise tourism: Issues of cruise tourism and sustainability. *Journal of Hospitality and Tourism Management, 18*(1), 107–116. doi:10.1375/jhtm.18.1.107

Leite, R. A., & Azevedo, A. (2017). The role of digital marketing: A perspective from Porto Hotels' Managers. *International Journal of Marketing, Communication and New Media,* (2).

Li, Y., & Kwortnik, R. (2017). Categorizing cruise lines by passenger perceived experience. *Journal of Travel Research, 56*(7), 941–956. doi:10.1177/0047287516674602

London, W. R., & Lohmann, G. (2014). Power in the context of cruise destination stakeholders' interrelationships. *Research in Transportation Business & Management, 13*, 24–35. doi:10.1016/j.rtbm.2014.11.004

Magano, J., & Cunha, M. N. (2020). Digital marketing impact on tourism in Portugal: A quantitative study. *African Journal of Hospitality, Tourism and Leisure*, *9*(1), 1–19.

Manthiou, A., Kang, J., & Hyun, S. S. (2017). An integration of cognitive appraisal theory and script theory in the luxury cruise sector: The bridging role of recollection and storytelling. *Journal of Travel & Tourism Marketing*, *34*(8), 1071–1088. doi:10.1080/10548408.2016.1277575

Mathew, V., & Soliman, M. (2021). Does digital content marketing affect tourism consumer behavior? An extension of t echnology acceptance model. *Journal of Consumer Behaviour*, *20*(1), 61–75. doi:10.1002/cb.1854

Ministry of Heritage & Tourism. (2023). *Directorate General of Tourism Promotion*. MHT. https://mht.gov.om/tourism-promotion

Mkwizu, K. H. (2019). Digital marketing and tourism: Opportunities for Africa. *International Hospitality Review*, *34*(1), 5–12. doi:10.1108/IHR-09-2019-0015

Muscat Daily. (2021, September 9). Oman ranks first in GCC for sustainable tourism. *Muscat Daily*. https://www.muscatdaily.com/2021/03/13/oman-ranks-first-in-gcc-for-sustainable-tourism/

Oliver, R. L. (1980). A cognitive model of the antecedents and consequences of satisfaction decisions. *JMR, Journal of Marketing Research*, *17*(4), 460–469. doi:10.1177/002224378001700405

Papathanassis, A. (2017). Cruise tourism management: State of the art. *Tourism Review*, *72*(1), 104–119. doi:10.1108/TR-01-2017-0003

Papathanassis, A., & Beckmann, I. (2011). Assessing the 'poverty of cruise theory' hypothesis. *Annals of Tourism Research*, *38*(1), 153–174. doi:10.1016/j.annals.2010.07.015

Pino, G., & Peluso, A. M. (2018). The development of cruise tourism in emerging destinations: Evidence from Salento, Italy. *Tourism and Hospitality Research*, *18*(1), 15–27. doi:10.1177/1467358415619672

Pop, R.-A., Săplăcan, Z., Dabija, D.-C., & Alt, M.-A. (2022). The impact of social media influencers on travel decisions: The role of trust in consumer decision journey. *Current Issues in Tourism*, *25*(5), 823–843. doi:10.1080/13683500.2021.1895729

Rowley, J. (2001). Remodelling marketing communications in an Internet environment. *Internet Research*, *11*(3), 203–212. doi:10.1108/10662240110397017

Ružić, D., Bosnić, I., & Kelić, I. (2018). Marketing communication in the river cruise industry. *International Journal of Multidisciplinarity in Business and Science*, *4*(5), 67–73.

Soliman, M. (2021). Extending the theory of planned behavior to predict tourism destination revisit intention. *International Journal of Hospitality & Tourism Administration*, *22*(5), 524–549. doi:10.1080/15256480.2019.1692755

Soliman, M., & Al Balushi, M. K. (2023). Unveiling destination evangelism through generative AI tools. *ROBONOMICS: The Journal of the Automated Economy, 4*, 54. https://journal.robonomics.science/index.php/rj/article/view/54.

Soliman, M., Cardoso, L., de Almeida, G. F., Araújo, A., & Vila, N. (2021). Mapping smart experiences in tourism: A bibliometric approach. *European Journal of Tourism Research*, *28*, 2809–2809. doi:10.54055/ejtr.v28i.2254

Soliman, M., Gulvady, S., Lyulyov, O., & Pimonenko, T. (2023). Research trends and themes in the top-tier tourism, leisure and hospitality journals: A bibliometric and network analysis before and during the COVID-19 era. *International Journal of Hospitality and Tourism Systems*, *16*(1).

Statistica Research Department. (2024, January 22). *Topic: Sustainable tourism worldwide*. Statista. https://www.statista.com/topics/1916/green-tourism/#editorsPicks

Sun, X., Feng, X., & Gauri, D. K. (2014). The cruise industry in China: Efforts, progress and challenges. *International Journal of Hospitality Management*, *42*, 71–84. doi:10.1016/j.ijhm.2014.05.009

Sundaram, R., Sharma, D. R., & Shakya, D. A. (2020). Power of digital marketing in building brands: A review of social media advertisement. *International Journal of Management*, *11*(4).

Surucu-Balci, E., & Balci, G. (2023). Building social capital in cruise travel via social network sites. *Current Issues in Tourism*, *26*(7), 1096–1111. doi:10.1080/13683500.2022.2047904

Tiago, F., Couto, J., Faria, S., & Borges-Tiago, T. (2018). Cruise tourism: Social media content and network structures. *Tourism Review*, *73*(4), 433–447. doi:10.1108/TR-10-2017-0155

Tsai, F. M., & Bui, T.-D. (2021). Impact of word of mouth via social media on consumer intention to purchase cruise travel products. *Maritime Policy & Management*, *48*(2), 167–183. doi:10.1080/03088839.2020.1735655

Wang, D., Xiang, Z., & Fesenmaier, D. R. (2014). Adapting to the mobile world: A model of smartphone use. *Annals of Tourism Research*, *48*, 11–26. doi:10.1016/j.annals.2014.04.008

Wirtz, J., & Lovelock, C. (2022). *Services Marketing*. World scientific.

World Travel & Tourism Council. (2022). *Travel & Tourism Economic Impact 2022*. WTTC. https://wttc.org/Portals/0/Documents/Reports/2022/EIR2022-Global%20Trends.pdf

Yasmin, A., Tasneem, S., & Fatema, K. (2015). Effectiveness of digital marketing in the challenging age: An empirical study. *International Journal of Management Science and Business Administration*, *1*(5), 69–80. doi:10.18775/ijmsba.1849-5664-5419.2014.15.1006

Chapter 6
The Potentialities of CRM to Increase Personalization in Hospitality

Rashed Isam Ashqar
https://orcid.org/0000-0001-5078-5449
Al Zaytona University of Science and Technology, Palestine & CinTurs, Portugal

Célia Maria M.Q. Ramos
https://orcid.org/0000-0002-3413-4897
ESGHT, CinTurs, University of Algarve, Portugal

ABSTRACT

Personalization allows customers to access customized information more efficiently at any time. The importance of applying personalization in smart technology expanded during the COVID-19 pandemic. This chapter aims to present how can use the data about the clients from customer relationship management (CRM) to use them on customer lifetime value (CLV) models to classify the potentialities of customers. In addition, the authors suggested using personalization to make promotions for specific clients. The motivation of this chapter is to increase the competitiveness of the hotels and offer attractive services to achieve the loyalty of current and new clients. Also, to offer exclusive products or services to increase user satisfaction.

DOI: 10.4018/979-8-3693-0960-5.ch006

INTRODUCTION

Organizations are progressively implementing cutting-edge technologies and tactics to enhance the functionalities of Customer Relationship Management (CRM) systems in the ever-evolving domain of customer-centric business models (Rane et al., 2023). Also, the segmentation of databases based on CLV is the cornerstone of CRM. To implement CRM strategies, the hospitality industry relies heavily on loyalty programs to track customer behavior (Webb et al., 2022).

According to Alt & Klein (2011), there has been a movement in the marketplace toward customers having more power and control. Businesses need to use technology to interact with customers more personally since they are involved in production and consumption (Buhalis & Law, 2008; Pine et al., 1999).

Consequently, personalization makes it possible for clients to obtain tailored information more quickly and easily at any moment (Nyheim et al., 2015). Personalization provides a means for businesses to cultivate enduring relationships with their (Nyheim et al., 2015). Personalized services allow customers to spend less time looking for information and get services that are more specifically tailored to their needs based on the information they have provided (Nyheim et al., 2015; Piccoli et al., 2017). In order to provide customization, businesses must be able to discern their clients' wants, which may require them to divulge sensitive information such as purchasing patterns, location data, and personal profiles (Ho, 2012)

Gathering consumer data on preferences, buying habits, purchase histories, and demographics may provide a solid basis for creating effective marketing campaigns and gaining long-term competitive advantages (Erevelles et al., 2016). Additionally, Wattal, Telang, & Mukhopadhyay (2009) deduced that personalization is thought to boost the value of the entire consumption experience in e- and m-commerce contexts, especially by improving the fit between a product's qualities and the demands of the customer.

Furthermore, personalization was defined by Bilgihan, Kandampully, & Zhang (2016) as the extent to which information is customized to meet the demands of an individual user, and as such, it is a significant factor in determining pleasant experiences. Using data mining techniques, information is tailored to each customer's needs and tastes, potentially increasing their degree of interest in purchasing (Zhang, Edwards, & Harding, 2007). Furthermore, one of the essential elements frequently linked to machine learning is personalization, which focuses mainly on optimizing personalization applications and developing algorithmic decision and prediction models that are ever more precise (Zanker et al., 2019). Thus, brands can use predictive personalization, which is the process of adapting content in real time using data analysis and profiling tools based on artificial intelligence and machine learning.

This chapter's goal is to demonstrate how customer lifetime value (CLV) models can be used to classify potential customers and calculate their value by utilizing data about them from customer relationship management (CRM). Market segmentation and the distribution of marketing resources for acquisition, retention, and cross-selling can benefit from using CLV models. In addition, the authors suggested using personalization to make promotions for specific clients. The motivation of this chapter is to increase the competitiveness of the hotels and offer attractive services to achieve the loyalty of current and new clients. Also, to offer exclusive products or services to increase user satisfaction.

The format of this chapter is as follows. In the second section, various implementable customer lifetime value (CLV) models are reviewed and the relevant literature regarding customer relationship management (CRM) is presented. In the third section, personalization in the hospitality industry is discussed along with relevant literature, the distinction between customization and personalization, and personalization metrics. A few new methods for utilizing smart technologies and experiencing personalization are shown in Section 4. The chapter is concluded in section five.

CUSTOMER RELATIONSHIP MANAGEMENT (CRM) AND CUSTOMER LIFETIME VALUE (CLV)

A collection of theories, tactics, procedures, and technological tools known as customer relationship management (CRM) helps businesses handle the interactions and transactions with their clients (Greenberg, 2010). Due to its ability to handle competition, foster differentiation, and increase customer value, CRM has emerged as a strategic requirement in the travel and hospitality industries (Debnath et al., 2016; Sheth, 2017).

In tourism and hospitality businesses, gathering and combining customer data to customize transactions has many advantages. By using CRM, for instance, businesses can increase customer lifetime value, customer satisfaction, and retention as well as business profits (Daghfous & Barkhi, 2009; Kasim & Minai, 2009; Lo et al., 2010; Wongsansukcharoen et al., 2015). They can also identify and retain the most profitable customers and improve the profitability of less profitable customers (Wang & Feng, 2012; Wongsansukcharoen et al., 2015; Wu & Lu, 2012).

The establishment and maintenance of long-term connections with clients is becoming an increasingly important source of revenue for businesses as modern economies become more and more service-oriented. Marketing functions to maximize customer lifetime value (CLV) and customer equity, which is the total of the customers' lifetime values for the business, in such an environment (Gupta et al., 2006). The objective of presenting the CLV is to classify potential customers and calculate their value by utilizing data about them from CRM.

In both academia and industry, CLV is becoming a more significant marketing indicator. For instance, 1) businesses are under increasing pressure to hold marketing accountable; 2) financial metrics, like stock price and the total profit of the company or a business unit, do not always address the issue; and 3) advancements in information technology have made it simple for businesses to gather vast amounts of transactional data from customers (Gupta et al., 2006).

The present value of all future profits derived from a client throughout that customer's association with a business is the general definition of CLV. The CLV for a customer (without the customer subscript) is derived from Reinartz & Kumar (2003) and Gupta et al. (2004). The following formula shows the calculation of CLV.

$$CLV = \sum_{t=0}^{T} \frac{(p_t - c_t) r_t}{(1+i)^t} - AC \qquad (1)$$

where

p_t = price paid by a consumer at time t,
c_t = direct cost of servicing the customer at time t,
i = discount rate or cost of capital for the firm,
r_t = probability of customer repeat buying or being "alive" at time t,
AC = acquisition cost, and
T = time horizon for estimating CLV.

In the following sections, the authors present the metrics that are used in customer analytics. The authors presented the traditional marketing metrics, popular customer-based value metrics, customer acquisition and customer activity metrics, lifetime value models, customer equity models, recency, frequency, monetary value (RFM) models, and probability models.

Traditional Marketing Metrics

Market share (MS) is one of the most widely used indicators to assess marketing effectiveness. It can be defined as the proportion of a company's sales to the total sales of all companies—across all clients—in a particular market. MS is a totality of the customers' measurements. It can be computed using a volumetric or monetary approach depending on Gupta et al. (2006). The following formula shows the calculation of the market share.

$$MS \text{ of firm } j\,(\%) = 100 \times \left[\frac{S_i}{\sum_{i=1}^{I} S_i} \right] \tag{2}$$

Where

i = focal firm
S_i = sales of firm i
I = all firms in the market

Moreover, the brand, product, or company's sales growth is determined by comparing the volume or value of sales during a certain time to the same period the previous year. It is therefore expressed in percentage. It serves as a warning sign for management and shows how much the sales performance has improved across two or more periods. According to Gupta et al. (2006), negative sales growth or sales growth that is slower than the rest of the market is typically the reason for concern. The following formula shows the calculation of the sales growth.

$$\text{Sales growth in period } t\,(\%) = 100 \times \left[\frac{{}'' S_{jt}}{S_{jt-1}} \right] \tag{3}$$

Where

i = focal firm,
t = time period
$'' S_{jt}$ = change in sales in period t from period t – 1
S_{jt-1} = sales of firm j in period t – 1

Popular Customer-Based Value Metrics

The size of the wallet is the amount of a buyer's overall expenditure in a particular category, or, to put it another way, the total amount of category sales made by all businesses to one client. The wallet's size is expressed in monetary terms using the following formula.

$$\text{Size of wallet } (\$) \text{ of customer i in a category } = \textstyle\sum_{j=1}^{J} S_{ij} \tag{4}$$

Where

i = a particular customer
i = firm
J = all firms offering products in the considered category
S_{ij} = sales value (in category) to customer i by firm i, i = 1, …, J

Moreover, Share of Category Requirement (SCR) is the percentage of category volume that a brand or focal company accounts for within its customer base. When specific purchase data are not available, this measure is frequently calculated at the aggregate level as the following formula.

$$\text{SCR}\left(\%\right)\text{of a firm (or brand })j_0\text{ in a category} = \frac{\sum_{i=1}^{I} V_{ij_0}}{\sum_{i=1}^{I}\sum_{j=1}^{J} V_{ij}} \times 100 \quad (5)$$

Where

j_0 = focal firm or brand
i = customer
I = all customers buying in the focal category
J = all firms or brands available in the focal category
V_{ij} = purchase volume of customer i from a firm (or brand) j

Also, Share of Wallet (SW) is the percentage of a category's value that a focal brand or focal company accounts for among its customer base. Both an aggregate level (i.e., segment level or total customer base) and an individual customer level can be used to measure it.

In addition, Individual Share of Wallet (iSW) is the percentage of a buyer's category value that comes from all of the brands she purchases fall into the category that a focal brand or focal business accounts for, It shows the extent to which a consumer finds a main brand or company to meet her needs in the category. According to Gupta et al. (2006), it is calculated by dividing the value of sales (S) of the focal firm (j0) to a buyer i in a category by the size of the same customer's wallet within a predetermined time frame as follows.

$$iSW\left(\%\right)\text{of firm } j_0 \text{ to customer } i = \frac{S_{ij_0}}{\sum_{j=1}^{J} S_{ij}} \times 100 \quad (6)$$

Where

i = firm
i = customer
S_{ij} = sales of firm j to customer i

Also, the aggregate share of wallet (aSW) is the percentage of a category's value that a focal brand or focal company accounts for throughout its whole customer base. It shows the extent to which, on average, clients of a focal firm in a category with a focal firm meet their needs as follows.

$$aSW\left(\%\right)\text{of firm}=\ j_0=\frac{\sum_{i=1}^{I}S_{ij_0}}{\sum_{j=1}^{J}\sum_{i=1}^{I}S_{ij}}\times 100 \quad (7)$$

Where

i = customer
j = firm
I = all customers
J = all firms who offer the category under consideration
S_{ij} = sales (value) of firm j to customer i

Additionally, there is a metric known as "past customer value," or PCV, that assumes that a customer's past transactional outcomes would predict their future contributions. A customer's value is established by taking into account their whole historical contribution (to earnings). This modeling approach assumes that a customer's historical performance predicts their level of profitability going forward. All transactions need to be adjusted for the time value of money since customers purchase goods and services at various times during their lives (Gupta et al., 2006).

$$\text{PCV of customer } i=\sum_{t=0}^{I}GC_{i(t_0-t)}*(1+\delta)^t \quad (8)$$

Where

i = customer
t = time index
δ = applicable discount rate (for example 1.25% per month)
t_0 = current time period
T = number of time periods prior to the current period that should be considered

GC_{it} = gross contribution of transactions of customer i period

Customer Acquisition and Customer Activity Metrics

When businesses want to recruit new clients, they usually have a target group in mind. For instance, a European credit card company may focus on the Italian student market. The acquisition rate—that is, the percentage of prospects who become customers—is a crucial performance metric for assessing the effectiveness of the acquisition effort. According to Gupta et al. (2006), it is computed by dividing the percentage of prospects obtained by the total number of prospects sought.

$$\text{Acquisition rate}(\%) = 100 \times \frac{\#\text{ of prospects acquired}}{\#\text{ of prospects targeted}} \tag{9}$$

The acquisition cost (AC) is the second important measure in client acquisition. The acquisition rate gauges a campaign's receptivity, but it says nothing about how cost-effective a campaign is. AC can be defined as the amount spent on acquisition campaigns divided by the total number of prospects obtained. The monetary value of AC is determined by (Gupta et al., 2006) as follows.

$$\text{Acquisition cost}(\$)\text{per prospect acquired} = \frac{\text{Acquisition spending}(\$)}{\text{Number of prospect acquired}} \tag{10}$$

Also, Average Inter-Purchase Time (AIT) is the mean duration between purchases. It is expressed in terms of discrete time intervals, such as days, weeks, or months. Based on Gupta et al. (2006), it is calculated by taking the inverse of the number of purchase incidents per time period as follows.

$$\text{AIT of a customer} = \frac{1}{\text{Number of purchases during a prespecified period}} \tag{11}$$

Moreover, defection and retention are akin to opposing sides of a single coin. One can be deduced from the other, and the appropriate usage of each metric depends on the circumstances. The retention rate in period t (Rr_t) is defined as the average likelihood that a customer purchases from the focal firm in a period (t), given that this customer has also purchased in the period before (t − 1). According to Gupta et al. (2006), the defection rate is the average probability that a customer will leave the focus firm in a period (t) assuming that the client was making purchases up to period (t − 1).

$$Rr_t(\%) = 100 \times \left[\frac{Number\ of\ customers\ in\ cohort\ buying\ in(t)|customer\ in(t-1)}{Total\ number\ of\ customers\ in\ cohort\ buying\ in(t-1)} \right] \tag{12}$$

Also, survival is another idea that is intimately related to defection and retention. The percentage of consumers who have endured (or, to put it another way, stayed clients) until a point t from when these customers were first observed is known as the survival rate (SR). Cohorts of customers—a group of customers acquired within a given time frame—are used to measure customer retention (SR). The SR provides a summary estimate of the number of customers that survived between the beginning of the formation of a cohort and any point in time subsequently, even while the retention rate and defection rate only offer information for a certain period of time. According to Gupta et al. (2006), the SR at time t is the product of the retention rate at time t and the SR during the immediately prior period (t − 1) as follows.

$$SR_t(\%) = 100 \times Rr_t \times SR_{t-1} \tag{13}$$

In non-contractual settings, it can be difficult to determine how long a client has been affiliated with a business because the consumer does not always declare the duration of their relationship. It is crucial in these kinds of circumstances to be able to forecast a customer's lifetime duration by the observation of purchasing trends and other explanatory variables. A crucial component of determining a client's lifetime value—a crucial strategic metric—is knowing how long they stay a customer. Moreover, it affects customer replacement, churn management, and lifespan duration driver management.

For one cohort of customers the avg. lifetime duration is defined based on Gupta et al. (2006) as:

$$\text{Avg. lifetime duration} = \frac{\sum_{t=1}^{T} \left(\begin{array}{c} t \times \text{Number of retained} \\ \text{customers in } t \end{array} \right)}{N} \tag{14}$$

Where

N = cohort size
t = time period
T = time horizon
(t × Number of retained customers in t) represents the number of active customer periods for the cohort at time t

Knowing if a specific consumer is likely to transact within a specific time frame may be helpful in a noncontractual situation. Stated differently, the authors are interested in learning P(Active), the likelihood that a client will be active at time t. A simple approach for computing the probability of being active, P(Active), is via the following formula (Schmittlein & Morrison, 1985):

$$P(\text{Active}) = \tau^{n} \tag{15}$$

Where

n = the number of purchases in a given period
τ = the time of the last purchase (expressed as a fraction of the observation period)

Lifetime Value (LTV) Models

LTV with splitted revenues and costs, the gross contribution can be dissected into its constituent parts according to Gupta et al. (2006). The following formula shows the calculation of LTV with splitted revenues and costs.

$$LTV_i = \sum_{t=1}^{T} \left((S_{it} - DC_{it}) - MC_{it} \right) \left(\frac{1}{1+\delta} \right)^{t} \tag{16}$$

Where

i = customer

t = time period
T = observation time horizon
δ = interest (or discount) rate
S_{it} = sales value to customer i at time t
DC_{it} = direct costs of products purchased by customer i at time t
MC_{it} = marketing costs directed at customer i at time t
LTV_i = lifetime value of an individual customer
i in net present value at time t = 0

LTV including customer retention probabilities, up until now, an assumption was that all customers remain fully active during the period of interest. In actuality, though, a growing number of clients end their business engagement with the company over time. Thus, taking into account the likelihood of retaining customers is the following stage. This has to do with the reality that clients typically stick around in relationships with a certain likelihood, which is roughly represented by the average retention rate (Rr). Additionally, the value of the customer is now reduced by the acquisition cost (AC) (Gupta et al., 2006). The following formula shows the calculation of LTV including customer retention probabilities.

$$LTV_i = \left(\left(\sum_{t=1}^{T} \left(\prod_{k=1}^{K} Rr_k \right) GC_{it} \left(\frac{1}{1+\delta} \right)^t \right) \right) - AC_i \quad (17)$$

Where

i = customer
t = time period
T = time horizon under consideration
δ = interest (or discount) rate
Rr_k = average retention rate at time t (it is possible to use an individual level retention probability)
GC_{it} = gross contribution of customer i at time t

LTV with constant retention rate and gross contribution, assuming that T → ∞, the retention rate (Rr) remains constant over time, and the gross contribution of the customer (GC) remains constant over time (Gupta et al., 2006). The following formula shows the calculation of LTV with coa nstant retention rate and gross contribution.

$$LTV_i = GC_i\left(\frac{Rr}{1 - Rr + \delta}\right) - AC_i \qquad (18)$$

Customer Equity

The authors can aggregate the LTV measure across consumers by expanding on the definition of LTV. Customer equity (CE) is the measure that shows how much the company is worth at a given moment as a result of its customer management initiatives based on Gupta et al. (2006).

An alternative metric to market share that takes the lifetime value of customers into account is the customer equity share (CES). The CES for a brand j can be calculated using the following formula:

$$CES_j = \frac{CE_j}{\sum_{K=1}^{K} CE_k} \qquad (19)$$

Where

i = focal brand
K = all brands a firm offers
CE_j = customer equity of brand i

RFM Models

RFM stands for recency, frequency, and monetary value. This method, which is frequently employed in practice, makes use of these three measures to assess consumer behavior and value. RFM's basic concept is to categorize clients according to their RFM measure. The resulting client groupings are linked to specific purchase behaviors, such as the propensity to react to a marketing effort. RFM tracks consumer behavior over time in a state space, which is comparable to the transition matrix approach. That is, clients travel via space over time while exhibiting specific, predetermined activity states.

Three factors are used by RFM models to form "clusters" or groups of customers: *R*ecency, *F*requency, and *M*onetary value of their previous transactions. The most basic models divide consumers into five groups according to each of these three variables. This yields 125 cells, or 5 x 5 × 5. Since RFM and other scoring models aim to forecast future consumer behavior, they are inadvertently connected to CLV (Gupta et al., 2006). The following are the three factors of RFM.

1. Recency: An indicator of how much time has passed since a client placed an order with the business.
2. Frequency: An indicator of how frequently a client places an order with the business within a predetermined time frame.
3. Monetary value: The typical transaction amount spent by a consumer.

Probability Models

A probability model is a picture of the world in which the behavior that is observed is understood to be the product of an underlying random process that is controlled by latent (unobserved) behavioral traits that differ between people. As with any regression model, the goal of the model-building process is not to explain changes in observed behavior as a function of variables but rather to tell a straightforward paramorphic story that defines (and predicts) the observed behavior. The assumption that consumer behavior varies throughout the population according to some probability distribution is usually one that the modeler is quite willing to make. The Pareto/NBD model, which analyzes the flow of transactions in a non-contractual situation, was developed by Schmittlein, Morrison, & Colombo (1987) and is one of the first models to explicitly address these difficulties. Some adjustments must be performed in order to include the profit from the transactions and estimate the CLV, as the Pareto/NBD model only predicts the probability of activity and the number of transactions of a customer (Glady et al., 2009). Therefore, like in Fader et al. (2005), the Gamma/Gamma submodel is employed. This Pareto/NBD-based model for CLV prediction makes the important assumption that a customer's transaction volume and profit per transaction are independent of one another.

In conclusion, as modern economies become more and more service-based, businesses are relying more and more on the development and maintenance of long-term relationships with their clients to generate revenue. Marketing's goal in this context is to maximize customer equity, or the total of the customers' lifetime values, and customer lifetime value (CLV) (Gupta et al., 2006). The authors examined a number of workable CLV models in this part, which are helpful for market segmentation and the distribution of marketing funds for acquisition, retention, and cross-selling.

Integrating CRM data into these CLV models involves extracting and cleaning relevant CRM data, creating meaningful features, and choosing between different CLV models. Features engineered from CRM data, such as purchase history and demographic information, are used to train and validate the model. Customers are then scored and segmented based on their predicted lifetime value, allowing businesses to tailor marketing strategies and allocate resources towards high-potential customers more efficiently. This process requires continuous monitoring and optimization to refine the model and strategies based on new data and market changes, ultimately enhancing customer experiences and driving profitability.

PERSONALIZATION IN THE HOSPITALITY

Experiences have been a key notion in tourism production and research for more than 50 years (Uriely, 2005). It has been said that the core of the hospitality sector is the development of happy experiences (Pizam, 2010). For instance, Barsky & Nash (2010) demonstrated how price and location can be important factors when choosing a hotel. Nonetheless, they concluded that the most important consideration when selecting a hotel is experience. Furthermore, Kim (2002) defined personalization as the capacity to meet the unique requirements and preferences of an individual or a group of individuals by providing information or services that are relevant to them in terms of their habits, lifestyles, preferences, likes, and dislikes.

Most of the literature has focused on customized information goods, such as recommendation systems (Ho & Bodoff, 2014; Lee, Hu, Cheng, & Hsieh, 2012; Parsons & Ralph, 2014; Zhang, Agarwal, & Lucas Jr, 2011) or the information exchange environment and customized websites (Chan, 2014; Thongpapanl & Ashraf, 2011). Another body of literature investigated the influence of some factors on personalization such as smart technologies (Neuhofer et al., 2015), customer hedonism (Lim, 2014), customer expectations (Ariffin & Maghzi, 2012), hotel guests' intentions to use Mobile apps (Morosan & DeFranco, 2016), consumers' behaviors in-service mobile apps (Kang & Namkung, 2019), IT-enabled customer service (Piccoli et al., 2017), the firm-customer interaction process (Lei, Wang, & Law, 2021), and the travelers' perception of personalized mobile travel advice (Lei, Chan, Tang, & Ye, 2022).

On the other hand, according to Mercan et al. (2020), the Internet of Things (IoT)[1] the Internet of Things (IoT) improved the individualized and customized service experience when the coronavirus disease 2019 (COVID-19) emerged. IoT is used to make judgments in real-time about large events, hotel occupancy, guest eating alternatives (including outdoor dining), and cruise line reservations in hospitality areas that are significantly impacted by the epidemic. In addition, the IoT used big data to help service providers anticipate and meet customer needs and wishes, customize the service experience, and expedite service recovery in order to deliver an all-around improved customer experience (Antons & Breidbach, 2018; Peters et al., 2016).

Moreover, another example is travel blogging which is simply a blog where the entire focus is on the world of travel. Travel blogging is anticipated to become increasingly significant in the decision-making process of consumers traveling in the coming years. Travel blogging addresses every phase of travelers' decision-making process, including pre-trip planning, information search, purchase or consumption, and post-consumption or experience review (Chamboko-Mpotaringa & Tichaawa, 2021). This is the rationale behind this. Travelers may, for instance, look up travel-related information before making a purchase, such as the best places to go, things to see and do, travel advice, weather reports, currency rates, and current pricing (Díaz-Meneses, 2019). Travel bloggers thus publish messages on travel news, last-minute offers, and/or special offers while travelers heed travel advice and special offers. Blogging aids tourists in getting ready for their trips in this way (Díaz-Meneses, 2019).

Furthermore, as travel information is readily available and helps visitors make better travel decisions, travelers are likely to keep reading and using travel blogs (Chamboko-Mpotaringa & Tichaawa, 2021). Because they rely on the bloggers' firsthand knowledge to inform their choices, prospective travelers are turning more and more to travel bloggers for advice (Díaz-Meneses, 2019). For this reason, advertisers pay for social media influencers—online personalities with a significant following—in order to influence their followers through blogging and content sharing. Through the content they share on social media, these influencers market travel destinations and enterprises to their followers as well as the organization's target audience (Chamboko-Mpotaringa & Tichaawa, 2021).

Moreover, incorporating digital storytelling—which involves narrating personal stories through audio and graphic visualization—in travel blogs helps draw visitors and promote tourism to destinations (Kim & Hall, 2020). Additionally, digital storytelling makes it possible to visualize travel experiences through images, films, and audio clips, providing tangible proof of the experiences (An et al., 2020). By extending the experience for visitors and stimulating their imagination, digital storytelling encourages a desire to travel. As a result, as tourism digital marketers develop into contemporary digital storytellers that can grab the interest of potential visitors, the practice of leveraging influencers as travel bloggers in conjunction with digital storytelling will only grow more common (Chamboko-Mpotaringa & Tichaawa, 2021).

Customization vs. Personalization

Experiences need to be personalized, but services may be tailored. Although these phrases are frequently used synonymously, it's crucial to understand the differences when thinking about creating extraordinary experiences (Rosenbaum et al., 2021).

Thus, customization refers to giving the customer the option to choose specific amenities, while personalization refers to the interaction between the customer and provider during the experience (e.g., sending a guest a cake with their initials along with their favorite beverage). The significance of hyper-personalizing items to provide unique consumer experiences has been acknowledged by luxury goods (Rosenbaum et al., 2021). Because unsolicited recommendations result in increased customer satisfaction, it is critical to understand what customers want without their asking (Barnes et al., 2016; Crotts et al., 2008).

Consumers vary in how sensitive they are to tailored interactions, therefore hotels must consider the values and interests of each guest. Therefore, the best-customized experience requires a human touch and sincere concern for the client. Some guests could view personalization attempts as an intrusion into their privacy, thus it is significant that the provider has a system for identifying guests that would be amenable to such personalization efforts (LaTour & Brant, 2021).

Measurements of the Personalization

In this section, the authors present some personalization evidence from the literature and some measurements of personalization.

For instance, Ariffin & Maghzi (2012) found that personal aspects including gender, the reason for the visit, nationality, and the private domain of hospitality[2] affect the expectations of hotel hospitality. The five characteristics of commercial hospitality in hotel services were also established by Ariffin & Maghzi (2012). These dimensions are personalized, warm welcoming, special relationships, straight from the heart, and comfort. Moreover, Lim (2014) found that customization has a favorable impact on consumer hedonism. As a result, they conclude that hospitality providers ought to provide patrons with the option to tailor experiences and service offerings. For example, they ought to keep track of patrons' requirements, preferences, likes, and dislikes in order to deliver more customized services during their stay.

Additionally, Morosan & DeFranco (2016) demonstrated that it is possible to forecast how customers will engage in mobile commerce in hotels based on their perceptions of privacy and customization as well as their reflections on inherent consumer traits. As well, they stressed that the ability to customize mobile apps bearing hotel brands enhances customer-hotel relations, suggesting that marketers should implement more complex customized solutions. Also, Piccoli et al. (2017) discovered that IT-enabled service systems have the power to alter the dynamic of the guest-hotel relationship and that service customization improves guests' assessments of value and service. Furthermore, they disclosed that the hotel gains monetarily from the revenue share shift from expensive intermediated to direct distribution channels brought about by IT-enabled service customization.

According to a recent study by Kang & Namkung (2019), there are important correlations between perceived risks and benefits and the personalization of mobile apps. Furthermore, they concluded that mobile apps' personalized services could be a double-edged sword because customers perceive both various benefits and privacy-related risks of disclosing their personal information when they use mobile apps. However, consumers believe that adopting branded mobile apps will provide more advantages than disadvantages, such as the potential for privacy invasion, misuse, or disclosure of personal information. Customers therefore appear to think that using mobile apps is more beneficial than not (Kang & Namkung, 2019).

In addition, Lei et al. (2022) discovered that passengers' intentions to follow mobile travel guidance may be influenced by personalization cues such as self-reference and content relevancy. Furthermore, they emphasize the significance of taking into account users' perceived personalization rather than concentrating solely on the personalization technique by implying that the impacts of personalization depend on the recipients' interpretation and knowledge of what personalization means to them. Table 1 presents the measurement of personalization from different studies.

Table 1. Measurements of the personalization

N.	Measurements	References
1	The six elements are the following: 1) I value Web pages that are personalized for the device (e.g. computer, palm, mobile phone, etc.), browser (e.g. Netscape, Internet Explorer), and operating system (e.g. Windows, Unix) that I use. 2) I value Web sites that are personalized for my usage experience preferences. 3) I value Web sites that acquire my personal preferences and personalize the services and products themselves. 4) I value goods and services that are personalized based on information that is collected automatically (such as IP address, pages viewed, and access time) but cannot identify me as an individual. 5) I value goods and services that are personalized on information that I have voluntarily given out (such as age range, salary range, and Zip Code) but cannot identify me as an individual. 6) I value goods and services that are personalized on information I have voluntarily given out and can identify me as an individual (such as name, shipping address, and credit card information).	(Ameen, Tarhini, Reppel, & Anand, 2021)
2	The three elements are the following: 1) recommendation agents understand my needs, 2) recommendation agents know what I want, and 3) recommendation agents take my needs as their own preferences.	(Komiak & Benbasat, 2006)
3	The three elements are the following: 1) Mobile Coupon[3] service can provide me with personalized deals/ads tailored to my activity context, 2) Mobile Coupon service can provide me with more relevant promotional information tailored to my preferences or personal interests, and 3) Mobile Coupon service can provide me with the kind of deals/ads that I might like.	(Xu, Luo, Carroll, & Rosson, 2011)
4	The five elements are the following: 1) the hotel staff knew my name and/or nationality, 2) the hotel staff treated me with full respect, 3) the hotel staff made eye contact with me during the conversation, 4) the hotel made me feel like an important person, 5) and the hotel staff gave me authentic smiles all the time.	(Ariffin & Maghzi, 2012)
5	The five items are the following: 1) personalization allows me to project a spark of creativity, 2) Personalization gives me a sense of natural authenticity, and 3) I am delighted when service providers have the flexibility to adapt the offer to my needs (i.e., requests), 4) the opportunity to customize an offering is something that I consider fun and exciting, and 5) overall, personalization is an important consideration when I engage with hospitality services.	(Lim, 2014)
6	Three Likert-scale items, anchored in five points, ranging from "strongly disagree" to "strongly agree": 1) The hotel app can provide me with personalized services, products, or information tailored to my specific hotel stay. 2) The hotel app can provide me with more relevant services, products, or information tailored to my preferences or personal interests. 3) The hotel app can provide me with the kind of personalized services, products, or information that I might like.	(Li, Sarathy, & Xu, 2011; Morosan & DeFranco, 2016)
7	Seven Likert-scale items, anchored in seven points, ranging from "strongly disagree" to "strongly agree": 1) I feel that the WeChat promotional materials should display a personalized message to me. 2) I feel that the WeChat promotional materials should be personalized for my usage. 3) Contents in WeChat promotional material should be personalized.	(Sam & Chatwin, 2019; Xu, 2006)
8	Five Likert-scale items, anchored in seven points, ranging from "strongly disagree" to "strongly agree": 1) The message seems to be designed specifically for me. 2) The message targets me as a unique individual. 3) Overall, this message is tailored to my situation. 4) This message makes me feel that I am unique. 5) I believe this message is customized to my needs.	(Lei et al., 2022)

Source: Author's elaboration.

THE USE OF ELECTRONIC RESERVATION SYSTEMS AND PERSONALIZATION IN THE HOSPITALITY INDUSTRY

The tourism industry makes use of several smart technologies, including the Internet of Things, the Internet of Everything, 5G, RFID, wearable smartphones and devices, 3D printing, apps with APIs, cryptocurrency and blockchain, sensor and beacon networks, pervasive computing, gamification, and enhanced analytical capabilities made possible by Artificial Intelligence (AI) and machine learning (ML) (Buhalis & Sinarta, 2019; Tussyadiah, Jung, & tom Dieck, 2018). According to Buhalis (2019), these technologies collectively establish the info structure and smart digital grid that facilitate the smooth collaboration of all parties involved. Furthermore, a few cutting-edge methods for utilizing smart technologies and experiencing personalization include chatbots, augmented reality (AR), virtual reality (VR), and the Internet of Things (IoT). The framework for smart technology and personalization in the hotels is shown in Figure 1 based on (Ashqar, Ramos, Sousa, & Matos, 2023).

Figure 1. The framework for electronic reservation systems and personalization in the hotels
Source: Ashqar et al. (2023).

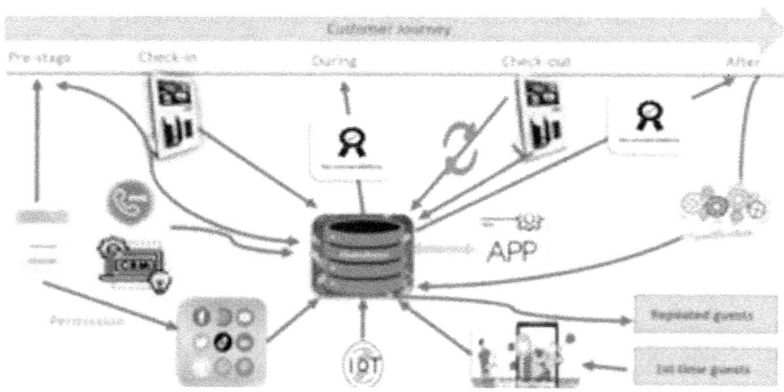

The framework for using the electronic reservation systems connected with CRM and property management system (PMS) with the experience personalization in the hotels during the five stages of the customer journey—pre-stage, check-in, during, check-out, and after—was depicted by the authors in Figure 1. For this reason, users join in the Pre-stage using a website or app on their phone and grant access to their social media accounts. The database is created using this data as well as the PMS and CRM data. Additionally, the check-in process can update the database with information about the services that clients have used. The Database can get data from the IoT and recommendations while traveling. The system has the ability to update consumer information as they are checking out. For returning visitors, the system can send app recommendations after the trip. Furthermore, gamification can be employed by the system to communicate, share, and collaborate with partners, employees, and customers. The authors propose that the cold start problem be used by the system to anticipate the needs of incoming visitors.

CONCLUSION

This chapter aims to present how can use the data about the clients from CRM in order to use them on CLV models to classify the potentialities of customers. Integrating CRM data into CLV models involves extracting and cleaning relevant CRM data, creating meaningful features, and choosing between different CLV models. Features engineered from CRM data, such as purchase history and demographic information, are used to train and validate the model. Customers are then scored and segmented based on their predicted lifetime value, allowing businesses to tailor marketing strategies and allocate resources towards high-potential customers more efficiently. This process requires continuous monitoring and optimization to refine the model and strategies based on new data and market changes, ultimately enhancing customer experiences and driving profitability. In addition, the authors suggested using personalization to make promotions for specific clients. The motivation of this chapter is to increase the competitiveness of the hotels and offer attractive services to achieve the loyalty of current and new clients. Also, to offer exclusive products or services to increase user satisfaction. In addition, the authors recommend that future studies look at the use of mobile apps and how they interact with in-person interactions in hotels, as well as the adoption, implementation, and impact of smart technology solutions in the years to come. Furthermore, future research ought to keep contrasting the outcomes of various personalization techniques and might gather information from various participant groups.

REFERENCES

Alt, R., & Klein, S. (2011). Twenty years of electronic markets research—Looking backward towards the future. *Electronic Markets*, *21*(1), 41–51. doi:10.1007/s12525-011-0057-z

Ameen, N., Tarhini, A., Reppel, A., & Anand, A. (2021). Customer experiences in the age of artificial intelligence. *Computers in Human Behavior, 114*, 106548. doi:10.1016/j.chb.2020.106548 PMID:32905175

An, Q., Ma, Y., Du, Q., Xiang, Z., & Fan, W. (2020). Role of user-generated photos in online hotel reviews: An analytical approach. *Journal of Hospitality and Tourism Management, 45*, 633–640. doi:10.1016/j.jhtm.2020.11.002

Antons, D., & Breidbach, C. F. (2018). Big data, big insights? Advancing service innovation and design with machine learning. *Journal of Service Research, 21*(1), 17–39. doi:10.1177/1094670517738373

Ariffin, A. A. M., & Maghzi, A. (2012). A preliminary study on customer expectations of hotel hospitality: Influences of personal and hotel factors. *International Journal of Hospitality Management, 31*(1), 191–198. doi:10.1016/j.ijhm.2011.04.012

Ashqar, R. I., Ramos, C., Sousa, C., & Matos, N. (2023). CRM and Smart Technologies in the Hospitality. In *Marketing and Smart Technologies: Proceedings of ICMarkTech 2022* (Vol. 2, pp. 113–124). Springer. doi:10.1007/978-981-19-9099-1_9

Barnes, D. C., Meyer, T., & Kinard, B. R. (2016). Implementing a delight strategy in a restaurant setting: The power of unsolicited recommendations. *Cornell Hospitality Quarterly, 57*(3), 329–342. doi:10.1177/1938965515626296

Barsky, J., & Nash, L. (2010). What is more important than location in selecting a hotel? [Online]. *Hotel & Motel Management*.

Bilgihan, A., Kandampully, J., & Zhang, T. C. (2016). Towards a unified customer experience in online shopping environments: Antecedents and outcomes. *International Journal of Quality and Service Sciences, 8*(1), 102–119. doi:10.1108/IJQSS-07-2015-0054

Buhalis, D. (2019). Technology in tourism-from information communication technologies to eTourism and smart tourism towards ambient intelligence tourism: A perspective article. *Tourism Review*.

Buhalis, D., & Law, R. (2008). Progress in information technology and tourism management: 20 years on and 10 years after the Internet—The state of eTourism research. *Tourism Management, 29*(4), 609–623. doi:10.1016/j.tourman.2008.01.005

Buhalis, D., & Sinarta, Y. (2019). Real-time co-creation and nowness service: Lessons from tourism and hospitality. *Journal of Travel & Tourism Marketing, 36*(5), 563–582. doi:10.1080/10548408.2019.1592059

Chamboko-Mpotaringa, M., & Tichaawa, T. M. (2021). Tourism digital marketing tools and views on future trends: A systematic review of literature. *African Journal of Hospitality, Tourism and Leisure*, *10*(2), 712–726. doi:10.46222/ajhtl.19770720-128

Chan, I. (2014). Leveraging student course enrollment data to infuse personalization in a library website. *Library Hi Tech*, *32*(3), 450–466. doi:10.1108/LHT-07-2013-0096

Crotts, J. C., Pan, B., & Raschid, A. E. (2008). A survey method for identifying key drivers of guest delight. *International Journal of Contemporary Hospitality Management*, *20*(4), 462–470. doi:10.1108/09596110810873552

Daghfous, A., & Barkhi, R. (2009). The strategic management of information technology in UAE hotels: An exploratory study of TQM, SCM, and CRM implementations. *Technovation*, *29*(9), 588–595. doi:10.1016/j.technovation.2009.05.007

Debnath, R., Datta, B., & Mukhopadhyay, S. (2016). Customer relationship management theory and research in the new millennium: Directions for future research. *Journal of Relationship Marketing*, *15*(4), 299–325. doi:10.1080/15332667.2016.1209053

Díaz-Meneses, G. (2019). A multiphase trip, diversified digital and varied background approach to analyzing and segmenting holidaymakers and their use of social media. *Journal of Destination Marketing & Management*, *11*, 166–182. doi:10.1016/j.jdmm.2017.07.005

Erevelles, S., Fukawa, N., & Swayne, L. (2016). Big Data consumer analytics and the transformation of marketing. *Journal of Business Research*, *69*(2), 897–904. doi:10.1016/j.jbusres.2015.07.001

Fader, P. S., Hardie, B. G. S., & Lee, K. L. (2005). RFM and CLV: Using iso-value curves for customer base analysis. *JMR, Journal of Marketing Research*, *42*(4), 415–430. doi:10.1509/jmkr.2005.42.4.415

Glady, N., Baesens, B., & Croux, C. (2009). A modified Pareto/NBD approach for predicting customer lifetime value. *Expert Systems with Applications*, *36*(2), 2062–2071. doi:10.1016/j.eswa.2007.12.049

Greenberg, P. (2010). The impact of CRM 2.0 on customer insight. *Journal of Business and Industrial Marketing*, *25*(6), 410–419. doi:10.1108/08858621011066008

Gupta, S., Hanssens, D., Hardie, B., Kahn, W., Kumar, V., Lin, N., Ravishanker, N., & Sriram, S. (2006). Modeling customer lifetime value. *Journal of Service Research*, *9*(2), 139–155. doi:10.1177/1094670506293810

Gupta, S., Lehmann, D. R., & Stuart, J. A. (2004). Valuing customers. *JMR, Journal of Marketing Research*, *41*(1), 7–18. doi:10.1509/jmkr.41.1.7.25084

Ho, S. Y. (2012). The effects of location personalization on individuals' intention to use mobile services. *Decision Support Systems*, *53*(4), 802–812. doi:10.1016/j.dss.2012.05.012

Ho, S. Y., & Bodoff, D. (2014). The effects of Web personalization on user attitude and behavior. *Management Information Systems Quarterly*, *38*(2), 497–A10. doi:10.25300/MISQ/2014/38.2.08

Kang, J.-W., & Namkung, Y. (2019). The role of personalization on continuance intention in food service mobile apps: A privacy calculus perspective. *International Journal of Contemporary Hospitality Management*, *31*(2), 734–752. doi:10.1108/IJCHM-12-2017-0783

Kasim, A., & Minai, B. (2009). Linking CRM strategy, customer performance measures, and performance in the hotel industry. *International Journal of Economics and Management*, *3*(2), 297–316.

Kim, M. J., & Hall, C. M. (2020). What drives visitor economy crowdfunding? The effect of digital storytelling on unified theory of acceptance and use of technology. *Tourism Management Perspectives*, *34*, 100638. doi:10.1016/j.tmp.2020.100638

Kim, W. (2002). Personalization: Definition, status, and challenges ahead. *Journal of Object Technology*, *1*(1), 29–40. doi:10.5381/jot.2002.1.1.c3

Komiak, S. Y. X., & Benbasat, I. (2006). The effects of personalization and familiarity on trust and adoption of recommendation agents. *Management Information Systems Quarterly*, *30*(4), 941–960. doi:10.2307/25148760

LaTour, K. A., & Brant, A. (2021). Social Listening to Create Bespoke Customer Experiences: Best Practices for Hospitality Operators. *Cornell Hospitality Quarterly*, 938965521993087.

Lee, Y.-H., Hu, P. J.-H., Cheng, T.-H., & Hsieh, Y.-F. (2012). A cost-sensitive technique for positive-example learning supporting content-based product recommendations in B-to-C e-commerce. *Decision Support Systems*, *53*(1), 245–256. doi:10.1016/j.dss.2012.01.018

Lei, S. I., Wang, D., & Law, R. (2021). Mobile-based value co-creation: Contextual factors towards customer experiences. *Tourism Review*.

Lei, S. S. I., Chan, I. C. C., Tang, J., & Ye, S. (2022). Will tourists take mobile travel advice? Examining the personalization-privacy paradox. *Journal of Hospitality and Tourism Management*, *50*, 288–297. doi:10.1016/j.jhtm.2022.02.007

Li, H., Sarathy, R., & Xu, H. (2011). The role of affect and cognition on online consumers' decision to disclose personal information to unfamiliar online vendors. *Decision Support Systems*, *51*(3), 434–445. doi:10.1016/j.dss.2011.01.017

Lim, W. M. (2014). The antecedents and consequences of customer hedonism in hospitality services. *Journal of Hospitality Marketing & Management*, *23*(6), 626–651. doi:10.1080/19368623.2014.846838

Lo, A. S., Stalcup, L. D., & Lee, A. (2010). Customer relationship management for hotels in Hong Kong. *International Journal of Contemporary Hospitality Management*, *22*(2), 139–159. doi:10.1108/09596111011018151

Mercan, S., Cain, L., Akkaya, K., Cebe, M., Uluagac, S., Alonso, M., & Cobanoglu, C. (2020). Improving the service industry with hyper-connectivity: IoT in hospitality. *International Journal of Contemporary Hospitality Management*.

Morosan, C., & DeFranco, A. (2016). Modeling guests' intentions to use mobile apps in hotels: The roles of personalization, privacy, and involvement. *International Journal of Contemporary Hospitality Management*, *28*(9), 1968–1991. doi:10.1108/IJCHM-07-2015-0349

Neuhofer, B., Buhalis, D., & Ladkin, A. (2015). Smart technologies for personalized experiences: A case study in the hospitality domain. *Electronic Markets*, *25*(3), 243–254. doi:10.1007/s12525-015-0182-1

Nyheim, P., Xu, S., Zhang, L., & Mattila, A. S. (2015). Predictors of avoidance towards personalization of restaurant smartphone advertising: A study from the Millennials' perspective. *Journal of Hospitality and Tourism Technology*, *6*(2), 145–159. doi:10.1108/JHTT-07-2014-0026

Parsons, J., & Ralph, P. (2014). Generating effective recommendations using viewing-time weighted preferences for attributes. *Journal of the Association for Information Systems*, *15*(8), 2. doi:10.17705/1jais.00369

Peters, C., Maglio, P., Badinelli, R., Harmon, R. R., Maull, R., Spohrer, J. C., Tuunanen, T., Vargo, S. L., Welser, J. J., & Demirkan, H. (2016). Emerging digital frontiers for service innovation. *Communications of the Association for Information Systems: CAIS*, *1*(39), online.

Piccoli, G., Lui, T.-W., & Grün, B. (2017). The impact of IT-enabled customer service systems on service personalization, customer service perceptions, and hotel performance. *Tourism Management*, *59*, 349–362. doi:10.1016/j.tourman.2016.08.015

Pine, B. J., Pine, J., & Gilmore, J. H. (1999). *The experience economy: work is theatre & every business a stage*. Harvard Business Press.

Pizam, A. (2010). *Creating memorable experiences.*

RaneN.ChoudharyS.RaneJ. (2023). Hyper-personalization for enhancing customer loyalty and satisfaction in Customer Relationship Management (CRM) systems. *Available at* SSRN 4641044. doi:10.2139/ssrn.4641044

Reinartz, W. J., & Kumar, V. (2003). The impact of customer relationship characteristics on profitable lifetime duration. *Journal of Marketing*, *67*(1), 77–99. doi:10.1509/jmkg.67.1.77.18589

Rosenbaum, M. S., Ramirez, G. C., Campbell, J., & Klaus, P. (2021). The product is me: Hyper-personalized consumer goods as unconventional luxury. *Journal of Business Research*, *129*, 446–454. doi:10.1016/j.jbusres.2019.05.017

Sam, K. M., & Chatwin, C. R. (2019). Understanding Wechat Users' Motivations, Attitudes and Intention of Reading Promotional Material. *Journal of Information Technology Management*, *30*(1), 25–37.

Schmittlein, D. C., & Morrison, D. G. (1985). Is the customer still active? *The American Statistician*, *39*(4), 291–295. doi:10.1080/00031305.1985.10479450

Schmittlein, D. C., Morrison, D. G., & Colombo, R. (1987). Counting your customers: Who-are they and what will they do next? *Management Science*, *33*(1), 1–24. doi:10.1287/mnsc.33.1.1

Sheth, J. (2017). Revitalizing relationship marketing. *Journal of Services Marketing*, *31*(1), 6–10. doi:10.1108/JSM-11-2016-0397

Thongpapanl, N., & Ashraf, A. R. (2011). Enhancing online performance through website content and personalization. *Journal of Computer Information Systems*, *52*(1), 3–13.

Tussyadiah, I. P., Jung, T. H., & tom Dieck, M. C. (2018). Embodiment of wearable augmented reality technology in tourism experiences. *Journal of Travel Research*, *57*(5), 597–611. doi:10.1177/0047287517709090

Uriely, N. (2005). The tourist experience: Conceptual developments. *Annals of Tourism Research*, *32*(1), 199–216. doi:10.1016/j.annals.2004.07.008

Wang, Y., & Feng, H. (2012). Customer relationship management capabilities: Measurement, antecedents and consequences. *Management Decision*, *50*(1), 115–129. doi:10.1108/00251741211194903

Wattal, S., Telang, R., & Mukhopadhyay, T. (2009). Information personalization in a two-dimensional product differentiation model. *Journal of Management Information Systems*, *26*(2), 69–95. doi:10.2753/MIS0742-1222260204

Webb, T., Cho, S. R., & Legg, M. (2022). Customer Lifetime Value: A Data Science Approach for Hospitality Applications. *International Journal of Gaming, Hospitality and Tourism, 2*(1).

Wongsansukcharoen, J., Trimetsoontorn, J., & Fongsuwan, W. (2015). Social CRM, RMO and business strategies affecting banking performance effectiveness in B2B context. *Journal of Business and Industrial Marketing*, *30*(6), 742–760. doi:10.1108/JBIM-02-2013-0039

Wu, S.-I., & Lu, C.-L. (2012). The relationship between CRM, RM, and business performance: A study of the hotel industry in Taiwan. *International Journal of Hospitality Management*, *31*(1), 276–285. doi:10.1016/j.ijhm.2011.06.012

Xu, D. J. (2006). The influence of personalization in affecting consumer attitudes toward mobile advertising in China. *Journal of Computer Information Systems*, *47*(2), 9–19.

Xu, H., Luo, X. R., Carroll, J. M., & Rosson, M. B. (2011). The personalization privacy paradox: An exploratory study of decision making process for location-aware marketing. *Decision Support Systems*, *51*(1), 42–52. doi:10.1016/j.dss.2010.11.017

Zanker, M., Rook, L., & Jannach, D. (2019). Measuring the impact of online personalisation: Past, present and future. *International Journal of Human-Computer Studies*, *131*, 160–168. doi:10.1016/j.ijhcs.2019.06.006

Zhang, T. (Catherine), Agarwal, R., & Lucas Jr, H. C. (2011). The value of IT-enabled retailer learning: Personalized product recommendations and customer store loyalty in electronic markets. *Management Information Systems Quarterly*, 859–881.

Zhang, X., Edwards, J., & Harding, J. (2007). Personalised online sales using web usage data mining. *Computers in Industry*, *58*(8–9), 772–782. doi:10.1016/j.compind.2007.02.004

ENDNOTES

1 The Internet of Things (IoT) is a name for the aggregate collection of network-enabled devices, excluding traditional computers like laptops and servers. Types of network connections can include Wi-Fi connections, Bluetooth connections, and near-field communication (NFC). The IoT includes devices such as "smart" appliances, like refrigerators and thermostats; home security systems; computer peripherals, like webcams and printers; wearable technology, such as Apple Watches and Fitbits; routers; and smart speaker devices, like Amazon Echo and Google Home.

2 The hospitality at private domain refers to the hospitality offered by individuals towards others in a more private setting such as at their homes.

3 A Mobile coupon is an electronic ticket solicited and/or delivered by mobile phone that can be exchanged for a financial discount or rebate when purchasing a product or service.

Chapter 7
3D-Printed Food for New Gastronomic Experiences:
A Study on Potential Application and Restaurant Consumer's Perception

Nuno Miguel Severino
Estoril Higher Institute for Tourism and Hotel Studies, Portugal

Cláudia Marcos Azevedo
https://orcid.org/0000-0001-8541-2669
Estoril Higher Institute for Tourism and Hotel Studies, Portugal

Maria Manuela Mendes Guerra
https://orcid.org/0000-0002-3655-9004
CiTUR, Portugal & Estoril Higher Institute for Tourism and Hotel Studies, Portugal

ABSTRACT

Digital gastronomy has been a common topic of conversation while talking about robotic breakthroughs in the hospitality sector. Most notably by producing highly personalized and imaginative goods via 3D food printing. Nevertheless, several studies have revealed its frequent association with negative notions. This derogatory idea is frequently the consequence of consumers' neophobia stemming from ignorance. It has been proposed that positive advertising of the technology's key advantages be utilized to boost the hedonic perception of food goods; however, no one has correlated the use of multiple avenues to share the information. For this purpose, this study used both a hedonic analysis and a presentation. Most of inquiries were aware of 3D printed food and linked it to favorable words. The practical approach had a positive effect on perception, while the theoretical had no significant correlation. The study's findings support the investment in this technology for small-scale food producing facilities.

DOI: 10.4018/979-8-3693-0960-5.ch007

INTRODUCTION/ BIBLIOGRAPHIC REVIEW

Robotics in Tourism

The rapid technological advancements of the last few years have been felt throughout the entire work environment leading to significant shifts in organizational behavior and worker dislocation. Some of the technologies which influenced this alteration are the following: electronic monitoring systems, robots, teleconferencing and wearable computing devices (Cascio and Montealegre, 2016). As predicted by Frey and Osborne (2017), around 47% of the total United States of America's job offers are in high risk of being automated in the next two decades, encompassing most of the transportation, logistics, office, administrative and production sectors. For this purpose, education will have to focus on the inherently human talents that computers still lack. These abilities which encompass creativity, problem solving, complex interpersonal communication and emotional intelligence will enable humanity to remain relevant in the new economy (Webster and Ivanov, 2019a).

Similar to other sectors tourism and hospitality have started to use these computational capabilities to their favor. Although the nature of tourism related jobs is innately different from tasks performed on traditional manufacturing positions, necessitating from a unique interpersonal relationship between the service producer and the customer (Webster and Ivanov, 2019b), with the purpose to create memorable experiences therefore increasing the consumer satisfaction (Seyitoglu and Ivanov, 2022). However, throughout the tourism sector, robots can already be seen performing various tasks such as provision of information, cleaning, room service, delivery items, serving, producing food and drinks and entertaining guests, and have found their way into hotels, restaurants, bars, food delivery services, museums and much more services (Ivanov et al, 2020). Robots as defined by the International Organization for Standardization (2012) are "actuated mechanism programmable in two or more axes with a degree of autonomy, moving within its environment, to perform intended tasks".

On one hand, robots can be used in tourism services to originate novel experiences, increase the service capacity, improve productivity, save employee's time and create additional revenues. However, they still are relatively expensive and present limited technologic functionalities (Webster and Ivanov, 2020). Their introduction on the market has been potentialized by the demographic crises the western countries have been facing, resulting in a future decreased employee base (Cristea et al., 2020). Nevertheless, stakeholders' perspectives have been guiding the technology to the opposite direction. It turns out that some customers reject the idea of integration of robots on tourism services, and the majority considers some activities not suitable to be performed by machines, most notably on positions that require sophisticated judgement call, such as security worker or on food and drink preparation on restaurants, often associated with a decreased quality and willingness to pay a premium price (Webster and Ivanov, 2020). However, when considering entertainment, information provision, booking processing, payment management and housekeeping were considered to be acceptable to be automated (Webster and Ivanov, 2019c, 5; Seyitoglu and Ivanov, 2020). From the manager's perspective, these machines have clear advantages such as the increase of service capacity, turn the planning of operations easier and more predictable, from a marketing standpoint, robots can be sold as a novel experience, reduce operational costs and make fewer mistakes, in short, being mostly adequate for repetitive, dull and dangerous tasks, though they were not intended to be implemented on the next few years by the majority of the managers interviewed on a Bulgarian study (Ivanov et al., 2020).

Digital Gastronomy

Digital transformation has also permeated the food production process over the past several decades, resulting in significant productivity improvements, product variance, food safety, shelf life, etc., even if these advancements are mostly invisible to customers. Although the term "digital gastronomy" is not new, the numerous advancements in digital cooking over the years make now the ideal moment to confirm its potential use, given the high degree of complexity displayed by the equipment already on the market. (Mizrahi et al., 2016). This idea proposes a more comprehensive strategy, enhancing the conventional cooking environment with new interactive possibilities, as opposed to substituting the chef with autonomous robots. Some of the technologies recommended for its use range from simple process enhancements, such as beating a cake in a continuous mixer, to far more complex and creative equipment, such as 3D Food Printing (Mizrahi et al., 2023; Lin et al., 2020), augmented reality and virtual reality (Chisik et al., 2018; Yildirim and Yildirim, 2022). Although many of its characteristics, such as comparing the usage of digital images to the food's actual form, have been previously researched in terms of how consumers perceive them (Harun et al., 2020), or whether there has been strong acceptance for the use of augmented and virtual reality (Çöl et al., 2023). But there were few studies that took in account how customers felt about 3D Food Printing being used on digital gastronomy, so it became necessary to find out what the public thought about this technology's application in the restaurant industry.

Associated to and often included onto digital gastronomy's umbrella definition is the word "smart gastronomy", this term which makes part of the designation of smart tourism. It is described by Zvirbule et al. (2023), as "a collection and compilation of information from tourism operators, infrastructures and people related to the respective destination. Then, by digitalizing the information, commercial value is created, focusing on sustainability, experience and efficiency.". This is often done by the use of technology-based digital applications that process and deliver the treated data, and contrasts with traditional tourism management approaches (Batal, 2023). When applied to gastronomy this concept can take various forms such as food order applications, like UberEATS and such, recipe applications, such as Sony AI's cooking recommender app RecipeBowl (Gim et al., 2021), food waste applications, like the Michelin awarded TooGoodToGo app (Hjalager, 2022), and health and nutrition applications (Suren and Kizileli, 2022). Other more concrete uses that were seen in the last few years in the food industry are for example, the use of 5G, sensors and beacons, Artificial Intelligence and Augmented Realities, as seen with Pepper, PizzaHut's and MasterCard's humanoid artificial intelligence that communicates with customers and accepts orders and payments (Ivanov et al., 2017), wearables combined with location-based treasure hunting games, like PokemonGo, cryptos, blockchain, ghost kitchens and even the advent of "foodstagramming", where social media turns into a place of sharing the consumer's gastronomic adventures (Hjalager, 2022).

Therefore, smart food tourism can ensure sustainable resource handling, simplification of logistics, and optimization production to match demand which most likely will arrive later in the technology evolution trajectory. Severe food crises, problems with food security, waste management, etc., may spur this kind of clever innovation. The topic has already received increased attention following the COVID-19 pandemic and during the European wars, though policymakers are unlikely to be first thinking about the implications and the tourism aspects of it (Vogt, S., 2017).

3D Food Printing

The American Society for Testing and Materials (ASTM) and the International Organization for Standardization (ISO) define additive manufacturing (AM) as the "process of joining materials to make parts from 3D model data, usually layer upon layer, as opposed to subtractive manufacturing and formative manufacturing methodologies", is also commonly called by one of its types of fabrication, 3D printing (3DP) (Bourell, 2016; ISO/ASTM 52900, 2015). It is comprised of seven types of procedures, from which only five of which have been applied to the production of food. These techniques are material extrusion, material jetting, binder jetting, powder bed fusion and laser sintering (Voon et al, 2019). All methods are founded on the same idea: from a digital model, freeform structured physical items are created through the direct layer-by-layer deposition of materials controlled by Computer Aided Design (CAD) data (Pinna et al., 2016).

Although this technology was firstly introduced in the 1980s by Kodama, only in the year of 2001, was patented the first model for a primitive 3D printer by Nanotek Instruments Inc. (Abdulhameed et al., 2019). In 2009 saw the release of the first extrusion-based printer created especially for the food industry, the Moléculaire concept design, which Nico Kläber presented at the Electrolux Design Lab 2009 competition. This printer could print a variety of materials using a tiny robotic arm. (Sun et al., 2015b). Many additional types of printers based on other AM technologies were created quickly after. (Soni et al., 2022). Many firms have developed their own printers in the past ten years, catering to both consumer and professional needs. A few of these companies are Natural Machines' Foodini, De Grood Innovations' Foodjet, and RIG's Foodform 3D. (Pinna et al., 2016).

Concerns exist about the adoption and use of AM technology in the food production industry. The primary cause of these issues is the type of inks used, as opposed to conventional 3DP applications. The term "food inks" refers to the completed printed form of edible materials used in additive food manufacturing (AFM), which typically takes the shape of pastes or gels. (Voon et al., 2019). Sun et al. (2015a), divides these inks into three categories: materials that can be printed naturally, conventional food materials that can't be printed, and substitute ingredients. Table 1 shows how these classifications are applied as well as some of the ingredients that each one uses.

The primary components of the ink must be correctly blended to obtain the desired texture for extrusion. These are mostly found in diet as fats, proteins, and carbs. We can control the intrinsic characteristics and binding processes of each deposited layer thanks to the synergy these compounds create and the interactions they form among themselves. This allows us to develop accurate and robust structures that would be difficult to design by hand. (Godoi et al., 2016; Cheng, et al., 2022).

Table 1. Classification of food inks and main ingredients used in AM technologies (adapted from Sun et al., 2015a)

	NATIVELY PRINTABLE MATERIALS	NON-PRINTABLE TRADITIONAL FOOD MATERIALS	ALTERNATIVE INGREDIENTS
DESCRIPTION	**Solid or semi-solid products that need minimal processing to be printed**	**Materials that need the addition of hydrocolloids to enable extrusion**	**Include various material not usually consumed for aesthetic or cultural reasons**
APPLICATIONS	Binder Jet, Powder bed Fusion, VAT Photopolymerization and Extrusion	Extrusion	Extrusion
PRODUCTS UTILIZED	Hydrogel, Cake frosting, Cheese, Chocolate and Sugar	Rice, Meat, Fruits and Vegetables	Insects and algae

Comparing the 3DP of food goods to conventional production methods, however, has shown certain advantages. These can be broadly divided into four categories: the first deals with how the food chain is really disrupted, shortened, and made more likely to produce highly customized and complicated items, which in turn lowers labor and food costs (Dabbene et al., 2018); the second focused on environmental issues and addressed issues including hunger, malnourishment, climate change, and decreasing food waste (Tran, 2018); the second one is health issues, such as lowering the amount of allergens and germs in food processing or even making it possible to create recipes for certain ailments like dysphagia (Kouzani et al., 2017); and lastly, as technology advances, it will be used into military and space facilities, making food production in these settings simpler and quicker (Tran, 2018; Caulier et al., 2020).

The ISO/ASTM has classified AM into these seven categories. These are Binder jetting, material jetting, extrusion of materials, powder bed fusion, directed energy deposition, sheet lamination, and vat photopolymerization. (ISO/ASTM 52900, 2015). Five have been applied to food production, however they are primarily relevant to non-food building. The most popular techniques among them are Liquid Binding, Fused Deposition Method (FDM), Selective Laser Sintering (SLS), and Selective Hot Air Sintering and Melting (SHASAM) (Mantihal et al., 2020). Other techniques that have been effectively implemented in the food manufacturing industry include VAT Photopolymerization, InkJet, and Bio-printing (Godoi et al., 2016; Lipton, 2017). Because ink has a wide range of physio-chemical properties, it can often be difficult to integrate these technologies into the food system.

The most popular additive manufacturing technologies nowadays are without a doubt extrusion techniques, which are derived from the Fused Deposition Modeling

(FDM) or Fused Filament Fabrication (FFF) process. In these processes, layers of thermoplastic polymeric material are deposited on top of one another using a syringe that moves in an x-y-z direction. This process differs from InkJet printing in that material is expelled from the nozzle in a continuous stream. (Nachal et al., 2019; Noort et al., 2017; Sher and Tutó, 2010). This indicates the material's characteristics must also alter. To be easily extruded by the printing nozzle in extrusion type prints, the ink needs to be in a semi-solid or viscous state, typically derived from fresh items. Consequently, a detailed comprehension of the thermal, rheological, and tribological characteristics of the food ingredients in the ink is required (Mantihal et al., 2020).

It can be divided into two categories for food uses. First, there is the syringe-based method, which is based on the ink feeding mechanism and can be categorized as follows: for highly viscous and mechanically intensive food materials, it is ideal because it allows for easy adjustment of the barometric pressure to accommodate changes in the viscosity of the extruded fluid and pushes the material through the nozzle in a controlled manner using a step motor that controls the extrusion in a linear motion through a syringe that has already been filled with the ink (Guo et al., 2019). Screw-based food processors produce fewer air bubbles because they feed food continuously through a screw-driven motor. However, they are not appropriate for high-viscosity and high-mechanical-strength food slurries because the food never reaches the necessary strength to support each layer, which frequently results in compression deformation (Guadagno et al., 2021; Guo et al., 2019; Kim et al, 2018). Alternatively, by air pressure, which consists of two parts: an encapsulated food cartridge and a pneumatic pump that regulates the extrusion rate, which varies depending on each printing head. This method is primarily used for liquid foods, as solid and semi-solid materials can frequently obstruct the print process by depositing at the nozzle tip (Lee, 2021; Singhal et al, 2020).

In a comparable manner extrusion-based food printers make up the great bulk of those on the market today. These can be further divided into two groups: fresh paste extruders, which are typically outfitted with all FDM functionalities, and chocolate printers, which solely have HME capabilities. The majority of fresh product printers can print at room temperature or even hotter temperatures, allowing for the creation of hydrogel-forming and hot-melt extrusions. When room temperature extrusion is the sole option, the printers from Micromake and ZMorph are among the ones that are specifically designed to include a self-heating plate for deposition. (Aniwaa, 2022; ZMorph, s.d.).

The market for 3D food printing was valued at approximately USD 201 million in 2022 and is projected to reach USD 1,941 million in 2027, growing at a compound yearly growth rate of 57,35%, beginning in 2022 (Scott, 2023). TNO (Netherlands), 3D Systems (USA), byFlow (Netherlands), Natural Machines (Spain), Systems and Materials Research Corporation (USA), Beehex (USA), ChocEdge (UK), Modern

Meadows (USA), Nu Food (UK), and North Branch Everbright (China) are the leading companies in the global distribution of 3D printers (Kunz, 2023). Currently, North America and Europe are the two largest markets (Aniket and Roshan, 2022); however, during the next ten years, the Asia-Pacific region is predicted to grow at the fastest rate (Scott, 2023).

There are now nine major players in the 3D food printing market: research institutes and universities, manufacturers of 3D printers, distributors, producers of food ingredients, food brands and restaurants, software developers, online platforms, marketplaces, and customers (Jayaprakash, 2017).

Studies indicate that 3DFP can be applied in a variety of use scenarios. These fall into five categories: 1) Food services: these comprise all aspects of the manufacturing and distribution of food, from vending machines to events, conferences, and on-demand food printing from larger businesses. Small-scale services like restaurants, bakeries, and food carts are included in this category (Jayaprakash et al., 2020; Rogers and Srivastava, 2021; Zoran, 2019); 2) Personalized nutrition: One of the greatest opportunities presented by this technology is personalized nutrition, which refers to the ability to print a range of food items with unique nutritional qualities tailored to the individual user. These products could be utilized in retirement communities, gyms, hospitals, universities, and educational institutions (Jayaprakash et al., 2020; Pinna et al., 2016); Medical and health-related: largely focused on treating food-related disorders including dysphagia, on which most study has been directed (Derrosi et al., 2021), immunocompromised people, food allergies, diabetes, and the microencapsulation of nutrients or medications in food products to serve as carriers for patients (Escalante-Aburto et al., 2021; Lorenz et al., 2022; Pinna et al., 2016); 4) Reducing food waste and sustainability: Some of the ways this technology can help combat environmental and ethical issues are through improved storage, reusing wasted food, creating edible packaging and cutlery, using alternative food sources like insects and algae, developing lab-grown meat, and developing meat analogs (Lupton and Turner, 2018a); 5) Special cases: these include home use, in which the user purchases a 3D printer and creates their own designs; they also include military and space missions, in which food supplies aren't available for extended periods of time and require food products to meet certain requirements, like being lightweight, portable, easy to store, and convenient to eat (Enfield et al., 2022; Lui et al., 2017).

Despite the interest shown by experts and financiers in the commercial sector—which includes bakeries, confectionaries, and restaurants—as well as the resurgence of the notion of digital gastronomy and the integration of 3D technology into fine dining, as seen on the study from Nassar and Fouad (2022), where the interest of Egyptian chefs was considered very high, especially when talking about young chefs. However, the majority of the consumer base appears to find this concept repulsive (Aniket and Roshan, 2022; Jayaprakash et al., 2020; Zoran, 2019).

The use of 3D food printers could only be considered in six different restaurant situations: Food Ink Restaurant, a pop-up restaurant based in the United Kingdom; Mélisse; La Enoteca at Hotel Arts; La Boscana; Wovega; and Miramar. The widespread use of this technology on the small-scale food production scene is still far away from the current status quo. (Dehue and Strikwerda, 2017; Nassar and Fouad, 2022). With the exception of the former restaurant, everyone else appears to employ the equipment to recycle leftover trimmings and food waste, creatively repurposing them in the meal. Even though larger food production firms like Barilla, Hershey's, and PepsiCo have been utilizing this technology for some time now, the transition to small scale food production still presents various obstacles (Peshave and Hodlur, 2022).

Consumer's Attitude on 3D Food Printing

To determine a customer's intention to buy, one must consider their attitudes and impressions about a product. The process of perception begins with the influence of the information disclosed to an individual, which then affects the response that results in acceptance or rejection (McCluskey et al., 2016). Perceived utility, or how the person believes the technology will improve their life, and perceived ease of use, or how much work the person believes he will need to put into the technology in order to use it, are the two main aspects that can be used to illustrate this awareness (Groot, 2019).

Few studies have examined how consumers perceive 3D food printing, despite the fact that it has been widely viewed positively in the media due to its mostly futuristic portrayal of the technology's creativity, healthfulness, efficiency, and sustainability (Lupton and Turner, 2018b; Zhu et al., 2020).

The two issues that are brought up on these sites the most are the general public's ignorance (Lupton & Turner, 2018b; Brunner et al., 2017; Feng et al., 2022; Mantihal et al., 2019; Manstan and McSweeney, 2020; Jenkins et al., 2021; Jayaprakash et al., 2020) together with the food technology neophobia associated with it (Brunner et al., 2017; Groot, 2019; Lupton & Turner, 2018b; Tuorila and Hartmann, 2020; Lupton and Turner, 2018a).

The scholarly literature isn't as constant when it comes to people's preference for printed foods over their conventional counterparts. Several studies show that when properly labeled (Feng et al., 2022; Manstan and McSweeney, 2020) or after being acquainted with food printers (Caulier et al., 2020) consumers are more likely to choose the printed item, although this does not mean they are more likely to use it (Manstan and McSweeney, 2020; Lupton and Turner, 2018b). Given that the other organoleptic qualities of the food are largely unchanged, it appears that people's preference for printed foods over their conventional counterparts depends on the type of food and how it is presented (Lupton and Turner, 2018b).

The impact of demographic factors including age, gender, and educational attainment on the acceptability of 3DFP, particularly with regard to food neophobia, is likewise equivocal. While it is frequently demonstrated that younger individuals, women, and those with more academic achievements respond more favorably to novel foods, this does not appear to be the case for 3DFPs. (Siegrist et al., 2013; Brunner et al., 2017; Manstan and McSweeney, 2020; Gosine et al., 2021).

Two more pertinent issues that arise from these findings are: people's perceptions of the 3DFP's utility in comparison to other techniques, which frequently cause them to wonder if the procedure is required or helpful (Lupton and Turner, 2018b; Gosine et al, 2021), and the fact that term "printer" is used to describe the device that produces food, even though it doesn't seem to be necessary in relation to chemicals and plastic goods (Lupton and Turner, 2018a).

Going back to the word "digital gastronomy," it is argued that most customers would not approve of its use on a manufacturing line in a high-end restaurant because of the widespread distaste for the use of 3DFP items and the neophobia towards food technology that is displayed throughout the majority of the bibliography. This is because to the unfavorable common impression of 3DFP products (Brunner et al., 2017; Lupton and Turner, 2018b).

METHODOLOGY

According to Sampieri et al. (2003), the conceptual paradigm used in this work might be characterized as mixed transversal non-experimental research. The study paradigm is characterized by the simultaneous gathering of data to characterize variables and examine their frequency and correlation.

The combination of research approaches and procedures utilized in this study forms the basis of the analysis employed in it, and are described as follows:

-Review of literature, media, and websites to ascertain how this technology is already being used, whether it may be applied to the restaurant industry, and what the primary barriers are to the integration of additive manufacturing in food production facilities;

- Analysis of consumer perception surveys conducted both before and after information was obtained, using a sample of primarily college students, and presenting the key features and applications of the technology along with a summary of its primary shortcomings at the moment;

- ◦ Hedonic sensorial analysis of two 3D printed food products was examined, and the resulting variation in the consumer's perception and perceived usefulness was also conducted in an academic setting.

Three classes from the Estoril Higher Institute for tourism and Hotel Studies (ESHTE) representing the two scientific fields of food production and tourist studies made up the panel for the presentation. The former exclusively included students pursuing bachelor's degrees, whilst the latter was divided into bachelor's and master's degrees.

The survey was completed twice: once prior to and once following the presentation of the technology. This information was provided in a 20-minute seminar on the subject, which included topics such as general use, application, and the main advantages and disadvantages of food additive production.

A demonstration of the technology was given alongside the presentation, with a spiral of instant potato puree printed using Natural Machines' 3D food printer, Foodini (Natural Machines, 2023). After the lecture, students had the opportunity to experience utilizing the technology and had their questions answered. At the start of the presentation, A4 printed sheets of paper with the questionnaires were delivered. Both parts of the survey were separate on each side of the paper. The quiz's first part was to be completed prior to the presentation, and the second part was to be completed following the talk.

The presentation was performed thrice, on May 11, 2023, on May 22, 2023 and on August 01, 2023. The second presentation was shown in the ESHTE chemical lab, while the first and last were shown in a typical classroom.

After the approximately 20-minute presentation, students were invited to ask any follow-up questions. Below is an outline of the lecture's structure:

- Brief introduction;
- Methodology of 3D printing;
- Usable inks on 3D food printing;
- Categories of 3D food printing;
- Commercially available 3D food Printers;
- Appliances of the technology;
- Gastronomic uses and Digital gastronomy;
- Limiting factors;
- Printing parameters;
- Future perspectives.

The panel utilized for this study's second questionnaire, the hedonic analysis, consisted of ESHTE students and faculty members, as well as other visitors who were in the institution at the time of the analysis. As done in the previous analysis, the questionnaire filling was divided into two different times, before and after the hedonic sensory analysis of both developed products.

In a similar vein, samples were gathered twice—preceding and following the hedonic analysis of the two printed products—in order to examine the variation in consumer perception of use of 3DFP technology on a restaurant environment.

The hedonic analysis adhered to ISO 1136:2014 since the goal was to determine what customers thought of each product. (Anzaldúa-Morales, 2005; Lawless and Heymann, 2010).

Prior to the experiment, certain tests using 3D printers were carried out to obtain the information needed to produce food products using an entirely different process as well as the variables that might render the final product unfeasible. Following this, a simpler rice cracker and kidney bean "tuna" sashimi were created independently. Ultimately, technical documentation and standards were developed for the finished prototypes and are seen in the following Table 2.

Kidney bean "tuna" sashimi	
Ingredients	**Quantity**
Kidney bean	64,75g
Water	27,75g
Xanthan gum	0,46g
Spirulina oil maceration	4g
Kombu oil maceration	2,5g
Ceps oil maceration	1g
Mono- and diglycerides of fatty acids	0,2g
Yeast extract	1g
Nutritional yeast	1g
Malic acid	0,8g
Konjac gum	1g
Yota carrageenan	1g

Table 2. Used products recipes (own source)

Rice cracker	
Ingredients	**Quantity**
Rice	200g
Water	400g + 100g
Salt	2g
Sunflower seed oil	50g

The Foodini 3D Printer from Natural Machines was the apparatus utilized in the research to extrude and 3D print the various pastes (Natural Machines, 2023).

The two distinct items that were assessed using the hedonic analysis were coded as follows—a rice cracker (code: K3C) printed in the shape of a sardine and a vegan tuna sashimi (code: P9D) made of kidney beans. The last item came with a sample of soy sauce and a toothpick. Throughout the study, a cup of water was provided as a palate cleanser.

To maintain their freshness, the food samples were prepared afresh to hold up to twenty samples at a time. They were arranged on single-use plastic dishes, spaced apart by a line that had been previously marked with each code.

A nine-point acceptability scale was applied to each sample: 1- Extremely dislike; 2- Dislike a lot; 3- Moderate dislike; 4- Slightly dislike; 5- Indifferent; 6- Slightly like; 7- Moderate like; 8- Like a lot; 9- Extremely like.

To determine the relationship between two variables the Spearman's Rank-order Correlation test and the Wilcoxon Signed-Rank test were used.

Both IBM SPSS Software and Microsoft Office Excel were used to carry out the computations.

RESULTS

The first sample was composed of a total of 86 participants. Table 2 displays the results of the first questionnaire's demographic variables.

Table 3. Presentation demographic variables results (own source)

Demographic variables	*n (N= 83)*	*Percentages*
Gender		
Masculine	43	50%
Feminine	43	50%
Prefer not to answer	0	0%
Age		
≤17	0	0%
18-27	74	86%
≥28	12	14%
Nationality		
Portuguese	81	94%
Other	5	6%
Academic degree		
High School	52	60%
Licentiate degree	29	34%
Master's degree	3	4%
Doctorate	2	2%
Scientific area		
Food production	58	67%
Tourism	18	21%
Management	1	1%
Other	9	11%

Following the inquiry regarding attendees' knowledge levels, it was found that 21 had never heard of the technology before, 57 had heard of it, 7 had knowledge of it, and 1 had used a 3D food printer before the presentation.

Figure 1. Sample's knowledge of 3D food printing percentages
(Own source)

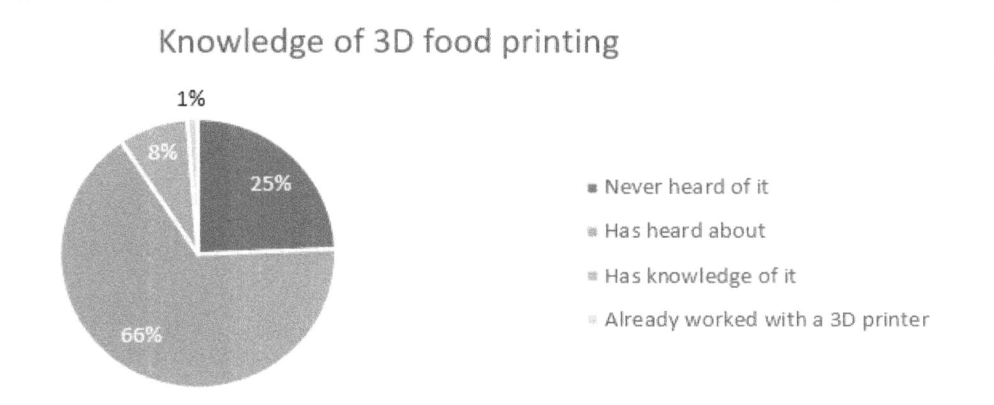

It was also looked at how the participants felt about eating things that had been 3D printed both before and after the lecture. And the findings showed that most of the responses were of interest, mostly attributed to the answer "Would choose if had the opportunity" both before and after the presentation. The variance was almost non-existent between both times.

Figure 2. Sample's disposition of consumption of 3D printed items
(Own source)

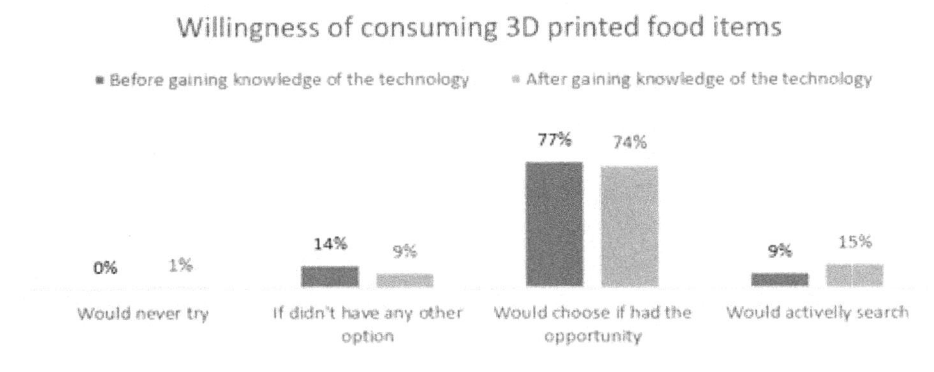

In a similar vein, both before and after the seminar, the effects of knowing that a food item was printed before its intake were investigated. While the majority of people voted on the option "innovative", counting with 49 and 46, before and after the presentation, respectively. While "artificial" had 29 and 20 votes respectively on the questionnaire before and after, it decreased drastically on the second time, leading to a majority of positive vocabulary to rein when perceiving 3DFP technologies. The "Other" words were the following: "Mysterious" and "Creative", before the explanation and "Creative", "Curious", "Different" and "Decorative", after the showcase.

Figure 3. Sample's words association when thinking about 3D food printing
(Own source)

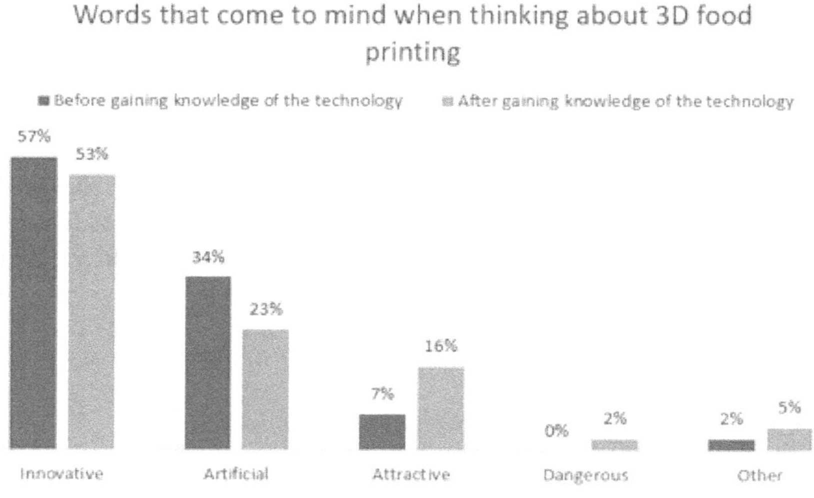

Prior to the presentation, there was an average of 3,86 and a standard deviation of 0,897 for interest in digital gastronomy. Conversely, the interest following contact with the printed materials had a standard deviation of 0.914 and a mean of 3,85.

A Spearman's rank-order correlation was run to determine the relationship between the perceptions before and after the presentation. There was a strong, positive correlation between both instances, which was statistically significant ($r_s(85) = 0{,}680$, $p < 0{,}001$).

The Wilcoxon signed-ranked test showed that the presentation did not elicit a statistically significant change in perception of use of 3DFP items in restaurants ($Z = -0{,}116$, $p = 0{,}908$). As expected, since both medians were rated as 3,86 and 3,85 before and after the presentation, respectively. Individual's 3D printed food trying interest decreased in average 0.012 points.

There were 242 subjects in the sample for the second assessment, mostly comprised by people present on the Estoril Higher Institute for Tourism and Hotel Studies, this led to a panel mostly composed of university students and professors, but as well a few other bystanders, gathered on multiple days of events happening at the school. The results of the demographic factors from the second questionnaire are shown in Table 4.

Table 4. Hedonic analysis demographic variables results (own source)

Demographic variables	*n (N= 242)*	*Percentages*
Gender		
Masculine	115	48%
Feminine	127	52%
Prefer not to answer	0	0%
Age		
≤17	9	4%
18-27	186	77%
≥28	47	19%
Nationality		
Portuguese	241	88%
Other	28	12%
Academic degree		
High School	151	62%
Licentiate degree	65	27%
Master's degree	19	8%
Doctorate	97	3%
Scientific area		
Food production	66	27%
Tourism	40	16%
Management	86	36%
Other	50	21%

The two different products—the rice cracker (code: K3C), which is printed like a sardine, and the vegan tuna sashimi (code: P9D), which is made of kidney beans—were subjected to a sensory study. An acceptability scale of nine points was utilized for every sample, in which the following description was attributed: 1- Extremely dislike; 2- Dislike a lot; 3- Moderate dislike; 4- Slightly dislike; 5- Indifferent; 6- Slightly like; 7- Moderate like; 8- Like a lot; 9- Extremely like.

For the first analysis the mean was 7,03, while both the mode and median were 7, and a standard deviation of 1,345.

Figure 4. K3C hedonic analysis result's bar chart
(Own source)

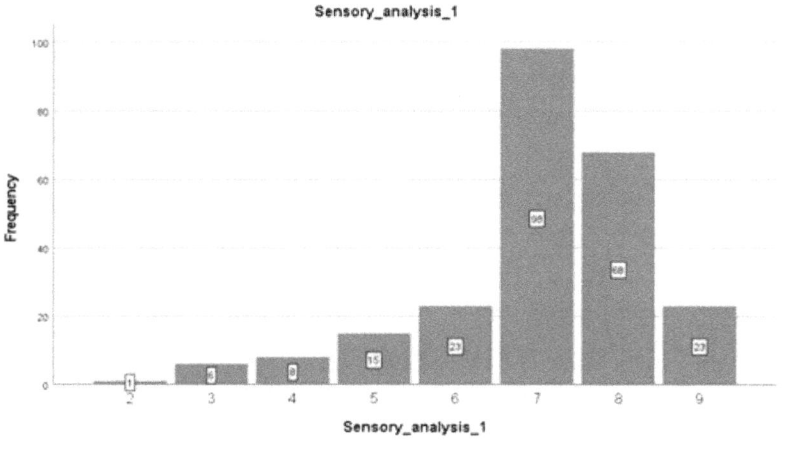

For the latter the mean was 6,02 and again both the mode and median were 7, while the standard deviation was 2,245.

Figure 5. P9D hedonic analysis result's bar chart
(Own source)

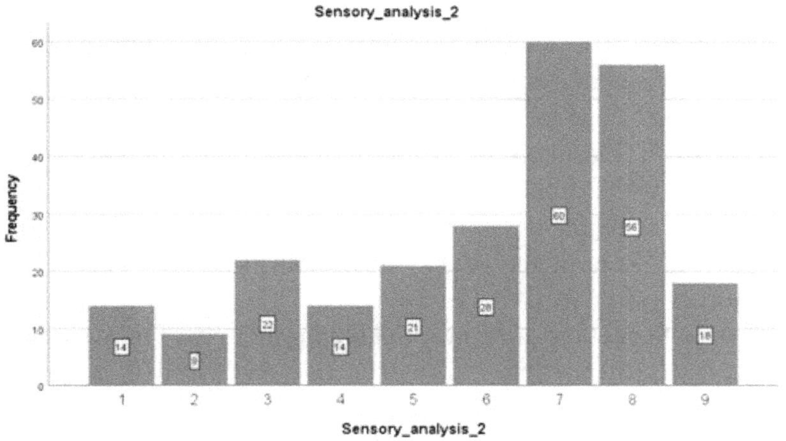

Prior to the hedonic analysis, interest in digital gastronomy had a mean of 3,55 and a standard deviation of 0,878. Conversely, the interest following interaction with the printed materials had a standard deviation of 1,053 and a mean of 3,81.

A Spearman's rank-order correlation was run to determine the relationship between the perceptions before and after the hedonic analysis. There was a moderate, positive correlation between both instances, which was statistically significant ($rs(242) = 0,433$, $p < 0,001$).

After the Wilcoxon signed-ranked test was run, we can say that the hedonic analysis had significant difference between both measurements. Thus, making it seem to indicate that the perception of digital gastronomy had a significant increase after the hedonic analysis ($Z = -3,834$, $p < 0,001$). After tasting the printed products, customers' interest in trying 3D printed food items in a restaurant setting grew by an average of 0.260 points.

DISCUSSION

The findings show that most people were at least aware of 3DFP technology and would be willing to give it a try if given the chance. This contradicts the majority of the examined studies done until this day. (Lupton and Turner, 2018b; Brunner et al., 2017 Feng et al., 2022; Manstan and McSweeney, 2020; Jenkins et al., 2021; Jayaprakash et al., 2020) and is consistent with Mantihal et al. (2019) given that both investigations were conducted in academic environments. It was also associated with a very low level of food technology neophobia among the majority of participants, as their taste experience was either positively or negatively impacted by their prior knowledge that the food product they were about to eat was 3D printed. However, more research is needed to determine whether or not knowing that a product was 3D printed before consumption affects the sensory analysis. The possible application of a Food Technology Neophobia Scale may also be used to corroborate these findings (Matin et al., 2012; Martins et al., 2019). This departure from previous research can be explained by the simple fact that during the time between the experiments, more information about the technology was made available through the media and publicity, enabling people to more easily assess both its perceived danger and utility (Chua, 2020).

Despite what the author suggested, 3D food printing was primarily associated with positive terms, such as Innovative, Attractive, and Creative, as opposed to the negative lexicon seen in the studies of Brunner et al. (2017) and Lupton and Turner (2018b). Thus, proving that the public's impression of the technology remained unaffected by the term "Printing" when referring to it (Brunner et al., 2017). This is important to note because word association has a significant impact on how people perceive food and food technologies (Lee et al., 2021). For instance, the term "lab grown meat" may emphasize the unnaturalness of the process more than other names, like "clean meat," which may even emphasize advantages. This word connection is easily applicable to 3DFP and may encourage the naturalistic fallacy in subsequent decision-making. (Bryant and Barnett, 2019).

It was possible to ascertain that there was a positive variance on public perception of 3D food printing after the acknowledgement on the practical approaches, while on the theoretical it was inexistent. The first result correlates to the statements made by Siegrist et al. (2013) and goes in accordance with the results shown by Lee et al. (2021), which demonstrated a positive effect on increasing the public perception of 3D food printing when focusing on specific attributes of the technology, most notably, health benefits, natural content, fun and creativity, from which "natural content" showed a higher increase on utilitarian value and hedonic perception of 3D printed food items. On the same manner, Manstan and McSweeney (2020) indicated that after cognitive reception of the technology, consumers found 3D food printed products had a lower degree of processing than conventional products and were healthier than non-printed foods. However, they were less likely to buy or consume these products.

Contrary to early assumptions, the majority of participants reacted favorably to the prospect of ingesting 3D printed products at restaurants. This may possibly be related to the tested sample's lower level of food technology neophobia and general higher level of knowledge compared to other samples on related studies, which led to a more culinary adventurous population. (Harun et al., 2020; Çöl et al., 2023). It is also feasible to ascertain that public perception of 3D food products in restaurant settings has improved as a result of publicity, specifically when practical acknowledgement was applied (Siegrist, 2013; Feng et al., 2022; Manstan and McSweeney, 2020).

Although there was a correlation between the perceptions on the theoretical approach, its stagnation of variance before and after the presentation might have been due to the small sample size used of the low diversity in terms of age and academic degree, since it used mainly university students (Sampieri et al., 2003). Other factor might have been due to the presentation itself, which could have led to the bias of the final result (Decullier & Chapuis, 2007).

Both of the developed items received positive feedback; the first received an average of 7,03 points on a 9-point scale, and the second received 6,02 points. Both products had a median score of 7. This has to do with the fact that both hedonic analyses had a beneficial impact on the participants' perceptions. Resulting in the deduction that the perception score increased with the perceived hedonic score. These outcomes are consistent with those of Feng et al. (2022), who demonstrated that a group of food technology neophobes rated 3D products higher on the perceived quality scale than conventionally produced foods, both with and without additional information. The non-food neophobic group did not exhibit the same variance in their hedonic ratings, despite having a more positive attitude towards the printed objects. Additional research is required to corroborate these findings, confirming whether the same holds true for other food items and whether the typical receipt of the used goods might affect perception in a similar way as demonstrated here.

Although five of the seven AM technology types have already been applied to food printing, as can be seen from the bibliographic research, their actual application and utility are still primarily limited to three of these: powder bed fusion, binder jetting, and material extrusion—by far the most popular. (Nachal et al., 2019; Noort et al., 2017; Godoi et al., 2016). The focus on these manufacturing types is primarily determined by the inks that are currently available, which are still very limited in most cases but should increase exponentially in the coming years due to the wider adoption and research conducted with 3DFP, as well as by the commercial printers that focus on the material extrusion methodology. Particularly for the extrusion of thick pastes, purees, and sculptures made of chocolate.

Though the term "digital gastronomy" has been around for a while, 3DFP is essentially nonexistent in the small-scale food production market and is generally viewed negatively, as evidenced by the bibliographic research. It is also largely absent from the restaurant scene, with only six instances recorded, most of which involve the reuse of discarded products. Notably, none of these instances occur in Portugal (Tran, 2018; Dehue and Strikwerda, 2017). The most recent technological developments have been suggested to spark more interest in using this equipment (Mizrahi et al., 2016). In addition to this, other computational abilities like machine learning, artificial intelligence, and virtual and augmented reality may be included (Chisik et al., 2018; Yildirim and Yildirim, 2022; Çölet al., 2023). Or even the inclusion of more concepts from smart gastronomy.

Consumer perception plays a major role in the success of food products and food technology. There are several methods to ascertain this perspective, including the language used to describe it and its perceived risk or utility (Groot, 2019). Thus, understanding the factors that influence perception and the best ways to communicate knowledge to customers, dispel ignorance-based presumptions, and pave the way for potential advancements in food technology Neophobia is crucial for assessing a technology's long-term viability (McCluskey et al., 2016). This is evident in a number of other culinary technologies, such as lab-grown beef and ractopamine pork, which the public became averse to due to ineffective marketing and informational efforts (Jenkins et al., 2021; Gayler et al., 2018; Bryant and Barnett, 2019). Conversely, we may look at examples of once-dreaded food production methods that have become commonplace today, such as microwaves, organic products, and genetically modified food, all of which can be attributed to successful customer awareness and demand (Hidalgo-Baz et al., 2017; Matin et al., 2012).

A few restrictions on the products and information still available on 3DFP technology, as well as the use of printers that are still in development—which requires users to define a number of parameters and pay close attention during the print process. Compared to traditional cooking, these factors pose a significant obstacle because of the way they function, converting an otherwise simple operation into a difficult one. One potential constraint on this study could have been the panel's exclusive focus on academics and the low number of inquiries on the first study. This could have resulted in the notion that additional research is necessary to validate certain findings, like the necessity of a more extensive age distribution and a wider range of academic accomplishments and scientific domains. An extra questionnaire, such as the proposed Food Technology Neophobia Scale, was necessary to provide support to the findings of this inquiry due to the lack of a concrete control for food technology neophobia (Matin et al., 2012; Martins et al., 2019). Furthermore, as was previously mentioned, perception is a complex topic with many contextual factors, including cultural and societal norms, which may have an impact on the evaluation of the technology and goods that are ultimately used.

CONCLUSION AND FUTURE RESEARCH PROPOSALS

The current study sought to ascertain whether Additive Manufacturing technology could be introduced into Portuguese small-scale food production lines, as well as to identify key players and suggest value chain models that would best facilitate the tech's appropriate popularization and influence on dietary habits. In addition, the effects they had on the perception of the 3D Food Printing population were examined using two distinct information transmission techniques.

For this purpose, it was suggested that two printed food items based on cereal and legumes be developed and optimized. A vegan "tuna" sashimi and a fish-shaped rice cracker were created specifically for this use. Both goods received positive feedback, concluding with average scores of 6,02 and 7,03 points, respectively, on their subsequent hedonic study. At the same time, the questionnaires showed that most people were aware of the technology prior to both approaches, and correlated it with positive words, such as "Innovative", "Attractive" and "Creative". It was also possible to determine a positive correlation between the practical cognitive approach and the perception of use of the technology in restaurant environments, although the theoretical had no effect on variance.

Aside from this, after the bibliographic examination it was found that five Additive Manufacturing technologies have been applied to the food manufacturing industry, with powder bed fusion, binder jetting, and material extrusion being the most widely utilized ones. (Nachal et al., 2019; Noort et al., 2017; Godoi et al., 2016). The sorts of printers that are now on the market also support this trend, with the Netherlands, the United States of America, Spain, China, and the United Kingdom being the countries with the largest printer development teams. (Kunz, 2023).

Food services (Jayaprakash et al., 2020; Pinna et al., 2016), personalized nutrition (Derrosi et al., 2021; Escalante-Aburto et al., 2021; Lorenz et al., 2022), sustainability food waste reduction (Lupton & Turner, 2018a), and, finally, in special cases, such as military spatial and domestic uses (Enfield et al., 2022; Lui et al., 2017), are the categories into which 3D food printing is proposed for use in this study. Although the possibility of using it on the restaurant production line has been suggested for a while, it is still rarely used for this purpose. However, as this study has shown, with the most recent developments in computational technology, such as machine learning, artificial intelligence, virtual reality, and augmented realities, now is the ideal time to invest in this manufacturing method. (Tran, 2018; Dehue & Strikwerda, 2017; Mizrahi et al., 2016; Chisik, Pons & Jaen, 2018; Yildirim & Yildirim, 2022; Çöl, Imre & Yıkmış, 2023).

Future research should confirm the presence of aversion to 3D Food Printing on the current market using the Food Technology Neophobia Scale as previously proposed, as the results of this study indicate a decrease in neophobia when compared to past investigations. These assessments should concentrate on other populations with historically different cognitive profiles, and compare the results presented here with different gastronomic customs. It is also necessary to consider the requirement for a study to examine a larger sample that is not limited to an academic setting. More diverse product categories and extrusion pastes should be taken into account, not just from a technical and design perspective but also with sustainability as the main goal. In conclusion, more research on the safety of food in relation to 3D food printing products is needed. This research should focus on microbiological assessments as well as the time it takes to print various products and compare it to traditional methods of production. Only then will it be possible to better understand the supply chains that this new technology proposes and develop potential solutions for any risks related to the printers.

REFERENCES

Abdulhameed, O., Al-Ahmari, A., & Mian, S. H. (2019). Additive manufacturing: Challenges, trends, and applications. *Advances in Mechanical Engineering*, *11*(2), 1–27. doi:10.1177/1687814018822880

Aniket, K., & Roshan, D. (2022). *Food 3D Printing Market Research, 2031*. Allied Market Research. https://www.alliedmarketresearch.com/food-3d-printing-market-A08587

Aniket, K., & Roshan, D. (2022). Food 3D Printing Market Research, 2031. *Allied Market Research*. https://www.alliedmarketresearch.com/food-3d-printing-market-A08587

Aniwaa (2022). *Food 3D Printer by Micromake*. Available at: https://www.aniwaa.com/product/3d-printers/micromake-food-3d-printer/ [accessed 6 February 2023].

Anzaldúa-Morales, A. (2005). *La evaluación sensorial de los alimentos en la teoria y la práctica*. Zaragoza: Editorial Acribia, S.A.

Bourell, D. L. (2016). Perspectives on Additive Manufacturing. *Annual Review of Materials Research*, *46*(1), 1–18. doi:10.1146/annurev-matsci-070115-031606

Brunner, T. A., Delley, M., & Denkel, C. (2017). Consumers' attitudes and change of attitude toward 3D-printed food. *Food Quality and Preference*, *68*(December), 389–396.

Cascio, W. F., & Montealegre, R. (2016). How Technology Is Changing Work and Organizations. *Annual Review of Organizational Psychology and Organizational Behavior*, *3*(1), 349–379. doi:10.1146/annurev-orgpsych-041015-062352

Caulier, S., Doets, E., & Noort, M. (2020). An exploratory consumer study of 3D printed food perception in a real-life military setting. *Food Quality and Preference*, *86*(June), 1–5. doi:10.1016/j.foodqual.2020.104001

Cheng, Y., Fu, Y., Ma, L., Yap, P. L., Losic, D., Wang, H., & Zhang, Y. (2022). Rheology of edible food inks from 2D/3D/4D printing, and its role in future 5D/6D printing. *Food Hydrocolloids, 132*(3), 1–34. doi:10.1016/j.foodhyd.2022.107855

Chisik, Y., Pons, P., & Jaen, J. (2018). Gastronomy Meets Ludology: Towards a Definition of What it Means to Play with Your (Digital) Food. In *CHI PLAY'18 Extended Abstracts* (pp. 155–168). Association for Computing Machinery. doi:10.1145/3270316.3272056

Chua, C. K. (2020). Publication Trends in 3D Bioprinting and 3D Food Printing. *International Journal of Bioprinting, 6*(1), 1–3. doi:10.18063/IJB.2017.01.003 PMID:32923736

Çöl, B. G., İmre, M., & Yıkmış, S. (2023). Virtual reality and augmented reality technologies in gastronomy: A review. *eFood, 4*(83), 1–16.

Cristea, M., Noja, G. G., Stefea, P., & Sala, A. L. (2020). The Impact of Population Aging and Public Health Support on EU Labor Markets. *International Journal of Environmental Research and Public Health, 17*(4), 1–27. doi:10.3390/ijerph17041439 PMID:32102277

Dabbene, L., Ramundo, L., & Terzi, S. (2018). Economic model for the evaluation of 3D food printing. In*: 2018 IEEE International Conference on Engineering, Technology and Innovation (ICE/ITMC)*. Stuttgart, Germany: ICE/ITMC. 10.1109/ICE.2018.8436285

Deculier, E., & Chapuis, F. (2007). Oral presentation bias: A retrospective cohort study. *Journal of Epidemiology and Community Health, 61*(3), 190–193. doi:10.1136/jech.2006.048603 PMID:17325393

Dehue, R., & Stikwerda, P. (2017). *4 Famous Restaurants that Use 3D Printers*. 3D Printing. https://3dprinting.com/food/4-famous-restaurants-that-use-3d-printers/

Enfield, R. E., Pandya, J. K., Lu, J., McClements, D. J., & Kinchia, A. J. (2022). The future of 3D food printing: Opportunities for space applications. *Critical Reviews in Food Science and Nutrition*, 1–14. PMID:35652158

Escalante-Aburto, A., Santiago, G. T., Álvarez, M. M., & Chuck-Hernández, C. (2021). Advances and prospective applications of 3D food printing for health improvement and personalized nutrition. *Comprehensive Reviews in Food Science and Food Safety, 20*(6), 5722–5741. doi:10.1111/1541-4337.12849 PMID:34643023

Feng, X., Kehemacheevakul, K., Siller, S. D. L., Wolodko, J., & Wismer, W. (2022). Effect of Labelling and Information on Consumer Perception of Foods Presented as 3D Printed. *Foods*, *11*(6), 1–15. doi:10.3390/foods11060809 PMID:35327230

Frey, C. B., & Osborne, M. A. (2017). The future of employment: How susceptible are jobs to computerisation? *Technological Forecasting and Social Change*, *114*, 254–280. doi:10.1016/j.techfore.2016.08.019

Gim, M., Park, D., Spranger, M., Maruyama, K., & Kang, J. (2021). RecipeBowl: A Cooking Recommender for Ingredients and Recipes Using Set Transformer. *IEEE Access : Practical Innovations, Open Solutions*, *9*, 143623–143633. doi:10.1109/ACCESS.2021.3120265

Godoi, F. C., Prakash, S., & Bhandari, B. R. (2016). 3d printing technologies applied for food design: Status and prospects. *Journal of Food Engineering*, *179*, 44–54. doi:10.1016/j.jfoodeng.2016.01.025

Gosine, L., Kean, B., Parsons, C., & McSweeney, M. B. (2021). Using a 3D food printer as a teaching tool: Focus groups with dietitians, teachers, and nutrition students. *Journal of Food Science Education*, *20*(1), 18–25. doi:10.1111/1541-4329.12216

Groot, S. (2019). *Effect of perceived risks, naturalness, usefulness and ease of use on the consumer acceptance of 3D food printing* [Bachelor's Thesis, Wageningen University, Netherlands].

Guadagno, M. C., Loss, J. M., & Pearce, J. M. (2021). Open Source 3D-Printable Planetary Roller Screw for Food Processing Applications. *Technologies*, *9*(2), 1–26. doi:10.3390/technologies9020024

Guo, C., Zhang, M., & Bhandari, B. (2019). A comparative study between syringe-based and screw-based 3D food printers by computational simulation. *Computers and Electronics in Agriculture*, *162*, 397–404. doi:10.1016/j.compag.2019.04.032

Hjalager, A. (2022). Digital Food and the Innovation of Gastronomic Tourism. *Journal of Gastronomy and Tourism*, *7*(1), 35–49. doi:10.3727/216929722X16354101932186

International Organization for Standardization. (2012). *ISO 8373:2012(en) Robots and robotic devices – Vocabulary*. ISO. https://www.iso.org/obp/ui/#iso:std:iso:8373:ed-2:v1:en:term:2.2, [accessed at 09/11/2023].

ISO/ASTM 52900. (2015). *Additive manufacturing — General principles — Terminology.* ISO/ASME International.

Ivanov, S., Seyitoğlu, F., & Markova, M. (2020). Hotel managers' perceptions towards the use of robots: A mixed-methods approach. *Information Technology & Tourism*, *22*(4), 505–535. doi:10.1007/s40558-020-00187-x

Ivanov, S., & Webster, C. (2019a). What should robots do? A comparative analysis of industry professionals, educators and tourists. In Pesonen, J., & Neidhardt, J. (Eds.) *Information and Communication Technologies in Tourism 2019, Proceedings of the International Conference in Nicosia*. Springer. 10.1007/978-3-030-05940-8_20

Ivanov, S., & Webster, C. (2019b). Perceived appropriateness and intention to use service robots in tourism. In Pesonen, J. & Neidhardt, J. (Eds.) *Information and Communication Technologies in Tourism 2019, Proceedings of the International Conference in Nicosia*. Springer. 10.1007/978-3-030-05940-8_19

Ivanov, S., Webster, C., & Berezina, K. (2017). Adoption of robots and service automation by tourism and hospitality companies. *Revista Tursmo & Desenvolvimento, n.º 27/28*, 1501-1517.

Jayaprakash, S. (2017). *Role of Prosumer Driven 3D Food Printingin Innovating Food Value Chains* [Master's Thesis, Aalto University, Finland].

Jayaprakash, S., Paasi, J., Pennamen, K., Ituarte, I. F., Lille, M., Partanen, J., & Sozer, N. (2020). Techno-economic prospects and desirability of 3d food printing: Perspectives of industrial experts, researchers and consumers. *Foods*, *9*(2), 1–23. doi:10.3390/foods9121725 PMID:33255289

Jenkins, S. C., Harris, A. J. L., & Osman, M. (2021). What drives risk perceptions? Revisiting public perceptions of food hazards associated with production and consumption. *Journal of Risk Research*, *24*(11), 1450–1464. doi:10.1080/13669877.2020.1871057

Kim, N., Cepeta, B., Kim, J., Yue, G., Kim, S., & Kim, H. (2018). IoT controlled screw-type 3d food printer using single line design technique. *Proceedings - 2018 International Conference on Computational Science and Computational Intelligence (CSCI)*. Las Vegas, USA: Association for Computing Machinery.

Kouzani, A. Z., Adams, S., Whyte, D. J., Oliver, R., Hemsley, B., Palmer, S., & Balandin, S. (2017). 3D Printing of Food for People with Swallowing Difficulties. *KnE Engineering*, *2*(2), 23–29. doi:10.18502/keg.v2i2.591

Kunz, E. (2023) 3D Food Printing Market Size & Share to Surpass $872.4 Million by 2028 | Vantage Market Research. *Vantage Market Research.* Globe News Wire. https://www.globenewswire.com/news-release/2023/03/09/2623870/0/en/3D-Food-Printing-Market-Size-Share-to-Surpass-872-4-Million-by-2028-Vantage-Market-Research.html

Lawless, H. T., & Heymann, H. (2010). *Sensory Evaluation of Food Principles and Practices* (2nd ed.). Springer. doi:10.1007/978-1-4419-6488-5

Lee, J. (2021). A 3D Food Printing Process for the New Normal Era: A Review. *Processes (Basel, Switzerland)*, *9*(9), 1–21. doi:10.3390/pr9091495

Lee, K. H., Hwang, K. H., Kim, M., & Cho, M. (2021). 3D printed food attributes and their roles within the value-attitude-behavior model: Moderating effects of food neophobia and food technology neophobia. *Journal of Hospitality and Tourism Management*, *48*, 46–54. doi:10.1016/j.jhtm.2021.05.013

Lin, Y., Punpongsanon, P., Wen, X., Iwai, D., Sato, K., Obrist, M., & Muller, S. (2020). FoodFab: Creating Food Perception Illusions using Food 3D Printing. In *CHI 2020* (pp. 1–13). Association for Computing Machinery. doi:10.1145/3313831.3376421

Lipton, J. L. (2017). Printable food: The technology and its application in human health. *Current Opinion in Biotechnology*, *44*, 198–201. doi:10.1016/j.copbio.2016.11.015 PMID:28327427

Lorenz, T., Iskandar, M. M., Baeghbali, V., Ngadi, M. O., & Kubow, S. (2022). 3D Food Printing Applications Related to Dysphagia:A Narrative Review. *Foods*, *11*(12), 1–15. doi:10.3390/foods11121789 PMID:35741992

Lupton, D., & Turner, B. (2018a). 'Both Fascinating and Disturbing': Consumer Responses to 3D Food Printing and Implications for Food Activism. In T. Schneider, K. Eli, C. Dolan, & S. Ulijaszek (Eds.), *Digital Food Activism* (pp. 151–167). Routledge.

Lupton, D., & Turner, B. (2018b). Food of the Future? Consumer Responses to the Idea of 3D-Printed Meat and Insect-Based Foods. *Food & Foodways*, *26*(4), 269–289. doi:10.1080/07409710.2018.1531213

Manstan, T., & McSweeney, M. B. (2020). Consumers' attitudes towards and acceptance of 3D printed foods in comparison with conventional food products. *International Journal of Food Science & Technology*, *55*(1), 323–331. doi:10.1111/ijfs.14292

Mantihal, S., Kobun, R., & Lee, B. (2020). 3D food printing of as the new way of preparing food: A review. *International Journal of Gastronomy and Food Science*, *22*, 1–10. doi:10.1016/j.ijgfs.2020.100260

Mantihal, S., Prakash, S., & Bhandari, B. (2019). Texture-modified 3D printed dark chocolate: Sensory evaluation and consumer perception study. *Journal of Texture Studies*, *50*(5), 386–399. doi:10.1111/jtxs.12472 PMID:31323141

McCluskey, J. J., Kalaitzandonakes, N., & Swinnen, J. (2016). Media coverage, public perceptions, and consumer behavior: Insights from new food technologies. *Annual Review of Resource Economics*, *8*(1), 467–486. doi:10.1146/annurev-resource-100913-012630

Mizrahi, A. B., Lachnish, A. Z., & Zoran, A. R. (2023). Digital gastronomy testcase: A complete pipeline of robotic induced dish variations. *International Journal of Gastronomy and Food Science*, *31*, 1–14.

Mizrahi, M., Golan, A., Mizrahi, A. B., Gruber, R., Lachnish, A. Z., & Zoran, A. (2016). Digital Gastronomy: Methods & Recipes for Hybrid Cooking. *In: UIST 2016 - Proceedings of the 29th Annual Symposium on User Interface Software and Technology*. Tokyo, Japan: Association for Computing Machinery.

Nachal, N., Moses, J. A., Karthik, P., & Anandharamakrishnan, C. (2019). Applications of 3D Printing in Food Processing. *Food Engineering Reviews*, *11*(3), 123–141. doi:10.1007/s12393-019-09199-8

Nassar, M. A., & Fouad, A. (2022). Tomorrow Taste Comes Today: Exploring Customers' Intention to Buy 3D Printed Food in Egyptian Restaurants. *Pharos International Journal of Tourism and Hospitality*, *1*(1), 31–48. doi:10.21608/pijth.2022.264346

Noort, M., van Bommel, K., & Renzetti, S. (2017). 3D-Printed Cereal Foods. *Cereal Foods World*, *62*(6), 272–277. doi:10.1094/CFW-62-6-0272

Peshave, J., & Hodlur, A. (2022). 3D Printing-The Future In Culinary Arts! *Multi-Disciplinary Journal*, *1*(2), 1–7.

Pinna, C., Ramundo, L., Sisca, F. G., Angioletti, C. M., Taisch, M., & Terzi, S. (2016). Additive Manufacturing applications within Food industry: an actual overview and future opportunities. XXI Summer School "Francesco Turco" - Industrial Systems Engineering, (pp. 18-24).

Rogers, H., & Srivastava, M. (2021). Emerging sustainable supply chain models for 3d food printing. *Sustainability (Basel)*, *13*(21), 1–18. doi:10.3390/su132112085

Sampieri, R. H., Collado, C. F., & Lucio, P. B. (2003). *Metodologia de Pesquisa* (3rd ed.). The McGraw-Hill Interamericana do Brasil Ltda.

Scott, E. (2023) 3D Food Printing Market Size, Share, and Key Insight. *Food and Agriculture Market News*. https://www.linkedin.com/pulse/3d-food-printing-market-size-share-key-insight-edward-scott/

Seyitoglu, F., & Ivanov, S. (2022). Understanding the robotic restaurant experience: A multiple case study. *Journal of Tourism Futures*, *8*(1), 55–72. doi:10.1108/JTF-04-2020-0070

Sher, D., & Tutó, X. (2010). Material characterisation and process development for chocolate additive layer manufacturing. *Virtual and Physical Prototyping*, *5*(2), 57–64. doi:10.1080/17452751003753212

Siegrist, M., Hartmann, C., & Keller, C. (2013). Antecedents of food neophobia and its association with eating behavior and food choices. *Food Quality and Preference*, *30*(2), 293–298. doi:10.1016/j.foodqual.2013.06.013

Singhal, S., Rasane, P., Kaur, S., Garba, U., Bankar, A., Singh, J., & Gupta, N. (2020). 3D food printing: Paving way towards novel foods. *Anais da Academia Brasileira de Ciências*, *92*(3), 1–26. doi:10.1590/0001-3765202020180737 PMID:33053099

Soni, R., Ponappa, K., & Tandon, P. (2022). A review on customized food fabrication process using Food Layered Manufacturing. *Lebensmittel-Wissenschaft + Technologie*, *161*(113411), 1–8. doi:10.1016/j.lwt.2022.113411

Sun, J., Peng, Z. Y., Liangkun, F., Jerry, Y. H., & Hong, G. S. (2015a). 3D food printing—An innovative way of mass customization in food fabrication. *International Journal of Bioprinting*, *1*(1), 27–38. doi:10.18063/IJB.2015.01.006

Sun, J., Zhou, W., Huang, D., Fuh, J. Y. H., & Hong, G. S. (2015b). An Overview of 3D Printing Technologies for Food Fabrication. *Food and Bioprocess Technology*, *8*(8), 1605–1615. doi:10.1007/s11947-015-1528-6

Tran, J. L. (2018). 3D-Printed Foods. *Minnesota Journal of Law, Science & Technology*, *17*(2), 856–880.

Tuorila, H., & Hartmann, C. (2020). Consumer responses to novel and unfamiliar foods. *Current Opinion in Food Science*, *33*, 1–8. doi:10.1016/j.cofs.2019.09.004

Vogt, S. (2017). *3D Food printing: What options the new technology offers*. DLG.

Voon, S. L., An, J., Wong, G., Zhang, Y., & Chua, C. K. (2019). 3D food printing: A categorised review of inks and their development. *Virtual and Physical Prototyping, 14*(3), 203–218. doi:10.1080/17452759.2019.1603508

Webster, C., & Ivanov, S. (2019). Robotics, artificial intelligence, and the evolving nature of work. In B. George & J. Paul (Eds.), *Business Transformation in Data Driven Societies*. Palgrave-MacMillan.

Webster, C., & Ivanov, S. (2020). *Robots in Travel, Tourism and Hospitality: Key Findings from a global study*. Zangador.

Yildirim, H., & Yildirim, Y. (2022). Digital Gastronomy and the Tables of Future. *Van Yüzüncü Yıl Üniversitesi İktisadi ve İdari Bilimler Fakültesi Dergisi, 8*(15), 1–14.

Zhu, S., Ribberink, M., Wit, M., Schutyser, M., & Stieger, M. (2020). Modifying sensory perception of chocolate coated rice waffles through bite-to-bite contrast: An application case study using 3D inkjet printing. *Food & Function, 11*(12), 10580–10587. doi:10.1039/D0FO01787F PMID:33188381

Zoran, A. (2019). Cooking With Computers: The Vision of Digital Gastronomy [Point of View]. *Proceedings of the IEEE, 107*(8), 1467–1473. doi:10.1109/JPROC.2019.2925262

Zvirbule, A., Auzina, A., & Griberta-Zalite, G. (2023). Gastronomic tourism and smart solutions used for its development: The case of a region of Latvia. *Worldwide Hospitality and Tourism Themes, 15*(5), 570–580. doi:10.1108/WHATT-06-2023-0076

Chapter 8
Circular Economy and Sustainable Tourism Management:
Uncertainties and Challenges Ahead

Josep Boyra
Escola Universitària Formatic Barcelona, University of Girona, Spain

Anna Alvado
Escola Universitària Formatic Barcelona, University of Girona, Spain

Jordi Garcia
Escola Universitària Formatic Barcelona, University of Girona, Spain

Jucinara Schena
Escola Universitària Formatic Barcelona, University of Girona, Spain

Joan Sorribes
Escola Universitària Formatic Barcelona, University of Girona, Spain

Joaquin Garcia-Lavernia
Escola Universitària Formatic Barcelona, University of Girona, Spain

ABSTRACT

This chapter will carry out an analysis of several factors of environmental and social change and its impacts in terms of tourism development and economic performance. A number of alternative mitigation measures will then be analyzed to counteract the negative effects on environmental and social components by the adoption of guidelines associated with more sustainable practices provided by a circular economy approach. Afterwards, the scope of tourism management practices and social media strategies for a sustainable tourism interactivity based on computational technologies will be discussed. Finally, a series of recommendations, further research directions and conclusions derived from the analysis conducted will be presented.

DOI: 10.4018/979-8-3693-0960-5.ch008

INTRODUCTION

Numerous factors of environmental decline have caused along the years an increasing awareness among public authorities and tourists about the need to adopt more sustainable patterns of consumption in order to guarantee the viability of destinations over time. Tourism industry and most local bodies consider nowadays sustainable development principles and practices as an opportunity to preserve their own territorial resources through integrated policy, sustainable planning and responsible management. Nevertheless, it has proven extremely difficult to go from theory to practice despite the time elapsed (Boyra, 2003, 2005, 2009) since environmental concern was internationally brought up in 1972 by Meadows et al.

Carrying capacity approaches to measure tourism impacts have been widely applied in tourism and recreation studies since the 1960s, although some authors trace its emergence to as far back as 1930. Although carrying capacity can be viewed as an important theoretical milestone (Coccossis et al., 2002) it has become less popular in recent years as sustainable tourism and its associated theoretical models have come to dominate discussions of the management of tourism and its impacts.

Some of the most recent models used today to analyze and forecast the development of a destination are: Limits of Acceptable Change (LAC), Visitor Impact Management (VIM), Visitor Experience and Resource Protection (VERP), Recreation Opportunity Spectrum (ROS), Visitor Activity Management Process (VAMP) and Tourism Optimization Management Model (TOMM) (Lindberg et al., 1997; Komsary et al., 2018). The aim of this chapter is to raise a series of questions that allow academic discussion and reflection and at the same time enrich the debate on how to continue to make tourism prosper in the digital era while overcoming the threats that loom over the future of human development.

BACKGROUND

The Pursuit of a Circular Economy for a Sustainable Development

Global economic consumption and production does not exist within a vacuum but relies on resource stocks and flows in our Earth System, acting as a limit to growth. By managing stocks and flows appropriately, and helping to preserve, restore and develop environmental and natural capital, a circular economy contributes to a steady system state, minimizing the risks from resource depletion significant interlinked policy challenges, and able to deliver a sustainable vision for the future (United Nations, 2020a). At the macroeconomic level, a circular economy implies an adaptation of economic growth based on the responsible use of natural resources and inputs.

Ideally, the rate of resource extraction ought to remain below the rate of resource consumption, and the rate of waste production ought to remain below the environment's ability to absorb and transform the waste. A circular economy (see figure 1) *can also be seen as a regenerative system in which resource input and waste, emissions, and energy leakages are minimized through long-lasting design, maintenance, repair, reuse, sharing, remanufacturing, refurbishing, and recycling activities* (United Nations Economist Network, 2023).

Figure 1. Circular economy
Source: United Nations, 2020b

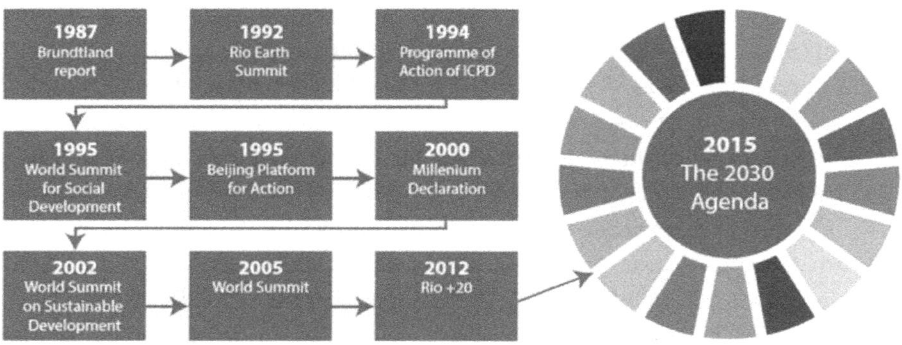

A circular economy is presented as "one of the current sustainable economic models, in which products and materials are designed in such a way that they can be reused, remanufactured, recycled or recovered (4-R) and thus maintained in the economy for as long as possible, along with the resources of which they are made, and the generation of waste, especially hazardous waste, is avoided or minimized, and greenhouse gas emissions are prevented or reduced". The definition highlights the 4-R framework for making the circular economy possible through more resource efficient processes, with life cycle considerations, and the prevention of programmed obsolescence. A circular economy thus provides an alternative to the "take-make-waste" linear model (United Nations, 2020c).

In this sense, different examples of solutions from the tourist industry as innovative greywater recycling in hotels, electric charging stations in tourist destinations, artificial intelligence for measuring food waste, biodigesters on board of cruises or nudging electric vehicle use constitute circular economy initiatives minimizing the impacts of the still predominant linear model of development. These types of initiatives have resulted in various benefits, including cost reduction, socioeconomic and environmental impacts, supply chain sustainability, energy efficiency, development of new skills and capabilities, enhanced brand reputation, and improved competitive advantage (Axhami et al. 2023).

Although the more recent examples for developing the implementation of suitable management practices in terms of circular economy and sustainable tourism the outcomes still clearly fragmentary and insufficient. Nevertheless, these practices, if generalized, demonstrate that is possible to reverse, at least to some extent the impacts of an extractive economic model still on place. As a sample of this management practices is relevant to note the agenda of the Economic Commission for Europe Committee on Environmental Policy Special session hold in Geneva, 9–12 May 2022 in the framework of the Ninth Environment for Europe Ministerial Conference and its substantive thematic documents dedicated to applying principles of circular economy to sustainable tourism (United Nations Economic Commission for Europe, 2022). Among the initiatives implemented until now this thematic document gather different legislative initiatives and management practices at different scales, that is, six current solutions on a macro level, six current solutions on a micro level, as well as 6 solutions on an organizational level. Among others it is worth highlighting, on a macro level, the Circular Economy Action Plan, as part of the European Green Deal, approved by the European Commission aiming at the implementation of a series of actions foreseen with regards to electronics and information and communication technologies, packaging, plastics, textiles, construction, buildings, and food which are highly relevant to accelerate a tourism industry transition towards a circular economic model that reduces its consumption footprint, increases its material circularity, and gives back to the planet more than it takes.

Another current solution is the CEnTOUR Project; CEnTOUR is a COSME EU project which aims to support tourism small and medium enterprises (SMEs) across five European countries. As SMEs often lack the necessary knowhow and tools to embrace circular economy in their operations this project is a relevant initiative. Among the ongoing outcomes of the project, they have developed a database of best practices implemented by SMEs in the transition towards circular economy which can be easily filtered by providers (e.g., campsites, restaurants, resorts…) likewise the project has led to the publication of a handbook called "Managing the transition to circular economy for tourism providers" (CEnTour, 2020).

The NH Hotels CORK2CORK initiative launched in 2011 is another current solution, on an organizational level, that the applying principles of circular economy to sustainable tourism gather by the United Nations Economic Commission for Europe (2022) thematic document highlights. The NH Hotel Group conceived the idea of recovering and reusing the cork stoppers from wine bottles with the leading producer of cork and cork covering materials Amorim. The recovered corks are turned into covering and insulation materials for subsequent use in the construction of new rooms. This initiative contributes to improve the hotel's energy efficiency as it acts as a heat insulator avoid the need for artificial temperature controls.

In terms of indicators to measure the progress towards circular tourism the thematic document of the Economic Commission for Europe published in 2022 states that circular tourism indicators are still in its infancy, specifically at a Pan-European level. This finding indicates that there is still a long way to go to reverse the effects of linear development.

The resilience of the tourist destination is based on the balance of its territorial nature components and its socioeconomic dimensions within and particular ecosystem that characterize it. In this sense, the quality of the tourist experience and the competitiveness of any local tourism industry is submitted through time to different factors of socioeconomic and environmental change. In fact, alike as one of many other economic activities competing in a territory, tourism development needs to be planned and managed within a sustainable and integrated framework if ecosystems are to be preserved.

Notwithstanding, the current model and pace of economic growth has proven unable to reverse social inequalities such as marginalization, poverty and hunger of a large number of people. Likewise, our means of production and consumption processes are bringing a series of negative impacts on the environment limiting thus the preservation of the ecosystems. The unlimited consumerism of postmodern societies is generating huge amount of greenhouse gas emissions causing climate change and toxic waste that cause and multiply human diseases that have serious effects on public health. Even so and despite the phenomenal and astonishing technological advances of this 21st century sovereign states have proven incapable of managing and combining their national interests with the needs of the international community as a whole.

These megatrends thus limit the probabilities of success and future development of the global community in the long term. In this context, any tourism development process is likely to be challenged by climate change sea level rise for different greenhouse gas and global warming pathways and other anthropogenic drivers such as overpopulation, land-use change, pollution, overexploitation of natural resources (Doxey, 1975; Settele et al. 2014). Therefore, it is essential to take into account the different means of production and consumption and its impacts on the environment to preserve the quality of both natural and social territorial resources at a regional scale on which tourist destinations are based adopting a more circular economy through more resource efficient use processes, the implementation of mechanisms for the integrated design of the life cycle of products and services, and the prevention of programmed obsolescence.

Nevertheless, and in the meanwhile, tourist destinations as well as their ecosystems, are increasingly sensitive and vulnerable to anthropogenic factors. An ever more growing concern about how to cope with and adapt to these further development challenges have been placed at the center of the international agenda. The report of the Program of Research on Climate Change Vulnerability, Impacts and Adaptation (United Nations Environment Program, 2013) analyzes a series of adaptation strategies to cope with widespread climate change impacts in specific human and natural systems affecting many weather and climate extremes with adverse impacts and related losses and damages to nature and people. Understanding adaptation in coupled human and natural systems requires understanding of the degree and nature of observed and projected climate impacts, current and future vulnerability, and the adaptive capacity of a country, region (IPCC, 2014) or tourist destination. Scientific information, knowledge and planning should contribute to lead to build an effective response to adverse impacts of climate change, thus reducing vulnerabilities and enhancing adaptive capacities as global warming keeps increasing. The period from 2015 to 2022 is constituted by the eight warmest years recorded to date (IPCC, 2023).

This secondary research chapter is fundamentally based on a process of identification, consultation and analysis of secondary documentary sources and it develops employing both a deductive and an inductive reasoning to conduct an explanatory and exploratory conceptual study that highlight the relevance of discussion and draw some specific conclusions to continue to make tourism prosper in the digital era while overcoming the threats that loom over the future of human development.

CHALLENGES AHEAD

The Implementation of the Objectives of the 2030 Agenda

The Intergovernmental Panel on Climate Change (IPCC) reports that climate-related illnesses, premature deaths, malnutrition in all its forms, and threats to mental health and well-being are increasing (Cissé et al., 2022). The IPCC further states that climate change and extreme events are projected to significantly increase ill health and premature deaths, as well as population exposure to heatwaves and heat-related morbidity and mortality. In addition, the global trend of rapid urbanization puts more people at risk of adverse health outcomes, as existing vulnerabilities to climate change may be aggravated in urban contexts. For example, air pollution is a major urban inconvenient to tourist destinations development (Cheung and Law, 2001) and a major threat to the health of the local urban population since its negative impacts are associated with nearly seven million premature deaths annually (World Meteorological Organization, 2023).

A growing global population, largely concentrated in cities, and a rising urban middle class, have led to an increase in the demands and pressures on urban infrastructure and government resources, and an increase in the consumption of resources in cities. Likewise, the increasing arrival of tourists in small, medium and large cities increases this pressure on resources and infrastructures.

The linear economy is hugely wasteful: most of the value in materials we use is 'lost' to landfills, and the things we make are consistently under-utilized. The waste generated through ineffective processes brings about additional costs due to waste management and collection spending which increases pressure on municipal budgets. In developing markets today, solid waste management and collection costs can sometimes reach 50% of municipal annual budgets. This trend is projected to increase, with the annual global cost of solid waste management expected to reach USD 375 billion by 2025. This is amplified in the urban context where analysis has found significant structural waste in key sectors such as mobility, food, and the built environment (Ellen Macarthur Foundation, 2017) all these sectors being closely related to tourist consumption processes with negative impacts on urban mobility systems, congestion and the resulting time lost to traffic city life and productivity.

Also, a series of large metropolitan areas around the world, such as for example in southern Europe, experience recurring episodes of drought that mean that more than half of the population regularly suffers from water stress. In southern Europe, water stress is typically greatest over the summer months, when water demand from agriculture and tourism is at its highest and precipitation is low.

Tourism industry is a major consumer of water putting further stress on water resources in destinations already suffering from some form of water scarcity and where further tourist developments are expected to exacerbate the problem even further in the not-so-distant future (Hadjikakou et al., 2013).

Inadequate responses until now have left us all more vulnerable. The consequences are felt most acutely by those with fewer assets and capabilities: those most dependent on ecosystems and least able to exercise their rights to human security, development, voice and dignity. The quest to achieve eight Millennium Development Goals (MDGs) demonstrates the power of Global Goals to realize progressive change (see figure 2).

Figure 2. Important milestones on the road to the Agenda 2030
Source: Publications Office of the European Union, (2022)

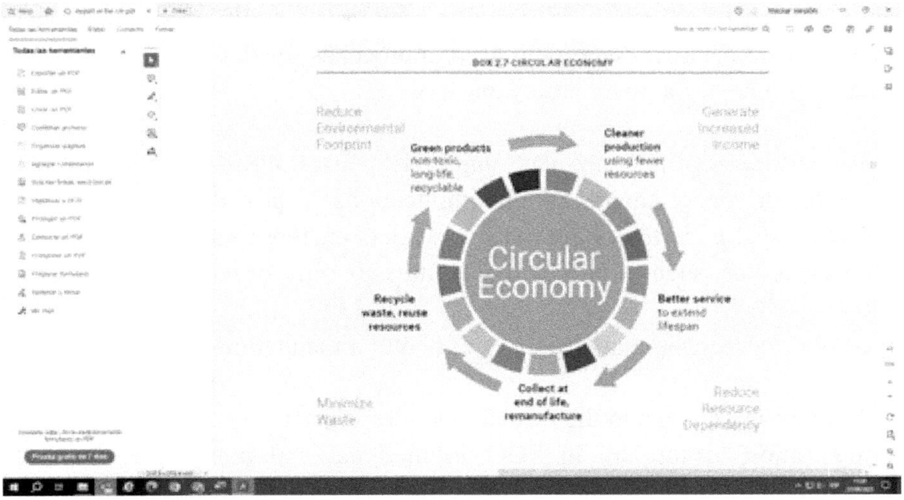

The MDGs played a role in lifting more than one billion people from extreme poverty. Notwithstanding and despite some progress the gap between the ambitions of the world's new global development agenda and collective action to date, leaves many doubtful about the SDG's prospects (United Nations Development Program, 2016). Therefore, it is crucial to keep carrying out a systematic analysis and monitoring of the set of indicators established for each of the MDG's to evaluate, plan and prioritize future actions in order to make further progress towards the implementation and achievement of the SDG's. In 2015, world leaders agreed on a new agenda to guide us towards 2030 - the Sustainable Development Goals (SDGs), officially known as *Transforming our world: the 2030 Agenda for Sustainable Development*.

Tourism is included specifically in three of the 17 universal SDGs of the 2030 Agenda for Sustainable Development:

1. Goal 8 on *Decent Work and Economic Growth*
2. Goal 12 on *Responsible Consumption and Production*
3. Goal 14 on *Life Below Water*

Yet the cross-cutting nature of tourism makes it an effective tool to contribute to all 17 Goals. Tourism can foster *Gender Equality* (Goal 5), *Help Build Sustainable Cities and Communities* (Goal 11) and *End poverty* (Goal 1). In so doing, it can increase its contribution to an overarching aim of the SDGs and of the United Nations: enhancing social progress, peace and human rights (United Nations World Tourism

Organization, 2017). In order to ensure progress towards the achievement of the SDG's it is equally necessary to increase scientific knowledge, develop research capacity and transfer technology as well as taking to use different approaches. In this sense, there are two commonly used approaches for developing scenarios of alternative futures for a given policy question.

a. The development-pressure-state-impact- response (DPSIR) framework explores the key drivers of change and the implications of these divers.
b. The critical uncertainty approach considers current trends in light of major uncertainties (such as future climate, the economy, or ecosystem response).

From the approaches analyzed, a series of recommendations are derived, such as

- Awareness-raising and the measurement of impact
- Integration of tourism in SDG-oriented national planning and business practices
- Effective partnerships for tourism and the SDGs
- Financing the tourism sector to implement the SDGs

While the following recommendations are geared towards all tourism stakeholders, the UN has a significant role to play in coordinating these stakeholders and to ensure that countries and the tourism private sector can maximize their impact. The global development partners from the United Nations System, including UNWTO, UNDP and other International Organizations, as well as OECD's Development Assistance Committee Members (DAC) and non-traditional donors should build a closer dialogue to facilitate tourism's contribution to the SDG system (United Nations World Tourism Organization, 2018).

In the short to medium-term, the most viable solution is to adopt a more circular economy approach for a more sustainable development based on renewable energies so that the need for fossil fuels can at least be curtailed. A more competitive and more responsible use of resources through technology, cooperation and planning is necessary to achieve our common 17th Sustainable Development Goals by 2030. Likewise, an ever more circular economy and the use of new technologies must contribute to a smarter sustainable tourism.

TOURISM ON THE HORIZON OF THE 2030 AGENDA

The development of organized leisure travel in Europe and North America is closely associated with several major processes of the modern period, including changing patterns of social and industrial organization, nation building, the rise of mass consumption and the emergence of a modern subjective consciousness (Pack, 2008). *Global tourism has experienced steady growth for over six decades, culminating in an estimated 1.5 billion international arrivals in 2019, representing an increase of 3.8% year-on-year, and well ahead of previous long-term forecasts. This strong growth is expected to continue, with arrivals in emerging markets in particular projected to grow at double the rate of advanced tourism economies. Demonstrating a similar pattern, global expenditures on travel more than tripled between 2000 and 2018, rising from USD 495 billion to USD 1.5 trillion and accounting for 7% of global exports in goods and services. In OECD countries, tourism directly accounts for, on average, 4.4% of GDP, 6.9% of employment and 21.5% of service exports* (UNWTO, 2019).

The significant growth in global tourism has benefitted greatly from the rise of globalization and technological advances that have led to cheaper airfares, making it easier for people to plan and book their own travel, and then to share their experiences with friends in real time. As more and more people engage in travel and tourism, the drive to ease travel facilitation through advanced technologies intensifies (Ioannou et al., 2020). While growth is projected to continue, changing demographics, improved connectivity for destinations, technological innovations, and increased recognition of the need for more sustainable and inclusive growth, are likely to dramatically transform the face of tourism by 2040, representing a range of opportunities and challenges for destinations (OECD, 2018).

Tourism, in the same way as any other economic sector, has developed and grown substantially as it has been analyzed in a linear model. This has been characterized, mainly, because of its connection to one continued economic growth and use and consumption of large amounts of materials, as well as of energy sources that turn out to be more economical and easier to access. However, the crucial challenge of tourism today is to adopt a more circular economy pursuing transform this traditional economic model and still predominant in order to bring it closer to a model similar to nature's biological cycle. In other words that is, optimizing the use of resources, so many times as possible, from sharing, renting, repair, renew or recycle. It is mainly a model that it is disconnected from the consumption of finite resources and promotes the transformation of the activity economic through, for example, sources of renewable energy (LABIIT, 2022).

Public procurement is a key factor in the economy of all countries, representing on average 13–20 per cent of GDP. It constitutes another crucial challenge as governments can leverage their purchasing power to drive markets towards greener and more innovative products and services, supporting sustainable development. In 2022, 67 national governments reported to the United Nations Environment Program on the implementation of sustainable public procurement policies and action plans, a 50 per cent increase from 2020.

However, data show a marked decline in the number of countries implementing tools to monitor the sustainable development impacts of tourism in 2020–2021, mainly due to disrupted statistical operations during the COVID-19 pandemic. While tourism contributes to creating jobs and promoting local culture and products, sustainable management of the sector's development is essential to protect its value. Countries must prioritize monitoring sustainable tourism practices as part of their recovery, ensuring economically viable and environmentally sustainable tourism (United Nations DESA, 2023).

At this point it is relevant to emphasize that coastal and marine tourism constitutes approximately 50 percent of all global tourism, equal to US$4.6 trillion or 5.2 percent of global gross domestic product (GDP) (Northrop et al., 2022). It is the largest segment of the tourism market worldwide and it is a crucial component of the economy of small islands and coastal communities. Because of the economic benefits that accrue from access to ocean navigation, coastal fisheries, industry, tourism and recreation, human settlements are often more concentrated in the coastal zone than elsewhere. *Presently about 40% of the world's population lives within 100 kilometers of the coast. As population density and economic activity in the coastal zone increases, pressures on coastal ecosystems increase. Among the most important pressures are habitat conversion, land cover change, pollutant loads, and introduction of invasive species. These pressures can lead to loss of biodiversity, coral reef bleaching, new diseases among organisms, hypoxia, harmful algal blooms, siltation, reduced water quality, and a threat to human health through toxins in fish and shellfish and pathogens such as cholera and hepatitis A residing in polluted water.*

Finally, it is important to recognize that a high population concentration in the low elevation coastal zone (defined as less than 10 meters elevation) increases a country's vulnerability to sea-level rise and other coastal hazards such as storm surges" (United Nations, 2007). Furthermore, oceans play a critical role as a climate regulator and buffer to climate change effects, which comes at the expense of their productivity and the health of marine ecosystems.

The ubiquitous degradation of coastal waters, marine ecosystems and oceans is a clear manifestation of the triple planetary crisis and the intricately connected threats of climate change, biodiversity loss and pollution. At the global level, two thirds of the oceans are significantly impacted by human activities that generate multiple pressures, ranging from excessive inputs of nutrients and hazardous substances (including plastics, microplastics and nano-plastics), unsustainable fishing (including illegal, unreported and unregulated (IUU) fishing) and habitat destruction due to coastal development (including for tourism) to extraction of natural resources.

Other detrimental environmental changes associated with climate change include ocean warming, acidification and deoxygenation, impacting the diversity and abundance of marine species (United Nations Economic Commission for Europe, & United Nations Environment Program (2022).

Therefore, coastal tourism destinations are at risk due increasing tourism massive flows that harm the environment on a global scale driving climate change because of the use and depletion of non-renewable energies for the transport phase associated with travel whereas coastal tourist destination development (see figure 3) alters environmental conditions on a local scale increasing pressure on natural resources (Boyra, 2009).

Figure 3. Dalian's Fujiazhuang beach (China)
Source: https://piximus.net/media/3766/beach-resorts-in-dalian-china-10.jpg

In the meantime, the so-called blue economy, which is steadily growing poses also sustainability challenges, since it involves income-generating activities in the ocean, such as the harvesting of food, shipping, seabed mining, offshore hydrocarbon exploration and exploitation, offshore wind energy, tourism and recreation. *Interest in seabed mining is on the rise, fueled in part by the increased demand for minerals and rare earth elements such as the cobalt needed in batteries for electric vehicles, as a climate change mitigation measure. The systematic nature of these challenges calls for the use of integrated and ecosystem-based management approaches,*

supported by spatially based assessments and the analysis of multiple pressures and cumulative impacts (EEA, 2020).

As global economy is growing at a rapid pace, and with it, the use of natural resources, resource consumption has more than tripled since 1970, a rate that significantly threatens the renewal capacity of our planet, and availability of finite resources for next generations. At our current consumption levels, we would need about 1.8 planets to continue to provide the resources we are consuming and absorb the waste we are generating. 2.3 planets will be needed by 2040 if the global population, demand and consumption for materials continue to grow at their present pace (MoEFCC & BCG, 2023).

To ensure that environment can sustainably replenish its renewable resources and extend the lifespan of finite resources for future generations, consumption of new materials should be reduced to a level that aligns with the resources of just one planet. This will help protect the climate, environment and provide greater societal equity. Resource efficiency and circular economy are therefore the key tools that can enable sustainable production and consumption of resources. The challenge calls-out for a plan of action to accelerate global transition towards circular economy and resource efficiency, through advancements in technology and innovation.

This is a priority and central challenge to avoid the risk posed to humanity as a whole by the failure to adopt more responsible growth.

A global industry coalition can address a number of structural and capability gaps that exist across the value chains. There are existing structural gaps that hinder progress in circularity, including fragmented actions by different stakeholders, insufficient integration of circular practices across value chains, and a limited scope of circular efforts primarily focused on sectors like plastics, textiles and so on. A global industry coalition can also play a crucial role in addressing capability gaps that hinder the progress of circular practices.

These gaps include a lack of expertise and capacity among small and medium enterprises (SMEs) and limited avenues for knowledge transfer between industries. By leveraging collective knowledge, experience, and resources, the coalition can help bridge these gaps and facilitate the advancement of circular practices across sectors (MoEFCC & BCG, 2023).

ADVANCEMENTS IN TECHNOLOGY: AN INFALLIBLE PATH TOWARDS SUSTAINABILITY?

As a campaign for progress in both literacy and technology, the March of Intellect was part of the so-called 'Machinery Question', that is, the public debate in England on the massive replacement of workers by industrial machines in the first half of the nineteenth century. An 1828 caricature by cartoonist William Heath (see figure 4) from the series 'March of Intellect' depicts a giant automaton advancing with long strides and holding a broom to sweep away a dusty mass of clerks, clergy and bureaucrats, representing figures of the old order and obsolete laws.

Figure 4. The March of Intellect (1828)
Source: William Heath, The March of Intellect (1828) © The Trustees of the British Museum. Pasquinelli, (2019)

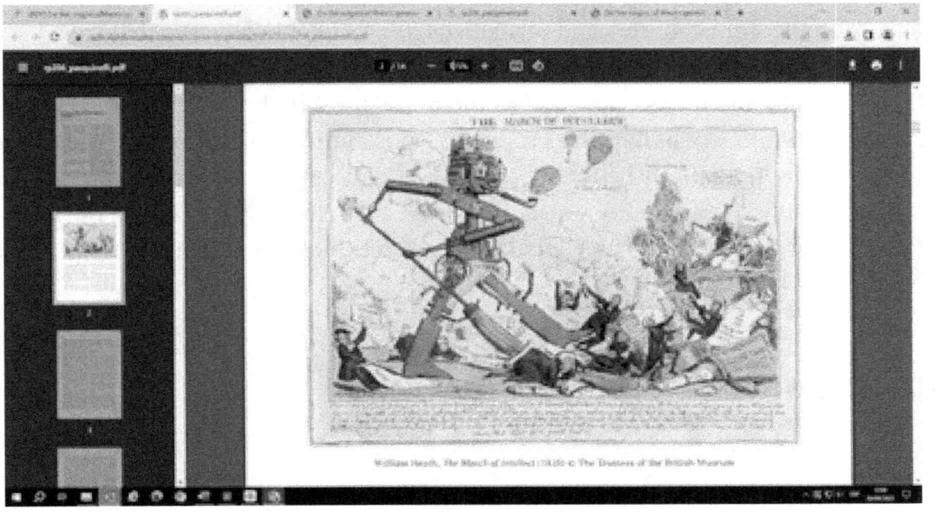

The digital revolution that began a little over half a century ago and continues to pick up pace is changing, in a similar way as it occurred in the first half of the nineteenth century, the landscape of the world's society, economics, and politics.

As Artificial intelligence (AI), including machine learning approaches and complex human enhancements, has flourished across various domains of our social life, the opaque nature of AI has been a sticky feature of discussions concerning AI. The employment of artificial intelligence in the twentieth century has abruptly reminded everyone that knowledge can be analyzed, measured and automated as successfully as manual labor (Pasquinelli, 2019). While there have been recent calls to define AI more broadly as it impacts life in the quotidian and the exceptional, from the mundane consumption of social media to medical emergencies, we are concerned primarily with AI systems based on machine learning techniques used for pattern recognition and predictive modelling (Arora & Sarkar, 2023).

These technologies facilitate human experiences, support critical business processes, and enable important governance aspects. From the customer perspective,

AI and robotics can provide structured automated services and enhanced experiences. From a firm perspective, they support customer engagement, the delivery of rich service, secure data acquisition, and increased employee productivity and efficiency. From a governance perspective, AI and robotics widen the action radius, allow for the adoption of new governance models, and propel efficiency to new levels (Koo et al., 2021).

Over the last years, due to the COVID-19 pandemic, there has been an accelerated learning curve in the use of digital technology and distanced work. This is bound to act as a fillip to the pace of technological advance in the years ahead. Nevertheless, the maroon theorem captures and formalizes the incipient concerns that have been expressed by scientists, scholars, and even popular media about the rise of artificial intelligence and the gig economy. This theoretical result shows formally how new technology, while expanding the production possibility frontier of the world and making all of us potentially better off, can leave significant sections of the population marooned, without bargaining power, and with a worse quality of life in the end—all depending on platform firms' legal capacity to exploit dominant positions (Basu & Caspi, 2021).

SOLUTIONS AND RECOMMENDATIONS

Social Media Strategies for Awareness and Sustainable Tourism Interactivity

In the field of marketing and commercialization, AI improves forecasting, adjusts prices and offers made to existing and potential customers, enhances customer relationship management (CRM) systems, helps develop personalized services and experiences through mass customization, allows the deployment of intelligent marketing, helps with the development of customized predictions, support agents and smart sales assistants, creates offers in real time that are sent to the user through a context-based and content-based approach, and allows for marketing to be used as a queue management tool.

One specific challenge that hotels must face is that big data is one of the foundations of the deployment of AI. However, it is difficult to describe the data sets available to hotels as big data. While the volume of data available to hotels is usually high, and there is some variety to the data, the data is usually limited to the guest's interaction with the hotel website before the trip, and his/her behavior in the hotel. Hotels have little data on their guests' profile, their interests and preferences, their preferred destinations and other characteristics, and their behavior outside the hotel. This means that hotels can only have big data about their guests by pairing with other businesses that can complement their data.

Nonetheless, to delegate these functions to advanced forms of computational technology will expurgate subjectivity and strengthen the role of instrumental rationality (Stocchetti, 2023) limiting human interactions and personalized services diminishing the qualitative communication inputs that characterize the tourist experience. In the final stage, when AI is fully developed and implemented in the hospitality industry and the systems are all integrated and can interoperate, almost all the tasks that are currently performed by humans will be able to be performed by robots, AI, and natural language systems.

However, this does not mean that the hospitality industry will be run without the presence of humans. Humans will continue to have two main functions. First, humans will develop a small set of tasks that are extremely difficult to automate, even with the development of the capabilities of robotics and AI. Second, the presence of humans will be used as a distinction and luxury; it will be a differential factor. In other words, if humans are inefficient from an economic perspective, their presence will be justified from a differentiation perspective or through an increase in quality, as is currently the case in gas stations (Bulchand-Gidumal, 2020).

Policies to mitigate the negative consequences of digitalization should include nimble and adaptive information and communication technology regulations capable of safeguarding and protecting consumers and infrastructure, without hampering innovation or investment in new digital technologies. Digitalization and data policies to secure and maximize value from the digital economy may involve aspects such as national data strategies, protections of the rights of individuals, open-data guidelines, standards for the interoperability of data functions and promotion of skills relevant for the data economy (United Nations (2020b). However, as Carvalho and Ivanov (2023) point out there are risks associated with the use of these new technologies such as overreliance on its output, the potential replacement of human workers, cybersecurity, and loss of human connection.

Once a futuristic dream, wearable technologies have now grown into the next frontier of consumer electronics and have revolutionized many aspects of human life, such as sports, healthcare, retail, tourism and education. Examples of wearable technologies include extended reality headsets, smart clothing, smart glasses, and smartwatches. Notable, the global market size of wearable technologies was USD 37.10 billion in 2020, and is expected to reach USD 104.39 billion by 2027. Smartwatches, in particular, have been widely commercialized, and have led the growth and market share of wearable technologies. A smartwatch is a personal computing device equipped with multiple functions (i.e. making phone calls, texting, timekeeping, health activities, and fitness tracking) that is worn on the wrist. Unlike the downturn trend seen in the demand for other consumer devices such as smartphones, the global demand for smartwatches has recorded impressive growth. Apple dominates the market and shipment volume, followed by Huawei and Garmin]. *Importantly, the cornerstone for sustainability and survival of the smartwatch industry is its continued use. This has been particularly true when the smartwatch market has moved beyond the early adoption stage. However, despite its high adoption rate, this highly prized innovation is facing an imminent threat: nearly one-third of users have discontinued using their smartwatch within a year, as they found it to be less useful and interesting.*

This undesired behavioral pattern implies that firms cannot efficiently harvest data, which represents the core valuation of the IoT industry, and the development of smartwatches may be impeded. More importantly, for individuals and society, discontinued usage means that consumers will not be able to garner the health benefits from smartwatch usage (e.g. maintaining a healthy lifestyle and monitoring health conditions based on the collected personal health-related data, and recommendations provided by smartwatches). This inadvertently represents a setback towards slowing progress in curbing prevailing medical problems (i.e. obesity, high blood pressure, and stress) in society. Hence, to ensure continued smartwatch usage, understanding smartwatch's value propositions and consumers' post-adoption behavior has emerged as an essential research area (Kamal Basha et al., 2022).

Today, a number of tourism businesses and destination marketing organizations (DMOs) are benefiting from the digital transformation of social media. Social networks services (SNSs) are connecting social media subscribers that may include prospective tourists to interactive websites and to other links that display promotional content and information on various destinations. They promote tourist attractions, points of interest as well as their amenities. The real time conversation capabilities of the digital media can encourage online users to engage with other online users in public domains. They could even motivate them to travel and to book their itineraries and hotel accommodation. A relevant review from the marketing literature suggests that there are a number of studies that investigated the individuals' perceptions on the use of interactive websites like social media (Camilleri & Kozak, 2022).

With the prevalent use of smartphones, digital personal assistants powered by natural language processing (NLP) and speech recognition program, such as Apple's Siri and Google's Allo, gradually become the apps of choice when it comes to searching for information and personalized recommendations for products and services. In travel and tourism, using a combination of NLP and machine learning, chatbots (typically integrated into popular messaging apps such as WhatsApp and Facebook Messenger) and robot concierges are readily available to assist tourists in making decision on flights, hotels, tour packages, attractions, etc. In tourism context, intelligent systems can be designed to influence consumer choices, not only from a marketing point of view, but also from a social perspective, such as promoting socially desirable choices to tourists. Hence, in order to support sustainable tourism development, chatbots and companion robots can be designed as persuasive agents in behavior modification and intervention efforts involving travel consumers promoting a more responsible travel behavior (Tussyadiah & Miller, 2019).

Adopting Large Language Model (LLM) applications in tourism can potentially transform the job market, tourist searching process, and tourist interaction with voice assistants and service robots, among other customer service supports. Furthermore, it can revolutionize business processes such as marketing and human resource management. It can also increase the complexity of security, privacy, and ethical challenges arising from AI implementation in tourism (Rahmani & Barzi, 2023). Public awareness campaigns can provide education on the impact of problematic use of smartphones and digital media and promote healthy behaviors in this regard. Various social media platforms have placed bans and restrictions on content related to self-harm (Abi-Jaoude et al., 2020).

FUTURE RESEARCH DIRECTIONS

Social networks on the internet are rapidly expanding in the context of the revolution of new information and communication technologies. This proliferation of information has as a consequence the increase in interaction and interactivity between the tourist consumers and the tourism industry components such as transport, catering and accommodation providers among others. The opinion expressed through comments and reviews by tourists on social networks is fundamental for all tourism companies in terms of their performance and profitability. While the habit and use of social networks by tourists grows to share their experiences either in the travel phase, the stay at the hotel and the tourist services consumed at the destination the dominant position of the digital platforms controlled by these means of communication grows proportionally.

The tourist experience thus becomes an experience that is lived and perceived more and more through the media where it is recreated and where more or less positive comments proliferate, affecting the behavior of the demand and consequently benefiting or harming the offer. Likewise, small businesses dedicated to tourist services that are not on social networks are increasingly invisible to a greater part of the demand that cannot identify them at the time of programming and planning their trips through the purchase of different tourist services thanks to the use of the main digital media search engines.

The prevalent use of smartphones and the interface between chatbots and tourists tends to accelerate the purchase of standardized products and services aimed at mass tourist consumption. In this context it is necessary to reflect on, on the one hand, the impacts that tourist massification can have on the territory, and on the other, the possible progressive lack of tourist attraction of the destinations as a result of the standardization of their assets. Indeed, the so-called knowledge society seems to have almost emancipated itself from work thanks to automatic production through the use of increasingly advanced technologies. That is, in fact, the ideal goal of a completely mechanized and automatized system of power production: the elimination of work: the universal achievement of leisure (Mumford, 1934) towards which the so-called developed societies seem to advance without limits.

The systematic acquisition of products and services through online shopping monitors and conditions the own individual tourist experience that tends towards a standardized collective experience. This means gladly sacrificing mere quantity in order to restore qualitative choice, shifting the seat of authority from the mechanical collective to the human personality and the autonomous group, favoring variety and ecological complexity, instead of stressing undue uniformity and standardization, above all, reducing the insensate drive to extend the system itself, instead of containing it within definite human and natural limits and thus releasing man himself for other purposes (Mumford, 1964).

Social media strategies for tourism interactivity should therefore focus on spreading sustainable values among societies in order to contribute to implement the Sustainable Development Goals. Likewise, assessing coupling interactions in a safe and just operating space for regional sustainability (Han et al., 2023) should be promote and further research should be carried on environmental analysis assessment to safeguard the intrinsically value of tourist destinations. Sustainable initiatives as slow tourism destinations should emerge as alternative forms of mass tourism promoting among the local community ecological food producers and restaurateurs rebalancing the relation between the natural environment through a more circular economy.

As G7 Leaders' Statement on the Hiroshima AI Process October 30th, 2023 declares there is a major need to manage risks and to protect individuals, society, and shared principles including the rule of law and democratic values, keeping humankind at the center. The Hiroshima Process International Guiding Principles for Organizations Developing Advanced AI Systems and the Hiroshima Process International Code of Conduct for Organizations Developing Advanced AI Systems propose new standards for AI safety and security promoting responsible innovation and competition avoiding relevant risks associated with the widespread use of AI as, for example, concerns about bias as all humans are biased (including, obviously, those who create AI algorithms), and bias is natural in humans, e.g., bias relating to race, gender, age, and economic status (Bulchand-Gidumal, 2020).

Likewise, artificial intelligence (AI) technologies can have a great potential to aid not only in promoting more sustainable tourist products and services, but also in influencing responsible travel behavior to support sustainability as they expand interactivity and share tourist experiences. Notwithstanding, ethical challenges remain ahead and need of further research and discussion as loss of privacy and fear of a society entirely guided by technology may not help to solve our common future.

CONCLUSION

The present chapter has analyzed and investigated the sustainable management strategies of tourism in a changing environment as a result of the emergence of new technologies and the uncertainty derived from global warming and the ecological crisis in a complex and unstable geopolitical context that can be interpreted as the beginning of a new world order. The last part especially sets out to identify the main trends and characteristics of the new tourist interface in the context of the digital revolution and hybrid intelligence. As the future of development moves forward on the path to the 2030 Agenda technology advances and its socialization process shape the paradigm of a renewed outlook on tourism consumption. In the meantime, as dominant models of development still in place with their emphasis on industrialization, resource exploitation and urbanization biodiversity and human interactions continue to erode with it, limiting sociotechnical options and opportunities as well as reducing our flexibility and adaptive capacity.

As analyzed rapid technological shifts are bringing new ways for tourists to interact with technology, and with each other, creating more novel uncertainties. Technological changes outpace our ability to understand their societal implications in terms of changing our lives in fundamental ways while disruptive phenomena as global warming and pollution are getting closer and closer to dangerous thresholds.

The lives of citizens depend in many ways on the services that marine ecosystems provide, including climate regulation, fish and seafood provision, coastal protection, cultural value, recreation and tourism. Against this backdrop, the European Commission and Member States have taken multiple steps to combat the loss of aquatic and coastal habitats and biodiversity, which poses a serious threat to human livelihoods food security and climate stability. Nevertheless, as Lenzen (2008) points out, in general, even extensive process analyses will not achieve reasonable system completeness, given the high number of important input paths. As a result, environmental impacts will be systematically underestimated in noncomparative conventional life-cycle assessment (LCA), thus leading to unreliable or incorrect conclusions.

Furthermore, the Anthropocene reality of shared challenges at the planetary scale requires cooperation—or, at a minimum, coordination—across countries (United Nations Development Program, 2022). Likewise, and in order to increase scientific knowledge, develop research capacity and transfer technology the university sector has to support more actively the emergence of innovative and sustainable initiatives and enterprises (Garcia et al., 2022). As student and researcher cohorts are becoming increasingly internationalized universities have to integrate and support their talent and knowledge within a social progress perspective enriching and transforming aspects for research and innovation, including the mainstreaming of Open Science and Open Access approaches to make scientific results and datasets more accessible, reinforcing co-operation with non-academic sectors, attracting, retaining and upskilling talent, and citizen and societal engagement to ensure progress towards the achievement of the Sustainable Development Goals.

REFERENCES

Abi-Jaoude, E., Naylor, K. T., & Pignatiello, A. (2020). Smartphones, social media use and youth mental health. Canadian Medical Association *Journal (CMAJ), 192*(6). https://www.cmaj.ca/content/192/6/E136 doi:10.1503/cmaj.190434

Arora, C., & Sarkar, D. (2023). Auditing Artificial Intelligence (AI) as a New Layer of Mediation: Introduction of a new black box to address another black box. *Hipertext*, (26), 65-68. doi:10.31009/hipertext.net.2023.i26.10

Axhami, M., Ndou, V., Milo, V., & Scorrano, P. (2023). Creating Value via the Circular Economy: Practices in the Tourism Sector. *Administrative Sciences*, *13*(7), 166. doi:10.3390/admsci13070166

Basha, K., Norazlyn, A., & Hui-Wen, S. (2022). Are we so over smartwatches? Or can technology, fashion, and psychographic attributes sustain smartwatch usage? Technology in Society. Elsevier.

Basha, N. K., Aw, E. C. X., & Chuah, S. H. W. (2022, May). Are we so over smartwatches? Or can technology, fashion, and psychographic attributes sustain smartwatch usage? *Technology in Society*, *69*, 101952. doi:10.1016/j.techsoc.2022.101952

BasuK.CaspiA. (2021). Markets and Regulation in the Age of Big Tech. Social Science Research Network. (SSRN). https://ssrn.com/abstract=3985585

Boyra, J. (2003). Sustainable tourism development convergence. In: *Proceedings of the II International Scientific Conference on Sustainable Tourism Development and the Environment*. University of the Aegean. Interdepartmental Program of Postgraduate Studies in Tourism Planning, Management and Policy. Chios Island, Greece.

Boyra, J. (2005). *Tourism and the Environment in Attica.* [PhD. Dissertation, University of Barcelona].

Boyra, J. (2009). Looking for Environmental Excellence in Tourist Destinations. *TOURISMOS: An International Multidisciplinary Refereed Journal of Tourism, 4*(2), 91-106. https://tourismosjournal.aegean.gr/article/view/110

Bulchand-Gidumal, J. (2020). *Impact of artificial intelligence in travel, tourism and hospitality. Handbook of e-tourism.* Springer. https://accedacris.ulpgc.es/bitstream/10553/106011/2/impact_artificial_intelligence.pdf

Camilleri, M. A., & Kozak, M. (2022). Interactive engagement through travel and tourism social media groups: A social facilitation theory perspective. *Technology in Society*, *71*, 102098. doi:10.1016/j.techsoc.2022.102098

Carvalho, I., & Ivanov, S. (2023). ChatGPT for tourism: applications, benefits and risks. Tourism Review, Vol. ahead-of-print (No. ahead-of-print). https://doi.org/doi:10.1108/TR-02-2023-0088

CEnTour. (2020). *Managing the transition to circular economy for tourism providers*. Circular Tourism. https://circulartourism.eu/wp-content/uploads/2021/02/CIRCULAR-ECONOMY-TRANSITION-FOR-TOURISM-PROVIDERS.pdf

Cheung, Y. Y., and Law, C. H. R. (2001). The impact of air quality on tourism: the case of Hong Kong. *Pacific tourism review, 5*(2018-02-01), 69-74.

Cissé, G., McLeman, R., Adams, H., Aldunce, P., Bowen, K., Campbell-Lendrum, D., Clayton, S., Ebi, K. L., Hess, J., Huang, C., Liu, Q., McGregor, G., Semenza, J., & Tirado, M. C. (2022). Health, Wellbeing, and the Changing Structure of Communities. In *Climate Change 2022: Impacts, Adaptation and Vulnerability. Contribution of Working Group II to the Sixth Assessment Report of the Intergovernmental Panel on Climate Change*, (pp. 1041–1170). Cambridge University Press. https://www.ipcc.ch/report/ar6/wg2/downloads/report/IPCC_AR6_WGII_Chapter07.pdf, doi:10.1017/9781009325844.009

Coccossis, H., Mexa, A., Collovini, A., Parpairis, A., & Kanstandoglou, M. (2002). Defining, Measuring, and Evaluating Carrying Capacity in European Destinations. B4-3040/2000/294577/MAR/D2 Final Report. Athens.

Doxey, G. (1975). A Causation Theory of Visitor–Resident Irritants: Methodology and Research Inferences. *The Impact of Tourism. In the Sixth Annual Conference Proceedings*, pp.195-198. San Diego: The Travel Research Association.

Ellen Macarthur Foundation. (2017). *Cities in the Circular Economy: An Initial Exploration*. Ellen Macarthur Foundation. https://www.ellenmacarthurfoundation.org/assets/downloads/publications/Cities-in-the-CE_An-Initial-Exploration.pdf

European Commission. (2020). *Directorate-General for Research and Innovation. Directorate G – Research & Innovation Outreach*. Europea. https://op.europa.eu/en/publication-detail/-/publication/a3cde934-12a0-11eb-9a54-01aa75ed71a1/

European Environment Agency (EEA). (2020). *Multiple pressures and their combined effects in Europe's seas*. ETC/ICM Technical Report 4/2019: European Topic Centre on Inland, Coastal and Marine waters. https://www.eea.europa.eu/downloads/e8fe9e1b961f48e3af7ac69adab8e696/1675956090/multiple-pressures-and-their-combined.pdf

Garcia, J., Alvado, A., Sorribes, J., & Boyra, J. (2022). The Challenges of Higher Education and its Contribution to Sustainable Development. *Higher Education Research, 7*(1). https://www.sciencepublishinggroup.com/journal/paperinfo?journalid=296&doi=10.11648/j.her.20220701.11 doi:10.11648/j.her.20220701.11

Hadjikakou, M. (2013). *Water and tourism*. Deakin University. https://dro.deakin.edu.au/articles/chapter/Water_and_tourism/20831107

Han, D., Yu, D. & Qiu, J. (2023). Assessing coupling interactions in a safe and just operating space for regional sustainability. *Nature Communications, Nature, 14*(1), 1-15. https://doi.org/ doi:10.1038/s41467-023-37073-z

Ioannou, A., Tussyadiah, I., & Miller, G. (2020). That's Private! Understanding travelers' privacy concerns and online data disclosure. *Journal of Travel Research*. https://openresearch.surrey.ac.uk/esploro/outputs/journalArticle/Thats-private-Understanding-travelers-privacy-concerns-and-online-data-disclosure/99512856502346

IPCC - Intergovernmental Panel on Climate Change. (2014). *Climate Change 2014: Impacts, Adaptation, and Vulnerability. Part A: Global and Sectoral Aspects*. Contribution of Working Group II to the Fifth Assessment Report of the Intergovernmental Panel on Climate Change [Field, C.B., V.R. Barros, D.J. Dokken, K.J. Mach, M.D. Mastrandrea, T.E. Bilir, M. Chatterjee, K.L. Ebi, Y.O. Estrada, R.C. Genova, B. Girma, E.S. Kissel, A.N. Levy, S. MacCracken, P.R. Mastrandrea, and L.L. White (eds.)]. Cambridge University Press, Cambridge, United Kingdom and New York, NY, USA. https://www.ipcc.ch/site/assets/uploads/2018/02/WGIIAR5-PartA_FINAL.pdf

IPCC - Intergovernmental Panel on Climate Change. (2023). *Climate Change 2023: Synthesis Report. Contribution of Working Groups I, II and III to the Sixth Assessment Report of the Intergovernmental Panel on Climate Change.* IPCC. https://www.ipcc.ch/report/ar6/syr/downloads/report/IPCC_AR6_SYR_FullVolume.pdf

Komsary, K. C., Tarigan, W. P., & Wiyana, T. (2018). Limits of acceptable change as tool for tourism development sustainability in Pangandaran West Java. *IOP Conference Series. Earth and Environmental Science*, *126*, 012129. https://iopscience.iop.org/article/10.1088/1755-1315/126/1/012129/pdf. doi:10.1088/1755-1315/126/1/012129

Koo, C., Xiang, Z., Gretzel, U., & Sigala, M. (2021). Artificial intelligence (AI) and robotics in travel, hospitality and leisure. *Electronic Markets*, *31*(3), 473–476. doi:10.1007/s12525-021-00494-z PMID:35603226

LABIIT - Laboratori d'Innovació i Intel·ligència Turística. (2022). *Departament de Consultoria Tecnològica del Centre Tecnològic Eurecat*. CDN. https://cdn.eurecat.org/PDF/InformeLabiit/Informe-LABIIT-1-2022-economiacircular-Eurecat-PTDT.pdf

Lenzen, M. (2008). Errors in Conventional and Input–Output-based Life Cycle Inventories. *Journal of Industrial Ecology*, *4*(4), 127–148. doi:10.1162/10881980052541981

Lindberg, K., McCool, S., & Stankey, G. (1997). Rethinking carrying capacity. *Annals of Tourism Research*, *24*(2), 461–465. https://www.researchgate.net/profile/Stephen-Mccool/publication/256987158_Rethinking_Carrying_Capacity/links/5a1c3b0b0f7e9bd1be5c5535/Rethinking-Carrying-Capacity.pdf. doi:10.1016/S0160-7383(97)80018-7

McCabe, S. (Ed.). (2014). *The Routledge Handbook of Tourism Marketing*. Routledge., https://perpus.univpancasila.ac.id/repository/EBUPT190874.pdf#page=514 doi:10.4324/9781315858265

Meadows, D. H., Meadows, D. L., Randers, J., Behrens, W., & Club of Rome. (1972). *The Limits to growth: A report for the Club of Rome's project on the predicament of mankind.* New York: Universe Books. https://www.donellameadows.org/wp-content/userfiles/Limits-to-Growth-digital-scan-version.pdf

MoEFCC & BCG - Ministry of Environment. (2023). *Encouraging Resource Efficiency and Circular Economy.* Ministry of Environment, Forest and Climate Change, New Delhi, India. https://www.g20.org/content/dam/gtwenty/gtwenty_new/document/G20_ECSWG-Resource_Efficiency_and%20_Circular_Economy_Industry_Coalition.pdf

Mumford, L. (1934). *Technics and Civilization*. Harcourt Brace & Company. https://ia801404.us.archive.org/10/items/in.ernet.dli.2015.49974/2015.49974.Technics-And-Civilization.pdf

Mumford, L. (1964). Authoritarian and Democratic Technics. *Technology and Culture*, *5*(1), 1–8. doi:10.2307/3101118

Northrop, E. (Ed.). (2022). *Opportunities for Transforming Coastal and Marine Tourism: Towards Sustainability, Regeneration and Resilience*. The High Level Panel for a Sustainable Ocean Economy (Ocean Panel). https://oceanpanel.org/publication/opportunities-for-transforming-coastal-and-marine-tourism-towards-sustainability-regeneration-and-resilience/

OECD. (2018). *OECD Tourism Trends and Policies 2018*. OECD Publishing. doi:10.1787/tour-2018-

OECD. (2020). Rethinking tourism success for sustainable growth. In *OECD Tourism Trends and Policies 2020*. OECD Publishing. doi:10.1787/82b46508-

Pack, S. (2008). Tourism, modernization, and difference: A twentieth-century Spanish paradigm. *Sport in Society*, *11*(6), 657–672. https://grupoturhis.files.wordpress.com/2012/06/tourism-modernisation-difference.pdf. doi:10.1080/17430430802283914

Pasquinelli, M. (2019). On the Origins of Marx's General Intellect. *Radical Philosophy, 2*, 06. https://kim.hfg-karlsruhe.de/marx-general-intellect/

Publications Office of the European Union. (2022). *Sustainable development in the European Union Monitoring report on progress towards the SDGs in an EU context 2022 edition*. Eurostat, Unit E2 — Environmental statistics and accounts; sustainable development. https://ec.europa.eu/eurostat/documents/15234730/15242025/KS-09-22-019-EN-N.pdf/a2be16e4-b925-f109-563c-f94ae09f5436?t=1667397761499

Rahmani, B., & Barzi, P. H. (2023). *What does ChatGPT show about the future impacts of large language model applications on tourism?* Conference paper. 6th International Conference on Management, Tourism and Technology (ICMTT) Penang, Malaysia. https://www.researchgate.net/publication/371119753_What_does_ChatGPT_show_about_the_future_impacts_of_large_language_model_applications_on_tourism

Settele, J., Scholes, R., Betts, R., Bunn, S., Leadley, P., Nepstad, D., Overpeck, J. T., & Taboada, M. A. (2014). Terrestrial and inland water systems. In *Climate Change 2014: Impacts, Adaptation, and Vulnerability. Part A: Global and Sectoral Aspects,* (pp. 271–359). Cambridge University Press. https://www.ipcc.ch/site/assets/uploads/2018/02/WGIIAR5-Chap4_FINAL.pdf

Stocchetti, M. (2023). A matter of meaning, life and death. Text, AI and the human condition. *Hipertext.net*, (26), 77-81. doi:10.31009/hipertext.net.2023.i26.12

Tussyadiah, I., & Miller, G. (2019). Perceived impacts of artificial intelligence and responses to positive behavior change intervention. In *Information and communication technologies in tourism 2019* (pp. 359–370). Springer. https://www.researchgate.net/publication/329685744_Perceived_Impacts_of_Artificial_Intelligence_and_Responses_to_Positive_Behaviour_Change_Intervention doi:10.1007/978-3-030-05940-8_28

United Nations. (2007a). *Percentage of total population living in coastal areas.* UN. https://www.un.org/esa/sustdev/natlinfo/indicators/methodology_sheets/oceans_seas_coasts/pop_coastal_areas.pdf

United Nations. (2020b). *Report of the UN Economist Network for the UN 75th Anniversary: Shaping the Trends of Our Time.* UN. https://digitallibrary.un.org/record/3884187?ln=es

United Nations. (2020c). *Executive Summary Report of the UN Economist Network for the UN 75th Anniversary: Shaping the Trends of Our Time.* UN. https://www.un.org/development/desa/publications/wp-content/uploads/sites/10/2020/10/20-124-UNEN-75Report-ExecSumm-EN-REVISED.pdf

United Nations DESA. (2023). *The Sustainable Development Goals Report 2023: Special Edition - July 2023.* UN DESA. https://unstats.un.org/sdgs/report/2023/

United Nations Development Program. (2016). From the MDGs to Sustainable Development for All: Lessons from 15 Years of Practice. https://www.undp.org/content/dam/undp/library/SDGs/English/From%20the%20MDGs%20to%20SD4All.pdf

United Nations Development Program. (2022). Human Development Report 2021-2022: Uncertain Times, Unsettled Lives: Shaping Our Future in a Transforming World. https://hdr.undp.org/content/human-development-report-2021-22

United Nations Economic Commission for Europe. (2022). *Applying principles of circular economy to sustainable tourism.* UN. https://unece.org/sites/default/files/2022-05/CEP-SS_Sustainable_Tourism.IP_.03.e.pdf

United Nations Economic Commission for Europe, & United Nations Environment Program. (2022). *Europe's Environment: The Seventh Pan-European Environmental Assessment.* UN. https://wedocs.unep.org/20.500.11822/40733

United Nations Economist Network. (2023). *New Economics for Sustainable Development: Circular Economy*. UN. https://www.un.org/en/desa/unen/policy-briefs

United Nations Environment Program. (2013). *PROVIA Guidance on Assessing Vulnerability, Impacts and Adaptation to Climate Change. Consultation document*. UN. https://www.adaptation-undp.org/sites/default/files/downloads/provia-guidance-nov2013.pdf

United Nations World Tourism Organization. (2017). *UNWTO Annual Report 2016*. UNWTO, Madrid. http://media.unwto.org/publication/unwto-annual-report-2016

United Nations World Tourism Organization. (2018). Tourism and the Sustainable Development Goals. Journey to 2030. https://www.e-unwto.org/doi/pdf/10.18111/9789284419401

World Meteorological Organization. (2023). United in Science 2023. *Sustainable development edition: A multi-organization high-level compilation of the latest weather-, climate and water-related sciences and services for sustainable development*. WMO. https://library.wmo.int/records/item/68235-united-in-science-2023

ADDITIONAL READING

Hall, C. M., Seyfi, S., & Koupaei, S. N. (2023). Politics and the sustainable development goals: Tourism Agenda 2030 perspective article. *Tourism Review*, *78*(2), 314–320. doi:10.1108/TR-10-2022-0498

Lenzen, M., Keyßer, L., & Hickel, J. (2022). Degrowth scenarios for emissions neutrality. *Nature Food*, *3*(5), 308–309. doi:10.1038/s43016-022-00516-9 PMID:37117569

Limna, P., & Kraiwanit, T. (2023). The Role of ChatGPT on customer service in the hospitality industry: An exploratory study of hospitality workers' experiences and perceptions. *Tourism and Hospitality Management*, *29*(4), 583–592. https://www.researchgate.net/publication/375005233_The_Role_of_ChatGPT_on_Customer_Service_in_the_Hospitality_Industry_An_Exploratory_Study_of_Hospitality_Workers'_Experiences_and_Perceptions#fullTextFileContent. doi:10.20867/thm.29.4.9

Noble, D. (1986). *Forces of Production. A Social History of Industrial Automation*. Oxford University Press. doi:10.4324/9780203791806

Rahmadian, E., Feitosa, D., & Zwitter, A. (2022). A systematic literature review on the use of big data for sustainable tourism. *Current Issues in Tourism*, *25*(11), 1711–1730. doi:10.1080/13683500.2021.1974358

Seetanah, B., Gopy-Ramdhany, N., & Bhattu-Babajee, R. (2023). Can tourism curb income inequality? Tourism Agenda 2030. *Tourism Review*, *78*(2), 646–664. doi:10.1108/TR-02-2022-0094

Tussyadiah, I. (2020). A review of research into automation in tourism: Launching the Annals of Tourism Research Curated Collection on Artificial Intelligence and Robotics in Tourism. *Annals of Tourism Research*, *81*, 102883. doi:10.1016/j.annals.2020.102883

Van der Aalst, W. M. P. (2021). Hybrid Intelligence: To automate or not to automate, that is the question. *International Journal of Information Systems and Project Management*, *9*(2), 2. https://aisel.aisnet.org/ijispm/vol9/iss2/2. doi:10.12821/ijispm090201

KEY TERMS AND DEFINITIONS

Adaptive Capacity: The general ability of institutions, systems, and individuals to adjust to potential damage, to take advantage of opportunities, or to cope with the consequences.

Artificial Intelligence: An area of computer science that deals with giving machines the ability to seem like they have human intelligence. The power of a machine to copy intelligent human behavior - a robot with *artificial intelligence* - abbreviation AI.

Drivers, Pressures, State, Impact, and Response Model of Intervention: A causal framework used to describe the interactions between society and the environment - abbreviation DPSIR.

Life Cycle Assessment: An analysis of the impact one object has on the world around it. The analysis of the environmental impact one object has on the world - abbreviation LCA.

Maroon Theorem: This theorem shows that as the platform becomes larger, the cost of trying to do business outside the platform gets higher.

Tourism Industry: Unlike with other industries, there is not one clear product or service. It incorporates many industries, including accommodation, transport, attractions, travel companies, etc.

Uncertainty: Scientific concept used in risk assessment to describe all types of limitations in available knowledge at the time an assessment is conducted, with the agreed resources, that affect the probability of possible outcomes to the assessment.

Chapter 9
Enhance Communication With Stakeholders Through Social Media in Protected Areas as Sustainable Tourism Destinations

Isabel Cristina Mañas-Álvarez
University of Almería, Spain

Mª del Carmen Caba-Pérez
University of Almeria, Spain

Juana Alonso-Cañadas
University of Almería, Spain

Federico Galán-Valdivieso
https://orcid.org/0000-0001-9632-2941
University of Almería, Spain

ABSTRACT

EUROPARC, the representative federation of protected areas, is adopting policies to disseminate information about its sustainable tourism strategies, safeguarding natural and cultural values, supporting local livelihoods and being economically viable. In this context, social networks play a key role in fostering sustainable tourism. This chapter aims to analyse the level of engagement achieved through social media (Twitter or X) in relation to sustainable tourism, and to examine the type of content disseminated. The main findings reveal notable trends in stakeholder engagement, with quick and simple actions such as "likes" and "retweets" predominating

DOI: 10.4018/979-8-3693-0960-5.ch009

over comments. Additionally, significant differences in the level of engagement are observed between protected areas in different countries and with respect to the type of content. These findings offer valuable perspectives for protected areas managers, providing guidance on how to improve their strategies to encourage greater stakeholder engagement through social media and therefore foster the preservation of these natural areas.

INTRODUCTION

The tourism sector is a fundamental pillar in the economic growth of many countries. In recent years, there has been a change in the preferences and lifestyle of society. This transformation, together with the COVID-19 health crisis, has encouraged the emergence of a new tourist profile characterised by the desire to disconnect from the crowds and the frenetic pace of cities. In this context, there is a growing interest in sustainable protected natural areas, representing spaces where the human footprint is minimal and environmental conservation is paramount (Mendieta-Aragón, 2022). These areas, supported by organisations such as EUROPARC, focus on the management and promotion of natural parks and spaces in Europe, ensuring that biodiversity, ecosystems, and cultural values are preserved for future generations. The work of EUROPARC and the designation of protected areas contribute to a more sustainable tourism, where visitors can connect with nature in a deeper and more respectful way.

Similarly, increasing environmental awareness leads to sustainable tourism, which seeks to strengthen the link with nature (Arkema et al., 2021). Sustainable tourism is characterised by sensitivity to the nature, culture, and way of life of the region, generating positive impacts and mitigating negative environmental, sociocultural, or economic impacts. Its three pillars are economic growth, inclusive development, and environmental sustainability (Monsalve-Peláez et al., 2023).

Effectively achieving sustainable tourism requires long-term commitment and the implementation of flexible policies by relevant authorities (Walker et al., 2021). Despite this, without proper management, natural spaces are vulnerable to the impact of human activities associated with tourism. In this situation, the administration of these spaces is faced with the dilemma of transforming them into attractive destinations that boost the local economy while ensuring the sustainability of their environment. This duality is in line with the Sustainable Development Goals, particularly numbers 12 and 15, which emphasise "responsible production and consumption" and "life on land" respectively (Luque-Martínez et al., 2019).

This sustainable approach acts as a regulator of the socio-environmental impacts of tourism. However, it should be noted that this sustainable approach to tourism not only mitigates adverse socioenvironmental impacts, but also entails multiple benefits such as job creation, heritage preservation, and increased tax revenues, improving the quality of local life (Falatoonitoosi et al., 2022). However, managing these destinations involves addressing various issues, from building trust to promoting more sustainable behaviour among travellers (Font et al., 2019). In the current era, the intersection between digital technology and sustainability opens new horizons for tourism management. Therefore, social networks are becoming invaluable tools for this purpose, as they favour the conservation of natural areas by promoting awareness campaigns, promoting collective financing, and allowing real-time monitoring of tourist areas (Zeng & Gerritsen, 2014).

Due to the relevance of these platforms in the current landscape of sustainable tourism, the central purpose of this research work is to analyse the level of engagement achieved through social networks in relation to sustainable tourism and to examine the type of content that is disseminated on these platforms.

In doing so, this study is structured as follows: Section 2 provides a review of the literature on protected areas and the role of social networks in the tourism sector. In Section 3 the methods developed and the data used are shown. Section 4 summarises the results obtained, and concluding remarks are provided in Section 5.

SOCIAL NETWORKS AS A TOOL TO FOSTER ENGAGEMENT IN THE CONTEXT OF PROTECTED AREAS

Today, the tourism sector is being impacted by social networks, which are being used to promote tourist destinations, specifically sustainable destinations, and in the decision making of today's tourists, so it is necessary to delve deeper into this impact. Social networks can provide information of great relevance today to determine where visitors usually go and why, how much time, what budget they spend on them, etc. The platforms allow users to share their location and specific time by associating them with the photographs they upload in their posts to their accounts. This provides the above information, thus enabling the management of destinations to offer services more in line with the interests of the predominant tourist profile, consolidate the positive aspects that they value most, and strengthen the protection measures of these areas. Likewise, these means allow us to estimate by the number of publications associated with the location the volume of tourists by zones and schedules and the most attractive geographical points, together with the habits they present according to the characteristics of this. Extracting these data is of vital importance as it facilitates sustainable tourism, for example, knowing where to invest in infrastructures with better access and amenities capable of supporting the tourist load and increasing its benefits, while ensuring the sustainability of the environment (Arkema et al., 2021).

Considering that the main attraction of this type of space is its natural character, the conservation of these means and their consolidation as sustainable tourist destinations is of vital importance. Therefore, the administration of these places must encourage visitors to take care of their practices during their stay and make them aware of the duty to protect the environment. Tourists not only drive economic activities in these destinations with their consumption habits (Ashley, 2000), but also contribute directly to the protection of the environment. That is why with the promotion by the management of the principles of sustainability, can generate changes (Becken, 2005), this being an incentive to preserve the tourist experience of a destination (Krutwaysho & Bramwell, 2010).

However, the focus should not be only on tourists, but also on other interest groups such as authorities, administrations of other natural spaces, and the population of the area; it is essential to include all of them in decision making in order to achieve the consolidation of a more sustainable space (Björk, 2000), since either actively or passively, they are involved in the process (Murphy, 1985). In fact, this is a main characteristic of sustainable tourism: investing in the community and individuals, creating better institutions and policies that promote the development of infrastructure (UN Conference on Trade and Development, 2013). Since it is a complex network of stakeholders, the activity on their social networks allows them to transmit these messages and practises more quickly and effectively to stakeholders (Luque-Martínez et al., 2019).

Social networks are a great engine in the tourism sector, as the search for information about destinations, decisions about crossing and staying, the promotion of these sites, and the interaction between institutions and consumers occurs in this virtual network (Zeng & Gerritsen, 2014). Currently, the most used by users are Facebook (2,960 million), Instagram (2,000 million), TikTok (814.5 million) and Twitter (556 million). Taking into account the level of connection between such a large volume of people in these social networks, it is vital to establish a good communication and engagement strategy to consolidate sustainable tourism. Abbassi et al. (2023) showed that consumers perceive the value of entertainment, information, credibility, and personalization from the images of the destination published on social networks. In fact, the analysis conducted by Soboleva et al. (2017) shows that especially Twitter provides a space for communication content in which the socialisation process is easier and more convenient. Galiano-Coronil et al. (2023) highlight in their study the value of using Twitter as a communication tool from the perspective of happiness and social marketing in the context of tourism. This point is relevant since social networks have become a vital source of information in decision making when choosing a destination and tourism plan (Fotis et al., 2012; Tham et al., 2020; Yuan et al., 2022).

Similarly, Moon & Han (2019) concluded that there is a correlation between social networking use and the perception of the tourist destination finally chosen, and the same correlation is present in sustainable tourism and the decision-making of tourists (Asmelash & Kumar, 2019; Rasoolimanesh et al., 2020). Especially from the COVID pandemic, tourists consider the environment that surrounds the destination (Lewis et al., 2021), whose positive mental image is largely on promotion on social networks. Platforms such as Facebook, Instagram, Twitter, and YouTube raise environmental awareness and encourage users to participate in sustainable tourism activities, according to a study conducted by Chiwaridzo & Masengu (2023). Even this same analysis determined that the feedback produced by the tourists themselves when sharing their participation and experiences in these sustainable environments influence the behaviour of other tourists.

The sustainable tourism supply chain must take advantage of the direct correlation between the resources and influences offered by new technologies and social networks (Chiwaridzo & Masengu, 2023). In this way, the efficiency and effectiveness of sustainable tourism initiatives can be improved. Gartner et al. (2020) concluded in their analysis of social networks in tourism that they are important to support sustainability and create sustainable value and strategies for success and focus on tourism. In fact, in the study by Galiano-Coronil et al. (2023) it is interesting that the issues that generate the most impact on the social network Twitter are those related to nature and culture within the framework of sustainable tourism.

The participation of stakeholders is not homogeneous. Depending on the strategy adopted, management can encourage manipulative participation, which leaves no decision-making power or information; passive participation, which consists of reporting on decisions that have already been taken; participation by consultation, which allows questions to be asked, but without taking into account their views; functional participation, which only allows decision making to external agents that help achieve the objectives; interactive participation, where they participate in the analysis and development of action plans; and mobilisation itself, whereby stakeholders take initiative independently of external institutions. The advantage of social networks is the possibility of checking that the message has been received, in the case of Twitter, for example, through "like" and "retweet", and also which kind of reactions generate, checking the comments on the publications. In this way, interactive participation is achieved between the organisation and the different stakeholders (Leung et al., 2018).

Although platforms such as Facebook, Twitter, Instagram, etc., are often used to make urgent announcements on topics such as fires, or related to the community of followers who share an interest in the protected area, they can also be used to influence the relationship with stakeholders. There are different ways in which protected areas can use social media communication. First, communication focused on social impact highlights the message and the benefits it brings to the individual and society. Second, long-term bi-directional communication emphasises the beneficial relationships between the administrations of protected areas and interest groups. Third, collaboration with digital ambassadors, such as influencers, allows one to expand the promotion of these spaces to their followers, increasing the benefits for both. Finally, the promotion of experiences in these spaces gives the opportunity to immerse the visitor in a unique and personalised experience. The idea is to create a positive impact on stakeholders, not only for the potential benefits, but also to share their philosophy and sustainable vision, managing to create greater awareness about the need to protect these areas (Leung et al., 2018).

RESEARCH DESIGN

In the research design, we will focus on the process of gathering and analyzing data carried out in this chapter, exposing the data collection and the methodology used.

SAMPLE AND DATA COLLECTION

The EUROPARC Federation represents one of the main European networks dedicated to the management and conservation of protected areas. Its management provides a holistic approach to the environment that helps the practical conservation of nature and the sustainable development of European biodiversity (EUROPARC, 2023). Therefore, to achieve the objectives established objectives, we work with a sample of 20 natural spaces attached to EUROPARC located in 5 different countries (Finland, France, Italy, Spain, and the United Kingdom).

Similarly, among all social networks in which these entities have a presence, Twitter is chosen for two fundamental reasons: first, because of the character limitation of this platform, which simplifies the identification and analysis of the content of the tweets, and second, because of the public nature of the content by default, which allows reaching more users (Gómez-Carrasco et al., 2021).

Regarding the study period, the activity of the accounts was analysed for 12 months, as it is considered an acceptable time to analyse the information present on the social network (Mariani et al., 2016). Specifically, the study conducted in September 2023 focused on publications between September 1, 2022, and August 31, 2023.

Data extraction and processing are carried out using ad hoc software for extracting and analysing content published on social networks (following Alonso-Cañadas et al.

(2019). The software employed consisted of four modules: i) the extraction module based on the social network Graph API based on Power Query M language; ii) the analysis module, based on the expressions of data analysis (DAX language) for the multidimensional exploitation of extracted information, calculating the different items defined in this study; iii) the visualisation module which uses Microsoft Power View technology to carry out the graphical representation of the results for a dynamic analysis of the information; and iv) the content analysis module, based on Learning Machine technology, analysed and classified in different topics, previously identified and parameterized, the content posted on social networks.

ANALYSIS OF STAKEHOLDER ENGAGEMENT VIA TWITTER

The engagement index (E) is calculated to determine the level of participation of the stakeholders (Table 1). This metric was initially conceived by Bonsón and Ratkai (2013) to quantify the level of online engagement in the field of governments and in the case of Facebook. However, it has been applied in other areas of research such as the tourism sector (Gálvez-Rodríguez et al., 2017), and an adaptation has been made in the case of this study for its measurement on Twitter.

Within Twitter, user engagement is manifested through its interactions. 'likes' (P) signal a foundational appreciation or acknowledgement of the content, typically demonstrating a low to medium level of commitment. Replies or comments (C) indicate a more profound engagement, as they suggest an intention to actively participate in a dialogue about the topic at hand. In contrast, retweets (V) embody a medium level of commitment, with the user disseminating the content to their audience, underscoring its pertinence or worth. Collectively, these interactions provide an overview of the content's impact and resonance on the platform.

Table 1. Metrics used to measure online engagement with the organisation through Twitter

Name	Sign	Formula	Measures
Popularity	P	Total Likes / Total Tweets	Average number of Likes per tweet
Commitment	C	Total Comments/ Total Tweets	Average number of comments per tweet
Virality	V	Total Retweets / Total Tweets	Average number of retweets per tweet

Engagement Index: $E = P + C + V$

RESULTS

Level of Engagement via Twitter

To contextualise the online engagement of users with protected areas, a descriptive analysis is performed in which some of the main characteristics of the published tweets are reflected.

First, Table 2 shows that the 6,369 tweets published during the analysed period receive 55,381 likes, 6,437 comments and 16,104 retweets. For all protected areas, the average number of likes per tweet is 8.67, while the number of comments is 1.01 and the shares is 2.52. Given these initial results, there is a predominance of quick and simple actions in line with previous literature (Gálvez-Rodríguez et al. 2017; Alonso-Cañadas et al. 2019) since the average of "likes" and "retweets" per publication is higher than the average of "comments".

Table 2. Main quantitative parameters used for Twitter interaction

	Total tweets	Total likes	Total comments	Total retweets
Total	6,369	55,381	6,437	16,104
Average	696.93	8.67	1.01	2.52

The results of the estimated level of engagement are shown in Table 3, which details the average values of the index of engagement (E), as well as their respective dimensions: popularity (P), commitment (C), and virality (V). The value that yields E presents a low level of heterogeneity in terms of the engagement achieved by users with the entity, estimating an average value of 12.18 and a level of deviation of 7.17. Regarding the mean value of the popular dimension (8.66), it can be observed that it is significantly higher than commitment (1.01) and virality (2.52). Unlike the E index, the standard deviation results for dimensions C, P, and V would indicate less variability between the values observed in these three components.

Table 3. Results of the average engagement of stakeholders on Twitter

	Commitment (E)	Popularity (P)	Commitment (C)	Virality (V)
M	12,18	8,66	1,01	2,52
Maximum	26,05	17,16	5,83	4,87
Minimum	1,33	0,92	0,00	0,25
SD	7,17	4,81	1,50	1,45

Note. N = 20

As mentioned above, protected areas are located in different geographical areas, specifically in 5 different countries. As Table 4 shows, Spain is the country with the highest number of publications, representing almost 56% of the total number of tweets in the sample. Similarly, it yields the highest values in terms of "likes" and "retweets", with Finland standing out in interactions that require greater commitment from stakeholders, such as "comments", although Italy presents the largest number of natural parks (a total of 10), holding the second position in terms of publications and "likes" achieved. Similarly, Italy gets the second-best mark in virality; however, it is still far from the more than 3 thousand comments achieved by Finland. In this ranking by countries, the worst position belongs to France since the publications made by its three protected areas do not reach the levels of interaction of the other countries.

When it comes to direct interactions (that is, without considering the number of tweets published), in all countries, stakeholders prefer to click to give a "like" than investing their time and effort in making a comment. With a total of 55,381 likes, it is the preferred form of interaction, representing 71.07% of total direct interactions, followed by the number of retweets (16,104), which represents 20.67%.

Table 4. Aggregated Twitter account by country

	Nº Protected Areas	Nº Tweets	Nº Likes	Nº Comments	Nº Retweets
Finland	1	555	9,027	3,233	2,195
France	3	291	2,312	46	467
Italy	10	1,594	10,848	359	2,700
Spain	5	3,569	27,984	1,216	8,859
United Kingdom	1	387	5,210	1,583	1,883
Total	**20**	**6,396**	**55,381**	**6,437**	**16,104**

After calculating the popularity, commitment, and virality scores for all protected areas, we obtain further their mean values by country (see Figure 1). It should be noted that, on average, Finland achieves the best level of engagement with a value of 26.05, followed by the United Kingdom with a value of 22.42. Unlike what was verified by reviewing the scores of direct interactions, Spain is in the third position, which indicates that not publishing more generates greater engagement. The confirmation of this is found in the case of Finland and the United Kingdom, both countries with a low number of publications, but thus obtaining the best levels of commitment of the whole sample.

Figure 1. Popularity, commitment, and virality metrics, and mean engagement scores by country

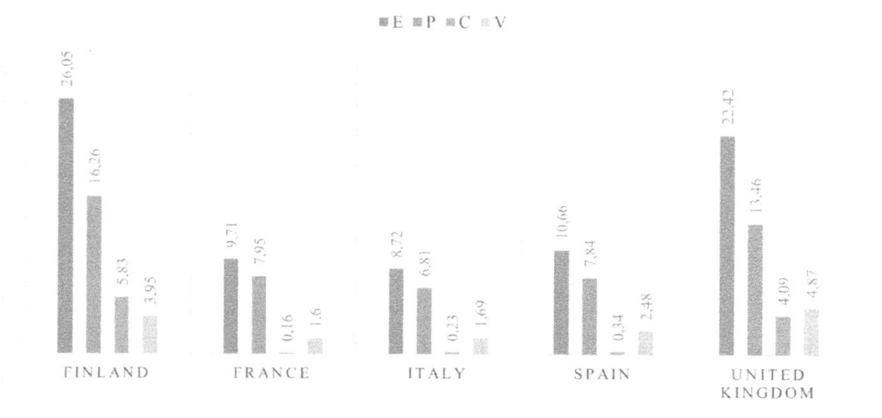

Particularising, we can see how the top five protected areas with the best scores in terms of engagement level (see Table 5) (for being above average) are reached by the natural spaces of Pallas-Yllästunturi National Park (Finland), Cairngomrs National Park (United Kingdom), followed by Parc Natural de l'Alt Pirineu (Spain), Cairngomrs National Park (United Kingdom), Montseny Nature Park (Spain), and Tretino Reti di Riserve Network (Italy).

Table 5. Aggregated Twitter account by protected natural areas

Twitter Account	Country	Average Engagement	Average Popularity	Average Community	Average Virality
Nature Services	Finland	26.05	16.26	5.83	3.95
Pnaltpyrineu	Spain	22.61	17.16	0.75	4.69
Cairngormsnews	United Kingdom	22.42	13.46	4.09	4.87
Montseny	Spain	15.23	10.74	0.53	3.96
Visittrentino	Italy	13.75	11.57	0.32	1.86
Pngranparadiso	Italy	11.66	9.11	0.12	2.44
Mercantour	France	10.18	8.59	0.17	1.42
Png971	France	9.89	6.04	0.11	3.75
Parcscat	Spain	9.75	7.31	0.27	2.17
Network of parks	Spain	9.51	6.55	0.35	2.61
Parco5terre	Italy	9.22	7.19	0.00	2.03
ParcoBeigua	Italy	8.15	5.88	0.17	2.10
ParcoAlpiLiguri	Italy	7.89	5.79	0.43	1.67
ParcoPaneveggio	Italy	4.96	4.00	0.07	0.89
Pnrlat	France	3.70	2.80	0.10	0.80
Torreguaceto	Italy	3.50	2.92	0.06	0.53
Heritage	Spain	3.33	2.39	0.07	0.87
Tuscan Islands	Italy	2.68	1.67	0.06	0.95
ParkSirenteVel	Italy	1.48	1.23	0.00	0.25
Parcomsrm	Italy	1.33	0.92	0.00	0.42
Total general		12.18	8.66	1.01	2.52

Analysis of Content and Level of Engagement Achieved Through Twitter

After descriptively analysing the engagement index and its components, it is imperative to dive into the main topics communicated through Twitter related to the sustainability and conservation of natural parks. Therefore, we have used content analysis, a methodological approach that makes easier to decipher and categorise the essence of the messages, allowing to identify key trends. From this analysis, we have identified 10 recurring topics, presented in Table 6. These categories help to structure and understand information related to sustainability, environmental management, and actions of protected areas for their conservation, which are communicated to the public through tweets.

Table 6. Informational content spread through Twitter

Topic	Denomination	Informative content disclosed
Topic 1	Ecosystem Restoration	Information related to the restoration of natural ecosystems. In this context, certain areas can be restored or help and benefit various species of flora and fauna.
Topic 2	Water Safety	It addresses safety-related tips and precautions when swimming or enjoying bodies of water in the natural environment, highlighting the importance of being prepared and safe.
Topic 3	Citizen Participation	Information on public participation in decision-making and policymaking related to the management of natural parks and the environment.
Topic 4	Conservation collaboration	This category includes initiatives and collaborative projects with external organisations or institutions for the conservation and protection of fauna and flora.
Topic 5	Environmental awareness	Messages that promote environmental awareness and individual responsibility in the conservation of the environment and respect for natural areas.
Topic 6	Outdoor Tips	Practical tips and recommendations are provided for outdoor activities, such as responsibly camping.
Topic 7	Education and Communication	This category includes messages related to environmental education and communication, such as welcome groups visiting the park or interviews with conservation experts.
Topic 8	Preservation of natural parks	It focusses on the preservation and conservation of natural parks, as well as the importance of maintaining their beauty and exploring them responsibly.
Topic 9	Promotion of online resources	It includes links and references to online resources that offer additional information on environmental issues and activities in the park.
Topic 10	Promoting individual responsibility	It emphasises the importance of people taking individual responsibility for protecting the environment and following outdoor guidelines and codes of conduct.

Based on the content analysis, we have extracted significant data that shed light on the predominant themes and their representation in Twitter posts. These results reflect not only the frequency with which certain topics are addressed but also their relevance and the way in which they are presented to the audience. In the following, we detail the main categories identified, their frequency, and some pertinent observations.

Table 7. Main results of content analysis

Topic	Nº Tweets	% Topic	Engagement	P	C	V
Topic 1	270	4,22%	16,67	12,75	0,44	3,47
Topic 2	77	1,20%	12,82	9,68	0,51	2,64
Topic 3	254	3,97%	22,57	7,71	11,98	2,89
Topic 4	482	7,54%	12,13	9,00	0,37	2,76
Topic 5	408	6,38%	14,83	11,17	0,31	3,36
Topic 6	476	7,44%	13,00	10,12	0,32	2,56
Topic 7	1.715	26,81%	10,88	7,61	1,16	2,10
Topic 8	1.931	30,19%	10,92	8,26	0,31	2,35
Topic 9	593	9,27%	8,29	6,07	0,20	2,01
Topic 10	190	2,97%	20,88	15,32	0,42	5,15
Total	6.396	100%	12,18	8,66	1,01	2,52

The content analysis of the tweets published by the set of natural parks has revealed a diverse range of topics addressed, each with varying levels of engagement and interaction with the public. The themes of Parks Preservation (Topic 8) and Environmental Education and Communication (Topic 7) stand out for their frequency, covering 30.19% and 26.81%, respectively, of the total tweets analysed. This underscores the importance and emphasis that parks place on education and the promotion of sustainable conservation practices, which is critical in a world increasingly aware of environmental challenges.

However, the frequency of a topic does not necessarily translate into a high level of engagement. For example, although Topic 3 (Public Participation in Decisions) represents only 3.97% of the total, it has a remarkable level of engagement with a value of 22.57. Particularly striking is its high value in metric C (11.98), suggesting that issues of governance and citizen participation are not only well received but also incite debate and conversation. On the other hand, Topic 10 (Individual Responsibility), although less prevalent (2.97%), boasts high engagement (20.88) and a significant popularity (P) of 15.32, reflecting a strong connection with the audience regarding the importance of the individual role in environmental protection.

It is also remarkable that some topics, despite their intrinsic relevance, do not achieve optimal engagement. In particular, Topic 9, which focusses on offering online resources, has the lowest engagement, at 8.29. Although it represents 9.27% of all tweets issued, its low popularity level (P) and low number of retweets (V) suggest that this type of content may not resonate adequately with the audience.

Shared resources may not be considered essential or may require a more engaging presentation to engage the audience.

On the other hand, although Topic 7 (Environmental Education and Communication) and Topic 8 (Park Preservation) dominate in terms of frequency, together constituting more than 50% of tweets, their engagement levels are surprisingly low, located at 10.88 and 10.92 respectively. This suggests that, although they are central to management communication, the way they are presented may not be generating a deep connection with the audience or encourage the desired interaction. Similarly, Topic 2, which focusses on water security, also shows a lower engagement (12.82) despite the relevance of the topic. The low frequency of the topic could indicate that it is communicated sporadically or that, despite its importance, the audience does not feel the need to interact widely with such content.

The environmental, cultural, and social realities vary considerably between countries and these differences can manifest themselves in the way conservation and sustainability issues are communicated. By analysing content by country, we can not only identify region-specific patterns and trends, but also discern effective practises and opportunities to adapt and fine-tune communication at the local level. Next, we present the results of the content analysis segmented by countries, shedding light on how different geographies reflect and focus their communication on the preservation of natural spaces.

Table 8. Main results of the content analysis grouped by country

	Finland		France		Italy		Spain		United Kingdom	
Topic	**Nº Tweets**	**E**	**Nº Tweets**	**E**	**Nº Tweets**	**E**	**Nº Tweets**	**E**	**Nº Tweets**	**E**
Topic 1	65	29.78	11	10.18	31	8.77	140	11.92	23	22.22
Topic 2	6	18.33	5	11.00	15	6.67	37	14.92	14	12.14
Topic 3	50	73.52	4	15.25	26	6.23	127	9.93	47	12.21
Topic 4	57	18.72	44	7.14	72	7.11	275	12.47	34	15.41
Topic 5	40	50.23	27	10.89	95	9.71	210	11.40	36	12.06
Topic 6	49	12.69	14	12.57	165	12.50	216	13.40	32	13.56
Topic 7	94	15.44	84	8.38	460	8.99	1,006	9.63	71	37.68
Topic 8	174	18.68	66	11.15	506	7.60	1,122	10.83	63	17.33
Topic 9	9	11.44	29	10.24	179	8.46	350	7.42	26	15.50
Topic 10	11	20.91	7	10.86	45	8.47	86	16.53	41	45.34
Total	555	26.05	291	9.71	1,594	8.72	3,569	10.66	387	22.42

Table 8 breaks down the engagement by country and topic. In Spain, a remarkable number of tweets are observed in each category, suggesting a high emphasis on communication. In particular, topic 8, relating to the Preservation and Conservation of Parks, is outstanding. Given the vast biodiversity and the extensive network of protected areas in Spain, this emphasis is consistent, although the level of engagement could be affected by the possible saturation of information.

Finland shows a marked engagement in topic 3, which focuses on Public Participation in Decisions. This could be aligned with the well-known Finnish tradition of transparency and citizen participation. Furthermore, topic 1, which refers to the restoration of ecosystems, has a significant impact on the sample, which may reflect cultural respect for the environment in this country.

Continuing with the analysis in the United Kingdom, it is observed that the engagement achieved with topic 10, related to Individual Responsibility in Environmental Protection, stands out significantly. In line with the arguments made so far, this may be correlated with British culture and its emphasis on civic responsibility and traditional valuing of the natural environment.

Italy, on the other hand, reflects a concentration of tweets in topics 7 and 8, which address Environmental Education and Communication and the Preservation and Conservation of Parks, respectively. Undoubtedly, the geographical richness and the Italian natural heritage contribute to the communicative emphasis on these topics. However, the modest level of engagement achieved could suggest familiarity or even thematic saturation in the audience.

Finally, France exhibits lower levels of engagement through the different topics. This could be due to France's long history of conservation and its geographical diversity, which could be causing the audience to already have a solid knowledge base, which could influence the moderate levels of interaction achieved through social networks.

CONCLUSION

Digital interaction on platforms such as Twitter has become an essential tool for protected areas, and this study sheds light on the complexity and nuances of this relationship in the European context, especially in protected areas linked to EUROPARC.

Analysis of online stakeholder engagement with protected areas reveals significant trends in interaction. There is a marked preference for quick and simple actions, such as giving "likes" and "retweets", over actions that require more effort, such as commenting. This trend coincides with previous literature, noting that low-effort actions, such as clicking to "like," dominate social media interaction. Therefore, when breaking down this index into its three components, popularity (P), commitment (C), and virality (V), it is observed that popularity has the highest value, followed by virality, and finally commitment.

Geographically, although Spain leads in the number of publications and likes, Finland shows the highest commitment from its stakeholders, followed by the United Kingdom. This suggests that a higher volume of posts does not necessarily translate into greater engagement. Finland and the United Kingdom, despite having fewer publications, achieve the highest levels of engagement rates. In terms of individual protected areas, Pallas-Yllästunturi National Park in Finland and Cairngomrs National Park in the UK are leaders in engagement, demonstrating that the quality and possibly content of publications are key factors for engagement.

Tweets are not simply messages; they transmit values, information, and, in many cases, invite action. In the context of protected areas, we observe that the themes of Environmental Education and Communication, as well as the Preservation and

Conservation of Parks, dominate the publications. This is understandable given the mission and objectives of protected areas. However, a key finding is that the frequency of a topic does not necessarily translate into greater engagement. For example, although Citizen Participation in Decisions constitutes only a small percentage of total tweets, it generates a remarkable level of engagement. This finding highlights the importance of relevant and timely content that resonates with the public's concerns and values of the public. Therefore, care must be taken not to saturate the audience with repeated themes, ensuring the diversity and relevance of the shared content.

Another key dimension is the nature of the interaction. In the digital world, not all interactions are created equally. Our analysis shows that certain forms of interaction, such as comments, can be indicative of deeper engagement. Unlike a "like" or a "retweet," which are quick, passive actions, comments represent a level of active engagement. They indicate a willingness to dialogue, debate, and reflect on the content. In this context, the high value in the engagement metric for issues such as Citizen Participation is remarkable, suggesting that certain topics, particularly those that touch on governance and public participation, are not only well received but also generate discussion and dialogue.

For topics with lower metrics (such as promoting online resources or water safety), they can offer opportunities to review and adjust communication strategies. It is essential to understand the reason behind these metrics and consider presenting the information in a more engaging or relevant way to the audience. A deep reflection on the content can be useful in improving engagement and interaction with these specific topics.

Despite the findings made, this work is not without limitations. One of them is the exclusive focus on Twitter. Although this is a social network with a notorious presence in the digital world, it is only one among many. Each platform has its own dynamic, and what works on Twitter might not be effective on, say, Instagram or Facebook. Therefore, while this study provides a valuable understanding of Twitter engagement, a more complete picture would require considering multiple platforms.

Additionally, the analysis was based on a specific time period. Digital dynamics is fluid and constantly changing. A significant event, be it a natural disaster or a political initiative, could drastically change the dynamics of interaction in a short period of time. Therefore, it could be relevant to use a longer study period.

Precisely, opportunities can arise from weaknesses, and in this case a possible avenue for future studies would be to explore digital interaction on other social platforms to obtain a more complete picture of the digital landscape. In addition, it would be valuable to conduct longitudinal studies to observe how the dynamics of the interaction changes over time. Another interesting direction would be to further explore the relationship between content and engagement, even identifying statistically significant relationships that could occur. It would also be interesting to investigate how different geographical, cultural and socioeconomic contexts influence the level of engagement achieved by protected areas.

REFERENCES

Abbasi, A. Z., Tsiotsou, R. H., Hussain, K., Rather, R. A., & Ting, D. H. (2023). Investigating the impact of social media images' value, consumer engagement, and involvement on eWOM of a tourism destination: A transmittal mediation approach. *Journal of Retailing and Consumer Services*, *71*, 103231. doi:10.1016/j.jretconser.2022.103231

Alonso-Cañadas, J., Galán-Valdivieso, F., Saraite-Sariene, L., & Caba-Perez, M. D. C. (2019). Unpacking the Drivers of Stakeholder Engagement in Sustainable Water Management: NGOs and the Use of Facebook. *Water (Basel)*, *11*(4), 775. doi:10.3390/w11040775

Arkema, K. K., Fisher, D. M., Wyatt, K., Wood, S. A., & Payne, H. J. (2021). Advancing sustainable development and protected area management with social media-based tourism data. *Sustainability (Basel)*, *13*(5), 2427. doi:10.3390/su13052427

Ashley, C. (2000). *The impacts of tourism on rural livelihoods: Namibia's experience*. Overseas Development Institute.

Asmelash, A. G., & Kumar, S. (2019). The structural relationship between tourist satisfaction and sustainable heritage tourism development in Tigrai, Ethiopia. *Heliyon*, *5*(3), e01335. doi:10.1016/j.heliyon.2019.e01335 PMID:30957037

Becken, S. (2005). The role of tourist icons for sustainable tourism. *Journal of Vacation Marketing*, *11*(1), 21–30. doi:10.1177/1356766705050840

Björk, P. (2000). Ecotourism from a conceptual perspective, an extended definition of a unique tourism form. *International Journal of Tourism Research*, *2*(3), 189–202. doi:10.1002/(SICI)1522-1970(200005/06)2:3<189::AID-JTR195>3.0.CO;2-T

Bonsón, E., & Ratkai, M. (2013). A set of metrics to assess stakeholder engagement and social legitimacy on a corporate Facebook page. *Online Information Review*, *37*(5), 787–803. doi:10.1108/OIR-03-2012-0054

Chiwaridzo, O. T., & Masengu, R. (2023). The impact of social media branding and technology adoption on green tourism: The role of tourist behavior as a mediator in developing countries post-COVID-19—context of Zimbabwe. *Future Business Journal*, *9*(1), 63. doi:10.1186/s43093-023-00249-6

Europarc Federation. (2023). *Who we are.* Europarc. https://www.europarc.org/who-we-are/

Falatoonitoosi, E., Schaer, V., & Kerr, D. (2022). Does sustainable tourism development enhance destination prosperity? *Journal of Hospitality & Tourism Research (Washington, D.C.)*, *46*(5), 1056–1082. doi:10.1177/1096348020988328

Font, X., Higham, J., Miller, G., & Pourfakhimi, S. (2019). Research engagement, impact and sustainable tourism. *Journal of Sustainable Tourism*, *27*(1), 1–11. doi:10.1080/09669582.2019.1560673

Fotis, J., Buhalis, D., & Rossides, N. (2012). Social media use and impact during the holiday travel planning process. In *Information and communication technologies in Tourism* (pp. 13–24). Springer. doi:10.1007/978-3-7091-1142-0_2

Galiano-Coronil, A., Blanco-Moreno, S., Tobar-Pesantez, L. B., & Gutiérrez-Montoya, G. A. (2023). Social media impact of tourism managers: A decision tree approach in happiness, social marketing and sustainability. *Journal of Management Development*, *42*(6), 436–457. doi:10.1108/JMD-04-2023-0131

Gálvez-Rodríguez, M. del M., Saraite-Sariene, L., Alonso-Cañadas, J., & Caba-Pérez, M. del C. (2017). Stakeholder Engagement via Social Media in the Hospitality Sector. In M. Dhiman (Ed.), *Opportunities and Challenges for Tourism and Hospitality in the BRIC Nations* (pp. 15–30). IGI Global. doi:10.4018/978-1-5225-0708-6.ch002

Gartner, S., Nicholson, A., & Christou, E. (2020). *Tourism marketing and distribution through social media: Assessing business economic performance. MPRA Paper 99194*. University Library of Munich.

Gómez-Carrasco, P., Guillamón-Saorín, E., & García Osma, B. (2021). Stakeholders versus firm communication in social media: The case of Twitter and corporate social responsibility information. *European Accounting Review*, *30*(1), 31–62. doi:10.1080/09638180.2019.1708428

Krutwaysho, O., & Bramwell, B. (2010). Tourism policy implementation and society. *Annals of Tourism Research*, *37*(3), 670–691. doi:10.1016/j.annals.2009.12.004

Leung, Y. F., Spenceley, A., Hvenegaard, G., Buckley, R., & Groves, C. (2018). *Tourism and visitor management in protected areas: Guidelines for sustainability* (Vol. 27). IUCN., doi:10.2305/IUCN.CH.2018.PAG.27.en

Lewis, C., Prayag, G., & Pour, S. (2021). Linking travel motives to identity and travel behavior of the Australian LGBT market during COVID-19. *Journal of Travel & Tourism Marketing*, *38*(7), 725–741. doi:10.1080/10548408.2021.1985039

Luque-Martínez, T., Faraoni, N., & Doña-Toledo, L. (2019). Auditing the marketing and social media communication of natural protected areas. How marketing can contribute to the sustainability of tourism. *Sustainability (Basel)*, *11*(15), 4014. doi:10.3390/su11154014

Mariani, M., Di Felice, M., & Mura, M. (2016). Facebook as a destination marketing tool: Evidence from Italian regional Destination Management Organizations. *Tourism Management*, *56*, 321–343. doi:10.1016/j.tourman.2015.12.008

Mendieta-Aragón, A. (2022). Changes in tourism behaviour after COVID-19: Towards a new profile of tourists and leisure travel in Spain. *Rect@. Electronic Journal of Communications and Works of ASEPUMA*, *23*(1), 37–51.

Monsalve-Pelaez, M., Tovar-Meléndez, A., & Salazar-Araujo, E. (2023). Documentary Review on Sustainable Tourism in the Framework of the SDGs. *Revista Turismo & Desenvolvimento (Aveiro)*, *40*, 137–153. doi:10.34624/rtd.v40i0.31483

Moon, H., & Han, H. (2019). Tourist experience quality and loyalty to an island destination: The moderating impact of destination image. *Journal of Travel & Tourism Marketing*, *36*(1), 43–59. doi:10.1080/10548408.2018.1494083

Murphy, P. (1985). *Tourism: A community approach*. Methuen.

Rasoolimanesh, S. M., Ramakrishna, S., Hall, C. M., Esfandiar, K., & Seyf, S. (2020). A systematic scoping review of sustainable tourism indicators in relation to the sustainable development goals. *Journal of Sustainable Tourism*, *31*(7), 1–21. doi:10.1080/09669582.2020.1775621

Soboleva, A., Burton, S., Mallik, G., & Khan, A. (2017). 'Retweet for a chance to...': An analysis of what triggers consumers to engage in seeded eWOM on twitter. *Journal of Marketing Management*, *33*(13–14), 1120–1148. doi:10.1080/0267257X.2017.1369142

Tham, A., Mair, J., & Croy, G. (2020). Social media influence on tourists' destination choice: Importance of context. *Tourism Recreation Research*, *45*(2), 161–175. doi:10.1080/02508281.2019.1700655

United Nations Conference on Trade and Development (UNCTAD) (2013, January). *Sustainable tourism: Contribution to economic growth and sustainable development.* UN. https://unctad.org/meetings/en/sessionaldocuments/ciem5d2_en.pdf

Walker, T., Lee, T. J., & Li, X. (2021). Sustainable development for small island tourism: Developing slow tourism in the Caribbean. *Journal of Travel & Tourism Marketing*, *38*(1), 115. doi:10.1080/10548408.2020.1842289

Yuan, Y., Chan, C-S., Eichelberger, S., Ma, H., Pikkemaat, B. (2022) The effect of social media on travel planning process by Chinese tourists: the way forward to tourism futures. *Journal of Tourism Futures*. doi:10.1108/JTF-04-2021-0094

Zeng, B., & Gerritsen, R. (2014). What do we know about social media in tourism? A review. *Tourism Management Perspectives*, *10*, 27–36. doi:10.1016/j.tmp.2014.01.001

Chapter 10
Mindful Consumers and New Marketing Strategies for the Restaurant Business:
Evidence of Bangladesh

Mohammad Badruddoza Talukder
https://orcid.org/0000-0001-7788-2732
International University of Business Agriculture and Technology, Bangladesh

Sanjeev Kumar
https://orcid.org/0000-0002-7375-7341
Lovely Professional University, India

Iva Rani Das
https://orcid.org/0009-0006-9805-4331
University of Dhaka, Bangladesh

ABSTRACT

People in Bangladesh know what they want and need to buy, which has changed the food business and made it necessary to use new marketing tactics. People who make purchases with ethics, sustainability, and health in mind are called mindful customers. The restaurant business should be honest, open, and socially responsible. In response to this new consumer trend, restaurant owners and marketers must develop new ways to draw and keep mindful consumers. This chapter focused on locally sourced products, showing sustainable practices, pushing healthy meal choices, and using social media and online platforms to express brand values. This chapter also talks about the problems the food industry faces and its strategies,

DOI: 10.4018/979-8-3693-0960-5.ch010

such as supply chain limits, educating customers, and competition. It could include a better brand image, loyal customers, and long-term sustainability. Overall, this chapter gives valuable information about how mindful customers are changing. It also gives restaurant owners and advertisers tips on using this new paradigm in the Bangladesh restaurant business.

INTRODUCTION

Bangladesh's food industry is changing because customers are becoming more aware. Mindful purchasers prioritize health, ethics, and sustainability when shopping.

This phenomenon can be observed from various perspectives, such as individuals' decision-making processes regarding their dining choices. Consumers today want businesses to be honest, open, and socially responsible beyond having good food and a lovely setting. So, restaurant owners and marketers must develop unique ways to market their businesses to attract and keep the growing number of health-conscious diners (Khalifa, 2015).

This chapter examines the idea of "mindful consumption" and what it means for the Bangladeshi food business. This study aims to find out what makes customers more aware, how their needs are changing, and what their buying habits mean for the business as a whole. By understanding how aware customers think and what their moral standards are, restaurant owners and marketers can create effective marketing campaigns that meet their needs and help them stand out in a market where competition is fierce (Mohammad et al., 2024a).

Bangladesh has a diverse spectrum of culinary practices and experiences, providing it with an extraordinary capacity to satisfy the requirements of choosy clients (Siddique, 2020). The active culinary culture of the nation can successfully incorporate sustainable and ethical practices, resulting in an attractive coordination that connects with the growing demographic of conscious consumers (Oosterveer & Sonnenfeld, 2012). To succeed in the current market, restaurants must employ innovative and targeted marketing strategies that exceed traditional methods.

Bangladeshi restaurants have the potential to enhance their brand reputation, develop a devoted customer base, and contribute to the industry's growth by implementing mindful consumption practices and aligning their marketing strategies accordingly. The restaurant industry in Bangladesh is experiencing an essential change towards increased mindfulness and social responsibility (Reich et al., 2010). This response addresses customers' evolving preferences and presents a prospect for expansion and differentiation within a gradually competitive market (Arnold & Quelch, 1998).

In this chapter, we'll look at the idea of "mindful consumption" and what it means for the restaurant industry in Bangladesh through the lens of relevant studies and industry views. We aim to give restaurant owners and marketers practical advice by examining successful case studies and determining the best practices. These suggestions will help them make the most of the current paradigm shift and be successful in an age where customers are more aware.

This chapter aims to give restaurants in Bangladesh helpful information about the specific marketing tactics they can use to reach out to people who care about what they eat. In this study, we will look at different ways a restaurant can become more environmentally friendly and health-conscious. These strategies include prioritizing using locally sourced ingredients, promoting sustainable practices, offering a wide range of healthy menu options, using social media and digital platforms to their fullest potential, and getting the community involved by working together (Mohammad et al., 2023). We will also look at the problems and possible benefits of implementing these strategies, such as the limited supply of sustainable ingredients, the need to educate consumers, and the financial effects.

THE KNOWLEDGE OF SMART CUSTOMERS

In our modern society, which has many food choices and a wide range of tasty flavors, a group of people who call themselves "mindful consumers" has grown. These people, who have a strong sense of purpose and a desire for positive change, are fundamentally reshaping the food business and changing how we eat (Sanderson Bellamy et al., 2021). By understanding what makes consumers tick and who they are, we can learn more about the fundamentals of their choices and how they affect the global food scene.

The Meaning of "Mindful Consumers" and What Makes Them Picky

People who decide what they buy with more awareness and care are "mindful consumers (Kaczorowska et al., 2019)." People eat for more than just the pleasure of their taste buds. Their food choices are based on beliefs and ideals, including worries about health, the environment, and moral questions (Mohammad et al., 2024b).

Characteristics of Mindful Consumers:

- **Ethical Priorities:** Ethical practices and ideals are essential to customers who are paying attention. They look for businesses and goods that align with what they believe in. They support companies committed to fair labor methods, protecting the environment, and getting their products responsibly (Gunawan et al., 2020).

- **Health and well-being:** Mindful customers care about their health, which is apparent from choosing healthy options (Ditlevsen et al., 2019). They look for food that is good for the body and the mind, focusing on natural products that have been treated as little as possible.
- **Concern for the environment:** Being concerned about the environment is crucial for mindful customers. They know how what they buy affects the environment and tend to choose eco-friendly and healthy products.
- **Social responsibility:** Aware customers pay attention to social problems and the well-being of their communities (Ditlevsen et al., 2019). They actively back businesses that do good things for society through charitable work and activity in the community.

The Fundamental Basis of the Mindfulness Movement

The emergence of mindful consumerism can be attributed to various factors indicative of global trends and changes in societal awareness. In Bangladesh, similar to numerous other regions globally, this movement has garnered significant traction owing to a multitude of compelling factors:

- **The emergence of health and wellness awareness:** People are paying more attention to their well-being and are actively looking for food choices that help improve their physical health and general energy (Talukder & Kumar, 2023). More and more people are trying to live better lives, leading to a trend called "mindfulness," in which people actively look for and choose healthy food choices (Thiermann & Sheate, 2022).
- **Environmental concerns:** In light of global environmental problems such as climate change and resource depletion, there is a growing consciousness among individuals regarding their ecological footprint (Talukder, 2020). Like consumers in other regions, mindful consumers in Bangladesh actively pursue strategies to minimize their environmental impact by making sustainable and environmentally conscious decisions.
- **The availability of information:** With the rise of technology and the start of the digital age, customers now have easy access to a wide range of information. By turning on a digital screen, people can learn about how ethically companies act, where their ingredients come from, and the social effects of their food choices (Kumar et al., 2024). The availability of information has significantly impacted individuals' decision-making processes regarding consumption

and has played a crucial role in driving the growth of mindful movement (Kuziemski & Misuraca, 2020).

Implications for the Food Industry

The food sector is undergoing extraordinary change due to the expanding group of mindful consumers. Businesses must adopt new techniques and strategies to satisfy the demands of these moral customers for transparency, sustainability, and ethics.

Restaurants and other food businesses are pressured to offer more than delicious flavors. They must have a dedication to community involvement, environmental responsibility, and responsible sourcing. The expansion of plant-based menus, eco-friendly packaging, and programs to decrease food waste are examples of how conscious consumerism has affected the food business (M. J. Kim et al., 2020).

THE PRESENT CONDITION OF THE RESTAURANT INDUSTRY IN BANGLADESH

Overview of the Restaurant Industry

The restaurant industry in Bangladesh is experiencing significant growth and development, with solid foundations in the nation's diverse culinary heritage. Bangladesh's restaurant industry exhibits a remarkable diversity level and continues to experience steady expansion. Within the culinary landscape, one can find diverse dining establishments, covering both traditional eateries specializing in delectable regional cuisine and contemporary establishments offering a global selection of dishes (Talukder, 2021).

Growth and expansion: In Bangladesh, the food business has grown significantly over the past decade. As cities grow, the middle class grows, and social habits change, more and more people are eating out. As a result, there are many more restaurants in big cities than there used to be. This is because more people want to try different kinds of food. Bangladesh's food scene is changing, with a wide range of tastes that make for a lively, delicious food map (Talukder et al., 2023).

Challenges in the industry: Even though the food business is growing and doing well, there are still problems. In a market with many different eating options and competition, restaurants must constantly work to set themselves apart and offer unique value. The world of cuisine is a highly competitive field where only the bravest and most creative people can survive and do well (Tien, 2019).

Adapting to Consumer Preferences

Changing palettes: One's sense of taste and capacity to discriminate between flavors shifts as one's values and lifestyle shift. Traditional Bangladeshi food has always been popular and continues to draw fans from all walks of life. However, modern consumers are more open to trying new foods. They are likelier to try exotic spices and seasonings worldwide (Cai et al., 2021). Foods from other cultures and traditions tend to pique people's interest, and they are willing to try them. So they go from place to place searching for new and exciting cuisine. Thanks to this event, participants may sample foods from around the world without leaving their neighborhood.

Health and awareness: People are becoming more aware of their health and fitness, which means they are paying more attention to what they eat. People in this group are very interested in eating healthy and well-balanced meals. So, they actively look for places to eat that offer various healthier options. They are ready to work with different diets, such as vegetarian, vegan, and gluten-free. There is a growing trend toward healthy eating, which means that people are actively looking for meals that are good for their bodies and minds (Sogari et al., 2018).

Sustainable ethics: The rise of conscious customers has spread to the food business, where people look for places that share their morals. People who care about the environment are likelier to choose locations that use eco-friendly packaging and responsibly get their goods (Talukder et al., 2022). It is as if the table has turned, and guests are changing the world by what they eat.

Technology and convenience: In the fast-moving digital age, it is hard to say enough about how vital user-friendliness is. People usually expect businesses to use new technologies, like online booking systems, delivery services, and easy payment methods. Restaurants that do not change to meet the needs of tech-savvy customers risk falling behind in a field that is already very competitive. Eating at a restaurant has become a digital experience where ease is the most important thing.

MARKET ANALYSIS AND CUSTOMER FEEDBACK

Importance of Market Research for Conscious Buyers

The restaurant industry in Bangladesh is competitive. Thus, it is important to conduct market research to learn about Bangladeshi diners' specific wants and demands. The trend toward mindful eating necessitates constantly evolving marketing strategies to stay up with consumer preferences (Thiermann & Sheate, 2022). This will ensure that their success does not stop. To better understand their customers, restaurants might do extensive market research. This will help change menus to meet these customers' sophisticated preferences.

Understanding mindful consumers: Performing market research makes it easier to understand the motives and actions taken by mindful buyers. It assists in identifying the elements that influence their decisions, such as morality, ethics, and social responsibility. Restaurants can match their menus, buying procedures, and marketing plans with the preferences and ideals of their ethical customers based on the information supplied (Peters & Remaud, 2020). It requires recognizing the underlying causes that influence ethical customers' behavior.

Identifying trends and market gaps: Market research plays a pivotal role in assisting businesses in identifying emerging trends and potential gaps within the restaurant industry. Through researching customer preferences and habits, companies can uncover novel strategies for improving their services and providing distinctive options that resonate with discerning and well-informed customers (Ginter et al., 2018).

Methods and Tools for Gathering Consumer Insights

Surveys: Customer surveys serve as an effective instrument for collecting quantitative and qualitative data from many participants. Restaurants can conduct surveys among their clientele to gain insights into their preferences regarding food, dining habits, and attitudes toward socially and ecologically responsible practices (Sarmiento & El Hanandeh, 2018). The process resembles the compilation of perspectives from multiple individuals who observe and contemplate their environment.

Focus groups: Focus groups allow restaurants to engage in direct and meaningful discussions with a select group of mindful consumers. This interactive approach enables a more profound understanding of consumer emotions, values, and preferences, thereby achieving significant qualitative data that can inform decision-making processes (Alsharif et al., 2021). This platform can be compared to a culinary roundtable, allowing mindful customers to express their opinions and perspectives.

Social media monitoring: Contemporary platforms offer extensive data on present-day consumers. By monitoring social media platforms, restaurants can gain valuable insights into their customers' experiences, current preferences, and potential future trends (Vu et al., 2019).

Recent Studies on Mindful Restaurant Customers

Recent research and surveys have provided insights into mindful customers' behavioral patterns and preferences within the restaurant sector. These main conclusions are provided:

1. **Sustainability matters:** The findings of a survey show that many mindful customers in Bangladesh place a high level of importance on sustainability when deciding which restaurant to visit (Vu et al., 2019). They are more inclined to patronize restaurants that utilize eco-friendly packaging, legally source their goods, and avoid wasting much food.
2. **Healthy dining choices:** The carefulness shown by customers can be linked to their concern regarding their welfare. The research findings suggest that individuals actively pursue establishments that provide food options that promote nutrition and health, such as plant-based dishes made from organic ingredients (Blanco-Gutiérrez et al., 2020).
3. **Social impact:** Mindful consumers want to support restaurants that give back to the community (Thiermann & Sheate, 2022). The research highlighted that establishments involved in social initiatives and charity work gain favor among conscious diners.
4. **Transparency builds trust:** The study revealed that transparency is a critical factor in gaining the trust of mindful consumers. Restaurants that openly communicate their sourcing practices and ethical commitments are more likely to attract and retain conscious customers (Cho & Yoo, 2021).

ADAPTING MARKETING STRATEGIES FOR MINDFUL CONSUMERS

Limitations of Traditional Marketing for Mindful Consumers

Traditional marketing strategies, which often focus solely on product features and mass appeal, may fall short when targeting mindful consumers. These discerning diners seek more than just superficial messaging; they crave authenticity, transparency, and alignment with their values. Traditional marketing may not effectively communicate a restaurant's commitment to sustainability, ethical practices, and health-conscious offerings, leaving mindful consumers feeling disconnected and unengaged (De Villiers et al., 2020).

The Significance of Transparency, Authenticity, and Sustainability in Marketing

Transparency: Mindful consumers value transparency in their dining choices. They want to know the story behind their meals, from sourcing ingredients to the preparation process. Restaurants openly sharing information about their suppliers, sustainable practices, and environmental initiatives build trust and credibility with mindful consumers (Hwang & Lee, 2019).

Authenticity: Authenticity resonates deeply with mindful consumers. They seek genuine experiences and authentic connections with the brands they choose. Restaurants that stay true to their values and provide a consistent dining experience rooted in authenticity are more likely to earn the loyalty of conscious diners (M. Kim & Lee, 2022).

Sustainability: With environmental concerns at the forefront, sustainability is crucial for mindful consumers. Restaurants that prioritize eco-friendly practices and communicate their efforts to reduce waste and carbon footprint gain favor among this conscious audience (Dinh, 2020).

Examples of Successful Marketing Strategies for Mindful Consumers

International Example: Sweetgreen (United States)

Sweetgreen, a popular fast-casual salad chain in the United States, has successfully targeted mindful consumers with its marketing strategies. They prioritize transparency by displaying the sources of their ingredients on large chalkboards in their restaurants. Customers can learn about the farms and suppliers that provide the fresh produce, fostering a sense of trust and connection with the brand (Nakandala et al., 2020). Sweetgreen emphasizes sustainability by using compostable packaging and engaging in local community initiatives. Their marketing campaigns highlight their commitment to healthy, sustainable, and ethically sourced food, resonating with their conscious customer base.

Local Example: Nondon Park (Dhaka, Bangladesh)

Nondon Park, a local restaurant in Dhaka, Bangladesh, has embraced mindful marketing strategies to cater to conscious consumers. They promote their farm-to-table approach, showcasing the locally sourced ingredients used in their dishes. Nondon Park actively engages with customers through social media, sharing stories of their partnerships with local farmers and artisans. Their marketing campaigns focus on their dishes' health benefits and dedication to sustainable practices, appealing to health-conscious and environmentally aware diners in Bangladesh.

EMBRACING SUSTAINABILITY AND ETHICAL PRACTICES

Importance of Sustainability and Ethics in Restaurant Operations

Incorporating sustainability and ethical practices into restaurant operations is no longer a choice but necessary in today's conscious dining landscape (Liu & Lin, 2020). Mindful consumers seek more than just a delicious meal; they desire a dining experience that aligns with their values and contributes positively to society and the environment. Embracing sustainability and ethical practices not only satisfies this demand but also presents several benefits for restaurants:

Building customer loyalty: Mindful consumers are loyal to restaurants that share their values. By demonstrating a commitment to sustainability and ethics, restaurants build trust and forge meaningful connections with their conscious customer base.

Attracting new customers: According to Talukder & Bhuiyan (2022), sustainability is a growing trend, and many consumers actively seek out restaurants with eco-friendly and ethical practices. By incorporating such initiatives, restaurants can attract a broader customer base, including those who prioritize conscious dining choices.

Contributing to a better world: Restaurants are crucial in shaping consumption habits and positively impacting the environment and local communities(Higgins-Desbiolles & Wijesinghe, 2021). By implementing sustainable practices, they become change agents, contributing to a better and more conscious world.

Sustainable Initiatives in Restaurant Operations

1. **Sourcing Local and Organic Ingredients:** Restaurants can support local farmers and reduce their carbon footprint by sourcing ingredients locally. Using organic produce, they promote healthier options for their customers and contribute to the environment's well-being (Mendini et al., 2019). It's like bringing the farm-to-table concept to life, with every bite infused with freshness and responsibility!

2. **Reducing food waste:** Food waste is a significant issue in the restaurant industry. By reducing food waste through portion control, creative menu planning, and partnering with food donation programs, restaurants can minimize their environmental impact and make a positive social contribution. It's like turning food waste into a delicious opportunity to feed needy people!
3. **Eco-friendly packaging:** Restaurants can opt for eco-friendly and biodegradable packaging materials, reducing single-use plastics and minimizing waste (Varkey et al., 2021). This sustainable initiative showcases the restaurant's commitment to environmental conservation and resonates with mindful consumers. It's like wrapping their culinary creations with a sustainable bow!

Showcase of Sustainable Restaurants in Bangladesh

Example: The Atrium (Dhaka, Bangladesh)

The Atrium, a popular restaurant in Dhaka, Bangladesh, has successfully implemented sustainable practices, positively impacting its marketing efforts. They source a significant portion of their ingredients from local farmers, supporting the community and reducing transportation-related emissions. The Atrium actively participates in food donation programs, distributing excess food to needy people, and proudly communicates this initiative through its marketing channels. By embracing eco-friendly packaging and reducing single-use plastics, they showcase their commitment to environmental sustainability. Their marketing campaigns emphasize the importance of conscious dining, and they connect with mindful consumers through social media by sharing behind-the-scenes stories of their sustainable practices.

DIGITAL MARKETING AND SOCIAL MEDIA ENGAGEMENT

Role of Digital Marketing and Social Media in Reaching and Engaging Mindful Consumers

In the modern era of technology and connectivity, digital marketing and social media have emerged as essential tools for restaurants to reach and engage mindful consumers (Dabas et al., 2021). These platforms offer an unprecedented opportunity to connect with the target audience, share the restaurant's values and sustainability efforts, and foster meaningful relationships with conscious diners.

Global reach and accessibility: Digital marketing enables restaurants to transcend geographical boundaries and connect with mindful consumers beyond their local area. Social media platforms offer a borderless stage where restaurants can showcase their conscious dining experiences to a diverse audience. It's like serving up a flavorful culinary experience that reaches every corner of the globe!

Building community and brand loyalty: Social media facilitates the formation of an engaged community of conscious diners. By consistently sharing valuable content and insights, restaurants can build brand loyalty and trust among their audience. Engaging with followers through comments and messages fosters a sense of belonging and appreciation. It's like creating a mindful dining family, where everyone gathers around the virtual table to savor the experience!

Effective Strategies for Creating Impactful and Authentic Content

1. **Storytelling with purpose:** Mindful consumers value authenticity and meaningful narratives. Restaurants can tell compelling stories about their sustainability journey, highlighting the impact of their eco-friendly practices and ethical sourcing (Sarmiento & El Hanandeh, 2018). Stories that resonate emotionally with the audience are likelier to leave a lasting impression. It's like writing a flavorful tale that touches the heart and nourishes the soul!
2. **Visual delight:** High-quality visuals play a significant role in capturing the attention of mindful consumers on social media. Restaurants can use stunning images and engaging videos to showcase their sustainable dishes, ingredient sourcing, and eco-friendly practices. Visually appealing content leaves a lasting impression on conscious diners.
3. **Behind-the-scenes glimpse:** Transparency is critical to connecting with mindful consumers. Restaurants can offer behind-the-scenes glimpses into their kitchen and sourcing practices, showcasing the efforts to reduce waste, support local farmers, and promote sustainability (Sarmiento & El Hanandeh, 2018). This authenticity builds trust with the audience.

Use of Social Media Platforms to Communicate Sustainability Efforts

1. **Showcasing Eco-Friendly Initiatives:** Social media allows restaurants to highlight their eco-friendly initiatives and sustainable practices (Khalifa, 2015). Regular posts about composting, recycling, energy conservation, and

other green efforts demonstrate the restaurant's commitment to environmental responsibility.

2. **Interactive campaigns:** Restaurants can engage mindful consumers through interactive social media campaigns. For example, challenges related to sustainable dining habits or sharing tips can encourage meaningful participation and dialogue. These campaigns foster a sense of community and conscious living.
3. **Responding to feedback:** Social media platforms allow restaurants to listen and respond to consumer feedback. Promptly addressing questions, concerns, and suggestions shows that the restaurant values its customers' opinions and is committed to continuous improvement.

NEW MARKETING STRATEGIES FOR THE RESTAURANT BUSINESS

Sustainable Sourcing and Transparent Supply Chains

Sustainable sourcing is a vital aspect of mindful dining, reflecting a restaurant's commitment to ethical practices and environmental responsibility. By sourcing local, organic, and sustainable ingredients, restaurants support local farmers and reduce their carbon footprint (Gunawan et al., 2020). Transparent supply chains play a crucial role in building trust with mindful consumers, as they want to know the origins of their food and the ethical practices involved in its production.

Green Bistro: Green Bistro, located in Dhaka, Bangladesh, is a shining example of sustainable sourcing in the restaurant industry. They prioritize using locally sourced, organic ingredients in their dishes. They transparently showcase the local farms and suppliers they partner with through engaging social media posts and in-house displays. This has resonated with conscious diners, creating a loyal customer base that appreciates their commitment to sustainable practices.

Health-Conscious Menus and Nutritional Transparency

As health consciousness increases among consumers, there is a growing demand for healthier food options in restaurants. Mindful consumers seek nutritious, well-balanced meals that contribute to their well-being (Thiermann & Sheate, 2022). Providing nutritional information on menus empowers diners to make informed choices aligning with their health goals and values.

Healthy Bites Café: Healthy Bites Café, situated in Chittagong, Bangladesh, has successfully developed a health-conscious menu that caters to mindful consumers. They offer many nutritious dishes, including plant-based options and gluten-free alternatives. The café provides detailed nutritional information for each menu item on its website and menu cards, allowing customers to make health-conscious choices. Their commitment to transparency and nutritional value has garnered praise from health-conscious diners and has contributed to their positive reputation.

Embracing Technology and Social Media Engagement

Technology and social media are pivotal in reaching and engaging mindful consumers. Social media platforms provide an interactive space where restaurants can showcase their sustainability efforts, share behind-the-scenes stories, and build a community of conscious diners(Presswood, 2019). Online reviews and food delivery apps influence consumer decisions, and restaurants can leverage these platforms to connect with their audience and receive valuable feedback.

Foodie Tales: Foodie Tales, a restaurant in Dhaka, Bangladesh, exemplifies the power of social media engagement. They actively engage with their followers through interactive posts, polls, and contests, creating a sense of community among their conscious audience. Foodie Tales encourages customers to share their dining experiences, which has resulted in user-generated content that showcases their ethical practices. They respond promptly to online reviews, showing they value their customers' feedback. These efforts have strengthened their connection with mindful consumers and have been instrumental in attracting new customers.

CHALLENGES AND OPPORTUNITIES

Challenges Faced by Restaurant Businesses in Adapting to Mindful Consumers

1. **Sourcing sustainable ingredients:** Finding local, organic, and ethically sourced ingredients can be challenging and may come with higher costs. Restaurants need to establish strong relationships with sustainable suppliers and navigate the complexities of seasonal availability (Gunawan et al., 2020).

2. **Changing menu preferences:** Changing mindful consumers' preferences might require significant changes. Restaurants must carefully balance introducing new conscious dishes while retaining their signature flavors. Managing this transition without alienating existing customers can be a delicate task.
3. **Communication and transparency:** Effectively communicating the restaurant's sustainable practices and ethical efforts is crucial. Restaurants need to be transparent and authentic in their messaging to gain the trust of mindful consumers (Hwang & Lee, 2019). Failing to convey their values adequately may result in missed opportunities.

Potential Solutions and Opportunities for Growth

1. **Collaboration and partnerships:** Restaurants can overcome ingredient sourcing challenges by collaborating with local farmers and suppliers committed to sustainable practices (Roy, 2022). Establishing partnerships can create a win-win situation, supporting the local economy and ensuring a steady supply of sustainable ingredients.
2. **Menu diversification:** Embracing mindful consumerism opens up opportunities for menu diversification. Restaurants can experiment with innovative plant-based dishes, introduce sustainable seafood options, and create unique menus catering to health-conscious and ethical diners (De Boer & Aiking, 2019).
3. **Engaging storytelling:** To effectively communicate sustainability efforts, restaurants can leverage engaging storytelling through social media, blog posts, and videos (Gruss et al., 2020). Sharing the restaurant's journey towards sustainability and its positive impact on the community and environment captivates mindful consumers and fosters loyalty.

Potential Benefits for Restaurants That Embrace Mindful Consumerism

1. **Customer loyalty:** Embracing mindful consumerism builds connections with conscious diners. Restaurants that authentically align with the values of their customers gain loyal patrons who return for both the culinary experience and the shared ethical principles (Severt et al., 2022).
2. **Positive reputation:** Restaurants promoting sustainability and ethical practices earn a positive reputation among customers and the broader community. A positive reputation leads to word-of-mouth referrals, media coverage, and increased brand visibility, attracting more mindful consumers (Putri, 2022).

3. **Financial success:** Although embracing mindful consumerism might involve initial investments, the potential for financial success is significant. The growing market of conscious consumers represents an opportunity for long-term profitability and growth. Conscious diners are willing to pay a premium for sustainable and ethical dining experiences (Gunawan et al., 2020).

CONCLUSION AND FUTURE RESEARCH

The rise of mindful consumers is transforming the restaurant industry in Bangladesh, leading to a shift towards sustainability, social responsibility, and personalized experiences. Mindful consumers prioritize ethical sourcing, sustainability, and health-conscious choices, driving restaurants to adopt new marketing strategies, embracing transparency, and collaborating with like-minded businesses. In response to these changing consumer preferences, restaurants in Bangladesh are adopting innovative practices, such as sourcing locally, offering plant-based options, implementing sustainable packaging, and engaging in community initiatives. Leveraging social media, interactive dining experiences, and personalized menus allows restaurants to connect with conscious diners and build brand loyalty.

The challenges restaurants face, such as sourcing sustainable ingredients, managing food waste, and balancing cost and affordability, are being addressed through creative solutions and a commitment to continuous improvement. By fostering transparency and authenticity, restaurants can build trust and credibility among mindful consumers, establishing themselves as leaders in the evolving landscape of conscious consumption. Understanding the evolving preferences and behaviors of mindful consumers in Bangladesh is crucial for developing targeted marketing strategies and sustainable practices. Future research can explore how age, income, and cultural backgrounds influence consumer choices and values. Investigating the impact of technological advancements, such as AI, robotics, and digital platforms, on the restaurant industry's sustainability efforts and customer experiences would provide valuable insights for restaurant owners and policymakers.

Exploring the implementation of circular economy practices in restaurants, including waste reduction strategies and the adoption of reusable packaging, can shed light on their environmental and economic benefits. Examining how restaurants can effectively communicate their sustainability initiatives to consumers and the influence of transparency and authenticity on consumer perception can inform best practices in messaging and branding. Research on the impact and effectiveness of collaborations and partnerships between restaurants and local farmers, suppliers, and other businesses in promoting sustainability and supporting local communities.

Studying the long-term effects of mindful consumption on consumer behavior and how restaurants can sustain consumer interest and engagement in sustainable practices over time. By addressing these research gaps, the restaurant industry in Bangladesh can further refine its strategies to cater to mindful consumers effectively and contribute to a more sustainable and socially responsible future. In conclusion, the era of mindful consumers presents both opportunities and challenges for the restaurant industry in Bangladesh. Embracing sustainability, transparency, authenticity, personalization, and collaboration is essential for restaurants to thrive in this evolving landscape. As the demand for conscious consumption grows, restaurants that proactively adapt to these changing preferences will position themselves as leaders and contribute to a more mindful and sustainable dining experience in Bangladesh.

REFERENCES

Alsharif, A. H., Salleh, N. Z. M., & Baharun, R. (2021). To better understand the role of emotional processes in decision-making. *International Journal of Academic Research in Economics and Management Sciences*, *10*(2), 49–67. doi:10.6007/IJAREMS/v10-i2/9883

Arnold, D. J., & Quelch, J. A. (1998). New strategies in emerging markets. *MIT Sloan Management Review*.

Blanco-Gutiérrez, I., Varela-Ortega, C., & Manners, R. (2020). Evaluating animal-based foods and plant-based alternatives using multi-criteria and SWOT analyses. *International Journal of Environmental Research and Public Health*, *17*(21), 7969. doi:10.3390/ijerph17217969 PMID:33138318

Cai, C. H., Ding, A., & Legendre, T. S. (2021). Exploring persuasive sales techniques to improve customer acceptance of sustainable but unfamiliar menu in restaurants. *International Journal of Contemporary Hospitality Management*, *33*(10), 3093–3114. doi:10.1108/IJCHM-08-2020-0924

Cho, M., & Yoo, J. J.-E. (2021). Customer pressure and restaurant employee green creative behavior: Serial mediation effects of restaurant ethical standards and employee green passion. *International Journal of Contemporary Hospitality Management*, *33*(12), 4505–4525. doi:10.1108/IJCHM-06-2021-0697

Dabas, S., Sharma, S., & Manaktola, K. (2021). Adoption of digital marketing tools in independent businesses: Experiences of restaurant entrepreneurs in India and United Kingdom. *Worldwide Hospitality and Tourism Themes*, *13*(2), 214–235. doi:10.1108/WHATT-09-2020-0120

De Boer, J., & Aiking, H. (2019). Strategies towards healthy and sustainable protein consumption: A transition framework at the levels of diets, dishes, and dish ingredients. *Food Quality and Preference*, *73*, 171–181. doi:10.1016/j.foodqual.2018.11.012

De Villiers, R., Tipgomut, P., & Franklin, A. (2020). *International market segmentation across consumption and communication categories: Identity, demographics, and consumer decisions and online habits.*

Dinh, T. T. H. (2020). *The Effect of Eco-Friendly Packaging on Consumer Behaviour in the Restaurant Business.*

Ditlevsen, K., Sandøe, P., & Lassen, J. (2019). Healthy food is nutritious, but organic food is healthy because it is pure: The negotiation of healthy food choices by Danish consumers of organic food. *Food Quality and Preference*, *71*, 46–53. doi:10.1016/j.foodqual.2018.06.001

Ginter, P. M., Duncan, W. J., & Swayne, L. E. (2018). *The strategic management of health care organizations*. John Wiley & Sons.

Gruss, R., Kim, E., & Abrahams, A. (2020). Engaging restaurant customers on Facebook: The power of belongingness appeals on social media. *Journal of Hospitality & Tourism Research (Washington, D.C.)*, *44*(2), 201–228. doi:10.1177/1096348019892071

Gunawan, J., Permatasari, P., & Tilt, C. (2020). Sustainable development goal disclosures: Do they support responsible consumption and production? *Journal of Cleaner Production*, *246*, 118989. doi:10.1016/j.jclepro.2019.118989

Higgins-Desbiolles, F., & Wijesinghe, G. (2021). The critical capacities of restaurants as facilitators for transformations to sustainability. In *Activating Critical Thinking to Advance the Sustainable Development Goals in Tourism Systems* (pp. 234–259). Routledge. doi:10.4324/9781003140542-14

Hwang, K., & Lee, B. (2019). Pride, mindfulness, public self-awareness, affective satisfaction, and customer citizenship behaviour among green restaurant customers. *International Journal of Hospitality Management*, *83*, 169–179. doi:10.1016/j.ijhm.2019.05.009

Kaczorowska, J., Rejman, K., Halicka, E., Szczebyło, A., & Górska-Warsewicz, H. (2019). Impact of food sustainability labels on the perceived product value and price expectations of urban consumers. *Sustainability (Basel)*, *11*(24), 7240. doi:10.3390/su11247240

Khalifa, G. S. A. (2015). Ethnic restaurants' meal experience: Egyptian customers' perceptions. *Journal of Faculty of Tourism and Hotels*, *9*(1), 92–112.

Kim, M., & Lee, G. (2022). The effect of servicescape on place attachment and experience evaluation: The importance of exoticism and authenticity in an ethnic restaurant. *International Journal of Contemporary Hospitality Management*, *34*(7), 2664–2683. doi:10.1108/IJCHM-07-2021-0929

Kim, M. J., Hall, C. M., & Kim, D.-K. (2020). Predicting environmentally friendly eating out behavior by value-attitude-behavior theory: Does being vegetarian reduce food waste? *Journal of Sustainable Tourism*, *28*(6), 797–815. doi:10.1080/09669582.2019.1705461

Kumar, S., Talukder, M. B., Kabir, F., & Kaiser, F. (2024). Challenges and Sustainability of Green Finance in the Tourism Industry: Evidence from Bangladesh. In S. Taneja, P. Kumar, S. Grima, E. Ozen, & K. Sood (Eds.), (pp. 97–111). Advances in Finance, Accounting, and Economics. IGI Global. doi:10.4018/979-8-3693-1388-6.ch006

Kuziemski, M., & Misuraca, G. (2020). AI governance in the public sector: Three tales from the frontiers of automated decision-making in democratic settings. *Telecommunications Policy*, *44*(6), 101976. doi:10.1016/j.telpol.2020.101976 PMID:32313360

Liu, X., & Lin, K.-L. (2020). Green organizational culture, corporate social responsibility implementation, and food safety. *Frontiers in Psychology*, *11*, 585435. doi:10.3389/fpsyg.2020.585435 PMID:33240175

Mendini, M., Pizzetti, M., & Peter, P. C. (2019). Social food pleasure: When sharing offline, online and for society promotes pleasurable and healthy food experiences and well-being. *Qualitative Market Research*, *22*(4), 544–556. doi:10.1108/QMR-06-2018-0067

Nakandala, D., Smith, M., & Lau, H. (2020). Shared power and fairness in trust-based supply chain relationships in an urban local food system. *British Food Journal*, *122*(3), 870–883. doi:10.1108/BFJ-05-2019-0309

Oosterveer, P., & Sonnenfeld, D. A. (2012). *Food, globalization and sustainability*. Routledge. doi:10.4324/9781849776790

Peters, K., & Remaud, P. H. (2020). Factors influencing consumer menu-item selection in a restaurant context. *Food Quality and Preference*, *82*, 103887. doi:10.1016/j.foodqual.2020.103887

Presswood, A. L. (2019). *Food Blogs, Postfeminism, and the Communication of Expertise: Digital Domestics*. Lexington Books.

Putri, S. V. (2022). The Impact of Electronic Word of Mouth (EWOM) Using Influencers on Brand Awareness and Purchase Intention. *CoverAge: Journal of Strategic Communication*, *13*(1), 11–25. doi:10.35814/coverage.v13i1.3913

Reich, A. Z., Xu, Y. H., & McCleary, K. W. (2010). The influence of social responsibility image relative to product and service quality on brand loyalty: An exploratory study of quick-service restaurants. *Hospitality Review*, *28*(1), 2.

Roy, H. (2022). Connecting Farmers' Markets to Foodservice Businesses: A Qualitative Exploration of Restaurants' Perceived Benefits and Challenges of Purchasing Food Locally. *International Journal of Hospitality & Tourism Administration*, 1–36. doi:10.1080/15256480.2022.2142994

Sanderson Bellamy, A., Furness, E., Nicol, P., Pitt, H., & Taherzadeh, A. (2021). Shaping more resilient and just food systems: Lessons from the COVID-19 Pandemic. *Ambio*, *50*(4), 782–793. doi:10.1007/s13280-021-01532-y PMID:33748902

Sarmiento, C. V., & El Hanandeh, A. (2018). Customers' perceptions and expectations of environmentally sustainable restaurant and the development of green index: The case of the Gold Coast, Australia. *Sustainable Production and Consumption*, *15*, 16–24. doi:10.1016/j.spc.2018.04.001

Severt, K., Shin, Y. H., Chen, H. S., & DiPietro, R. B. (2022). Measuring the relationships between corporate social responsibility, perceived quality, price fairness, satisfaction, and conative loyalty in the context of local food restaurants. *International Journal of Hospitality & Tourism Administration*, *23*(3), 623–645. doi:10.1080/15256480.2020.1842836

Siddique, S. B. (2020). *Taste matters: A qualitative study of eating traditional vegetables among Bangladeshi immigrants in Italy.*

Sogari, G., Velez-Argumedo, C., Gómez, M. I., & Mora, C. (2018). College students and eating habits: A study using an ecological model for healthy behavior. *Nutrients*, *10*(12), 1823. doi:10.3390/nu10121823 PMID:30477101

Talukder, M., Shakhawat Hossain, M., & Kumar, S. (2022). Blue Ocean Strategies in Hotel Industry in Bangladesh: A Review of Present Literatures' Gap and Suggestions for Further Study. SSRN *Electronic Journal*. doi:10.2139/ssrn.4160709

Talukder, M. B. (2020b). The Future of Culinary Tourism: An Emerging Dimension for the Tourism Industry of Bangladesh. I-Manager's. *Journal of Management, 15*(1), 27. doi:10.26634/jmgt.15.1.17181

Talukder, M. B. (2021). An assessment of the roles of the social network in the development of the Tourism Industry in Bangladesh. *International Journal of Business, Law, and Education, 2*(3), 85–93. doi:10.56442/ijble.v2i3.21

Talukder, M. B., & Hossain, M. M. (2021). Prospects of Future Tourism in Bangladesh: An Evaluative Study. I-Manager's. *Journal of Management, 15*(4), 1–8. doi:10.26634/jmgt.15.4.17495

Talukder, M. B. & Kumar, S. (2023). *The Effect of Food Service Quality on Customer Satisfaction in the Hotel Industry: A Conceptual Paper.* ResearchGate. https://www.researchgate.net/publication/371503829_The_Effect_of_Food_Service_Quality_on_Customer_Satisfaction_in_the_Hotel_Industry_A_Conceptual_Paper

Talukder, M. B., Kumar, S., Sood, K., & Grima, S. (2023). Information Technology, Food Service Quality and Restaurant Revisit Intention. *International Journal of Sustainable Development and Planning, 18*(1), 295–303. doi:10.18280/ijsdp.180131

Thiermann, U. B., & Sheate, W. R. (2022). How Does Mindfulness Affect Pro-environmental Behaviors? A Qualitative Analysis of the Mechanisms of Change in a Sample of Active Practitioners. *Mindfulness, 13*(12), 2997–3016. doi:10.1007/s12671-022-02004-4

Tien, N. H. (2019). Customization and Standardization of the Business Strategy of Foreign Enterprises in Vietnam: The McDonald's case and the fast-food sector. *International Journal of Research in Marketing Management and Sales, 1*(2), 44–50. doi:10.33545/26633329.2019.v1.i2a.16

Varkey, P. S., Walker, T. R., & Saunders, S. J. (2021). Identifying barriers to reducing single-use plastic use in a coastal metropolitan city in Canada. *Ocean and Coastal Management, 210*, 105663. doi:10.1016/j.ocecoaman.2021.105663

Vu, H. Q., Li, G., Law, R., & Zhang, Y. (2019). Exploring tourist dining preferences based on restaurant reviews. *Journal of Travel Research, 58*(1), 149–167. doi:10.1177/0047287517744672

Chapter 11
Exploring the Past and Identifying the Future Research Agenda for Social Media and Tourist Behavior: A Bibliometric Analysis

Nidhi Sharma
https://orcid.org/0000-0002-3014-2312
Chandigarh University, India

Bhanupriya Khatri
Chandigarh University, India

Shad Ahmad Khan
https://orcid.org/0000-0001-7593-3487
University of Buraimi, Oman

ABSTRACT

A bibliometric analysis was utilized in the study to incorporate current knowledge in the domain of social media and tourist behavior from 202 research papers published between 2012 and 2023. Scopus academic database was employed to collect the data. To recognize contributions from specific authors, sources and countries, the research conducted performance (recent trends), bibliometric analysis (bibliographic coupling, citation, co-citations, and co-word). Further, network analysis (thematic maps) was used to find out the emerging themes in the field of social media and tourist behavior providing major insights into past study in the topic and suggesting future research directions. The VOS viewer and R software were used for all analyses.

DOI: 10.4018/979-8-3693-0960-5.ch011

INTRODUCTION

Since becoming one of the most effective online networking platforms, social media (SM) has been interwoven into "real-world social and economic life". It can be defined as "a group of Internet-based applications that build on the ideological and technological foundations of Web 2.0, and that allow the creation and exchange of user-generated content" (Kaplan and Haenlein, 2010, p.61). The concepts "social networking" and "social media" must be studied together (Sharma et al., 2023a; 2023b). A social networking site (SNs) is a platform, service, or website that focuses on enabling the creation of social networks or relationships between individuals who, for instance, have similar interests, hobbies, histories, or real-life connections (Saleem *et al.*, 2022; 2023). Since Social networking is the process of using SM tools to connect and communicate directly with people you are already connected to or would like to be connected to. SM tools are thought of as tools or means of communication that allow one to communicate, reach, and impact a large group of people (Khan *et al.*, 2023; Saleem *et al.*, 2022; 2023). By combining IT Communications, socialization, and the creation of text, photographs, videos, and audio, SM has changed as the new means for persons to connect globally. It is not merely a new means to connect; it is a whole online world built on the inputs and interactions of members. In recent times, the expansion of SM has been phenomenal. SM which was coined in the late 1990s, has grown in popularity to the point that in 2020. SM has changed communication among businesses as well as customers by connecting everyone in previously inconceivable ways (Kietzmann *et al.*, 2011). With the advancement of technology and availability of the internet, the number of people using social networking sites is rapidly increasing (Khan and Magd, 2023; 2021; Khan, 2023; Saleem *et al.*, 2023). New avenues to socialize and participate are created by SNs such as Facebook and Twitter. Users can connect, communicate, and exchange information with one another using SM websites and applications. These sites let users customize their pages, follow similar interests, and communicate with others. Also, the new means to search and obtain knowledge about the huge variety of goods as well as services available have arisen as a consequence of the SM revolution. It has facilitated customers to contact and compare brands with each other in a quick and effortless manner (Powers *et al.*, 2012). Random individuals in digital environments are quickly affecting consumer's perceptions toward goods as well as services, which further influence the physical world sentiments (Naim and Khan, 2023; Kamal *et al.*, 2022). Since marketers have limited control on the content, duration, or frequency of online conversations with clients, SM has given them a competitive advantage (Mangold and Faulds, 2009; Khan, 2023).

Furthermore, the growth of SM, search engines (Xiang and Gretzel, 2010) and mobile technologies (Leung *et al.*, 2013; Khatri *et al.*, 2023), has already had profound effects on tour related information exploration, making decisions, and the exchange of ideas and remembrance of travel experiences. Travel decisions are influenced by SM by promoting an engaged as well as informed customer (Xiang *et al.,* 2015). The social media's impact on tourism extends to all areas of a travel (Chung and Buhalis, 2008; Sharma *et al.*, 2023a). SNs has become an essential tool for many travellers (Law, Buhalis and Cobanoglu, 2014; Lu, Chen and Law, 2018). User-generated content (UGC) available on SM significantly influence the thoughts and choices of many other travellers or users (Xiang and Gretzel, 2010). Credibility of UGC extends much beyond the information provided by particular destination since it is based on the travel experiences of users who have no personal stake in the destinations (Jacobsen and Munar, 2012). Furthermore, when these contents are shared via SM by friends and colleagues, the WOM impact enhances the effect on attitudes and tourism-related behaviors of other individuals (Ladhari and Michaud, 2015). Also, with the advancement of mobile technology, travel experiences start with the seeking for details and continue between the travel and beyond.

SM not just has altered consumer behavior and tourist sector, but additionally tourism as a research focus. Recognizing the significance of SM in travel decisions and planning a trip, researchers have revealed a rising interest in exploring the functions and implications of it in the tourism domain across the past couple of decades. Prior studies investigated SM and tourist behavior in different contexts using different quantitative and qualitative approach. Zeng and Gerritsen, (2014) and Zarezadeh et al., (2018) emphasized on social media's review in tourism, Huertas, (2018) discussed about role of live videos on tourist behavior. Furthermore, Ghosh & Mukherjee, (2022); Ramos and Hassan, (2021) and Xu et al., (2021) talked about social media's influence on tourist behavior. However, there is no bibliometric study conducted on SM and tourist behavior to comprehend the development of this research area. So, the current study used different bibliometrics to fill the research gap by conducting a bibliometric analysis of SM and tourist behavior literature. To expose and display the large picture and evolution of this research topic. This study will specifically address the following questions:

RQ1: What is the current publication trend in the area of SM and tourist behavior?

Examining publication trends enables scholars to obtain insights on the dynamics and evolution of scholarly discourse in their discipline. Understanding publication trends can provide valuable information, such as allowing researchers to identify areas of high activity and interest within a discipline, as well as benchmarks for evaluating the impact and productivity of individual researchers, research groups, institutions, and countries within a specific field. By studying the current publication trend in a certain area, bibliometric research may provide useful insights into the state of the field, aid in dissemination of knowledge, and support evidence-based decision-making in academia and beyond. Performance analysis investigates the contributions of research constituents to a certain field (Ramos-Rodríguez and Ruíz-Navarro, 2004; Cobo *et al.*, 2011).

RQ2: Who are the crucial contributors in the area of SM and tourist behavior?

Identifying crucial contributors aims to identify and assess prominent researchers, institutions, or nations who have made major contributions to a certain field of study. Overall, using bibliometric analysis to determine who the most important contributors are in a certain subject helps to gain a better knowledge of the research landscape, enables cooperation and networking, and supports evidence-based decision-making in academia and beyond.

RQ3: What are the mature and emerging themes in the field of SM and tourist behavior?

Mature and developing topics in an area are frequently chosen as research questions in bibliometric studies because they provide useful information on the evolution, trends, and present level of study in that field.

The remainder of the paper has been divided into some sections. Section two discusses literature review. Research methodology used to explore the phenomena is explained in section three. The result of the study is discussed in section four. Discussions and conclusions are explained in section five. Section six includes the implications of the study followed by limitations in section seven.

LITERATURE REVIEW

Social media platforms have transformed the way people connect, interact, and exchange information throughout the globe. With the introduction of social media, the tourism sector has seen substantial changes in how visitors plan, enjoy, and share their travel adventures. This literature review will look at significant topics, trends, and study findings linked to social media and tourist behavior. Social media sites such as Facebook, Instagram, and TripAdvisor have a significant impact on visitors' travel decisions (Hays et al., 2013). Litvin, Goldsmith and Pan, (2008) and Sharma *et al.*, (2023a) found that user-generated content on social media platforms had a considerable influence on travellers' destination and lodging selections. Furthermore, Kim and Fesenmaier, (2008) discovered that social media suggestions and reviews alter travellers' impressions of places and experiences, influencing their decision-making throughout the trip process. Destination marketing organisations (DMOs) use social media platforms to promote destinations, engage tourists, and improve destination branding. Similarly, Buhalis and Foerste, (2015) address the importance of social media-based destination branding and its influence on visitor perceptions and destination competitiveness. Tourists use social media platforms to discuss their experiences, seek suggestions, and interact with other travellers (Xiang and Gretzel, 2010). Sharma and Arora, (2023a) investigates visitors' intentions for utilising social media for destination selection. Furthermore, Wang et al. (2016) look at the impact of social media in improving visitors' overall travel experiences, emphasizing the significance of real-time communication and personalized suggestions.

To summarize, social media has a complex impact on tourist behavior, impacting travel decision-making processes, destination marketing tactics, destination image development, and crisis management in the tourism sector. This literature review emphasizes the interconnection between social media use and tourist behavior, emphasizing the need for more study to investigate developing trends, problems, and possibilities in this dynamic sector.

METHODOLOGY

We employ bibliometric technique, which entails the examination of bibliometric and bibliographic data using quantitative methods (Pritchard, 1969). Bibliometric reviews, unlike traditional systematic literature reviews, have the ability to deliver information across areas with huge volumes of bibliometrics and bibliographic data. Four-step method of (Donthu *et al.*, 2021) was used for bibliometric reviews- (a) specifying the scope and goals of the review; (b) selecting analysis techniques; (c) gathering information for analysis; and (d) carrying out the analysis and reporting the results.

To recognize contributions from specific authors, sources and countries, the research conducted performance (recent trends), bibliometric analysis ("bibliographic coupling (BC), citation, co-citations and co-word"). Further, network analysis (thematic maps) was used to find out the emerging themes in the domain of SM and tourist behavior using the "VOSviewer software and Bibliometrix package from R software". VOSviewer is a trusted software which can evaluate bibliometric data and present the results in a variety of ways (Van Eck and Waltman, 2014). However, R has several packages for many sorts of research. Bibliometrix, on the other hand, is especially well suited to scientific mapping (Aria and Cuccurullo, 2017), and it has been utilized in an increasing number of articles (Linnenluecke, Marrone and Singh, 2020).

Table 1. Overview of the study

Research Questions	Analysis	Database/ Tools
Q1. What is the current publication trend in the area of SM and tourist behavior?	No. of documents a) Per year b) By Source c) By Authors d) By countries	Scopus
Q2. Who are the crucial contributors in the area of SM and tourist behavior?	1. BC 2. Citation analysis 3. Co-occurrence 4. Co-citation	VOS viewer
Q3. What are the mature and emerging themes in the field of SM and tourist behavior?	Thematic Maps	RStudio

Data Collection

The "Scopus database" was used to obtain data for the current study, which has a wider coverage of the author's work. While other databases, such as Web of Science and Google Scholar, dispense citation data and are commonly used for bibliometric studies, Scopus is frequently chosen due to its better coverage, larger dataset, easiness in downloading data (Harzing and Alakangas, 2016) and user-friendly citation analysis interface. Also, Scopus surpasses its nearest competition with almost 2.4 billion cited references, accounting for 10-15% more citations per indexed paper on average. The number of citations provides numerous advantages which allows for more detailed examination of bibliometric and historical patterns like it provides more detailed author biographies and citation histories, improves the accuracy and reliability of h-index assessments for writers (Scopus). An examination of data from the "Scopus database" is more pertinent and beneficial for specialized study, on the other hand, has provided additional insights to the findings. Furthermore, because cited references are available in the Scopus database, co-citation analysis may be done more precisely (Zupic and Čater, 2015;Khatri et al., 2022). The process to reach at a final collection of 202 articles is shown in table 2. Data collected from "Scopus, or any other search engine", may contain inaccurate information because of the reporting of the primary research article in successive papers (Baker et al., 2021; Magd et al., 2023). As a result, interpreting such records directly without first cleansing the data risks erroneous evaluation. As indicated by Donthu et al., (2021), such a technique leads to suitable study of "bibliometric and bibliographic data, visualization, and interpretation of results".

Table 2. Selection of articles

Filtering Criteria	Accept	Reject
"Search Engine: Scopus"		
"Search Date: 15 February 2023"		
"Search term: ("Social media" OR "SM networking" OR "SMplatforms" OR "Facebook" OR "Instagram" OR "YouTube" OR "SNSs" OR "social networking sites" OR "Twitter" AND "traveller behavio*" OR "tourist behavio*")	274	
"Subject Area: (Business, management and accounting, Psychology, Multidiscipline, Social Sciences, Arts and humanities and Economics, Econometrics and Finance)"	237	37
"Document Type: Articles and Reviews"	205	32
"Language screening: Include documents in English only"	**202**	**3**

"Note: The systematic process used to reach at the final 202 articles for review is detailed in this table."

RESULTS

RQ1. What is the Current Publication Trend in the Area of SM and Tourist Behavior?

Table 3. Current trends

Year Analysis		Source Analysis		Authors Analysis		Countries Analysis	
Year	Document	Sources	Documents	Author	Documents	Countries	Documents
2023	4	Tourism Management	26	Law, R.	6	China	45
2022	46	Sustainability Switzerland	24	Vu, H.Q.	5	United States	36
2021	42	Annals of Tourism Research	14	Li, G.	4	United Kingdom	28
2020	30	Journal of Travel Research	13	Andreu, L.	3	Spain	21
2019	22	Asia Pacific Journal of Tourism Research	11	Campo, S.	3	Australia	17
2018	19	Current Issues in Tourism	10	Pantano, E.	3	Hong Kong	17
2017	12	International Journal of Tourism Research	6	Zhang, Y.	3	South Korea	14
2016	9	Journal of Hospitality and Tourism Technology	6	Abd Rahman, A.	2	India	8
2015	6	Journal of Sustainable Tourism	6	Ardoin, N.M.	2	Italy	8
2014	4	Tourism Management	26	Aziz, Y.A.	2	Malaysia	8
2013	5						
2012	3						

Figure 1. Distribution of SM and tourist behavior articles found in Scopus on an annual basis from 2012 to 2023

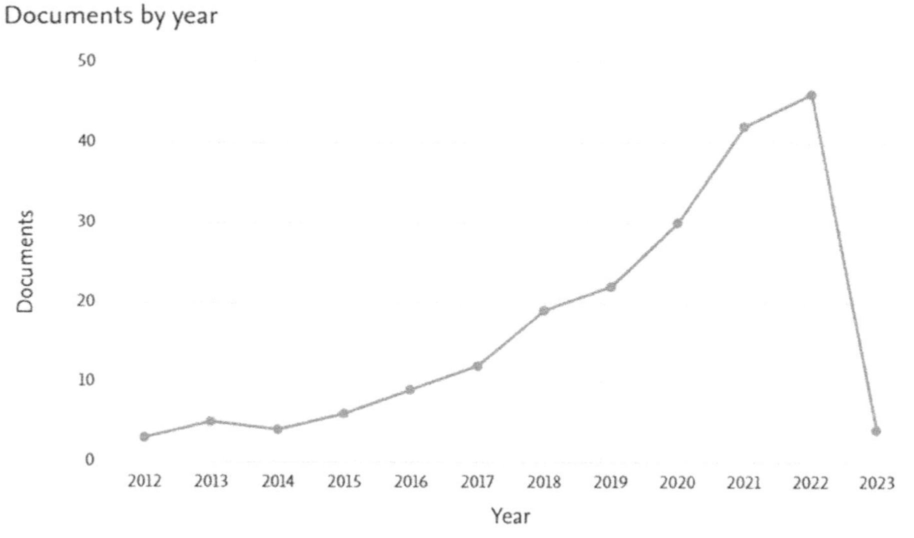

Figure 2. Distribution of SM and tourist behavior articles found in Scopus on the basis of sources from 2012 to 2023

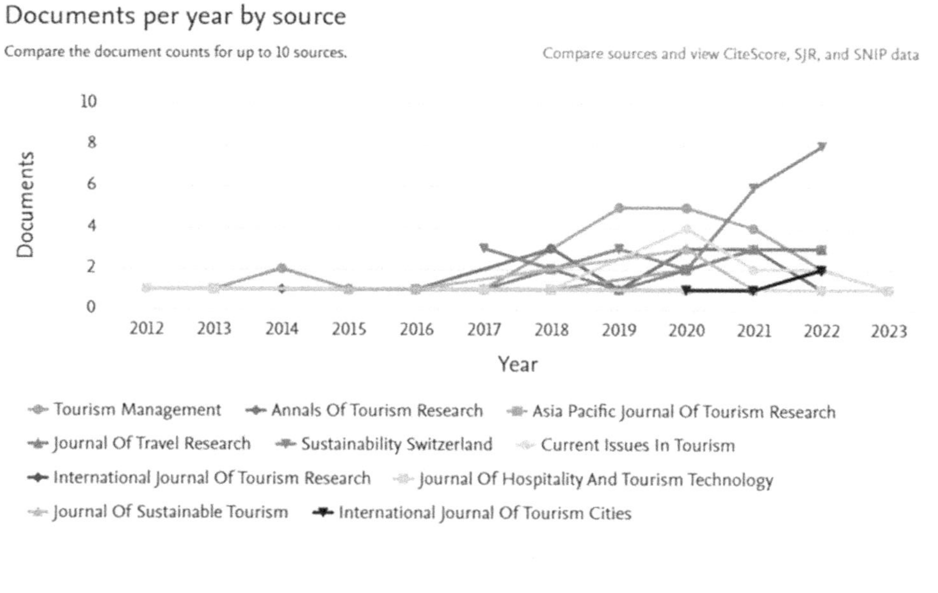

Figure 3. Distribution of SM and tourist behavior articles found in Scopus on the basis of number of articles by authors

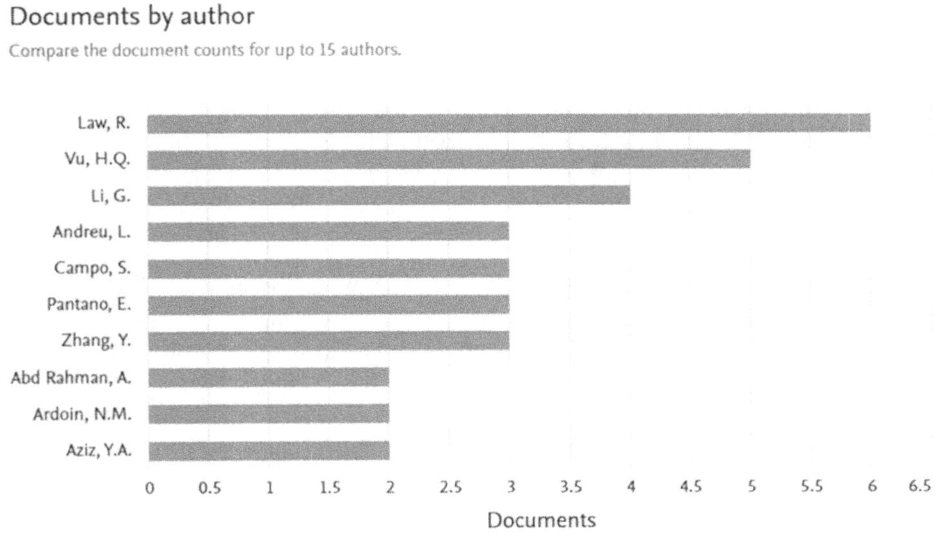

Figure 4. Distribution of SM and tourist behavior articles found in Scopus on the basis of number of articles by countries

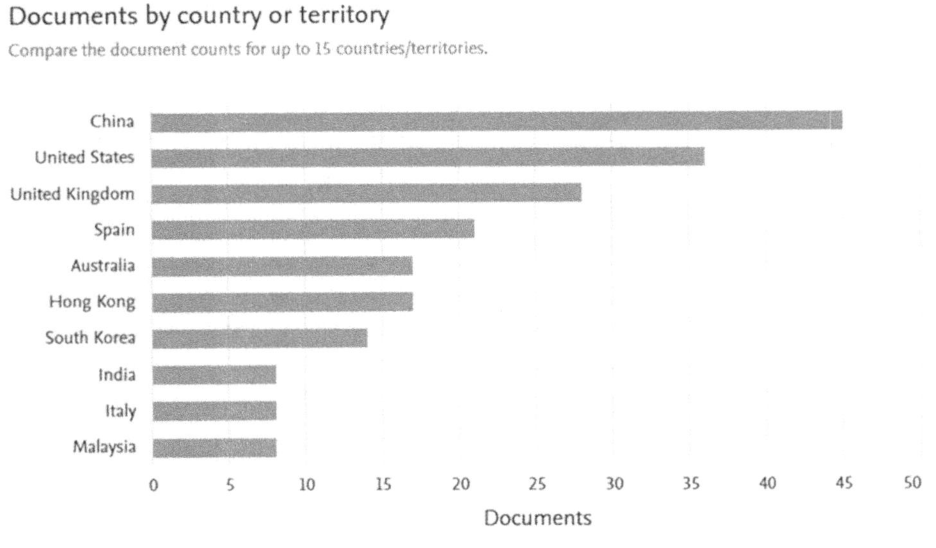

RQ2. Who Are the Crucial Contributors in the Area of SM and Tourist Behavior?

BC

"BC is used to compare two publications which refers to the same document because similar references suggest that the publications have a lot in common in terms of intellectual capital" (Shin and Perdue, 2019). The most prominent authors, nations and journals contributed significant publications to the study's sample is depicted in table 4. Law R. looks to be the most notable and influential author in the SM and tourist behavior domains followed by Vu H.Q. with 884 and 865 link strength respectively. Among countries, China has made the most intellectual contributions in the domains of SM and tourist behavior, subsequently surpassed by the United States. Among journals, Annals of Tourism Research displays the highest inspiration. However, some have criticized the BC approach, which is based on backward citations clustering, for its inability in assessing older publications (van Eck and Waltman, 2014) .

Table 4. BC

Authors	Link Strength	Countries	Link Strength	Sources	Link Strength
Law R.	884	China	5181	Annals of Tourism Research	1007
Vu H.Q.	865	United States	3585	Asia Pacific Journal of Tourism Research	770
Li G.	841	United Kingdom	3544	Current Issues in Tourism	745
Zhang Y.	557	Hong Kong	3257	International Journal of Tourism Research	712
Chen Y.	160	Australia	2118	Journal Of Hospitality and Tourism Technology	587
Campo S.	138	Spain	2108	Journal of Sustainable Tourism	427
Andreu L.	128	South Korea	1816	Journal of Travel Research	346
Liu Y.	45	Macau	1594	Sustainability (Switzerland)	298
Pantano E.	24	Malaysia	1197	Tourism Management	246
Law R.	884	India	1174	Annals of Tourism Research	1007

Citation Analysis

"The citation count of a published document is used in this approach to determine the degree of recognition it has received in academia (Caviggioli and Ughetto, 2019)". The topmost authors, in SM and tourist behavior research, along with countries and sources at time of authorship with no. grounded on citations, are shown in table 5. Based on the no. of citations Vu H.Q., Pantano E. and Law R. seems as the most significant authors in SM and tourist behavior domain. Amid nations, United States with 1184 and United Kingdom with 1043 citations has the greatest intellectual contributions in SM and tourist behavior domain based on top citations. Among journals, Tourism management has top citations with 2235 followed by Journal of Travel Research with 519 citations.

Table 5. Citations analysis

Authors	TP	TC	Countries	TP	TC	Sources	TP	TC
Vu H.Q.	5	328	United States	36	1184	Tourism Management	26	2235
Pantano E.	3	188	China	44	1043	Journal of Travel Research	13	519
Law R.	6	174	Australia	17	1040	Annals of Tourism Research	14	507
Zhang Y.	6	156	Spain	21	717	Sustainability (Switzerland)	24	264
Liu Y.	4	141	Norway	3	615	Journal of Sustainable Tourism	6	226
Campo S.	3	130	Hong Kong	17	522	Journal of Hospitality and Tourism Technology	6	218
Li G.	4	115	United Kingdom	28	474	Current Issues in Tourism	10	168
Chen Y.	6	86	South Korea	14	259	International Journal of Tourism Research	6	152
Andreu L.	3	84	Macau	7	250	Asia Pacific Journal of Tourism Research	11	143
Vu H.Q.	5	328	United States	36	1184	Tourism Management	26	2235

Co-Occurrences

"The keywords utilized by the authors and journal indexers in the papers under consideration give a picture of the literature on a study issue" (Khanra, Dhir and Mäntymäki, 2020). Table 6 depicts the most frequent words used in SM and tourist behavior research is SM with 140 occurrences and 304 total link strength followed by tourist behavior with 134 occurrences. Other words which are used most frequently in in SM and tourist behavior research are tourist destination, tourism, tourism management, travel behavior etc. The visualization of co-occurrences is shown in Figure 5.

Table 6. Co-Occurrences

Words	Occurrences	Total Link Strength
Social Media	140	304
Tourist Behavior	134	315
Tourist Destination	61	174
Tourism	42	76
Tourism Management	29	81
Tourism Market	24	80
Travel Behavior	24	73
China	21	72
Internet	20	62
Social Network	20	59

Figure 5. Words co-occurrences

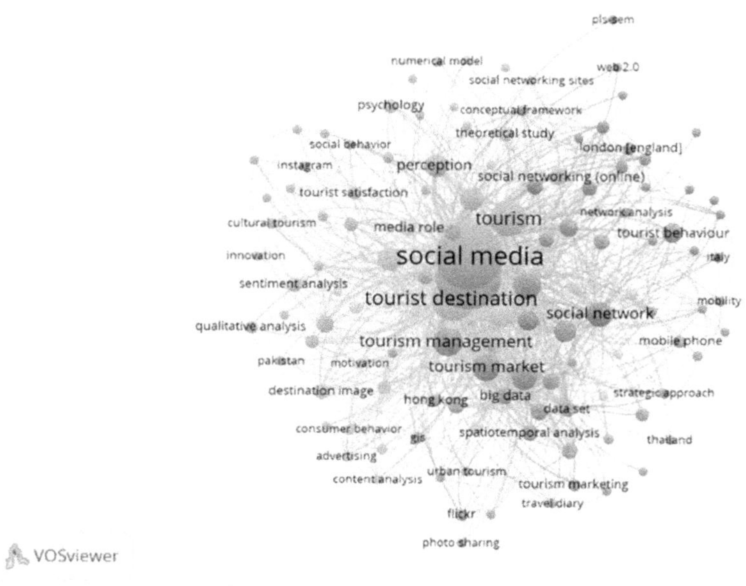

Co-Citations Analysis

"When two publications cite the same pair of publications, the pair is referred to as co-cited" (Xu *et al.*, 2018) . In table 7 the topmost authors, sources on the basis of co-citations in SM and tourist behavior research are depicted. Law, R. tends to be the most significant author in SM and tourist behavior study, with 248 citations, surpassed by Gretzel, U. with 194 citations. Among sources Tourism Management is most dominant source followed by Annals of Tourism Research. The visualization of sources and authors co-citations is shown in Figure 6 and 7 respectively.

Table 7. Co-citations analysis

Author	TC	TP	Sources	TC	TP
Law, R.	248	1581	Tourism Management	969	15328
Gretzel, U.	194	1642	Annals of Tourism Research	530	10040
Buhalis, D.	157	1364	Journal of Travel Research	455	9299
Fesenmaier, D.R.	114	1107	International Journal of Hospitality Management	180	4184
Xiang, Z.	106	932	Journal of Travel & Tourism Marketing	170	3906
Mckercher, B.	89	544	Current Issues in Tourism	151	3517
Kim, J.	60	479	International Journal of Contemporary Hospitality Management	133	3024
Hall, C.M.	49	1296	Journal of Business Research	122	2721
Saarinen, J.	25	1204	Computers in Human Behavior	134	2621
Stewart, E.J.	18	1005	Journal of Sustainable Tourism	118	2408

Figure 6. Co-Citation sources

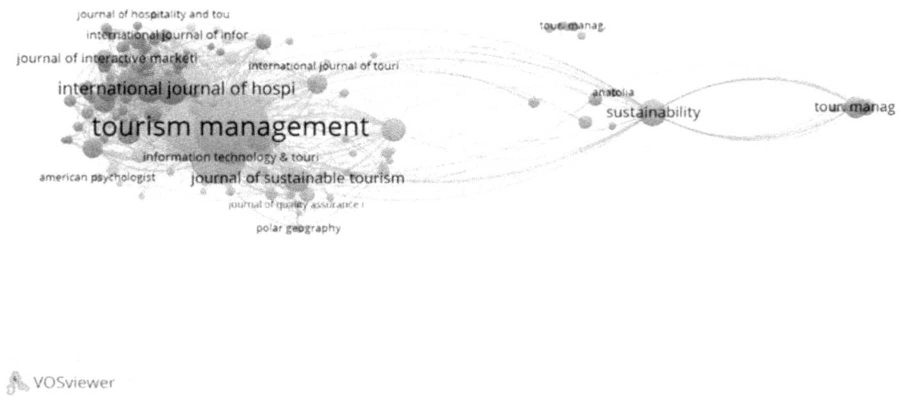

Figure 7. Co-Citation authors

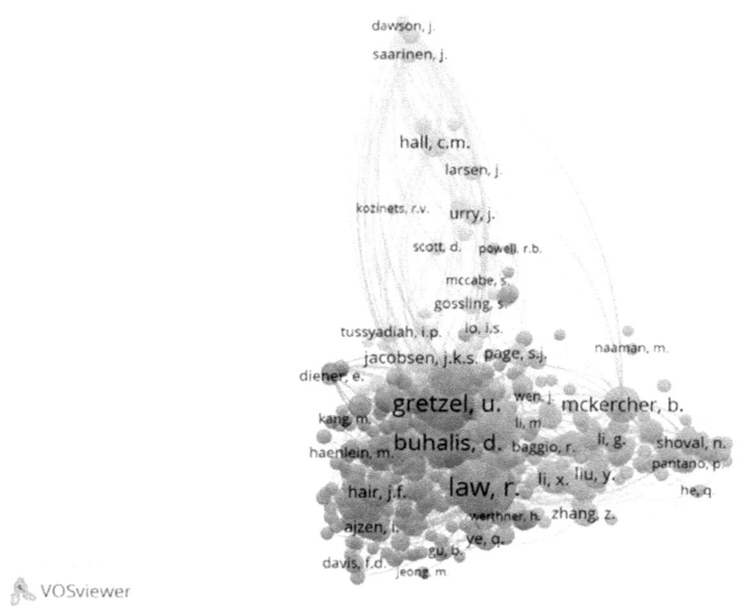

What Are the Mature and Emerging Themes in the Area of SM and Tourist Behavior?

Emerging themes in bibliometric analysis are subjects or areas of research that are gaining traction within a certain discipline but have not yet matured in terms of publication number or citations. When employing bibliometric analysis to analyse emergent themes, researchers often look for recent publications, follow citation increase over time, and examine patterns of collaboration among academics and institutions (Goyal and Kumar, 2021; Sharma and Arora, 2023b). By displaying the progression of themes through time, the thematic map gives insights into "patterns, trends, seasonality, and outliers of research topics" (Aria and Cuccurullo, 2017). Thematic maps are easy to understand since themes are divided into "four quadrants depending on their centrality (X-axis) and density (Y-axis)". Based on the quadrants, themes can be classified into four categories i.e., "Niche themes, Motor themes, Basic themes and Emerging themes". Niche themes include specialized topics or keywords among researchers and are thus largely hermetic, in the sense that they do not impact or are influenced by other topics. Motor themes are those keywords which are well developed and have the potential to affect the research field (Forliano, De Bernardi and Yahiaoui, 2021). Basic themes imply keywords which might be transversal for a discipline. Emerging themes include keywords that are either underdeveloped or have the potential to be explored further. Figure 8 shows how the field of SM and tourist behavior (2012-2023) is grouped in terms of research topics. Consumer behavior, nature-based tourism, online reviews are the emerging themes in SM and tourism behavior domain where future research can be done by researchers as these themes are not much explored yet.

Figure 8. Thematic maps

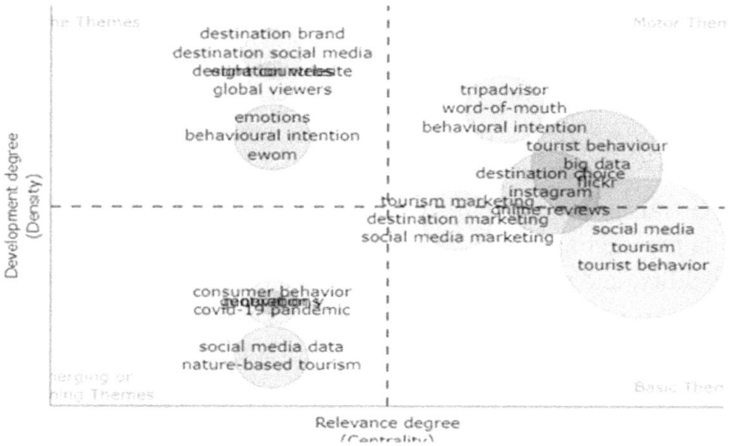

DISCUSSION AND CONCLUSION

The current research provides a comprehensive review of SM and tourist behavior research by conducting bibliometric analyses of articles published between 2012 and 2023. To answer the research question of the study, we conduct the performance analysis using recent trends in the domain and bibliometric and network analysis using "BC, citation analysis, co-citation analysis and thematic maps". Our findings offer the data in a way that shows the big picture of literature.

The first question for the study was to look at current trends in SM and tourist behavior. To address this question, we looked at yearly trends, the most active journals, top countries, and renowned authors in the fields of SM and tourist behavior. Our initial discovery is that there is an increasing body of literature on the subject, as indicated by a consistent growth in the number of papers from 2012 (3 documents) to 2022 (46 documents). The results of the bibliometric study on SM and tourist behavior explain that academics from "developed and developing countries" have made substantial research advances. Furthermore, Tourism Management and Sustainability Switzerland have the highest no. of papers on SM and tourist behavior. The contributions from many nations demonstrate that experts have paid close attention to SM and tourist behavior. "China, the United States, and the United Kingdom" are the top publishing nations in terms of SM and tourist behavior. Finally, Law, R.

and Vu, H.Q. are the top contributing researchers in the domains of SM and tourist behavior, with six and five articles, respectively.

Prior research on SM and tourist behavior is dispersed among journals, and evidence that the current structure of the literature is inadequate. The second research question of this study was to identify the major contributors to the field of SM and tourist behavior research. Different bibliometrics are used to answer this question. Using BC the results indicates that Law R. looks to be the most notable and influential author in the SM and tourist behavior domains followed by Vu H.Q. with 884 and 865 link strength respectively. Among countries, China has made the most intellectual contributions in the domains of SM and tourist behavior, subsequently surpassed by the United States. Amid journals, Annals of Tourism Research display the highest inspiration. Furthermore, on the basis of the number of citations, Vu H.Q., Pantano E., and Law R. are the most prominent authors in the domains of SM and tourist behavior, with 328, 188, and 174 citations, respectively. Based on top citations, the United States has 1184 citations, and the United Kingdom has 1043 citations in the sphere of SM and tourist behavior. Tourism management has the most citations with 2235, followed by Journal of Travel Research with 519 citations. The most frequent words used in SM and tourist behavior research is SM with 140 occurrences and 304 total link strength followed by tourist behavior with 134 occurrences. Lastly, Law, R. tends to be the most significant author in SM and tourist behavior study, with 248 citations, surpassed by Gretzel, U. with 194 citations. Amid sources Tourism Management is the most dominant source with 969 citations followed by Annals of Tourism Research with 530 citations.

Furthermore, to address the third question the study discussed mature and emerging themes in the field of SM and tourist behavior with the help of thematic maps. The results revealed that consumer behavior, nature-based tourism, online reviews are the emerging themes in SM and tourism behavior domain where future research can be done by researchers as these themes are not much explored yet. The study also provides future research opportunities in the area of SM and tourist behavior. We claim that thematic maps provide a clear mechanism for separating future study routes, such as Niche themes, which may hold theoretical contributions to the discipline owing to their low centrality, and emerging themes, which may provide researchers with unexplored topics. Niche cluster includes keyword destination brand, destination social media, behavioral intention and e-WOM.

IMPLICATIONS

The study shed light on the evolving landscape of research on social media and tourist behavior, including emerging subjects, popular research approaches, and notable scholars. By analysing the current literature, the study identified the gaps in research on social media and tourist behavior, directing future research goals and priorities. The findings of the study can help policymakers, tourism industry experts, and destination marketers understand the trends, difficulties, and possibilities associated with the use of social media in tourism. This information may be utilised to create more successful destination marketing or customer engagement. The study also revealed the patterns of collaboration among scholars, organisations, and nations investigating social media and tourist behavior. This information can help academia, business, and government organisations collaborate more effectively, resulting in multidisciplinary research and knowledge sharing.

LIMITATIONS

The usage of only one database (Scopus) is a key limitation of our research. While Scopus is expected to include the most important academic research, using other databases such as Web of Science, Google Scholar, or ABDC can broaden the scope of study coverage. This study used bibliometric analysis like performance analysis, co-word analysis, co-citations, bibliographic coupling and thematic maps in the field of SM and tourist behavior. Other sorts of analysis, like content analysis, can be used to support future research, bolstering the findings with the researchers' approach, data analysis, and so on. This study excluded the noteworthy books, book chapters, and dissertations that may limit the breadth of the study's scope. Scholars can deepen and broaden their research by adding noteworthy books, book chapters, and dissertations into future study, developing a more holistic knowledge of the complex issues underlying SM and tourist behavior.

REFERENCES

Aria, M., & Cuccurullo, C. (2017). bibliometrix : An R-tool for comprehensive science mapping analysis. *Journal of Informetrics*, *11*(4), 959–975. doi:10.1016/j.joi.2017.08.007

Baker, H. K., Kumar, S., & Pattnaik, D. (2021). Research constituents, intellectual structure, and collaboration pattern in the Journal of Forecasting : A bibliometric analysis. *Journal of Forecasting*, *40*(4), 577–602. doi:10.1002/for.2731

Buhalis, D., & Foerste, M. (2015). SoCoMo marketing for travel and tourism: Empowering co-creation of value. *Journal of Destination Marketing & Management*, *4*(3), 151–161. doi:10.1016/j.jdmm.2015.04.001

Caviggioli, F., & Ughetto, E. (2019). A bibliometric analysis of the research dealing with the impact of additive manufacturing on industry, business and society. *International Journal of Production Economics*, *208*, 254–268. doi:10.1016/j.ijpe.2018.11.022

Chung, J. Y., & Buhalis, D. (2008). Information Needs in Online Social Networks. *Information Technology & Tourism*, *10*(4), 267–281. doi:10.3727/109830508788403123

Cobo, M. J., López-Herrera, A. G., Herrera-Viedma, E., & Herrera, F. (2011). An approach for detecting, quantifying, and visualizing the evolution of a research field: A practical application to the Fuzzy Sets Theory field. *Journal of Informetrics*, *5*(1), 146–166. doi:10.1016/j.joi.2010.10.002

Donthu, N., Kumar, S., Mukherjee, D., Pandey, N., & Lim, W. M. (2021). How to conduct a bibliometric analysis: An overview and guidelines. *Journal of Business Research*, *133*, 285–296. doi:10.1016/j.jbusres.2021.04.070

Forliano, C., De Bernardi, P., & Yahiaoui, D. (2021). Entrepreneurial universities: A bibliometric analysis within the business and management domains. *Technological Forecasting and Social Change*, *165*, 120522. doi:10.1016/j.techfore.2020.120522

Ghosh, P., & Mukherjee, S. (2022). Understanding tourist behaviour towards destination selection based on SMinformation: an evaluation using unsupervised clustering algorithms. *Journal of Hospitality and Tourism Insights*. doi:10.1108/JHTI-11-2021-0317

Goyal, K., & Kumar, S. (2021). Financial literacy: A systematic review and bibliometric analysis. *International Journal of Consumer Studies*, *45*(1), 80–105. doi:10.1111/ijcs.12605

Harzing, A.-W., & Alakangas, S. (2016). Google Scholar, Scopus and the Web of Science: A longitudinal and cross-disciplinary comparison. *Scientometrics*, *106*(2), 787–804. doi:10.1007/s11192-015-1798-9

Hays, S., Page, S. J., & Buhalis, D. (2013). Social media as a destination marketing tool: Its use by national tourism organisations. *Current Issues in Tourism*, *16*(3), 211–239. doi:10.1080/13683500.2012.662215

Huertas, A. (2018). How live videos and stories in SMinfluence tourist opinions and behaviour. *Information Technology & Tourism*, *19*(1–4), 1–28. doi:10.1007/s40558-018-0112-0

Jacobsen, J. K. S., & Munar, A. M. (2012). Tourist information search and destination choice in a digital age. *Tourism Management Perspectives*, *1*, 39–47. doi:10.1016/j.tmp.2011.12.005

Kamal, S., Naim, A., Magd, H., Khan, S. A., & Khan, F. M. (2022). The Relationship Between E-Service Quality, Ease of Use, and E-CRM Performance Referred by Brand Image. In A. Naim & S. Kautish (Eds.), *Building a Brand Image Through Electronic Customer Relationship Management* (pp. 84–108). IGI Global. doi:10.4018/978-1-6684-5386-5.ch005

Kaplan, A. M., & Haenlein, M. (2010). Users of the world, unite! The challenges and opportunities of Social Media. *Business Horizons*, *53*(1), 59–68. doi:10.1016/j.bushor.2009.09.003

Khan, S. A. (2023). E-Marketing, E-Commerce, E-Business, and Internet of Things: An Overview of Terms in the Context of Small and Medium Enterprises (SMEs). In A. Naim & V. Devi (Eds.), *Global Applications of the Internet of Things in Digital Marketing* (pp. 332–348). IGI Global. doi:10.4018/978-1-6684-8166-0.ch017

Khan, S. A., & Magd, H. (2021). Empirical Examination of MS Teams in Conducting Webinar: Evidence from International Online Program conducted in Oman. *Journal of Content. Community and Communication*, *14*(8), 159–175. doi:10.31620/JCCC.12.21/13

Khan, S. A., & Magd, H. (2023). New Technology Anxiety and Acceptance of Technology: An Appraisal of MS Teams. In *Advances in Distance Learning in Times of Pandemic* (pp. 105–134). CRC Press, Taylor and Francis., doi:10.1201/9781003322252-5

Khan, S. A., Narula, S., Kansra, P., Naim, A., & Kalra, D. (2023). Should Marketing and Public Relations be Part of the Institutional Accreditation Criterion of Business Schools? An Appraisal of Accreditation Criterion of Selected Accreditation Agencies. In A. Naim (Ed.), *Accreditation Processes and Frameworks in Higher Education* (pp. 349–375). Nova Science Publishers. doi:10.52305/QUVJ6658

Khanra, S., Dhir, A., & Mäntymäki, M. (2020). Big data analytics and enterprises: A bibliometric synthesis of the literature. *Enterprise Information Systems*, *14*(6), 737–768. doi:10.1080/17517575.2020.1734241

Khatri, B., Arora, S., Magd, H., & Khan, S. A. (2022). Bibliometric Analysis of Social Entrepreneurship. In H. Magd, D. Singh, R. Syed, & D. Spicer (Eds.), *International Perspectives on Value Creation and Sustainability Through Social Entrepreneurship* (pp. 46–60). IGI Global. doi:10.4018/978-1-6684-4666-9.ch003

Khatri, B., Shrimali, H., Khan, S. A., & Naim, A. (2023). Role of HR Analytics in Ensuring Psychological Wellbeing and Job Security: Learnings From COVID-19. In R. Yadav, M. Sinha, & J. Kureethara (Eds.), *HR Analytics in an Era of Rapid Automation* (pp. 36–53). IGI Global. doi:10.4018/978-1-6684-8942-0.ch003

Kietzmann, J. H., Hermkens, K., McCarthy, I. P., & Silvestre, B. S. (2011). Social media? Get serious! Understanding the functional building blocks of social media. *Business Horizons*, *54*(3), 241–251. doi:10.1016/j.bushor.2011.01.005

Kim, H., & Fesenmaier, D. R. (2008). Persuasive Design of Destination Web Sites: An Analysis of First Impression. *Journal of Travel Research*, *47*(1), 3–13. doi:10.1177/0047287507312405

Ladhari, R., & Michaud, M. (2015). eWOM effects on hotel booking intentions, attitudes, trust, and website perceptions. *International Journal of Hospitality Management*, *46*, 36–45. doi:10.1016/j.ijhm.2015.01.010

Law, R., Buhalis, D., & Cobanoglu, C. (2014). Progress on information and communication technologies in hospitality and tourism. *International Journal of Contemporary Hospitality Management*, *26*(5), 727–750. doi:10.1108/IJCHM-08-2013-0367

Leung, D., Law, R., van Hoof, H., & Buhalis, D. (2013). SMin Tourism and Hospitality: A Literature Review. *Journal of Travel & Tourism Marketing*, *30*(1–2), 3–22. doi:10.1080/10548408.2013.750919

Linnenluecke, M. K., Marrone, M., & Singh, A. K. (2020). Conducting systematic literature reviews and bibliometric analyses. *Australian Journal of Management*, *45*(2), 175–194. doi:10.1177/0312896219877678

Litvin, S. W., Goldsmith, R. E., & Pan, B. (2008). Electronic word-of-mouth in hospitality and tourism management. *Tourism Management*, *29*(3), 458–468. doi:10.1016/j.tourman.2007.05.011

Lu, Y., Chen, Z. W., & Law, R. (2018). Mapping the progress of SMresearch in hospitality and tourism management from 2004 to 2014. *Journal of Travel & Tourism Marketing*, *35*(2), 102–118. doi:10.1080/10548408.2017.1350249

Magd, H., Khan, S. A., Khatri, B., Sharma, N., & Arora, S. (2023). Understanding the Relationship Between IoT and Digital Marketing: A Bibliometric Analysis. In A. Naim & V. Devi (Eds.), *Global Applications of the Internet of Things in Digital Marketing* (pp. 123–140). IGI Global. doi:10.4018/978-1-6684-8166-0.ch007

Mangold, W. G., & Faulds, D. J. (2009). Social media: The new hybrid element of the promotion mix. *Business Horizons*, *52*(4), 357–365. doi:10.1016/j.bushor.2009.03.002

Naim, A., & Khan, S. A. (2023). Impact and Assessment of Electronic Commerce on Consumer Buying Behaviour. In A. Naim & V. Devi (Eds.), *Global Applications of the Internet of Things in Digital Marketing* (pp. 264–289). IGI Global. doi:10.4018/978-1-6684-8166-0.ch014

Powers, T., Advincula, D., Austin, M. S., Graiko, S., & Snyder, J. (2012). Digital and SMIn the Purchase Decision Process. *Journal of Advertising Research*, *52*(4), 479–489. doi:10.2501/JAR-52-4-479-489

Pritchard, A. (1969). Statistical bibliography or bibliometrics. *The Journal of Documentation*, *25*, 348.

Ramos, C. M. Q., & Hassan, A. (2021). Evaluation of the tourist experience using a framework for the analysis of the influence of SMon tourist behaviour. *International Journal of Tourism Policy*, *11*(3), 207. doi:10.1504/IJTP.2021.118663

Ramos-Rodríguez, A., & Ruíz-Navarro, J. (2004). Changes in the intellectual structure of strategic management research: A bibliometric study of the Strategic Management Journal, 1980–2000. *Strategic Management Journal*, *25*(10), 981–1004. doi:10.1002/smj.397

Saleem, M., Khan, S. A., Al Shamsi, I. R., & Magd, H. (2023). Digital Marketing Through Social Media Best Practices: A Case Study of HEIs in the GCC Region. In A. Naim & V. Devi (Eds.), *Global Applications of the Internet of Things in Digital Marketing* (pp. 17–30). IGI Global. doi:10.4018/978-1-6684-8166-0.ch002

Saleem, M., Khan, S. A., & Magd, H. (2022). Content Marketing Framework for Building Brand Image: A Case Study of Sohar International School, Oman. In A. Naim & S. Kautish (Eds.), *Building a Brand Image Through Electronic Customer Relationship Management* (pp. 64–83). IGI Global. doi:10.4018/978-1-6684-5386-5.ch004

Sharma, N., & Arora, N. (2023). Past, Present, and Future of Cultural Marketing: A Bibliometric Analysis. In Cultural Marketing and Metaverse for Consumer Engagement (pp. 234-248). IGI Global.

Sharma, N. and Arora, N. (2023a). Do Instagram reels influence travelers' behavioral and e-WOM intentions for the selection of ecotourism destination?. *Journal of Hospitality and Tourism Insights*. . doi:10.1108/JHTI-03-2023-0135

Sharma, N., Khatri, B., & Khan, S. A. (2023b). Do e-WOM Persuade Travelers Destination Visit Intentions? An investigation on how Travelers Adopt the Information from the Social Media Channels. *Journal of Content. Community and Communication, 17*(9), 147–161. doi:10.31620/JCCC.06.23/11

Sharma, N., Khatri, B., Khan, S. A., & Shamsi, M. S. (2023a). Extending the UTAUT Model to Examine the Influence of social media on Tourists' Destination Selection. *Indian Journal of Marketing, 53*(4), 47–64. doi:10.17010/ijom/2023/v53/i4/172689

Shin, H., & Perdue, R. R. (2019). Self-Service Technology Research: A bibliometric co-citation visualization analysis. *International Journal of Hospitality Management, 80*, 101–112. doi:10.1016/j.ijhm.2019.01.012

Statista Research Department. (2022). *Number of global social network users 2017-2025*. Statista. https://www.statista.com/statistics/278414/number-of-worldwide-social-network-users/

van Eck, N. J., & Waltman, L. (2014). Visualizing Bibliometric Networks. In Y. Ding, R. Rousseau, & D. Wolfram (Eds.), *Measuring Scholarly Impact: Methods and Practice* (pp. 285–320). Springer International Publishing., doi:10.1007/978-3-319-10377-8_13

Wang, D., Xiang, Z., & Fesenmaier, D. R. (2016). Smartphone Use in Everyday Life and Travel. *Journal of Travel Research, 55*(1), 52–63. doi:10.1177/0047287514535847

Xiang, Z., & Gretzel, U. (2010). Role of social media in online travel information search. *Tourism Management, 31*(2), 179–188. doi:10.1016/j.tourman.2009.02.016

Xiang, Z., & Gretzel, U. (2010). Role of SMin online travel information search. *Tourism Management, 31*(2), 179–188. doi:10.1016/j.tourman.2009.02.016

Xiang, Z., Magnini, V. P., & Fesenmaier, D. R. (2015). Information technology and consumer behavior in travel and tourism: Insights from travel planning using the internet. *Journal of Retailing and Consumer Services, 22*, 244–249. doi:10.1016/j.jretconser.2014.08.005

Xiang, Z., Magnini, V. P., & Fesenmaier, D. R. (2015). Information technology and consumer behavior in travel and tourism: Insights from travel planning using the internet. *Journal of Retailing and Consumer Services, 22*, 244–249. doi:10.1016/j.jretconser.2014.08.005

Xu, H., Lovett, J., Cheung, L. T. O., Duan, X., Pei, Q., & Liang, D. (2021). Adapting to social media: The influence of online reviews on tourist behaviour at a world heritage site in China. *Asia Pacific Journal of Tourism Research*, *26*(10), 1125–1138. doi:10.1080/10941665.2021.1952460

Xu, X., Chen, X., Jia, F., Brown, S., Gong, Y., & Xu, Y. (2018). Supply chain finance: A systematic literature review and bibliometric analysis. *International Journal of Production Economics*, *204*, 160–173. doi:10.1016/j.ijpe.2018.08.003

Zarezadeh, Z. Z., Rastegar, H. R., & Gretzel, U. (2018). Reviewing the Past to Inform the Future: A Literature Review of SMin Tourism. *Czech Journal of Tourism*, *7*(2), 115–131. doi:10.1515/cjot-2018-0006

Zeng, B., & Gerritsen, R. (2014). What do we know about SMin tourism? A review. *Tourism Management Perspectives*, *10*, 27–36. doi:10.1016/j.tmp.2014.01.001

Zupic, I., & Čater, T. (2015). Bibliometric Methods in Management and Organization. *Organizational Research Methods*, *18*(3), 429–472. doi:10.1177/1094428114562629

Compilation of References

Abbasi, A. Z., Tsiotsou, R. H., Hussain, K., Rather, R. A., & Ting, D. H. (2023). Investigating the impact of social media images' value, consumer engagement, and involvement on eWOM of a tourism destination: A transmittal mediation approach. *Journal of Retailing and Consumer Services*, *71*, 103231. doi:10.1016/j.jretconser.2022.103231

Abdulhameed, O., Al-Ahmari, A., & Mian, S. H. (2019). Additive manufacturing: Challenges, trends, and applications. *Advances in Mechanical Engineering*, *11*(2), 1–27. doi:10.1177/1687814018822880

Abdullaeva, S., & Oripova, D. (2023). Development of Main Directions for Achieving Sustainability in Tourism. *International Journal of Social Science Research and Review*, *6*(6), 154–159. doi:10.47814/ijssrr.v6i6.1358

Abdullahi, M., Kilili, R., & Günay, T. (2021). E-tourism and digital marketing in africa: Opportunities and challenges. *Linguistica Antverpiensia*, *21*(1), 244–261.

Abdullah, M., Dias, C., Muley, D., & Shahin, M. (2020). Exploring the impacts of COVID-19 on travel behavior and mode preferences. *Transportation Research Interdisciplinary Perspectives*, *8*, 100255. doi:10.1016/j.trip.2020.100255 PMID:34173481

Abi-Jaoude, E., Naylor, K. T., & Pignatiello, A. (2020). Smartphones, social media use and youth mental health. Canadian Medical Association *Journal (CMAJ)*, *192*(6). https://www.cmaj.ca/content/192/6/E136 doi:10.1503/cmaj.190434

Afrisal, A. (2022). Collaborative Governance in Tourism Development Policy. *Journal of Social Sciences*, *3*(6), 1266–1270. doi:10.46799/jss.v3i6.478

Aguinis, H., Kraus, S., Poček, J., Meyer, N., & Jensen, S. H. (2023). The why, how, and what of public policy implications of tourism and hospitality research. *Tourism Management*, *97*, 104720. doi:10.1016/j.tourman.2023.104720

Ahmad, N., Harun, A., Khizar, H. M. U., Khalid, J., & Khan, S. (2022). Drivers and barriers of travel behaviors during and post COVID-19 pandemic: a systematic literature review and future agenda. *Journal of Tourism Futures*, 1-23. doi:10.1108/JTF-01-2022-0023

Ahn, J., & Back, K. J. (2020). The structural effects of affective and cognitive elaboration in formation of customer–brand relationship. *Service Industries Journal*, *40*(3-4), 226–242. doi:10.1080/02642069.2018.1460358

Akadiri, S. saint, Alola, A. A., & Uzuner, G. (2020). Economic policy uncertainty and tourism: evidence from the heterogeneous panel. In Current Issues in Tourism, 23(20), 2507–2514). Routledge. doi:10.1080/13683500.2019.1687662

Aldao, C., Blasco, D., & Espallargas, M. P. (2022). Lessons from COVID-19 for the future: destination crisis management, tourist behavior and tourism industry trends. *Journal of Tourism Futures*, 1-15. doi:10.1108/JTF-02-2022-0059

Al-Fuqaha, A., Guizani, M., Mohammadi, M., Aledhari, M., & Ayyash, M. (2015). Internet of Things: A Survey on Enabling Technologies, Protocols, and Applications. *IEEE Communications Surveys and Tutorials*, *17*(4), 2347–2376. doi:10.1109/COMST.2015.2444095

Alonso-Cañadas, J., Galán-Valdivieso, F., Saraite-Sariene, L., & Caba-Perez, M. D. C. (2019). Unpacking the Drivers of Stakeholder Engagement in Sustainable Water Management: NGOs and the Use of Facebook. *Water (Basel)*, *11*(4), 775. doi:10.3390/w11040775

Alsharif, A. H., Salleh, N. Z. M., & Baharun, R. (2021). To better understand the role of emotional processes in decision-making. *International Journal of Academic Research in Economics and Management Sciences*, *10*(2), 49–67. doi:10.6007/IJAREMS/v10-i2/9883

Alt, R., & Klein, S. (2011). Twenty years of electronic markets research—Looking backward towards the future. *Electronic Markets*, *21*(1), 41–51. doi:10.1007/s12525-011-0057-z

Alves, G. M., Sousa, B. M., & Machado, A. (2020). The role of digital marketing and online relationship quality in social tourism: A tourism for all case study. In *Digital marketing strategies for tourism, hospitality, and airline industries* (pp. 49–70). IGI Global. doi:10.4018/978-1-5225-9783-4.ch003

Ameen, N., Tarhini, A., Reppel, A., & Anand, A. (2021). Customer experiences in the age of artificial intelligence. *Computers in Human Behavior*, *114*, 106548. doi:10.1016/j.chb.2020.106548 PMID:32905175

Amelung, B., Nicholls, S., & Viner, D. (2007). Implications of Global Climate Change for Tourism Flows and Seasonality. *Journal of Travel Research*, *45*(3), 285–296. doi:10.1177/0047287506295937

Amoiradis, C., Velissariou, E., & Stankova, M. (2021). Tourism as a Socio-Cultural Phenomenon: A Critical Analysis. *The Social Science Journal*, *4*(2), 10–21. doi:10.31014/aior.1991.04.02.271

Andrade, M. J., Costa, J. P., & Jiménez-Morales, E. (2021). Challenges for European tourist-city-ports: Strategies for a sustainable coexistence in the cruise post-COVID context. *Land (Basel)*, *10*(11), 1269. doi:10.3390/land10111269

Aniket, K., & Roshan, D. (2022). *Food 3D Printing Market Research, 2031*. Allied Market Research. https://www.alliedmarketresearch.com/food-3d-printing-market-A08587

Aniwaa (2022). *Food 3D Printer by Micromake*. Available at: https://www.aniwaa.com/product/3d-printers/micromake-food-3d-printer/ [accessed 6 February 2023].

An, Q., Ma, Y., Du, Q., Xiang, Z., & Fan, W. (2020). Role of user-generated photos in online hotel reviews: An analytical approach. *Journal of Hospitality and Tourism Management*, *45*, 633–640. doi:10.1016/j.jhtm.2020.11.002

Antons, D., & Breidbach, C. F. (2018). Big data, big insights? Advancing service innovation and design with machine learning. *Journal of Service Research*, *21*(1), 17–39. doi:10.1177/1094670517738373

Anzaldúa-Morales, A. (2005). *La evaluación sensorial de los alimentos en la teoria y la práctica*. Zaragoza: Editorial Acribia, S.A.

Arabadzhyan, A., Figini, P., García, C., González, M., Lam-González, Y., & León, C. (2020). Climate change, coastal tourism, and impact chains – a literature review. *Current Issues in Tourism*, *24*(16), 2233–2268. doi:10.1080/13683500.2020.1825351

Aria, M., & Cuccurullo, C. (2017). bibliometrix : An R-tool for comprehensive science mapping analysis. *Journal of Informetrics*, *11*(4), 959–975. doi:10.1016/j.joi.2017.08.007

Ariffin, A. A. M., & Maghzi, A. (2012). A preliminary study on customer expectations of hotel hospitality: Influences of personal and hotel factors. *International Journal of Hospitality Management*, *31*(1), 191–198. doi:10.1016/j.ijhm.2011.04.012

Arkema, K. K., Fisher, D. M., Wyatt, K., Wood, S. A., & Payne, H. J. (2021). Advancing sustainable development and protected area management with social media-based tourism data. *Sustainability (Basel)*, *13*(5), 2427. doi:10.3390/su13052427

Arnold, D. J., & Quelch, J. A. (1998). New strategies in emerging markets. *MIT Sloan Management Review*.

Arora, C., & Sarkar, D. (2023). Auditing Artificial Intelligence (AI) as a New Layer of Mediation: Introduction of a new black box to address another black box. *Hipertext*, (26), 65-68. doi:10.31009/hipertext.net.2023.i26.10

Artal-Tur, A., Villena-Navarro, M., & Alamá-Sabater, L. (2018). The relationship between cultural tourist behaviour and destination sustainability. *Anatolia*, *29*(2), 237–251. doi:10.1080/13032917.2017.1414444

Ashley, C. (2000). *The impacts of tourism on rural livelihoods: Namibia's experience*. Overseas Development Institute.

Ashqar, R. I., Ramos, C., Sousa, C., & Matos, N. (2023). CRM and Smart Technologies in the Hospitality. In *Marketing and Smart Technologies: Proceedings of ICMarkTech 2022* (Vol. 2, pp. 113–124). Springer. doi:10.1007/978-981-19-9099-1_9

Asmelash, A. G., & Kumar, S. (2019). The structural relationship between tourist satisfaction and sustainable heritage tourism development in Tigrai, Ethiopia. *Heliyon*, *5*(3), e01335. doi:10.1016/j.heliyon.2019.e01335 PMID:30957037

Atef, T. M., & Al-Balushi, M. (2017). Cruising Market in Oman: Current trends and future perspectives. *Journal of Tourism and Hospitality Management*, *5*(1), 1–14. doi:10.15640/jthm.v5n1a1

Atef, T., & Al Balushi, M. (2017). Omani tourism and hospitality students' employment intentions and job preferences: Ramifications on Omanization plans. *Quality Assurance in Education*, *25*(4), 440–461. doi:10.1108/QAE-04-2016-0022

Awedyk, M., & Niezgoda, A. (2016). New opportunities for future tourism after 25 years of political and socioeconomic transformation – foresight in Poland's tourism planning. *Journal of Tourism Futures*, *2*(2), 137–154. doi:10.1108/JTF-05-2015-0031

Axhami, M., Ndou, V., Milo, V., & Scorrano, P. (2023). Creating Value via the Circular Economy: Practices in the Tourism Sector. *Administrative Sciences*, *13*(7), 166. doi:10.3390/admsci13070166

Aziz, H., El-Said, O., & Bontenbal, M. (2020). An analytical approach to cruise tourism as an option for development: A case study of the Sultanate of Oman. *Tourism in Marine Environments*, *15*(2), 95–109. doi:10.3727/154427320X15828792518754

Baker, H. K., Kumar, S., & Pattnaik, D. (2021). Research constituents, intellectual structure, and collaboration pattern in the Journal of Forecasting : A bibliometric analysis. *Journal of Forecasting*, *40*(4), 577–602. doi:10.1002/for.2731

Bąk, I., & Szczecińska, B. (2020). Global Demographic Trends and Effects on Tourism. *European Research Studies*, *4*(4), 571–585. doi:10.35808/ersj/1701

Baloglu, S., & Brinberg, D. (1997). Affective Images of Tourism Destinations. *Journal of Travel Research*, *35*(4), 11–15. doi:10.1177/004728759703500402

Barnes, D. C., Meyer, T., & Kinard, B. R. (2016). Implementing a delight strategy in a restaurant setting: The power of unsolicited recommendations. *Cornell Hospitality Quarterly*, *57*(3), 329–342. doi:10.1177/1938965515626296

Barsky, J., & Nash, L. (2010). What is more important than location in selecting a hotel? [Online]. *Hotel & Motel Management*.

Basha, K., Norazlyn, A., & Hui-Wen, S. (2022). Are we so over smartwatches? Or can technology, fashion, and psychographic attributes sustain smartwatch usage? Technology in Society. Elsevier.

Basha, N. K., Aw, E. C. X., & Chuah, S. H. W. (2022, May). Are we so over smartwatches? Or can technology, fashion, and psychographic attributes sustain smartwatch usage? *Technology in Society*, *69*, 101952. doi:10.1016/j.techsoc.2022.101952

BasuK.CaspiA. (2021). Markets and Regulation in the Age of Big Tech. Social Science Research Network. (SSRN). https://ssrn.com/abstract=3985585

Becken, S. (2005). The role of tourist icons for sustainable tourism. *Journal of Vacation Marketing*, *11*(1), 21–30. doi:10.1177/1356766705050840

Beerli, A., & Martín, J. D. (2004). Factors influencing destination image. *Annals of Tourism Research*, *31*(3), 657–681. doi:10.1016/j.annals.2004.01.010

Begum, H., Er, A. C., Alam, A. S. A. F., & Sahazali, N. (2014). Tourist's Perceptions towards the Role of Stakeholders in Sustainable Tourism. *Procedia: Social and Behavioral Sciences*, *144*, 313–321. doi:10.1016/j.sbspro.2014.07.301

Bianchi, R. (2018). The political economy of tourism development: A critical review. *Annals of Tourism Research*, *70*, 88–102. doi:10.1016/j.annals.2017.08.005

Bilgihan, A., Kandampully, J., & Zhang, T. C. (2016). Towards a unified customer experience in online shopping environments: Antecedents and outcomes. *International Journal of Quality and Service Sciences*, *8*(1), 102–119. doi:10.1108/IJQSS-07-2015-0054

Björk, P. (2000). Ecotourism from a conceptual perspective, an extended definition of a unique tourism form. *International Journal of Tourism Research*, *2*(3), 189–202. doi:10.1002/(SICI)1522-1970(200005/06)2:3<189::AID-JTR195>3.0.CO;2-T

Blanco-Gutiérrez, I., Varela-Ortega, C., & Manners, R. (2020). Evaluating animal-based foods and plant-based alternatives using multi-criteria and SWOT analyses. *International Journal of Environmental Research and Public Health*, *17*(21), 7969. doi:10.3390/ijerph17217969 PMID:33138318

Blas, S. S., & Carvajal-Trujillo, E. (2014). Cruise passengers' experiences in a Mediterranean port of call. The case study of Valencia. *Ocean and Coastal Management*, *102*, 307–316. doi:10.1016/j.ocecoaman.2014.10.011

Bonsón, E., & Ratkai, M. (2013). A set of metrics to assess stakeholder engagement and social legitimacy on a corporate Facebook page. *Online Information Review*, *37*(5), 787–803. doi:10.1108/OIR-03-2012-0054

Borges, B. (2009). *Marketing 2.0: Bridging the gap between seller and buyer through social media marketing*. Wheatmark.

Bosque, I. R., & Martin, H. S. (2008). Tourist Satisfaction a Cognitive-Affective Model. *Annals of Tourism Research*, *35*(2), 551–573. doi:10.1016/j.annals.2008.02.006

Bouhalleb, A., & Smida, A. (2020). *Exploring the relationship between scenario planning and strategic flexibility and complexity*. European J. of International Management., doi:10.1504/EJIM.2020.107033

Bourell, D. L. (2016). Perspectives on Additive Manufacturing. *Annual Review of Materials Research*, *46*(1), 1–18. doi:10.1146/annurev-matsci-070115-031606

Bowen, J., & Whalen, E. (2017). Trends that are changing travel and tourism. *Worldwide Hospitality and Tourism Themes*, *9*(6), 592–602. doi:10.1108/WHATT-09-2017-0045

Boyd, D., & Ellison, N. (2008). Social Network Sites: Definition, History, and Scholarship. *Journal of Computer-Mediated Communication, 13*(1), 210–230. doi:10.1111/j.1083-6101.2007.00393.x

Boyra, J. (2003). Sustainable tourism development convergence. In: *Proceedings of the II International Scientific Conference on Sustainable Tourism Development and the Environment.* University of the Aegean. Interdepartmental Program of Postgraduate Studies in Tourism Planning, Management and Policy. Chios Island, Greece.

Boyra, J. (2005). *Tourism and the Environment in Attica.* [PhD. Dissertation, University of Barcelona].

Boyra, J. (2009). Looking for Environmental Excellence in Tourist Destinations. *TOURISMOS: An International Multidisciplinary Refereed Journal of Tourism, 4*(2), 91-106. https://tourismosjournal.aegean.gr/article/view/110

Brendehaug, E., Aall, C., & Dodds, R. (2017). Environmental policy integration as a strategy for sustainable tourism planning: Issues in implementation. *Journal of Sustainable Tourism, 25*(9), 1257–1274. doi:10.1080/09669582.2016.1259319

Brida, J. G., Bukstein, D., & Tealde, E. (2015). Exploring cruise ship passenger spending patterns in two Uruguayan ports of call. *Current Issues in Tourism, 18*(7), 684–700. doi:10.1080/13683500.2013.861391

Brida, J. G., & Zapata, S. (2010). Cruise tourism: Economic, socio-cultural and environmental impacts. *International Journal of Leisure and Tourism Marketing, 1*(3), 205–226. doi:10.1504/IJLTM.2010.029585

Brodie, R. J., Ilic, A., Juric, B., & Hollebeek, L. (2013). Consumer engagement in a virtual brand community: An exploratory analysis. *Journal of Business Research, 66*(1), 105–114. doi:10.1016/j.jbusres.2011.07.029

Brunner, T. A., Delley, M., & Denkel, C. (2017). Consumers' attitudes and change of attitude toward 3D-printed food. *Food Quality and Preference, 68*(December), 389–396.

Buckley, R., Guitart, D., & Shakeela, A. (2017). Contested surf tourism resources in the Maldives. *Annals of Tourism Research, 64*, 185–199. doi:10.1016/j.annals.2017.03.005

Buhalis, D., & Sinarta, Y. (2022). Tourism marketing in the smart era. In The Routledge Handbook of Tourism Experience Management and Marketing. Routledge.

Buhalis, D. (2019). Technology in tourism-from information communication technologies to eTourism and smart tourism towards ambient intelligence tourism: A perspective article. *Tourism Review, 75*(1), 267–272. doi:10.1108/TR-06-2019-0258

Buhalis, D., & Foerste, M. (2015). SoCoMo marketing for travel and tourism: Empowering co-creation of value. *Journal of Destination Marketing & Management, 4*(3), 151–161. doi:10.1016/j.jdmm.2015.04.001

Buhalis, D., & Law, R. (2008). Progress in information technology and tourism management; 20 years on and 10 years after the Internet the state of eTourism research. *Tourism Management, 29*(4), 606–623. doi:10.1016/j.tourman.2008.01.005

Buhalis, D., Papathanassis, A., & Vafeidou, M. (2022). Smart cruising: Smart technology applications and their diffusion in cruise tourism. *Journal of Hospitality and Tourism Technology, 13*(4), 626–649. doi:10.1108/JHTT-05-2021-0155

Buhalis, D., & Sinarta, Y. (2019). Real-time co-creation and nowness service: Lessons from tourism and hospitality. *Journal of Travel & Tourism Marketing, 36*(5), 563–582. doi:10.1080/10548408.2019.1592059

Bulchand-Gidumal, J. (2020). *Impact of artificial intelligence in travel, tourism and hospitality. Handbook of e-tourism.* Springer. https://accedacris.ulpgc.es/bitstream/10553/106011/2/impact_artificial_intelligence.pdf

Buzzi, N. S., Menéndez, M. C., Truchet, D. M., Delgado, A. L., & Severini, M. D. F. (2022). An overview on metal pollution on touristic sandy beaches: Is the COVID-19 pandemic an opportunity to improve coastal management? *Marine Pollution Bulletin, 174*, 113275. doi:10.1016/j.marpolbul.2021.113275 PMID:35090269

Cai, C. H., Ding, A., & Legendre, T. S. (2021). Exploring persuasive sales techniques to improve customer acceptance of sustainable but unfamiliar menu in restaurants. *International Journal of Contemporary Hospitality Management, 33*(10), 3093–3114. doi:10.1108/IJCHM-08-2020-0924

Camilleri, M. A., & Kozak, M. (2022). Interactive engagement through travel and tourism social media groups: A social facilitation theory perspective. *Technology in Society, 71*, 102098. doi:10.1016/j.techsoc.2022.102098

Campos-Soriaa, J. A., Inchausti-Sintes, F., & Eugenio-Martin, J. L. (2015). Understanding tourists' economizing strategies during the global economic crisis. *Tourism Management, 48*, 164–173. doi:10.1016/j.tourman.2014.10.019

Can, Y., Gaberli, Ü., & Güler, M. (2022). Impact of Political Stability and Absence of Violence/Terrorism on Tourism: A Panel Co-Integration Analysis. *Yönetim ve Ekonomi Araştırmaları Dergisi, 20*(4), 387–400. doi:10.11611/yead.1168124

Cao, B., Zhao, J., Lv, Z., & Yang, P. (2021). Diversified Personalized Recommendation Optimization Based on Mobile Data. *IEEE Transactions on Intelligent Transportation Systems, 22*(4), 2133–2139. doi:10.1109/TITS.2020.3040909

Carvalho, I., & Ivanov, S. (2023). ChatGPT for tourism: applications, benefits and risks. Tourism Review, Vol. ahead-of-print (No. ahead-of-print). https://doi.org/ doi:10.1108/TR-02-2023-0088

Casado-Díaz, A. B., Navarro-Ruiz, S., Nicolau, J. L., & Ivars-Baidal, J. (2021). Expanding our understanding of cruise visitors' expenditure at destinations: The role of spatial patterns, onshore visit choice and cruise category. *Tourism Management, 83*, 104199. doi:10.1016/j.tourman.2020.104199

Cascio, W. F., & Montealegre, R. (2016). How Technology Is Changing Work and Organizations. *Annual Review of Organizational Psychology and Organizational Behavior*, *3*(1), 349–379. doi:10.1146/annurev-orgpsych-041015-062352

Caulier, S., Doets, E., & Noort, M. (2020). An exploratory consumer study of 3D printed food perception in a real-life military setting. *Food Quality and Preference*, *86*(June), 1–5. doi:10.1016/j.foodqual.2020.104001

Caviggioli, F., & Ughetto, E. (2019). A bibliometric analysis of the research dealing with the impact of additive manufacturing on industry, business and society. *International Journal of Production Economics*, *208*, 254–268. doi:10.1016/j.ijpe.2018.11.022

CEnTour. (2020). *Managing the transition to circular economy for tourism providers*. Circular Tourism. https://circulartourism.eu/wp-content/uploads/2021/02/CIRCULAR-ECONOMY-TRANSITION-FOR-TOURISM-PROVIDERS.pdf

Chaffey, D., & Smith, P. R. (2022). *Digital marketing excellence: planning, optimizing and integrating online marketing*. Taylor & Francis. doi:10.4324/9781003009498

Chamboko-Mpotaringa, M., & Tichaawa, T. M. (2021). Tourism Digital Marketing Tools and Views on Future Trends: A Systematic Review of Literature. *African Journal of Hospitality, Tourism and Leisure*, *10*(2), 712–726. doi:10.46222/ajhtl.19770720-128

Chang, Y.-T., Lee, S., & Park, H. K. (2017). Efficiency analysis of major cruise lines. *Tourism Management*, *58*, 78–88. doi:10.1016/j.tourman.2016.10.012 PMID:32287747

Chan, I. (2014). Leveraging student course enrollment data to infuse personalization in a library website. *Library Hi Tech*, *32*(3), 450–466. doi:10.1108/LHT-07-2013-0096

Checkland, P. B., & Scholes, J. (1990). *Soft systems methodology in action*. John Wiley & Sons.

Cheng, X., Xue, T., Yang, B., & Ma, B. (2023). A digital transformation approach in hospitality and tourism research. *International Journal of Contemporary Hospitality Management*, *35*(8), 2944–2967. doi:10.1108/IJCHM-06-2022-0679

Cheng, Y., Fu, Y., Ma, L., Yap, P. L., Losic, D., Wang, H., & Zhang, Y. (2022). Rheology of edible food inks from 2D/3D/4D printing, and its role in future 5D/6D printing. *Food Hydrocolloids*, *132*(3), 1–34. doi:10.1016/j.foodhyd.2022.107855

Chen, H., & Jai, T. (2019). Cyber alarm: Determining the impacts of hotel's data breach messages. *International Journal of Hospitality Management*, *82*, 326–334. doi:10.1016/j.ijhm.2018.10.002

Chen, S., Law, R., Zhang, M., & Si, Y. (2021). Mobile communications for tourism and hospitality: A review of historical evolution, present status, and future trends. *Electronics (Basel)*, *10*(15), 1804. doi:10.3390/electronics10151804

Chen, Y., & Zhang, C. (2019). A survey on the internet of things security. *Journal of Network and Computer Applications*, *126*, 46–70.

Cheung, Y. Y., and Law, C. H. R. (2001). The impact of air quality on tourism: the case of Hong Kong. *Pacific tourism review, 5*(2018-02-01), 69-74.

Chisik, Y., Pons, P., & Jaen, J. (2018). Gastronomy Meets Ludology: Towards a Definition of What it Means to Play with Your (Digital) Food. In *CHI PLAY'18 Extended Abstracts* (pp. 155–168). Association for Computing Machinery. doi:10.1145/3270316.3272056

Chitadze, N. (2023). International Tourism and its Impact on World Politics and World Economy. *Journal of Social Sciences, 8*(2). doi:10.31578/jss.v8i2.146

Chiwaridzo, O. T., & Masengu, R. (2023). The impact of social media branding and technology adoption on green tourism: The role of tourist behavior as a mediator in developing countries post-COVID-19—context of Zimbabwe. *Future Business Journal, 9*(1), 63. doi:10.1186/s43093-023-00249-6

Cho, M., & Yoo, J. J.-E. (2021). Customer pressure and restaurant employee green creative behavior: Serial mediation effects of restaurant ethical standards and employee green passion. *International Journal of Contemporary Hospitality Management, 33*(12), 4505–4525. doi:10.1108/IJCHM-06-2021-0697

Chua, B.-L., Lee, S., Goh, B., & Han, H. (2015). Impacts of cruise service quality and price on vacationers' cruise experience: Moderating role of price sensitivity. *International Journal of Hospitality Management, 44*, 131–145. doi:10.1016/j.ijhm.2014.10.012

Chua, C. K. (2020). Publication Trends in 3D Bioprinting and 3D Food Printing. *International Journal of Bioprinting, 6*(1), 1–3. doi:10.18063/IJB.2017.01.003 PMID:32923736

Chung, J. Y., & Buhalis, D. (2008). Information Needs in Online Social Networks. *Information Technology & Tourism, 10*(4), 267–281. doi:10.3727/109830508788403123

Cissé, G., McLeman, R., Adams, H., Aldunce, P., Bowen, K., Campbell-Lendrum, D., Clayton, S., Ebi, K. L., Hess, J., Huang, C., Liu, Q., McGregor, G., Semenza, J., & Tirado, M. C. (2022). Health, Wellbeing, and the Changing Structure of Communities. In *Climate Change 2022: Impacts, Adaptation and Vulnerability. Contribution of Working Group II to the Sixth Assessment Report of the Intergovernmental Panel on Climate Change*, (pp. 1041–1170). Cambridge University Press. https://www.ipcc.ch/report/ar6/wg2/downloads/report/IPCC_AR6_WGII_Chapter07.pdf, doi:10.1017/9781009325844.009

Cobo, M. J., López-Herrera, A. G., Herrera-Viedma, E., & Herrera, F. (2011). An approach for detecting, quantifying, and visualizing the evolution of a research field: A practical application to the Fuzzy Sets Theory field. *Journal of Informetrics, 5*(1), 146–166. doi:10.1016/j.joi.2010.10.002

Coccossis, H., Mexa, A., Collovini, A., Parpairis, A., & Kanstandoglou, M. (2002). Defining, Measuring, and Evaluating Carrying Capacity in European Destinations. B4-3040/2000/294577/MAR/D2 Final Report. Athens.

Coelho, P. S., Rita, P., & Santos, Z. R. (2018). On the relationship between consumer-brand identification, brand community, and brand loyalty. *Journal of Retailing and Consumer Services*, *43*, 101–110. doi:10.1016/j.jretconser.2018.03.011

Çöl, B. G., İmre, M., & Yıkmış, S. (2023). Virtual reality and augmented reality technologies in gastronomy: A review. *eFood*, *4*(83), 1–16.

Collazos, A., Obando, J., López, J., & García, L. (2023). Public policy and its impact on innovation, competitiveness, and performance in the tourism sector. *Cogent Social Sciences*, *9*(2), 2249692. Advance online publication. doi:10.1080/23311886.2023.2249692

Correia, A., Kozak, M., & Ferradeira, J. (2011). Impact of culture on tourist decision-making styles. *International Journal of Tourism Research*, *13*(5), 433–446. doi:10.1002/jtr.817

Costello, L., McDermott, M.-L., & Wallace, R. (2017). Netnography: Range of practices, misperception. *International Journal of Qualitative Methods*, *16*(1), 1–1. doi:10.1177/1609406917700647

Cozzio, C., Orlandi, L. B., & Zardini, A. (2018). Food sustainability as a strategic value driver in the hotel industry. *Sustainability (Basel)*, *10*(10), 3404. doi:10.3390/su10103404

Cristea, M., Noja, G. G., Stefea, P., & Sala, A. L. (2020). The Impact of Population Aging and Public Health Support on EU Labor Markets. *International Journal of Environmental Research and Public Health*, *17*(4), 1–27. doi:10.3390/ijerph17041439 PMID:32102277

Croce, V. (2018). With growth comes accountability: Could a leisure activity turn into a driver for sustainable growth? *Journal of Tourism Futures*, *4*(3), 218–232. doi:10.1108/JTF-04-2018-0020

Crompton, J. (1979). Motivations for Pleasure Vacation. *Annals of Tourism Research*, *6*(4), 408–424. doi:10.1016/0160-7383(79)90004-5

Crotts, J. C., Pan, B., & Raschid, A. E. (2008). A survey method for identifying key drivers of guest delight. *International Journal of Contemporary Hospitality Management*, *20*(4), 462–470. doi:10.1108/09596110810873552

Cruise Lines International Association. (2022). *2022 Global Market Report*. CLIA. https://cruising.org/-/media/clia-media/research/2023/2022-1r-clia-001-overview-global-final.ashx

Cruise Market Watch. (2023). *Cruise travel is back but economic uncertainty may cool future demand.* Market Watch. https://www.marketwatch.com/video/sectorwatch/cruise-travel-is-back-but-economic-uncertainty-may-cool-future-demand/C979F72A-DF95-48FC-8C94-34E658E96C3C.html

Dabas, S., Sharma, S., & Manaktola, K. (2021). Adoption of digital marketing tools in independent businesses: Experiences of restaurant entrepreneurs in India and United Kingdom. *Worldwide Hospitality and Tourism Themes*, *13*(2), 214–235. doi:10.1108/WHATT-09-2020-0120

Dabbene, L., Ramundo, L., & Terzi, S. (2018). Economic model for the evaluation of 3D food printing. In*: 2018 IEEE International Conference on Engineering, Technology and Innovation (ICE/ITMC)*. Stuttgart, Germany: ICE/ITMC. 10.1109/ICE.2018.8436285

Ďaďová, I., & Soviar, J. (2021). The application of online marketing tools in marketing communication of the entities with the tourism offer in 2020 in Slovakia. *Transportation Research Procedia*, *55*, 1791–1799. doi:10.1016/j.trpro.2021.07.170

Daghfous, A., & Barkhi, R. (2009). The strategic management of information technology in UAE hotels: An exploratory study of TQM, SCM, and CRM implementations. *Technovation*, *29*(9), 588–595. doi:10.1016/j.technovation.2009.05.007

Damnjanović, V., Lončarić, D., & Dlačić, J. (2020). Digital marketing strategy of Accor Hotels: Shaping the future of hospitality. *Tourism and Hospitality Management*, *26*(1), 233–244.

Darcy, S., Mckercher, B., & Schweinsberg, S. (2020). From tourism and disability to accessible tourism: A perspective article. *Tourism Review*, *75*(1), 140–144. doi:10.1108/TR-07-2019-0323

de Amorim, L. A., Sousa, B. B., Dias, A. L., & Santos, V. R. (2022). Exploring the outcomes of digital marketing on historic sites' visitor behaviour. *Journal of Cultural Heritage Management and Sustainable Development*. doi:10.1108/JCHMSD-11-2021-0202

De Boer, J., & Aiking, H. (2019). Strategies towards healthy and sustainable protein consumption: A transition framework at the levels of diets, dishes, and dish ingredients. *Food Quality and Preference*, *73*, 171–181. doi:10.1016/j.foodqual.2018.11.012

de Bruyn, C., Said, F. B., Meyer, N., & Soliman, M. (2023). Research in tourism sustainability: A comprehensive bibliometric analysis from 1990 to 2022. *Heliyon*, *9*(8), e18874. doi:10.1016/j.heliyon.2023.e18874 PMID:37636413

De Villiers, R., Tipgomut, P., & Franklin, A. (2020). *International market segmentation across consumption and communication categories: Identity, demographics, and consumer decisions and online habits*.

Debnath, R., Datta, B., & Mukhopadhyay, S. (2016). Customer relationship management theory and research in the new millennium: Directions for future research. *Journal of Relationship Marketing*, *15*(4), 299–325. doi:10.1080/15332667.2016.1209053

Deculier, E., & Chapuis, F. (2007). Oral presentation bias: A retrospective cohort study. *Journal of Epidemiology and Community Health*, *61*(3), 190–193. doi:10.1136/jech.2006.048603 PMID:17325393

Dehue, R., & Stikwerda, P. (2017). *4 Famous Restaurants that Use 3D Printers*. 3D Printing. https://3dprinting.com/food/4-famous-restaurants-that-use-3d-printers/

Delgado, A., Rodriguez, R., & Staszewska, A. (2023). Tackling Food Waste in the Tourism Sector: Towards a Responsible Consumption Trend. *Sustainability (Basel)*, *15*(17), 13226. doi:10.3390/su151713226

Demiralay, S., & Kilincarslan, E. (2019). The impact of geopolitical risks on travel and leisure stocks. *Tourism Management*, *75*, 460–476. doi:10.1016/j.tourman.2019.06.013

Demir, E., Gozgor, G., & Paramati, S. R. (2019). Do geopolitical risks matter for inbound tourism? *Eurasian Business Review*, *9*(2), 183–191. doi:10.1007/s40821-019-00118-9

Derbisheva, E., & Kyzy, E. (2022). Regulatory Regulation of Construction of Tourist Facilities. *The herald of KSUCTA n a N Isanov*. . doi:10.35803/1694-5298.2022.2.769-776

Dewantara, M., Gardiner, S., & Jin, X. (2022). Travel Vlog Ecosystem in Tourism Digital Marketing Evolution: A Narrative Literature Review. *. *Current Issues in Tourism*, 2022.

Dias, Á., González-Rodríguez, M. R., & Hallak, R. (2022). Nascent entrepreneurship: A critical perspective and research agenda in tourism and hospitality. *International Journal of Contemporary Hospitality Management*. doi:10.1108/IJCHM-07-2022-0853

Díaz-Meneses, G. (2019). A multiphase trip, diversified digital and varied background approach to analyzing and segmenting holidaymakers and their use of social media. *Journal of Destination Marketing & Management*, *11*, 166–182. doi:10.1016/j.jdmm.2017.07.005

Dinh, T. T. H. (2020). *The Effect of Eco-Friendly Packaging on Consumer Behaviour in the Restaurant Business.*

Ditlevsen, K., Sandøe, P., & Lassen, J. (2019). Healthy food is nutritious, but organic food is healthy because it is pure: The negotiation of healthy food choices by Danish consumers of organic food. *Food Quality and Preference*, *71*, 46–53. doi:10.1016/j.foodqual.2018.06.001

Dong, X., Liu, S., Li, H., Yang, Z., Liang, S., & Deng, N. (2020). Love of nature as a mediator between connectedness to nature and sustainable consumption behavior. *Journal of Cleaner Production*, *242*, 118451. doi:10.1016/j.jclepro.2019.118451

Donthu, N., Kumar, S., Mukherjee, D., Pandey, N., & Lim, W. M. (2021). How to conduct a bibliometric analysis: An overview and guidelines. *Journal of Business Research*, *133*, 285–296. doi:10.1016/j.jbusres.2021.04.070

Doxey, G. (1975). A Causation Theory of Visitor–Resident Irritants: Methodology and Research Inferences. *The Impact of Tourism. In the Sixth Annual Conference Proceedings*, pp.195-198. San Diego: The Travel Research Association.

Duan, J., Xie, C., & Morrison, A. M. (2021). Tourism Crises and Impacts on Destinations: A Systematic Review of the Tourism and Hospitality Literature. *Journal of Hospitality & Tourism Research (Washington, D.C.)*, *46*(4), 667–695. doi:10.1177/1096348021994194

Ellen Macarthur Foundation. (2017). *Cities in the Circular Economy: An Initial Exploration.* Ellen Macarthur Foundation. https://www.ellenmacarthurfoundation.org/assets/downloads/publications/Cities-in-the-CE_An-Initial-Exploration.pdf

Elliot, S., Papadopoulos, N., & Kim, S. S. (2011). An Integrative Model of Place Image: Exploring Relationships Between Destination, Product, and Country Images. *Journal of Travel Research*, *50*(5), 520–534. doi:10.1177/0047287510379161

Enfield, R. E., Pandya, J. K., Lu, J., McClements, D. J., & Kinchia, A. J. (2022). The future of 3D food printing: Opportunities for space applications. *Critical Reviews in Food Science and Nutrition*, 1–14. PMID:35652158

Ercan, F. (2020). An examination on the use of immersive reality technologies in the travel and tourism industry. *Business & Management Studies: An International Journal*, *8*(2), 2348–2383. doi:10.15295/bmij.v8i2.1510

Erevelles, S., Fukawa, N., & Swayne, L. (2016). Big Data consumer analytics and the transformation of marketing. *Journal of Business Research*, *69*(2), 897–904. doi:10.1016/j.jbusres.2015.07.001

Escalante-Aburto, A., Santiago, G. T., Álvarez, M. M., & Chuck-Hernández, C. (2021). Advances and prospective applications of 3D food printing for health improvement and personalized nutrition. *Comprehensive Reviews in Food Science and Food Safety*, *20*(6), 5722–5741. doi:10.1111/1541-4337.12849 PMID:34643023

Estevão, C., & Costa, C. (2020). Natural disaster management in tourist destinations: A systematic literature review. *European Journal of Tourism Research*, *25*, 2502. doi:10.54055/ejtr.v25i.417

Etemad, H. (2020). Managing uncertain consequences of a global crisis: SMEs encountering adversities, losses, and new opportunities. *Journal of International Entrepreneurship*, *18*(2), 125–144. doi:10.1007/s10843-020-00279-z

Eugenio-Martin, J. (2003). Modelling Determinants of Tourism Demand as a Five-Stage Process: A Discrete Choice Methodological Approach. *Tourism and Hospitality Research*, *4*(4), 341–354. doi:10.1177/146735840300400407

Eugenio-Martin, J. L., & Campos-Soria, J. A. (2014). Economic crisis and tourism expenditure cutback decision. *Annals of Tourism Research*, *44*(1), 53–73. doi:10.1016/j.annals.2013.08.013

Europarc Federation. (2023). *Who we are.* Europarc. https://www.europarc.org/who-we-are/

European Commission. (2020). *Directorate-General for Research and Innovation. Directorate G – Research & Innovation Outreach.* Europea. https://op.europa.eu/en/publication-detail/-/publication/a3cde934-12a0-11eb-9a54-01aa75ed71a1/

European Environment Agency (EEA). (2020). *Multiple pressures and their combined effects in Europe's seas.* ETC/ICM Technical Report 4/2019: European Topic Centre on Inland, Coastal and Marine waters. https://www.eea.europa.eu/downloads/e8fe9e1b961f48e3af7ac69adab8e696/1675956090/multiple-pressures-and-their-combined.pdf

Fader, P. S., Hardie, B. G. S., & Lee, K. L. (2005). RFM and CLV: Using iso-value curves for customer base analysis. *JMR, Journal of Marketing Research*, *42*(4), 415–430. doi:10.1509/jmkr.2005.42.4.415

Falatoonitoosi, E., Schaer, V., & Kerr, D. (2022). Does sustainable tourism development enhance destination prosperity? *Journal of Hospitality & Tourism Research (Washington, D.C.)*, *46*(5), 1056–1082. doi:10.1177/1096348020988328

Feng, X., Kehemacheevakul, K., Siller, S. D. L., Wolodko, J., & Wismer, W. (2022). Effect of Labelling and Information on Consumer Perception of Foods Presented as 3D Printed. *Foods*, *11*(6), 1–15. doi:10.3390/foods11060809 PMID:35327230

Filippo, M., Colangelo, D., & Farnia, L. (2017). *Innovation and new business models in tourism*, 149-168. doi:10.3280/RISS2017-001010

Fisher, D., & Wilder-Smith, A. (2020). The global community needs to swiftly ramp up the response to contain COVID-19. *Lancet*, *395*(10230), 1109–1110. doi:10.1016/S0140-6736(20)30679-6 PMID:32199470

Flinta, N. (2022). Modern electronic booking and reservation systems in the hotel business. *Scientific Herald of Chernivtsi University. Geography (Sheffield, England)*, *839*(839), 40–49. doi:10.31861/geo.2022.839.40-49

Font, X., Higham, J., Miller, G., & Pourfakhimi, S. (2019). Research engagement, impact and sustainable tourism. *Journal of Sustainable Tourism*, *27*(1), 1–11. doi:10.1080/09669582.2019.1560673

Forliano, C., De Bernardi, P., & Yahiaoui, D. (2021). Entrepreneurial universities: A bibliometric analysis within the business and management domains. *Technological Forecasting and Social Change*, *165*, 120522. doi:10.1016/j.techfore.2020.120522

Fossgard, K., & Stensland, S. (2021). Broadening the scope of resources in nature: An explorative study of nature-based tourism firms. *Journal of Ecotourism*, *20*(1), 35–50. doi:10.1080/14724049.2020.1751650

Fotis, J., Buhalis, D., & Rossides, N. (2012). Social media use and impact during the holiday travel planning process. In M. Fuchs, F. Ricci, & L. Cantoni (Eds.), *Information and Communication Technologies in Tourism* (pp. 13–24). Springer. doi:10.1007/978-3-7091-1142-0_

Fotis, J., Buhalis, D., & Rossides, N. (2012). Social media use and impact during the holiday travel planning process. In *Information and communication technologies in Tourism* (pp. 13–24). Springer. doi:10.1007/978-3-7091-1142-0_2

Frey, C. B., & Osborne, M. A. (2017). The future of employment: How susceptible are jobs to computerisation? *Technological Forecasting and Social Change*, *114*, 254–280. doi:10.1016/j.techfore.2016.08.019

Fu, H., Okumus, F., Wu, K., & Köseoglu, M. A. (2019). The entrepreneurship research in hospitality and tourism. *International Journal of Hospitality Management*, *78*, 1–12. doi:10.1016/j.ijhm.2018.10.005

Galiano-Coronil, A., Blanco-Moreno, S., Tobar-Pesantez, L. B., & Gutiérrez-Montoya, G. A. (2023). Social media impact of tourism managers: A decision tree approach in happiness, social marketing and sustainability. *Journal of Management Development*, *42*(6), 436–457. doi:10.1108/JMD-04-2023-0131

Gálvez-Rodríguez, M. del M., Saraite-Sariene, L., Alonso-Cañadas, J., & Caba-Pérez, M. del C. (2017). Stakeholder Engagement via Social Media in the Hospitality Sector. In M. Dhiman (Ed.), *Opportunities and Challenges for Tourism and Hospitality in the BRIC Nations* (pp. 15–30). IGI Global. doi:10.4018/978-1-5225-0708-6.ch002

Gam, A., Bahri-Ammari, N., & Soliman, M. (2023). Intelligent customer experience and behavioral brand loyalty: Empirical evidence from the commerce environment. *International Journal of Human-Computer Interaction*, *39*(10), 2090–2101. doi:10.1080/10447318.2022.2074120

Garcia, J., Alvado, A., Sorribes, J., & Boyra, J. (2022). The Challenges of Higher Education and its Contribution to Sustainable Development. *Higher Education Research, 7*(1). https://www.sciencepublishinggroup.com/journal/paperinfo?journalid=296&doi=10.11648/j.her.20220701.11 doi:10.11648/j.her.20220701.11

Gartner, S., Nicholson, A., & Christou, E. (2020). *Tourism marketing and distribution through social media: Assessing business economic performance. MPRA Paper 99194*. University Library of Munich.

Garvey, A. M., & Bolton, L. E. (2017). Eco-product choice cuts both ways: How pro-environmental licensing versus reinforcement is contingent on environmental consciousness. *Journal of Public Policy & Marketing*, *36*(2), 284–298. doi:10.1509/jppm.16.096

Gautam, B. P., Asami, H., Batajoo, A., & Fujisaki, T. (2016). Regional Revival Through IoT Enabled Smart Tourism Process Framework (STPF): A Proposal. *2016 Joint 8th International Conference on Soft Computing*.

Ghaderi, Z., & Henderson, J. C. (2013). Japanese tsunami debris and the threat to sustainable tourism in the Hawaiian Islands. *Tourism Management Perspectives*, *8*, 98–105. doi:10.1016/j.tmp.2013.09.001

Ghaderi, Z., Saboori, B., & Khoshkam, M. (2017). Does security matter in tourism demand? *Current Issues in Tourism*, *20*(6), 552–565. doi:10.1080/13683500.2016.1161603

Ghalia, T., Fidrmuc, J., Samargandi, N., & Sohag, K. (2019). Institutional quality, political risk, and tourism. *Tourism Management Perspectives*, *32*, 100576. doi:10.1016/j.tmp.2019.100576

Ghobadian, A., Han, T., Zhang, X., O'Regan, N., Troise, C., Bresciani, S., & Narayanan, V. (2022). COVID-19 pandemic: The interplay between firm disruption and managerial attention focus. *British Journal of Management*, *33*(1), 390–409. doi:10.1111/1467-8551.12556

Ghosh, P., & Mukherjee, S. (2022). Understanding tourist behaviour towards destination selection based on SMinformation: an evaluation using unsupervised clustering algorithms. *Journal of Hospitality and Tourism Insights*. doi:10.1108/JHTI-11-2021-0317

Gim, M., Park, D., Spranger, M., Maruyama, K., & Kang, J. (2021). RecipeBowl: A Cooking Recommender for Ingredients and Recipes Using Set Transformer. *IEEE Access : Practical Innovations, Open Solutions*, *9*, 143623–143633. doi:10.1109/ACCESS.2021.3120265

Ginter, P. M., Duncan, W. J., & Swayne, L. E. (2018). *The strategic management of health care organizations*. John Wiley & Sons.

Giurea, R., Precazzini, I., Ragazzi, M., Achim, M., Cioca, L., Conti, F., Torretta, V., & Rada, E. (2018). Good Practices and Actions for Sustainable Municipal Solid Waste Management in the Tourist Sector. *Resources*, *7*(3), 51. doi:10.3390/resources7030051

Glady, N., Baesens, B., & Croux, C. (2009). A modified Pareto/NBD approach for predicting customer lifetime value. *Expert Systems with Applications*, *36*(2), 2062–2071. doi:10.1016/j.eswa.2007.12.049

Godoi, F. C., Prakash, S., & Bhandari, B. R. (2016). 3d printing technologies applied for food design: Status and prospects. *Journal of Food Engineering*, *179*, 44–54. doi:10.1016/j.jfoodeng.2016.01.025

Gomes, S., & Lopes, J. (2023). Insights for Pro-Sustainable Tourist Behavior: The Role of Sustainable Destination Information and Pro-Sustainable Tourist Habits. *Sustainability (Basel)*, *15*(11), 8856. doi:10.3390/su15118856

Gómez-Carrasco, P., Guillamón-Saorín, E., & García Osma, B. (2021). Stakeholders versus firm communication in social media: The case of Twitter and corporate social responsibility information. *European Accounting Review*, *30*(1), 31–62. doi:10.1080/09638180.2019.1708428

Gosine, L., Kean, B., Parsons, C., & McSweeney, M. B. (2021). Using a 3D food printer as a teaching tool: Focus groups with dietitians, teachers, and nutrition students. *Journal of Food Science Education*, *20*(1), 18–25. doi:10.1111/1541-4329.12216

Gössling, S., Scott, D., & Hall, C. (2020). Pandemics, tourism, and global change: A rapid assessment of COVID-19. *Journal of Sustainable Tourism*, *29*(1), 1–20. doi:10.1080/09669582.2020.1758708

Goyal, K., & Kumar, S. (2021). Financial literacy: A systematic review and bibliometric analysis. *International Journal of Consumer Studies*, *45*(1), 80–105. doi:10.1111/ijcs.12605

Gozgor, G., Lau, M. C. K., Zeng, Y., Yan, C., & Lin, Z. (2022). The Impact of Geopolitical Risks on Tourism Supply in Developing Economies: The Moderating Role of Social Globalization. *Journal of Travel Research*, *61*(4), 872–886. doi:10.1177/00472875211004760

Greenberg, P. (2010). The impact of CRM 2.0 on customer insight. *Journal of Business and Industrial Marketing*, *25*(6), 410–419. doi:10.1108/08858621011066008

Gretzel, U. (2006). Consumer generated content – trends and implications for branding. *e-Review of Tourism Research*, *4*(3), 9–11

Gretzel, G., Fesenmaier, D. R., Formica, S., & O'Leary, J. T. (2006). Searching for the Future: Challenges Faced by Destination Marketing Organizations. *Journal of Travel Research*, *45*(2), 116–126. doi:10.1177/0047287506291598

Gretzel, U., Fesenmaier, D. R., & O'Leary, J. T. (2006). The transformation of consumer behaviour. *Tourism Business Frontiers: Consumers. Products and Industry*, *9*, 18.

Gretzel, U., Murphy, J., Pesonen, J., & Blanton, C. (2019). Food waste in tourist households: A perspective article. *Tourism Review*, *75*(1), 235–238. doi:10.1108/TR-05-2019-0170

Gretzel, U., Werthner, H., Koo, C., & Lamsfus, C. (2015). Conceptual foundations for understanding smart tourism ecosystems. *Computers in Human Behavior*, *50*, 558–563. doi:10.1016/j.chb.2015.03.043

Gretzel, U., & Yoo, K. H. (2019). The Transformation of Consumer Behavior. In *Information and Communication Technologies in Tourism 2020* (pp. 12–25). Springer.

Gretzel, U., & Yoo, K. H. (2021). The future of robots in the hospitality industry: A Delphi study. *Tourism Management*, *82*, 104209.

Gretzel, U., Yuan, Y. L., & Fesenmaier, D. R. (2000). Preparing for the New Economy: Advertising Strategies and Change in Destination Marketing Organizations. *Journal of Travel Research*, *39*(2), 146–156. doi:10.1177/004728750003900204

Groot, S. (2019). *Effect of perceived risks, naturalness, usefulness and ease of use on the consumer acceptance of 3D food printing* [Bachelor's Thesis, Wageningen University, Netherlands].

Gruss, R., Kim, E., & Abrahams, A. (2020). Engaging restaurant customers on Facebook: The power of belongingness appeals on social media. *Journal of Hospitality & Tourism Research (Washington, D.C.)*, *44*(2), 201–228. doi:10.1177/1096348019892071

Guadagno, M. C., Loss, J. M., & Pearce, J. M. (2021). Open Source 3D-Printable Planetary Roller Screw for Food Processing Applications. *Technologies*, *9*(2), 1–26. doi:10.3390/technologies9020024

Gudz, O. (2020). *Organizational and information aspects of management of modern enterprise development*., 31. Taylor & Francis. . doi:10.31673/2415-8089.2020.010510

Gu, J., Song, C., Jiang, W., Wang, X., & Liu, M. (2020). Enhancing Personalized Trip Recommendation with Attractive Routes. *Proceedings of the AAAI Conference on Artificial Intelligence*. IEEE. 10.1609/aaai.v34i01.5407

Gunawan, J., Permatasari, P., & Tilt, C. (2020). Sustainable development goal disclosures: Do they support responsible consumption and production? *Journal of Cleaner Production*, *246*, 118989. doi:10.1016/j.jclepro.2019.118989

Guo, C., Zhang, M., & Bhandari, B. (2019). A comparative study between syringe-based and screw-based 3D food printers by computational simulation. *Computers and Electronics in Agriculture*, *162*, 397–404. doi:10.1016/j.compag.2019.04.032

Guo, Y., Jiang, J., & Li, S. (2019). A sustainable tourism policy research review. *Sustainability (Basel)*, *11*(11), 3187. Advance online publication. doi:10.3390/su11113187

Gupta, K., & Sharma, S. (2021). Kiosks as self-service technology in hotels: Opportunities and challenges. *Worldwide Hospitality and Tourism Themes*, *13*(2), 236–251. doi:10.1108/WHATT-10-2020-0125

Gupta, S., Hanssens, D., Hardie, B., Kahn, W., Kumar, V., Lin, N., Ravishanker, N., & Sriram, S. (2006). Modeling customer lifetime value. *Journal of Service Research*, *9*(2), 139–155. doi:10.1177/1094670506293810

Gupta, S., Lehmann, D. R., & Stuart, J. A. (2004). Valuing customers. *JMR, Journal of Marketing Research*, *41*(1), 7–18. doi:10.1509/jmkr.41.1.7.25084

Gursoy, D., Chi, C. G., & Lu, L. (2019). Antecedents and outcomes of travelers' information-seeking behavior: A meta-analysis. *Tourism Management*, *70*, 230–243.

Gutberlet, M. (2017). *Searching for an oriental paradise?: Imaginaries, tourist experiences and socio-cultural impacts of mega-cruise tourism in the sultanate of Oman* [Dissertation, Rheinisch-Westfälische Technische Hochschule Aachen, 2017].

Gutberlet, M. (2016). Socio-cultural impacts of large-scale cruise tourism in Souq Mutrah, Sultanate of Oman. *Fennia-International Journal of Geography*, *194*(1), 46–63. doi:10.11143/46532

Hadjikakou, M. (2013). *Water and tourism*. Deakin University. https://dro.deakin.edu.au/articles/chapter/Water_and_tourism/20831107

Hakkarainen, T. (2016). *Opportunities and challenges of content marketing as a way of digital marketing communications.*

Han, D., Yu, D. & Qiu, J. (2023). Assessing coupling interactions in a safe and just operating space for regional sustainability. *Nature Communications, Nature, 14*(1), 1-15. https://doi.org/doi:10.1038/s41467-023-37073-z

Han, H., & Hyun, S. S. (2019). Cruise travel motivations and repeat cruising behaviour: Impact of relationship investment. *Current Issues in Tourism*, *22*(7), 786–805. doi:10.1080/13683500.2017.1313204

Han, S. H., Lee, J., Edvardsson, B., & Verma, R. (2021). Mobile technology adoption among hotels: Managerial issues and opportunities. *Tourism Management Perspectives*, *38*, 100811. doi:10.1016/j.tmp.2021.100811

Harzing, A.-W., & Alakangas, S. (2016). Google Scholar, Scopus and the Web of Science: A longitudinal and cross-disciplinary comparison. *Scientometrics*, *106*(2), 787–804. doi:10.1007/s11192-015-1798-9

Ha, T. K. D., Nguyen, T. K., Pham, T. M. N., Nguyen, D. Q., Truong, B. T., Le, V. S., & Nguyen, H. T. (2022). Influence of Macro Environment on Tourism Value Chain in Vietnam. *Geo Journal of Tourism and Geosites*, *41*(2), 400–407. doi:10.30892/gtg.41209-843

Hays, S., Page, S. J., & Buhalis, D. (2019). Social media as a destination marketing tool: Its use by national tourism organisations. *Current Issues in Tourism*, *22*(9), 1052–1069.

Heikkinen, H. I., Bjørst, R., Pashkevich, A., & Fi, H. I. H. (2020). Challenging Tourism Landscapes of Southwest Greenland: Identifying Social and Cultural Capital for Sustainable Tourism Development. *Arctic Anthropology*, *57*(2), 212–228. doi:10.3368/aa.57.2.212

Heinonen, K., & Medberg, G. (2018). Netnography as a tool for understanding customers: Implications for service research and practice. *Journal of Services Marketing*, *32*(6), 657–679. doi:10.1108/JSM-08-2017-0294

Higgins-Desbiolles, F., & Wijesinghe, G. (2021). The critical capacities of restaurants as facilitators for transformations to sustainability. In *Activating Critical Thinking to Advance the Sustainable Development Goals in Tourism Systems* (pp. 234–259). Routledge. doi:10.4324/9781003140542-14

Hjalager, A. (2022). Digital Food and the Innovation of Gastronomic Tourism. *Journal of Gastronomy and Tourism*, *7*(1), 35–49. doi:10.3727/216929722X16354101932186

Ho, S. Y. (2012). The effects of location personalization on individuals' intention to use mobile services. *Decision Support Systems*, *53*(4), 802–812. doi:10.1016/j.dss.2012.05.012

Ho, S. Y., & Bodoff, D. (2014). The effects of Web personalization on user attitude and behavior. *Management Information Systems Quarterly*, *38*(2), 497–A10. doi:10.25300/MISQ/2014/38.2.08

Hou, K. M., Diao, X., Shi, H., Ding, H., Zhou, H., & de Vaulx, C. (2023). Trends and Challenges in AIoT/IIoT/IoT Implementation. *. *Sensors (Basel)*, *23*(11), 2023. doi:10.3390/s23115074 PMID:37299800

Huber, D., Milne, S., & Hyde, K. (2019). Conceptualizing Senior Tourism Behaviour: A Life Events Approach. *Tourist Studies*, *19*(4), 407–433. doi:10.1177/1468797619832318

Huertas, A. (2018). How live videos and stories in SMinfluence tourist opinions and behaviour. *Information Technology & Tourism*, *19*(1–4), 1–28. doi:10.1007/s40558-018-0112-0

Hussain, K., Alam, M. M. D., Malik, A., & Al Balushi, M. K. (2024). Capitalizing social media content for attracting tourists: Implications for digital transformation of Oman's tourism sector. *2nd International Conference on Strategies for Empowering Oman as a Competitive Economy*, Arab University Oman Faculty of Business Studies, Muscat, Oman.

Hwang, K., & Lee, B. (2019). Pride, mindfulness, public self-awareness, affective satisfaction, and customer citizenship behaviour among green restaurant customers. *International Journal of Hospitality Management*, *83*, 169–179. doi:10.1016/j.ijhm.2019.05.009

Iglesias-Sánchez, P. P., López-Delgado, P., Correia, M. B., & Jambrino-Maldonado, C. (2020). How do external openness and R&D activity influence open innovation management and the potential contribution of social media in the tourism and hospitality industry? *Information Technology & Tourism*, *22*(2), 1–27. doi:10.1007/s40558-019-00165-y

International Organization for Standardization. (2012). *ISO 8373:2012(en) Robots and robotic devices – Vocabulary*. ISO. https://www.iso.org/obp/ui/#iso:std:iso:8373:ed-2:v1:en:term:2.2, [accessed at 09/11/2023].

Ioannou, A., Tussyadiah, I., & Miller, G. (2020). That's Private! Understanding travelers' privacy concerns and online data disclosure. *Journal of Travel Research*. https://openresearch.surrey.ac.uk/esploro/outputs/journalArticle/Thats-private-Understanding-travelers-privacy-concerns-and-online-data-disclosure/99512856502346

Ip, C., Lee, H., & Law, R. (2012). Profiling the Users of Travel Websites for Planning and Online Experience Sharing. *Journal of Hospitality & Tourism Research (Washington, D.C.)*, *36*(3), 418–426. doi:10.1177/1096348010388663

IPCC - Intergovernmental Panel on Climate Change. (2014). *Climate Change 2014: Impacts, Adaptation, and Vulnerability. Part A: Global and Sectoral Aspects*. Contribution of Working Group II to the Fifth Assessment Report of the Intergovernmental Panel on Climate Change [Field, C.B., V.R. Barros, D.J. Dokken, K.J. Mach, M.D. Mastrandrea, T.E. Bilir, M. Chatterjee, K.L. Ebi, Y.O. Estrada, R.C. Genova, B. Girma, E.S. Kissel, A.N. Levy, S. MacCracken, P.R. Mastrandrea, and L.L. White (eds.)]. Cambridge University Press, Cambridge, United Kingdom and New York, NY, USA. https://www.ipcc.ch/site/assets/uploads/2018/02/WGIIAR5-PartA_FINAL.pdf

IPCC - Intergovernmental Panel on Climate Change. (2023). *Climate Change 2023: Synthesis Report. Contribution of Working Groups I, II and III to the Sixth Assessment Report of the Intergovernmental Panel on Climate Change*. IPCC. https://www.ipcc.ch/report/ar6/syr/downloads/report/IPCC_AR6_SYR_FullVolume.pdf

Iranmanesh, M., Ghobakhloo, M., Nilashi, M., Tseng, M. L., Yadegaridehkordi, E., & Leung, N. (2022). Applications of disruptive digital technologies in hotel industry: A systematic review. *International Journal of Hospitality Management*, *107*, 103304. doi:10.1016/j.ijhm.2022.103304

Işık, C., Sirakaya-Turk, E., & Ongan, S. (2020). Testing the efficacy of the economic policy uncertainty index on tourism demand in USMCA: Theory and evidence. *Tourism Economics*, *26*(8), 1344–1357. doi:10.1177/1354816619888346

ISO/ASTM 52900. (2015). *Additive manufacturing — General principles — Terminology*. ISO/ASME International.

Ivanov, S., & Webster, C. (2019a). What should robots do? A comparative analysis of industry professionals, educators and tourists. In Pesonen, J., & Neidhardt, J. (Eds.) *Information and Communication Technologies in Tourism 2019, Proceedings of the International Conference in Nicosia*. Springer. 10.1007/978-3-030-05940-8_20

Ivanov, S., & Webster, C. (2019b). Perceived appropriateness and intention to use service robots in tourism. In Pesonen, J. & Neidhardt, J. (Eds.) *Information and Communication Technologies in Tourism 2019, Proceedings of the International Conference in Nicosia*. Springer. 10.1007/978-3-030-05940-8_19

Ivanov, S., Webster, C., & Berezina, K. (2017). Adoption of robots and service automation by tourism and hospitality companies. *Revista Tursmo & Desenvolvimento, n.º 27/28*, 1501-1517.

Ivanov, S., Seyitoğlu, F., & Markova, M. (2020). Hotel managers' perceptions towards the use of robots: A mixed-methods approach. *Information Technology & Tourism*, *22*(4), 505–535. doi:10.1007/s40558-020-00187-x

Jaas, A. (2022). E-Marketing and its strategies: Digital opportunities and challenges. *Open Journal of Business and Management*, *10*(2), 822–845. doi:10.4236/ojbm.2022.102046

Jacobsen, J. K. S., & Munar, A. M. (2012). Tourist information search and destination choice in a digital age. *Tourism Management Perspectives*, *1*, 39–47. doi:10.1016/j.tmp.2011.12.005

Jashari, A., Tiberius, V., & Dabić, M. (2022). Tracing the progress of scenario research in business and management. *Futures & Foresight Science*, *4*(2), e109. doi:10.1002/ffo2.109

Jayaprakash, S. (2017). *Role of Prosumer Driven 3D Food Printingin Innovating Food Value Chains* [Master's Thesis, Aalto University, Finland].

Jayaprakash, S., Paasi, J., Pennamen, K., Ituarte, I. F., Lille, M., Partanen, J., & Sozer, N. (2020). Techno-economic prospects and desirability of 3d food printing: Perspectives of industrial experts, researchers and consumers. *Foods*, *9*(2), 1–23. doi:10.3390/foods9121725 PMID:33255289

Jena, R. K., & Dwivedi, Y. (2021). Prioritizing the barriers to tourism growth in rural India: an integrated multi-criteria decision making (MCDM) approach. *Journal of Tourism Futures*, 1-24. doi:10.1108/JTF-10-2020-0171

Jenkins, S. C., Harris, A. J. L., & Osman, M. (2021). What drives risk perceptions? Revisiting public perceptions of food hazards associated with production and consumption. *Journal of Risk Research*, *24*(11), 1450–1464. doi:10.1080/13669877.2020.1871057

Jiao, Y., Hou, Y., & Lau, Y.-y. (2021). Segmenting cruise consumers by motivation for an emerging market: A case of China. *Frontiers in Psychology*, *12*, 606785. doi:10.3389/fpsyg.2021.606785 PMID:33790831

Jiménez-Guerrero, J. F., Piedra-Muñoz, L., Galdeano-Gómez, E., & Pérez-Mesa, J. C. (2021). The Global Economic Crisis and International Tourism: A Sub-Continental Analysis. *Tourism Planning & Development*, *18*(1), 1–24. doi:10.1080/21568316.2019.1683887

Johnson, A. (2018). The impact of the Internet of Things on tourism. *Information and Communication Technologies in Tourism*, *2018*, 63–74.

Juvan, E., & Dolnicar, S. (2017). Drivers of pro-environmental tourist behaviours are not universal. *Journal of Cleaner Production*, *166*, 879–890. doi:10.1016/j.jclepro.2017.08.087

Kaczorowska, J., Rejman, K., Halicka, E., Szczebyło, A., & Górska-Warsewicz, H. (2019). Impact of food sustainability labels on the perceived product value and price expectations of urban consumers. *Sustainability (Basel)*, *11*(24), 7240. doi:10.3390/su11247240

Kamal, S., Naim, A., Magd, H., Khan, S. A., & Khan, F. M. (2022). The Relationship Between E-Service Quality, Ease of Use, and E-CRM Performance Referred by Brand Image. In A. Naim & S. Kautish (Eds.), *Building a Brand Image Through Electronic Customer Relationship Management* (pp. 84–108). IGI Global. doi:10.4018/978-1-6684-5386-5.ch005

Kang, J.-W., & Namkung, Y. (2019). The role of personalization on continuance intention in food service mobile apps: A privacy calculus perspective. *International Journal of Contemporary Hospitality Management*, *31*(2), 734–752. doi:10.1108/IJCHM-12-2017-0783

Kannan, P., & Li, H. A. (2017). Digital marketing: A framework, review and research agenda. *International Journal of Research in Marketing*, *34*(1), 22–45. doi:10.1016/j.ijresmar.2016.11.006

Kaplan, A. M., & Haenlein, M. (2010). Users of the world, unite! The challenges and opportunities of Social Media. *Business Horizons*, *53*(1), 59–68. doi:10.1016/j.bushor.2009.09.003

Kaplan, A., & Haenlein, M. (2009). Consumer Use and Business Potential of Virtual Worlds: The Case of "Second Life". *International Journal on Media Management*, *11*(3-4), 93–101. doi:10.1080/14241270903047008

Kasim, A., & Minai, B. (2009). Linking CRM strategy, customer performance measures, and performance in the hotel industry. *International Journal of Economics and Management*, *3*(2), 297–316.

Kavoura, A., & Bitsani, E. (2013). Managing the World Heritage Site of the Acropolis, Greece. *International Journal of Culture, Tourism and Hospitality Research*, *7*(1), 58–67. doi:10.1108/17506181311301363

Kemp, B. S. (2023). *Digital 2023: Oman - DataReportal – Global Digital Insights*. Data Portal.

Ketter, E. (2020). Millennial travel: Tourism micro-trends of European Generation Y. *Journal of Tourism Futures*, *7*(2), 192–196. doi:10.1108/JTF-10-2019-0106

Khalid, U., Okafor, L. E., & Shafiullah, M. (2020). The Effects of Economic and Financial Crises on International Tourist Flows: A Cross-Country Analysis. *Journal of Travel Research*, *59*(2), 315–334. doi:10.1177/0047287519834360

Khalifa, G. S. A. (2015). Ethnic restaurants' meal experience: Egyptian customers' perceptions. *Journal of Faculty of Tourism and Hotels*, *9*(1), 92–112.

Khan, K., Su, C. W., Xiao, Y. D., Zhu, H., & Zhang, X. (2021). Trends in tourism under economic uncertainty. *Tourism Economics*, *27*(4), 841–858. doi:10.1177/1354816620909608

Khan, M., Siddique, M., Yasir, M., Qureshi, M. I., Khan, N., & Safdar, M. Z. (2022). The Significance of Digital Marketing in Shaping Ecotourism Behaviour through Destination Image. *Sustainability (Basel)*, *14*(12), 14. doi:10.3390/su14127395

KhanN.HassanA. U.FahadS.NaushadM. (2020). Factors affecting the tourism industry and its impacts on the global economy of the world. SSRN. https://ssrn.com/abstract=3559353 or doi:10.2139/ssrn.3559353

Khanra, S., Dhir, A., & Mäntymäki, M. (2020). Big data analytics and enterprises: A bibliometric synthesis of the literature. *Enterprise Information Systems*, *14*(6), 737–768. doi:10.1080/17517575.2020.1734241

Khan, S. A. (2023). E-Marketing, E-Commerce, E-Business, and Internet of Things: An Overview of Terms in the Context of Small and Medium Enterprises (SMEs). In A. Naim & V. Devi (Eds.), *Global Applications of the Internet of Things in Digital Marketing* (pp. 332–348). IGI Global. doi:10.4018/978-1-6684-8166-0.ch017

Khan, S. A., & Magd, H. (2021). Empirical Examination of MS Teams in Conducting Webinar: Evidence from International Online Program conducted in Oman. *Journal of Content. Community and Communication*, *14*(8), 159–175. doi:10.31620/JCCC.12.21/13

Khan, S. A., & Magd, H. (2023). New Technology Anxiety and Acceptance of Technology: An Appraisal of MS Teams. In *Advances in Distance Learning in Times of Pandemic* (pp. 105–134). CRC Press, Taylor and Francis., doi:10.1201/9781003322252-5

Khan, S. A., Narula, S., Kansra, P., Naim, A., & Kalra, D. (2023). Should Marketing and Public Relations be Part of the Institutional Accreditation Criterion of Business Schools? An Appraisal of Accreditation Criterion of Selected Accreditation Agencies. In A. Naim (Ed.), *Accreditation Processes and Frameworks in Higher Education* (pp. 349–375). Nova Science Publishers. doi:10.52305/QUVJ6658

Khatri, B., Arora, S., Magd, H., & Khan, S. A. (2022). Bibliometric Analysis of Social Entrepreneurship. In H. Magd, D. Singh, R. Syed, & D. Spicer (Eds.), *International Perspectives on Value Creation and Sustainability Through Social Entrepreneurship* (pp. 46–60). IGI Global. doi:10.4018/978-1-6684-4666-9.ch003

Khatri, B., Shrimali, H., Khan, S. A., & Naim, A. (2023). Role of HR Analytics in Ensuring Psychological Wellbeing and Job Security: Learnings From COVID-19. In R. Yadav, M. Sinha, & J. Kureethara (Eds.), *HR Analytics in an Era of Rapid Automation* (pp. 36–53). IGI Global. doi:10.4018/978-1-6684-8942-0.ch003

Khosravi, F., & Jha-Thakur, U. (2019). Managing uncertainties through scenario analysis in strategic environmental assessment. *Journal of Environmental Planning and Management*, *62*(6), 1000–1979. doi:10.1080/09640568.2018.1456913

Kietzmann, J. H., Hermkens, K., McCarthy, I. P., & Silvestre, B. S. (2011). Social media? Get serious! Understanding the functional building blocks of social media. *Business Horizons*, *54*(3), 241–251. doi:10.1016/j.bushor.2011.01.005

Kim, B., & Ieng Lei, S. (2024). Millennials' interactions with social media content on cruise tourism. *Tourism Review*. doi:10.1108/TR-08-2023-0582

Kim, N., Cepeta, B., Kim, J., Yue, G., Kim, S., & Kim, H. (2018). IoT controlled screw-type 3d food printer using single line design technique. *Proceedings - 2018 International Conference on Computational Science and Computational Intelligence (CSCI)*. Las Vegas, USA: Association for Computing Machinery.

Kim, D., & Park, S. (2020). Rethinking millennials: How are they shaping the tourism industry? *Asia Pacific Journal of Tourism Research*, *25*(1), 1–2. doi:10.1080/10941665.2019.1667607

Kim, H., & Fesenmaier, D. R. (2008). Persuasive Design of Destination Web Sites: An Analysis of First Impression. *Journal of Travel Research*, *47*(1), 3–13. doi:10.1177/0047287507312405

Kim, M. J., & Hall, C. M. (2020). What drives visitor economy crowdfunding? The effect of digital storytelling on unified theory of acceptance and use of technology. *Tourism Management Perspectives*, *34*, 100638. doi:10.1016/j.tmp.2020.100638

Kim, M. J., Hall, C. M., & Kim, D.-K. (2020). Predicting environmentally friendly eating out behavior by value-attitude-behavior theory: Does being vegetarian reduce food waste? *Journal of Sustainable Tourism*, *28*(6), 797–815. doi:10.1080/09669582.2019.1705461

Kim, M., & Lee, G. (2022). The effect of servicescape on place attachment and experience evaluation: The importance of exoticism and authenticity in an ethnic restaurant. *International Journal of Contemporary Hospitality Management*, *34*(7), 2664–2683. doi:10.1108/IJCHM-07-2021-0929

Kim, W. (2002). Personalization: Definition, status, and challenges ahead. *Journal of Object Technology*, *1*(1), 29–40. doi:10.5381/jot.2002.1.1.c3

Kim, Y., & Kim, H. (2020). Usability Evaluation and Improvements of Mobile Travel Apps. *International Journal of Internet. Broadcasting and Communication*, *12*, 27–36. doi:10.7236/IJIBC.2020.12.1.27

Kladou, S., & Kehagias, J. (2014). Assessing destination brand equity: An integrated approach. *Journal of Destination Marketing & Management*, *3*(1), 2–10. doi:10.1016/j.jdmm.2013.11.002

Kladou, S., & Mavragani, E. (2015). Assessing destination image: An online marketing approach and the case of TripAdvisor. *Journal of Destination Marketing & Management*, *4*(3), 187–193. doi:10.1016/j.jdmm.2015.04.003

Klein, R. A. (2011). Responsible cruise tourism: Issues of cruise tourism and sustainability. *Journal of Hospitality and Tourism Management*, *18*(1), 107–116. doi:10.1375/jhtm.18.1.107

Knani, M., Echchakoui, S., & Ladhari, R. (2022). Artificial intelligence in tourism and hospitality: Bibliometric analysis and research agenda. *International Journal of Hospitality Management*, *107*, 103317. doi:10.1016/j.ijhm.2022.103317

Komiak, S. Y. X., & Benbasat, I. (2006). The effects of personalization and familiarity on trust and adoption of recommendation agents. *Management Information Systems Quarterly*, *30*(4), 941–960. doi:10.2307/25148760

Komsary, K. C., Tarigan, W. P., & Wiyana, T. (2018). Limits of acceptable change as tool for tourism development sustainability in Pangandaran West Java. *IOP Conference Series. Earth and Environmental Science*, *126*, 012129. https://iopscience.iop.org/article/10.1088/1755-1315/126/1/012129/pdf. doi:10.1088/1755-1315/126/1/012129

Koo, C., Xiang, Z., Gretzel, U., & Sigala, M. (2021). Artificial intelligence (AI) and robotics in travel, hospitality and leisure. *Electronic Markets*, *31*(3), 473–476. doi:10.1007/s12525-021-00494-z PMID:35603226

Kosevich, A., Novikova, N., Gladkikh, V., Sharonin, P., & Smirnov, M. (2020). Improving Economic and Legal Regulation in the Tourism Sector. *Journal of Environmental Management and Tourism*, *11*(4), 979–984. doi:10.14505//jemt.v11.4(44).23

Kouzani, A. Z., Adams, S., Whyte, D. J., Oliver, R., Hemsley, B., Palmer, S., & Balandin, S. (2017). 3D Printing of Food for People with Swallowing Difficulties. *KnE Engineering*, *2*(2), 23–29. doi:10.18502/keg.v2i2.591

Kozinets, R. (2002). The field behind the screen: Using netnography for marketing research in online communities. *JMR, Journal of Marketing Research*, *39*(1), 61–72. doi:10.1509/jmkr.39.1.61.18935

Kozinets, R. V. (2010). *Netnography: Doing ethnographic research online*. Sage Publications.

Kozinets, R. V., Valck, K., Wojnicki, A., & Wilner, S. (2010). narratives: Understanding Word-of-Mouth marketing in online communities'. *Journal of Marketing*, *74*(2), 74. doi:10.1509/jm.74.2.71

Kozłowski, M., Brzozowska-Rup, K., & Piotrowska-Piątek, A. (2021). Information and Communication Technologies in Food and accommodation sector in EU Countries: Sticker or Challenge for tourism development? *Technological Forecasting and Social Change*, *171*, 120941. doi:10.1016/j.techfore.2021.120941

Krutwaysho, O., & Bramwell, B. (2010). Tourism policy implementation and society. *Annals of Tourism Research*, *37*(3), 670–691. doi:10.1016/j.annals.2009.12.004

Kumar, S., Talukder, M. B., Kabir, F., & Kaiser, F. (2024). Challenges and Sustainability of Green Finance in the Tourism Industry: Evidence from Bangladesh. In S. Taneja, P. Kumar, S. Grima, E. Ozen, & K. Sood (Eds.), (pp. 97–111). Advances in Finance, Accounting, and Economics. IGI Global. doi:10.4018/979-8-3693-1388-6.ch006

Kuncharia, K. (2019). Influence of family and culture on youth consumers. *Asian Journal of Development Matters*, *13*, 79–85.

Kunz, E. (2023) 3D Food Printing Market Size & Share to Surpass $872.4 Million by 2028 | Vantage Market Research. *Vantage Market Research.* Globe News Wire. https://www.globenewswire.com/news-release/2023/03/09/2623870/0/en/3D-Food-Printing-Market-Size-Share-to-Surpass-872-4-Million-by-2028-Vantage-Market-Research.html

Kuziemski, M., & Misuraca, G. (2020). AI governance in the public sector: Three tales from the frontiers of automated decision-making in democratic settings. *Telecommunications Policy*, *44*(6), 101976. doi:10.1016/j.telpol.2020.101976 PMID:32313360

LABIIT - Laboratori d'Innovació i Intel·ligència Turística. (2022). *Departament de Consultoria Tecnològica del Centre Tecnològic Eurecat.* CDN. https://cdn.eurecat.org/PDF/InformeLabiit/Informe-LABIIT-1-2022-economiacircular-Eurecat-PTDT.pdf

Ladhari, R., & Michaud, M. (2015). eWOM effects on hotel booking intentions, attitudes, trust, and website perceptions. *International Journal of Hospitality Management, 46*, 36–45. doi:10.1016/j.ijhm.2015.01.010

LaTour, K. A., & Brant, A. (2021). Social Listening to Create Bespoke Customer Experiences: Best Practices for Hospitality Operators. *Cornell Hospitality Quarterly*, 938965521993087.

Lawless, H. T., & Heymann, H. (2010). *Sensory Evaluation of Food Principles and Practices* (2nd ed.). Springer. doi:10.1007/978-1-4419-6488-5

Law, R., Buhalis, D., & Cobanoglu, C. (2014). Progress on information and communication technologies in hospitality and tourism. *International Journal of Contemporary Hospitality Management, 26*(5), 727–750. doi:10.1108/IJCHM-08-2013-0367

Lebrun, A. M., Corbel, R., & Bouchet, P. (2022). Impacts of Covid-19 on travel intention for summer 2020: A trend in proximity tourism mediated by an attitude towards Covid-19. *Service Business, 16*(3), 469–501. doi:10.1007/s11628-021-00450-z

Lee, C., & Chen, M. (2020). Do Country Risks Matter for Tourism Development? International Evidence. *Journal of Travel Research, 60*(7), 1445–1468. doi:10.1177/0047287520954539

Lee, C., Kang, S., Ahmad, M., Park, Y., Park, E., & Kang, C. (2021). Role of cultural worldview in predicting heritage tourists' behavioural intention. *Leisure Studies, 40*(5), 645–657. doi:10.1080/02614367.2021.1890804

Lee, J. (2021). A 3D Food Printing Process for the New Normal Era: A Review. *Processes (Basel, Switzerland), 9*(9), 1–21. doi:10.3390/pr9091495

Lee, K. H., Hwang, K. H., Kim, M., & Cho, M. (2021). 3D printed food attributes and their roles within the value-attitude-behavior model: Moderating effects of food neophobia and food technology neophobia. *Journal of Hospitality and Tourism Management, 48*, 46–54. doi:10.1016/j.jhtm.2021.05.013

Lee, Y.-H., Hu, P. J.-H., Cheng, T.-H., & Hsieh, Y.-F. (2012). A cost-sensitive technique for positive-example learning supporting content-based product recommendations in B-to-C e-commerce. *Decision Support Systems, 53*(1), 245–256. doi:10.1016/j.dss.2012.01.018

Lei, S. I., Wang, D., & Law, R. (2021). Mobile-based value co-creation: Contextual factors towards customer experiences. *Tourism Review.*

Lei, S. S. I., Chan, I. C. C., Tang, J., & Ye, S. (2022). Will tourists take mobile travel advice? Examining the personalization-privacy paradox. *Journal of Hospitality and Tourism Management, 50*, 288–297. doi:10.1016/j.jhtm.2022.02.007

Leite, R. A., & Azevedo, A. (2017). The role of digital marketing: A perspective from Porto Hotels' Managers. *International Journal of Marketing, Communication and New Media,* (2).

Leith, C. (2020). Tourism trends: Lifestyle developments and the links to solo tourism. *Journal of Tourism Futures, 6*(3), 251–255. doi:10.1108/JTF-11-2019-0126

Lenzen, M. (2008). Errors in Conventional and Input–Output-based Life Cycle Inventories. *Journal of Industrial Ecology*, *4*(4), 127–148. doi:10.1162/10881980052541981

Leonidou, L. C., Coudounaris, D. N., Kvasova, O., & Christodoulides, P. (2015). Drivers and Outcomes of Green Tourist Attitudes and Behavior: Sociodemographic Moderating Effects. *Psychology and Marketing*, *32*(6), 635–650. doi:10.1002/mar.20806

Leung, D., Law, R.,. van Hoof, H., & Buhalis, D. (2013). SMin Tourism and Hospitality: A Literature Review. *Journal of Travel & Tourism Marketing*, *30*(1–2), 3–22. doi:10.1080/10548408.2013.750919

Leung, Y. F., Spenceley, A., Hvenegaard, G., Buckley, R., & Groves, C. (2018). *Tourism and visitor management in protected areas: Guidelines for sustainability* (Vol. 27). IUCN., doi:10.2305/IUCN.CH.2018.PAG.27.en

Lewis, C., Prayag, G., & Pour, S. (2021). Linking travel motives to identity and travel behavior of the Australian LGBT market during COVID-19. *Journal of Travel & Tourism Marketing*, *38*(7), 725–741. doi:10.1080/10548408.2021.1985039

Li, H., Sarathy, R., & Xu, H. (2011). The role of affect and cognition on online consumers' decision to disclose personal information to unfamiliar online vendors. *Decision Support Systems*, *51*(3), 434–445. doi:10.1016/j.dss.2011.01.017

Lim, W. M. (2014). The antecedents and consequences of customer hedonism in hospitality services. *Journal of Hospitality Marketing & Management*, *23*(6), 626–651. doi:10.1080/19368623.2014.846838

Lindberg, K., McCool, S., & Stankey, G. (1997). Rethinking carrying capacity. *Annals of Tourism Research*, *24*(2), 461–465. https://www.researchgate.net/profile/Stephen-Mccool/publication/256987158_Rethinking_Carrying_Capacity/links/5a1c3b0b0f7e9bd1be5c5535/Rethinking-Carrying-Capacity.pdf. doi:10.1016/S0160-7383(97)80018-7

Linnenluecke, M. K., Marrone, M., & Singh, A. K. (2020). Conducting systematic literature reviews and bibliometric analyses. *Australian Journal of Management*, *45*(2), 175–194. doi:10.1177/0312896219877678

Lin, Y., Punpongsanon, P., Wen, X., Iwai, D., Sato, K., Obrist, M., & Muller, S. (2020). FoodFab: Creating Food Perception Illusions using Food 3D Printing. In *CHI 2020* (pp. 1–13). Association for Computing Machinery. doi:10.1145/3313831.3376421

Lipton, J. L. (2017). Printable food: The technology and its application in human health. *Current Opinion in Biotechnology*, *44*, 198–201. doi:10.1016/j.copbio.2016.11.015 PMID:28327427

Litvin, S. W., Goldsmith, R. E., & Pan, B. (2008). Electronic word-of-mouth in hospitality and tourism management. *Tourism Management*, *29*(3), 458–468. doi:10.1016/j.tourman.2007.05.011

Liu, X., & Lin, K.-L. (2020). Green organizational culture, corporate social responsibility implementation, and food safety. *Frontiers in Psychology*, *11*, 585435. doi:10.3389/fpsyg.2020.585435 PMID:33240175

Liu, X., Mehraliyev, F., Liu, C., & Schuckert, M. (2020). The roles of social media in tourists' choices of travel components. *Tourist Studies*, *20*(1), 27–48. doi:10.1177/1468797619873107

Liu, Z., & Chen, X. (2020). Research on Relation Extraction of Named Entity on Social Media in Smart Cities. *. *Soft Computing*, *24*(15), 2020. doi:10.1007/s00500-020-04742-w

Li, X., Wang, D., Liang, Y., & Huang, D. (2019). An empirical examination of tourists' adoption of smart tourism destinations. *Journal of Travel Research*, •••, 0047287519896017.

Li, Y., Huang, S. S., & Song, L. (2020). Opportunity and necessity entrepreneurship in the hospitality sector: Examining the institutional environment influences. *Tourism Management Perspectives*, *34*, 100665. doi:10.1016/j.tmp.2020.100665

Li, Y., & Kwortnik, R. (2017). Categorizing cruise lines by passenger perceived experience. *Journal of Travel Research*, *56*(7), 941–956. doi:10.1177/0047287516674602

Lo, A. S., Stalcup, L. D., & Lee, A. (2010). Customer relationship management for hotels in Hong Kong. *International Journal of Contemporary Hospitality Management*, *22*(2), 139–159. doi:10.1108/09596111011018151

London, W. R., & Lohmann, G. (2014). Power in the context of cruise destination stakeholders' interrelationships. *Research in Transportation Business & Management*, *13*, 24–35. doi:10.1016/j.rtbm.2014.11.004

López-Gamero, M. D., Claver-Cortés, E., & Molina-Azorín, J. F. (2011). Environmental perception, management, and competitive opportunity in Spanish hotels. *Cornell Hospitality Quarterly*, *52*(4), 480–500. doi:10.1177/1938965511420694

Lorenz, T., Iskandar, M. M., Baeghbali, V., Ngadi, M. O., & Kubow, S. (2022). 3D Food Printing Applications Related to Dysphagia:A Narrative Review. *Foods*, *11*(12), 1–15. doi:10.3390/foods11121789 PMID:35741992

Lupton, D., & Turner, B. (2018a). 'Both Fascinating and Disturbing': Consumer Responses to 3D Food Printing and Implications for Food Activism. In T. Schneider, K. Eli, C. Dolan, & S. Ulijaszek (Eds.), *Digital Food Activism* (pp. 151–167). Routledge.

Lupton, D., & Turner, B. (2018b). Food of the Future? Consumer Responses to the Idea of 3D-Printed Meat and Insect-Based Foods. *Food & Foodways*, *26*(4), 269–289. doi:10.1080/07409710.2018.1531213

Luque-Martínez, T., Faraoni, N., & Doña-Toledo, L. (2019). Auditing the marketing and social media communication of natural protected areas. How marketing can contribute to the sustainability of tourism. *Sustainability (Basel)*, *11*(15), 4014. doi:10.3390/su11154014

Lu, Y., Chen, Z. W., & Law, R. (2018). Mapping the progress of SMresearch in hospitality and tourism management from 2004 to 2014. *Journal of Travel & Tourism Marketing*, *35*(2), 102–118. doi:10.1080/10548408.2017.1350249

MacNeill, T., & Wozniak, D. (2018). The economic, social, and environmental impacts of cruise tourism. *Tourism Management*, *66*, 387–404. doi:10.1016/j.tourman.2017.11.002

Magano, J., & Cunha, M. N. (2020). Digital marketing impact on tourism in Portugal: A quantitative study. *African Journal of Hospitality, Tourism and Leisure*, *9*(1), 1–19.

Magd, H., Khan, S. A., Khatri, B., Sharma, N., & Arora, S. (2023). Understanding the Relationship Between IoT and Digital Marketing: A Bibliometric Analysis. In A. Naim & V. Devi (Eds.), *Global Applications of the Internet of Things in Digital Marketing* (pp. 123–140). IGI Global. doi:10.4018/978-1-6684-8166-0.ch007

Mandić, A., & Vuković, M. (2022). Millennials attitudes, choices and behaviour - integrative analysis. *Journal of Ecotourism*, *21*(1), 87–97. doi:10.1080/14724049.2021.1932925

Mangold, W. G., & Faulds, D. J. (2009). Social media: The new hybrid element of the promotion mix. *Business Horizons*, *52*(4), 357–365. doi:10.1016/j.bushor.2009.03.002

Manstan, T., & McSweeney, M. B. (2020). Consumers' attitudes towards and acceptance of 3D printed foods in comparison with conventional food products. *International Journal of Food Science & Technology*, *55*(1), 323–331. doi:10.1111/ijfs.14292

Manthiou, A., Kang, J., & Hyun, S. S. (2017). An integration of cognitive appraisal theory and script theory in the luxury cruise sector: The bridging role of recollection and storytelling. *Journal of Travel & Tourism Marketing*, *34*(8), 1071–1088. doi:10.1080/10548408.2016.1277575

Mantihal, S., Kobun, R., & Lee, B. (2020). 3D food printing of as the new way of preparing food: A review. *International Journal of Gastronomy and Food Science*, *22*, 1–10. doi:10.1016/j.ijgfs.2020.100260

Mantihal, S., Prakash, S., & Bhandari, B. (2019). Texture-modified 3D printed dark chocolate: Sensory evaluation and consumer perception study. *Journal of Texture Studies*, *50*(5), 386–399. doi:10.1111/jtxs.12472 PMID:31323141

Mardhiyani, N. L. (2020). Tourism 4.0: Strategi Komunikasi Pemasaran Pariwisata Kota Semarang, 2020.

Mariani, M., Di Felice, M., & Mura, M. (2016). Facebook as a destination marketing tool: Evidence from Italian regional Destination Management Organizations. *Tourism Management*, *56*, 321–343. doi:10.1016/j.tourman.2015.12.008

Marin, D. (2015). Study on the economic impact of tourism and of agrotourism on local communities. *Research Journal of Agricultural Science*, *47*, 160–163.

Marine-Roig, E., & Clavé, S. A. (2015). Tourism Analytics with Massive User-generated Content: A Case Study of Barcelona. *Journal of Destination Marketing and Management*, 5. (IF: 5)

Martins, L., Gan, Y., & Ferreira-Lopes, A. (2017). An empirical analysis of the influence of macroeconomic determinants on World tourism demand. *Tourism Management*, *61*, 248–260. doi:10.1016/j.tourman.2017.01.008

Masiero, L., Viglia, G., & Nieto-García, M. (2020). Strategic consumer behavior in online hotel booking. *Annals of Tourism Research, 83*, 102947. doi:10.1016/j.annals.2020.102947

Máthé, I. (2018). Multiculturality and Interculturality in Tourism. *Valahian Journal of Economic Studies, 9*(1), 39–46. doi:10.2478/vjes-2018-0004

Mathew, V., & Soliman, M. (2021). Does digital content marketing affect tourism consumer behavior? An extension of t echnology acceptance model. *Journal of Consumer Behaviour, 20*(1), 61–75. doi:10.1002/cb.1854

Maxim, C. (2015). Drivers of Success in Implementing Sustainable Tourism Policies in Urban Areas. *Tourism Planning & Development, 12*(1), 37–47. doi:10.1080/21568316.2014.960599

Maxim, C. (2019). Challenges faced by world tourism cities–London's perspective. *Current Issues in Tourism, 22*(9), 1006–1024. doi:10.1080/13683500.2017.1347609

McCabe, S. (Ed.). (2014). *The Routledge Handbook of Tourism Marketing*. Routledge., https://perpus.univpancasila.ac.id/repository/EBUPT190874.pdf#page=514 doi:10.4324/9781315858265

McCluskey, J. J., Kalaitzandonakes, N., & Swinnen, J. (2016). Media coverage, public perceptions, and consumer behavior: Insights from new food technologies. *Annual Review of Resource Economics, 8*(1), 467–486. doi:10.1146/annurev-resource-100913-012630

Mckercher, B., & Prideaux, B. (2020). *Tourism Theories*. Concepts and Models., doi:10.23912/9781911635352-4280

Meadows, D. H., Meadows, D. L., Randers, J., Behrens, W., & Club of Rome. (1972). *The Limits to growth: A report for the Club of Rome's project on the predicament of mankind.* New York: Universe Books. https://www.donellameadows.org/wp-content/userfiles/Limits-to-Growth-digital-scan-version.pdf

Mendieta-Aragón, A. (2022). Changes in tourism behaviour after COVID-19: Towards a new profile of tourists and leisure travel in Spain. *Rect@. Electronic Journal of Communications and Works of ASEPUMA, 23*(1), 37–51.

Mendini, M., Pizzetti, M., & Peter, P. C. (2019). Social food pleasure: When sharing offline, online and for society promotes pleasurable and healthy food experiences and well-being. *Qualitative Market Research, 22*(4), 544–556. doi:10.1108/QMR-06-2018-0067

Menon, D., Gunasekar, S., Dixit, S. K., Das, P., & Mandal, S. (2021). Present and prospective research themes for tourism and hospitality education post-COVID19: A bibliometric analysis. *Journal of Hospitality, Leisure, Sport and Tourism Education, 100360*. doi:10.1016/j.jhlste.2021.100360 PMID:34840528

Mercan, S., Cain, L., Akkaya, K., Cebe, M., Uluagac, S., Alonso, M., & Cobanoglu, C. (2020). Improving the service industry with hyper-connectivity: IoT in hospitality. *International Journal of Contemporary Hospitality Management.*

Merino, F., & Prats, M. A. (2020). Sustainable beach management and promotion of the local tourist industry: Can blue flags be a good driver of this balance? *Ocean and Coastal Management*, *198*, 105359. doi:10.1016/j.ocecoaman.2020.105359

Mestanza-Ramón, C., & Jiménez-Caballero, J. L. (2021). Nature tourism on the Colombian—Ecuadorian Amazonian border: History, current situation, and challenges. *Sustainability (Basel)*, *13*(8), 4432. doi:10.3390/su13084432

Ministry of Heritage & Tourism. (2023). *Directorate General of Tourism Promotion*. MHT. https://mht.gov.om/tourism-promotion

Mizrahi, M., Golan, A., Mizrahi, A. B., Gruber, R., Lachnish, A. Z., & Zoran, A. (2016). Digital Gastronomy: Methods & Recipes for Hybrid Cooking. *In: UIST 2016 - Proceedings of the 29th Annual Symposium on User Interface Software and Technology*. Tokyo, Japan: Association for Computing Machinery.

Mizrahi, A. B., Lachnish, A. Z., & Zoran, A. R. (2023). Digital gastronomy testcase: A complete pipeline of robotic induced dish variations. *International Journal of Gastronomy and Food Science*, *31*, 1–14.

Mkwizu, K. H. (2019). Digital marketing and tourism: Opportunities for Africa. *International Hospitality Review*, *34*(1), 5–12. doi:10.1108/IHR-09-2019-0015

MoEFCC & BCG - Ministry of Environment. (2023). *Encouraging Resource Efficiency and Circular Economy*. Ministry of Environment, Forest and Climate Change, New Delhi, India. https://www.g20.org/content/dam/gtwenty/gtwenty_new/document/G20_ECSWG-Resource_Efficiency_and%20_Circular_Economy_Industry_Coalition.pdf

Monsalve-Pelaez, M., Tovar-Meléndez, A., & Salazar-Araujo, E. (2023). Documentary Review on Sustainable Tourism in the Framework of the SDGs. *Revista Turismo & Desenvolvimento (Aveiro)*, *40*, 137–153. doi:10.34624/rtd.v40i0.31483

Montero, A. A., & López-Sánchez, J. A. (2021). Intersection of Data Science and Smart Destinations: A Systematic Review. *. *Frontiers in Psychology*, 2021. PMID:34393952

Moon, H., & Han, H. (2019). Tourist experience quality and loyalty to an island destination: The moderating impact of destination image. *Journal of Travel & Tourism Marketing*, *36*(1), 43–59. doi:10.1080/10548408.2018.1494083

Morosan, C., & DeFranco, A. (2016). Modeling guests' intentions to use mobile apps in hotels: The roles of personalization, privacy, and involvement. *International Journal of Contemporary Hospitality Management*, *28*(9), 1968–1991. doi:10.1108/IJCHM-07-2015-0349

Moyle, B. D., McLennan, C. J., Ruhanen, L., & Weiler, B. (2014). Terrorist incidents and tourism demand: Evidence from Greece. *Journal of Sustainable Tourism*, *22*(7), 1037–1051. doi:10.1080/09669582.2013.839694

Mumford, L. (1934). *Technics and Civilization*. Harcourt Brace & Company. https://ia801404.us.archive.org/10/items/in.ernet.dli.2015.49974/2015.49974.Technics-And-Civilization.pdf

Mumford, L. (1964). Authoritarian and Democratic Technics. *Technology and Culture*, *5*(1), 1–8. doi:10.2307/3101118

Muñoz, E., & Navia, R. (2015). Waste management in touristic regions. *Waste Management & Research*, *33*(7), 593–594. doi:10.1177/0734242X15594982 PMID:26185162

Murphy, P. (1985). *Tourism: A community approach*. Methuen.

Muscat Daily. (2021, September 9). Oman ranks first in GCC for sustainable tourism. *Muscat Daily*. https://www.muscatdaily.com/2021/03/13/oman-ranks-first-in-gcc-for-sustainable-tourism/

Nachal, N., Moses, J. A., Karthik, P., & Anandharamakrishnan, C. (2019). Applications of 3D Printing in Food Processing. *Food Engineering Reviews*, *11*(3), 123–141. doi:10.1007/s12393-019-09199-8

Naciye, G., & Adem, A. (2020). Impacts of COVID -19 on global tourism industry: A cross-regional comparison. *Journal of Tourism Management Perspective*, *36*

Nagarajan, N. R., Wada, M., Fang, M. L., & Sixsmith, A. (2019). Defining organizational contributions to sustaining an aging workforce: a bibliometric review. In European Journal of Ageing, 16(3). Springer Verlag. doi:10.1007/s10433-019-00499-w

Naim, A., & Khan, S. A. (2023). Impact and Assessment of Electronic Commerce on Consumer Buying Behaviour. In A. Naim & V. Devi (Eds.), *Global Applications of the Internet of Things in Digital Marketing* (pp. 264–289). IGI Global. doi:10.4018/978-1-6684-8166-0.ch014

Nakandala, D., Smith, M., & Lau, H. (2020). Shared power and fairness in trust-based supply chain relationships in an urban local food system. *British Food Journal*, *122*(3), 870–883. doi:10.1108/BFJ-05-2019-0309

Nam, K., Dutt, C. S., Chathoth, P., & Khan, M. S. (2021). Blockchain technology for smart city and smart tourism: Latest trends and challenges. *Asia Pacific Journal of Tourism Research*, *26*(4), 454–468. doi:10.1080/10941665.2019.1585376

Naseer, S., Khalid, S., Parveen, S., Abbass, K., Song, H., & Achim, M. (2023). COVID-19 outbreak: Impact on global economy. *Frontiers in Public Health*, *10*, 1009393. doi:10.3389/fpubh.2022.1009393 PMID:36793360

Nassar, M. A., & Fouad, A. (2022). Tomorrow Taste Comes Today: Exploring Customers' Intention to Buy 3D Printed Food in Egyptian Restaurants. *Pharos International Journal of Tourism and Hospitality*, *1*(1), 31–48. doi:10.21608/pijth.2022.264346

Neto, F. (2003). A new approach to sustainable tourism development: Moving beyond environmental protection. *Natural Resources Forum*, *27*(3), 212–222. doi:10.1111/1477-8947.00056

Neuhofer, B., Buhalis, D., & Ladkin, A. (2019). Technology as a catalyst of change: Enablers and barriers of the tourist experience and their consequences. The Routledge Handbook of Transport Economics, 112-132. Routledge.

Neuhofer, B., Buhalis, D., & Ladkin, A. (2019). Technology as a catalyst of change: Enablers and barriers of the tourist experience and their consequences. The Routledge Handbook of Transport Economics, 247

Neuhofer, B., Buhalis, D., & Ladkin, A. (2015). Smart technologies for personalized experiences: A case study in the hospitality domain. *Electronic Markets*, *25*(3), 243–254. doi:10.1007/s12525-015-0182-1

Nguyen, C. P., Thanh, S. D., & Nguyen, B. (2022). Economic uncertainty and tourism consumption. *Tourism Economics*, *28*(4), 920–941. doi:10.1177/1354816620981519

Nikolskaya, E., Zakharova, E., Galkin, D., Kovaleva, N., & Panova, N. (2021). *The Impact of Digital Technologies on the Transformation of the Tourism and Hospitality Industry*. Revista Gestão Inovação e Tecnologias. doi:10.47059/revistageintec.v11i4.2133

Noort, M., van Bommel, K., & Renzetti, S. (2017). 3D-Printed Cereal Foods. *Cereal Foods World*, *62*(6), 272–277. doi:10.1094/CFW-62-6-0272

Northrop, E. (Ed.). (2022). *Opportunities for Transforming Coastal and Marine Tourism: Towards Sustainability, Regeneration and Resilience*. The High Level Panel for a Sustainable Ocean Economy (Ocean Panel). https://oceanpanel.org/publication/opportunities-for-transforming-coastal-and-marine-tourism-towards-sustainability-regeneration-and-resilience/

Nuenen, T., & Scarles, C. (2021). Advancements in technology and digital media in tourism. *Tourist Studies*, *21*(1), 119–132. doi:10.1177/1468797621990410

Nusair, K. (2020). Developing A Comprehensive Life Cycle Framework for Social Media Research in Hospitality and Tourism. *International Journal of Contemporary Hospitality Management*, *3* (IF: 3)

Nyheim, P., Xu, S., Zhang, L., & Mattila, A. S. (2015). Predictors of avoidance towards personalization of restaurant smartphone advertising: A study from the Millennials' perspective. *Journal of Hospitality and Tourism Technology*, *6*(2), 145–159. doi:10.1108/JHTT-07-2014-0026

OECD. (2018). *OECD Tourism Trends and Policies 2018*. OECD Publishing. doi:10.1787/tour-2018-

OECD. (2020). Rethinking tourism success for sustainable growth. In *OECD Tourism Trends and Policies 2020*. OECD Publishing. doi:10.1787/82b46508-

Oliver, R. L. (1980). A cognitive model of the antecedents and consequences of satisfaction decisions. *JMR, Journal of Marketing Research*, *17*(4), 460–469. doi:10.1177/002224378001700405

Ooi, N., Duke, E., & O'Leary, J. (2018). Tourism in changing natural environments. *Tourism Geographies*, *20*(2), 193–201. doi:10.1080/14616688.2018.1440418

Ooi, N., Laing, J., & Mair, J. (2015). Sociocultural change facing ranchers in the Rocky Mountain West as a result of mountain resort tourism and amenity migration. *Journal of Rural Studies*, *41*(October), 59–71. doi:10.1016/j.jrurstud.2015.07.005

Oosterveer, P., & Sonnenfeld, D. A. (2012). *Food, globalization and sustainability*. Routledge. doi:10.4324/9781849776790

Oreja Rodríguez, J. R., Parra-López, E., & Yanes-Estévez, V. (2008). The sustainability of island destinations: Tourism area life cycle and teleological perspectives. The case of Tenerife. *Tourism Management*, *29*(1), 53–65. doi:10.1016/j.tourman.2007.04.007

Otero-Giráldez, M., Álvarez-Díaz, M., & González-Gómez, M. (2012). Estimating the long-run effects of socioeconomic and meteorological factors on the domestic tourism demand for Galicia (Spain). *Tourism Management*, *33*(6), 1301–1308. doi:10.1016/j.tourman.2012.04.005

Pack, S. (2008). Tourism, modernization, and difference: A twentieth-century Spanish paradigm. *Sport in Society*, *11*(6), 657–672. https://grupoturhis.files.wordpress.com/2012/06/tourism-modernisation-difference.pdf. doi:10.1080/17430430802283914

Page, S. J., & Connell, J. (2020). *Tourism: A modern synthesis*. Routledge. doi:10.4324/9781003005520

Pahrudin, P., Li- Wei, L., Shao-Yu, L. (2022). What is Role of Tourism Management and Marketing toward Sustainable Tourism? A Biblometric Analysis Approach. *Sustainability*, 14.

Pandey, D., & Kumar, R. (2022). Russia-Ukraine War and the global tourism sector: A 13-day tale. *Current Issues in Tourism*, *26*(5), 692–700. doi:10.1080/13683500.2022.2081789

Pan, S., Gao, M., Kim, H., Shah, K., Pei, S., & Chiang, P. (2018). Advances and challenges in sustainable tourism toward a green economy. *The Science of the Total Environment*, *635*, 452–469. doi:10.1016/j.scitotenv.2018.04.134 PMID:29677671

Papathanassis, A. (2017). Cruise tourism management: State of the art. *Tourism Review*, *72*(1), 104–119. doi:10.1108/TR-01-2017-0003

Papathanassis, A., & Beckmann, I. (2011). Assessing the 'poverty of cruise theory'hypothesis. *Annals of Tourism Research*, *38*(1), 153–174. doi:10.1016/j.annals.2010.07.015

Papatheodorou, A., Rosselló, J., & Xiao, H. (2010). Global economic crisis and tourism: Consequences and perspectives. *Journal of Travel Research*, *49*(1), 39–45. doi:10.1177/0047287509355327

Paré, G., Tate, M., Johnstone, D., & Kitsiou, S. (2016). Contextualizing the twin concepts of systematicity and transparency in information systems literature reviews. *European Journal of Information Systems*, *25*(6), 493–508. doi:10.1057/s41303-016-0020-3

Parsons, J., & Ralph, P. (2014). Generating effective recommendations using viewing-time weighted preferences for attributes. *Journal of the Association for Information Systems*, *15*(8), 2. doi:10.17705/1jais.00369

Pasquinelli, M. (2019). On the Origins of Marx's General Intellect. *Radical Philosophy, 2*, 06. https://kim.hfg-karlsruhe.de/marx-general-intellect/

Pasquinelli, C., Trunfio, M., Bellini, N., & Rossi, S. (2021). Sustainability in Overtourisified Cities? A Social Media Insight into Italian Branding Responses to Covid -19 Crisis. *Sustainability*, 13.

Pencarelli, T. (2019). The digital revolution in the travel and tourism industry. *Information Technology & Tourism*, *22*(3), 455–476. doi:10.1007/s40558-019-00160-3

Pérez-Tapia, G., Mercadé-Melé, P., Yeong-Hyeon, H., & Almeida-García, F. (2022). Cultural Context or Generational Cohort: Which Influences Tourist Behavior More? *Frontiers in Psychology*, *13*, 767035. doi:10.3389/fpsyg.2022.767035 PMID:35282202

Perles-Ribes, J., Ramón-Rodríguez, A., Sevilla-Jiménez, M., & Moreno-Izquierdo, L. (2016). Unemployment effects of economic crises on hotel and residential tourism destinations: The case of Spain. *Tourism Management*, *54*, 356–368. doi:10.1016/j.tourman.2015.12.002

Peshave, J., & Hodlur, A. (2022). 3D Printing-The Future In Culinary Arts! *Multi-Disciplinary Journal*, *1*(2), 1–7.

Peters, C., Maglio, P., Badinelli, R., Harmon, R. R., Maull, R., Spohrer, J. C., Tuunanen, T., Vargo, S. L., Welser, J. J., & Demirkan, H. (2016). Emerging digital frontiers for service innovation. *Communications of the Association for Information Systems: CAIS*, *1*(39), online.

Peters, K., & Remaud, P. H. (2020). Factors influencing consumer menu-item selection in a restaurant context. *Food Quality and Preference*, *82*, 103887. doi:10.1016/j.foodqual.2020.103887

Piccoli, G., Lui, T.-W., & Grün, B. (2017). The impact of IT-enabled customer service systems on service personalization, customer service perceptions, and hotel performance. *Tourism Management*, *59*, 349–362. doi:10.1016/j.tourman.2016.08.015

Pine, B. J., Pine, J., & Gilmore, J. H. (1999). *The experience economy: work is theatre & every business a stage*. Harvard Business Press.

Pinna, C., Ramundo, L., Sisca, F. G., Anglioletti, C. M., Taisch, M., & Terzi, S. (2016). Additive Manufacturing applications within Food industry: an actual overview and future opportunities. XXI Summer School "Francesco Turco" - Industrial Systems Engineering, (pp. 18-24).

Pino, G., & Peluso, A. M. (2018). The development of cruise tourism in emerging destinations: Evidence from Salento, Italy. *Tourism and Hospitality Research*, *18*(1), 15–27. doi:10.1177/1467358415619672

Pizam, A. (2010). *Creating memorable experiences.*

Plzáková, L., & Smeral, E. (2022). Impact of the COVID-19 crisis on European tourism. *Tourism Economics*, *28*(1), 91–109. doi:10.1177/13548166211031113

Podoshen, J. S. (2013). Dark tourism motivations: Simulation, emotional contagion and topographic comparison. *Tourism Management*, *35*, 263–271. doi:10.1016/j.tourman.2012.08.002

Pop, R., Saplacan, Z., Dabija, D., & Alt, M. (2021). The impact of social media influencers on travel decisions: The role of trust in consumer decision journey. *Current Issues in Tourism*, *25*(5), 823–843. doi:10.1080/13683500.2021.1895729

Postma, A., & Yeoman, I. (2021). A systems perspective as a tool to understand disruption in travel and tourism. *Journal of Tourism Futures*. . doi:10.1108/JTF-04-2020-0052

Postma, A., Cavagnaro, E., & Spruyt, E. (2017). Sustainable tourism 2040. *Journal of Tourism Futures*, *3*(1), 13–22. doi:10.1108/JTF-10-2015-0046

Powers, T., Advincula, D., Austin, M. S., Graiko, S., & Snyder, J. (2012). Digital and SMIn the Purchase Decision Process. *Journal of Advertising Research*, *52*(4), 479–489. doi:10.2501/JAR-52-4-479-489

Presswood, A. L. (2019). *Food Blogs, Postfeminism, and the Communication of Expertise: Digital Domestics*. Lexington Books.

Pritchard, A. (1969). Statistical bibliography or bibliometrics. *The Journal of Documentation*, *25*, 348.

Priya, G., Mathew, S., & Subbaiyan, G. (2019). Household Structure and the Travel Pattern of Senior Citizens for Leisure Trips. *Transportation Research*, *45*, 325–340. doi:10.1007/978-981-32-9042-6_26

Publications Office of the European Union. (2022). *Sustainable development in the European Union Monitoring report on progress towards the SDGs in an EU context 2022 edition*. Eurostat, Unit E2 — Environmental statistics and accounts; sustainable development. https://ec.europa.eu/eurostat/documents/15234730/15242025/KS-09-22-019-EN-N.pdf/a2be16e4-b925-f109-563c-f94ae09f5436?t=1667397761499

Pulido-Fernández, J. I., Cárdenas-García, P. J., & Espinosa-Pulido, J. A. (2019). Does environmental sustainability contribute to tourism growth? An analysis at the country level. *Journal of Cleaner Production*, *213*, 309–319. doi:10.1016/j.jclepro.2018.12.151

Pulido-Fernández, J., & Cárdenas-García, P. (2020). Analyzing the Bidirectional Relationship between Tourism Growth and Economic Development. *Journal of Travel Research*, *60*(3), 583–602. doi:10.1177/0047287520922316

Putri, S. V. (2022). The Impact of Electronic Word of Mouth (EWOM) Using Influencers on Brand Awareness and Purchase Intention. *CoverAge: Journal of Strategic Communication*, *13*(1), 11–25. doi:10.35814/coverage.v13i1.3913

Rahmani, B., & Barzi, P. H. (2023). *What does ChatGPT show about the future impacts of large language model applications on tourism?* Conference paper. 6th International Conference on Management, Tourism and Technology (ICMTT) Penang, Malaysia. https://www.researchgate.net/publication/371119753_What_does_ChatGPT_show_about_the_future_impacts_of_large_language_model_applications_on_tourism

Ramírez, R., Churchhouse, S., Palermo, A., & Hoffmann, J. (2017). Using scenario planning to reshape strategy. *MIT Sloan Management Review*, 58.

Ramos, C. M. Q., & Hassan, A. (2021). Evaluation of the tourist experience using a framework for the analysis of the influence of SMon tourist behaviour. *International Journal of Tourism Policy*, *11*(3), 207. doi:10.1504/IJTP.2021.118663

Ramos-Rodríguez, A., & Ruíz-Navarro, J. (2004). Changes in the intellectual structure of strategic management research: A bibliometric study of the Strategic Management Journal, 1980–2000. *Strategic Management Journal*, *25*(10), 981–1004. doi:10.1002/smj.397

RaneN.ChoudharyS.RaneJ. (2023). Hyper-personalization for enhancing customer loyalty and satisfaction in Customer Relationship Management (CRM) systems. *Available at* SSRN 4641044. doi:10.2139/ssrn.4641044

Rasoolimanesh, S. M., Ramakrishna, S., Hall, C. M., Esfandiar, K., & Seyf, S. (2020). A systematic scoping review of sustainable tourism indicators in relation to the sustainable development goals. *Journal of Sustainable Tourism*, *31*(7), 1–21. doi:10.1080/09669582.2020.1775621

Rasoolimanesh, S. M., Seyfi, S., Rastegar, R., & Hall, C. M. (2021). Destination image during the COVID-19 pandemic and future travel behavior: The moderating role of past experience. *Journal of Destination Marketing & Management*, *21*, 100620. doi:10.1016/j.jdmm.2021.100620

Raykova, M. (2021). Crisis Management in Tourism. *Socio-Economic Analyses*, *13*(1), 86–91. doi:10.54664/OYZN2909

Razumova, M., Ibáñez, J. L., & Palmer, J. R. M. (2015). Drivers of environmental innovation in Majorcan hotels. *Journal of Sustainable Tourism*, *23*(10), 1529–1549. doi:10.1080/09669582.2015.1062016

Reddy, M. V. (2008). Sustainable Tourism Rapid Indicators for Less- developed Islands: An Economic Perspective. *International Journal of Tourism Research*, *10*(6), 557–576. doi:10.1002/jtr.700

Reich, A. Z., Xu, Y. H., & McCleary, K. W. (2010). The influence of social responsibility image relative to product and service quality on brand loyalty: An exploratory study of quick-service restaurants. *Hospitality Review*, *28*(1), 2.

Reinartz, W. J., & Kumar, V. (2003). The impact of customer relationship characteristics on profitable lifetime duration. *Journal of Marketing*, *67*(1), 77–99. doi:10.1509/jmkg.67.1.77.18589

Ribeiro, H. N. R., & Pereira, B. R. (2022). The Age of Uncertainty: Prospects for Challenging Times. *IJTM International Journal of Trade and Management*, *1*(1), 148–161. doi:10.5281/zenodo.6564192

Rihova, I., Buhalis, D., Moital, M., & Gouthro, M. B. (2018). Visitor attractions and events: From insourcing to crowdsourcing of the visitor experience. *Tourism Management*, *66*, 308–321.

Robinson, P., Lück, M., & Smith, S. (2020). Tourism policy and planning. *Tourism (Zagreb)*. doi:10.1079/9781780642970.0391

Rodrigues, V., Eusébio, C., & Breda, Z. (2023). Enhancing sustainable development through tourism digitalization: A systematic literature review. *Information Technology & Tourism*, *25*(1), 13–45. doi:10.1007/s40558-022-00241-w

Rogers, H., & Srivastava, M. (2021). Emerging sustainable supply chain models for 3d food printing. *Sustainability (Basel)*, *13*(21), 1–18. doi:10.3390/su132112085

Roman, M., Kosiński, R., Bhatta, K., Niedziółka, A., & Krasnodębski, A. (2022). Virtual and Space Tourism as New Trends in Travelling at the Time of the COVID-19 Pandemic. *Sustainability (Basel)*, *14*(2), 628. doi:10.3390/su14020628

Rosenbaum, M. S., Ramirez, G. C., Campbell, J., & Klaus, P. (2021). The product is me: Hyper-personalized consumer goods as unconventional luxury. *Journal of Business Research*, *129*, 446–454. doi:10.1016/j.jbusres.2019.05.017

Rosselló, J., Becken, S., & Santana-Gallego, M. (2020). The effects of natural disasters on international tourism: A global analysis. *Tourism Management*, *79*, 104080. doi:10.1016/j.tourman.2020.104080 PMID:32287755

Rosselló, J., & Santana-Gallego, M. (2014). Recent trends in international tourist climate preferences: A revised picture for climatic change scenarios. *Climatic Change*, *124*(1–2), 119–132. doi:10.1007/s10584-014-1086-3

Rowley, J. (2001). Remodelling marketing communications in an Internet environment. *Internet Research*, *11*(3), 203–212. doi:10.1108/10662240110397017

Roy, H. (2022). Connecting Farmers' Markets to Foodservice Businesses: A Qualitative Exploration of Restaurants' Perceived Benefits and Challenges of Purchasing Food Locally. *International Journal of Hospitality & Tourism Administration*, 1–36. doi:10.1080/15256480.2022.2142994

Ruan, W., Kang, S., & Song, H. J. (2020). Applying protection motivation theory to understand international tourists' behavioural intentions under the threat of air pollution: A case of Beijing, China. *Current Issues in Tourism*, *23*(16), 2027–2041. doi:10.1080/13683500.2020.1743242

Ružić, D., Bosnić, I., & Kelić, I. (2018). Marketing communication in the river cruise industry. *International Journal of Multidisciplinarity in Business and Science*, *4*(5), 67–73.

Safko, L., & Brake, D. (2009). *The social media bible tactics tools and strategies for business success*. John Wiley & Sons.

Saleem, M., Khan, S. A., Al Shamsi, I. R., & Magd, H. (2023). Digital Marketing Through Social Media Best Practices: A Case Study of HEIs in the GCC Region. In A. Naim & V. Devi (Eds.), *Global Applications of the Internet of Things in Digital Marketing* (pp. 17–30). IGI Global. doi:10.4018/978-1-6684-8166-0.ch002

Saleem, M., Khan, S. A., & Magd, H. (2022). Content Marketing Framework for Building Brand Image: A Case Study of Sohar International School, Oman. In A. Naim & S. Kautish (Eds.), *Building a Brand Image Through Electronic Customer Relationship Management* (pp. 64–83). IGI Global. doi:10.4018/978-1-6684-5386-5.ch004

Sam, K. M., & Chatwin, C. R. (2019). Understanding Wechat Users' Motivations, Attitudes and Intention of Reading Promotional Material. *Journal of Information Technology Management*, *30*(1), 25–37.

Sampieri, R. H., Collado, C. F., & Lucio, P. B. (2003). *Metodologia de Pesquisa* (3rd ed.). The McGraw-Hill Interamericana do Brasil Ltda.

Sanderson Bellamy, A., Furness, E., Nicol, P., Pitt, H., & Taherzadeh, A. (2021). Shaping more resilient and just food systems: Lessons from the COVID-19 Pandemic. *Ambio*, *50*(4), 782–793. doi:10.1007/s13280-021-01532-y PMID:33748902

Santos, M. C., Veiga, C., & Águas, P. (2016). Tourism services: Facing the challenge of new tourist profiles. *Worldwide Hospitality and Tourism Themes*, *8*(6), 654–669. doi:10.1108/WHATT-09-2016-0048

Sarmiento, C. V., & El Hanandeh, A. (2018). Customers' perceptions and expectations of environmentally sustainable restaurant and the development of green index: The case of the Gold Coast, Australia. *Sustainable Production and Consumption*, *15*, 16–24. doi:10.1016/j.spc.2018.04.001

Schmittlein, D. C., & Morrison, D. G. (1985). Is the customer still active? *The American Statistician*, *39*(4), 291–295. doi:10.1080/00031305.1985.10479450

Schmittlein, D. C., Morrison, D. G., & Colombo, R. (1987). Counting your customers: Who-are they and what will they do next? *Management Science*, *33*(1), 1–24. doi:10.1287/mnsc.33.1.1

Schwarz, J., Ram, C., & Rohrbeck, R. (2019). Combining scenario planning and business wargaming to better anticipate future competitive dynamics. *Futures*, *105*, 133–142. Advance online publication. doi:10.1016/j.futures.2018.10.001

Scott, E. (2023) 3D Food Printing Market Size, Share, and Key Insight. *Food and Agriculture Market News*. https://www.linkedin.com/pulse/3d-food-printing-market-size-share-key-insight-edward-scott/

Scott, D. (2021). Sustainable tourism and the grand challenge of climate change. *Sustainability (Basel)*, *13*(4), 1–17. doi:10.3390/su13041966

Seal, P. P. (2023). Robots in the Hotel Kitchen: The Future Chef in Ed, Impactful Technologies Transforming the Food Industry. IGI -Global.

Senecal, S., & Nantel, J. (2004). The Influence of Online Product Recommendations on Consumers' Online Choices. *Journal of Retailing*, *80*(2), 159–169. doi:10.1016/j.jretai.2004.04.001

Settele, J., Scholes, R., Betts, R., Bunn, S., Leadley, P., Nepstad, D., Overpeck, J. T., & Taboada, M. A. (2014). Terrestrial and inland water systems. In *Climate Change 2014: Impacts, Adaptation, and Vulnerability. Part A: Global and Sectoral Aspects,* (pp. 271–359). Cambridge University Press. https://www.ipcc.ch/site/assets/uploads/2018/02/WGIIAR5-Chap4_FINAL.pdf

Severt, K., Shin, Y. H., Chen, H. S., & DiPietro, R. B. (2022). Measuring the relationships between corporate social responsibility, perceived quality, price fairness, satisfaction, and conative loyalty in the context of local food restaurants. *International Journal of Hospitality & Tourism Administration*, *23*(3), 623–645. doi:10.1080/15256480.2020.1842836

Seyfi, S., Hall, C. M., Saarinen, J., & Vo-Thanh, T. (2021). Understanding drivers and barriers affecting tourists' engagement in digitally mediated pro-sustainability boycotts. *Journal of Sustainable Tourism*. Advance online publication. doi:10.1080/09669582.2021.2013489

Seyitoğlu, F., & Costa, C. (2022a). A systematic review of scenario planning studies in tourism and hospitality research. *Journal of Policy Research in Tourism, Leisure & Events*, 1–18. doi:10.1080/19407963.2022.2032108

Seyitoğlu, F., & Costa, C. (2022b). A scenario planning framework for (post-) pandemic tourism in European destinations. *European Planning Studies*, *30*(12), 2554–2574. doi:10.1080/09654313.2022.2045571

Seyitoglu, F., & Ivanov, S. (2022). Understanding the robotic restaurant experience: A multiple case study. *Journal of Tourism Futures*, *8*(1), 55–72. doi:10.1108/JTF-04-2020-0070

Sharma, N. and Arora, N. (2023a). Do Instagram reels influence travelers' behavioral and e-WOM intentions for the selection of ecotourism destination?. *Journal of Hospitality and Tourism Insights*. . doi:10.1108/JHTI-03-2023-0135

Sharma, N., & Arora, N. (2023). Past, Present, and Future of Cultural Marketing: A Bibliometric Analysis. In Cultural Marketing and Metaverse for Consumer Engagement (pp. 234-248). IGI Global.

Sharma, N., Khatri, B., & Khan, S. A. (2023b). Do e-WOM Persuade Travelers Destination Visit Intentions? An investigation on how Travelers Adopt the Information from the Social Media Channels. *Journal of Content. Community and Communication*, *17*(9), 147–161. doi:10.31620/JCCC.06.23/11

Sharma, N., Khatri, B., Khan, S. A., & Shamsi, M. S. (2023a). Extending the UTAUT Model to Examine the Influence of social media on Tourists' Destination Selection. *Indian Journal of Marketing*, *53*(4), 47–64. doi:10.17010/ijom/2023/v53/i4/172689

Sher, D., & Tutó, X. (2010). Material characterisation and process development for chocolate additive layer manufacturing. *Virtual and Physical Prototyping*, *5*(2), 57–64. doi:10.1080/17452751003753212

Sheth, J. (2017). Revitalizing relationship marketing. *Journal of Services Marketing*, *31*(1), 6–10. doi:10.1108/JSM-11-2016-0397

Shijin, W., Yaqiong, M., Xueyan, Z., & Jia, X. (2020). Polar tourism and environment change: Opportunity, impact and adaptation. *Polar Science*, *25*, 100544. doi:10.1016/j.polar.2020.100544

Shin, H., & Perdue, R. R. (2019). Self-Service Technology Research: A bibliometric co-citation visualization analysis. *International Journal of Hospitality Management*, *80*, 101–112. doi:10.1016/j.ijhm.2019.01.012

Siddique, S. B. (2020). *Taste matters: A qualitative study of eating traditional vegetables among Bangladeshi immigrants in Italy*.

Siddiqui, S., & Imran, M. (2019). Impact of Climate Change on Tourism. *Environmental Impacts of Tourism in Developing Nations,* 68-83. doi:10.4018/978-1-5225-5843-9.ch004

Siegrist, M., Hartmann, C., & Keller, C. (2013). Antecedents of food neophobia and its association with eating behavior and food choices. *Food Quality and Preference*, *30*(2), 293–298. doi:10.1016/j.foodqual.2013.06.013

Sigala, M. (2020). Tourism and COVID-19: Impacts and implications for advancing and resetting industry and research. *Journal of Business Research*, *117*, 312–321. doi:10.1016/j.jbusres.2020.06.015 PMID:32546875

Singh, M., Kumari, M., Deogam, M., Gupta, L., Behra, L., Bharti, K. M., & Karmakar, S. (2020). *A Study on Layered Security Threats and Counter-Measures in Internet of Things: International Conference on Recent Trends in Artificial Intelligence, IOT, Smart Cities & Applications (ICAISC-2020)*. CompScirn: Software Network (Topic).

Singhal, S., Rasane, P., Kaur, S., Garba, U., Bankar, A., Singh, J., & Gupta, N. (2020). 3D food printing: Paving way towards novel foods. *Anais da Academia Brasileira de Ciências*, *92*(3), 1–26. doi:10.1590/0001-3765202020180737 PMID:33053099

Smeral, E. (2009). The impact of the financial and economic crisis on European tourism. *Journal of Travel Research*, *48*(1), 3–13. doi:10.1177/0047287509336332

Smith, S., Bergner, N., Ross, C., Tjernström, O., & Weinberg, C. (2020). The internet of things and new business models in tourism: A case study from Sweden. *Journal of Tourism Futures*, *6*(2), 133–144.

Sobhanifard, Y., & Vaeysi, M. (2020). Mixed modeling of the social network mechanisms for the sustainable development of tourism: The case of Iranian Kurdistan. *Sustainable Development (Bradford)*, *28*(1), 187–196. doi:10.1002/sd.1981

Soboleva, A., Burton, S., Mallik, G., & Khan, A. (2017). 'Retweet for a chance to...': An analysis of what triggers consumers to engage in seeded eWOM on twitter. *Journal of Marketing Management*, *33*(13–14), 1120–1148. doi:10.1080/0267257X.2017.1369142

Sofronov, B. (2018). The development of the travel and tourism industry in the world. Annals of Spiru Haret University. *Economic Series*, *18*(4), 123–137. doi:10.26458/1848

Sogari, G., Velez-Argumedo, C., Gómez, M. I., & Mora, C. (2018). College students and eating habits: A study using an ecological model for healthy behavior. *Nutrients*, *10*(12), 1823. doi:10.3390/nu10121823 PMID:30477101

Soliman, M., & Al Balushi, M. K. (2023). Unveiling destination evangelism through generative AI tools. *ROBONOMICS: The Journal of the Automated Economy, 4*, 54. https://journal.robonomics.science/index.php/rj/article/view/54.

Soliman, M. (2021). Extending the theory of planned behavior to predict tourism destination revisit intention. *International Journal of Hospitality & Tourism Administration*, *22*(5), 524–549. doi:10.1080/15256480.2019.1692755

Soliman, M., Cardoso, L., de Almeida, G. F., Araújo, A., & Vila, N. (2021). Mapping smart experiences in tourism: A bibliometric approach. *European Journal of Tourism Research*, *28*, 2809–2809. doi:10.54055/ejtr.v28i.2254

Soliman, M., Gulvady, S., Lyulyov, O., & Pimonenko, T. (2023). Research trends and themes in the top-tier tourism, leisure and hospitality journals: A bibliometric and network analysis before and during the COVID-19 era. *International Journal of Hospitality and Tourism Systems*, *16*(1).

Song, H., Livat, F., & Ye, S. (2019). Effects of terrorist attacks on tourist flows to France: Is wine tourism a substitute for urban tourism? *Journal of Destination Marketing & Management*, *14*, 100385. doi:10.1016/j.jdmm.2019.100385

Soni, R., Ponappa, K., & Tandon, P. (2022). A review on customized food fabrication process using Food Layered Manufacturing. *Lebensmittel-Wissenschaft + Technologie*, *161*(113411), 1–8. doi:10.1016/j.lwt.2022.113411

Soontiens-Olsen, A., Genge, L., Medeiros, A., Klein, G., Lin, S., & Sheehan, L. (2023). Coastal Adaptation and Vulnerability Assessment in a Warming Future: A Systematic Review of the Tourism Sector. *SAGE Open*, *13*(2), 21582440231179215. doi:10.1177/21582440231179215

Stankov, U., Lazić, L., & Dragicevic, V. (2010). The Extent of Use of Basic Facebook User-Generated Content by the National Tourism Organizations in Europe. *European Journal of Tourism Research*, *3*(2), 105–113. doi:10.54055/ejtr.v3i2.51

Statista Research Department. (2022). *Number of global social network users 2017-2025*. Statista. https://www.statista.com/statistics/278414/number-of-worldwide-social-network-users/

Statistica Research Department. (2024, January 22). *Topic: Sustainable tourism worldwide*. Statista. https://www.statista.com/topics/1916/green-tourism/#editorsPicks

Stocchetti, M. (2023). A matter of meaning, life and death. Text, AI and the human condition. *Hipertext.net*, (26), 77-81. doi:10.31009/hipertext.net.2023.i26.12

Sukunesan, S., Selvarajah, C., & Mellström, Z. (2020). Internationalization Via Instagram: An Exploratory Study of Small and Medium Enterprises. *Contemporary Management Research*, *16*(2), 77–121. doi:10.7903/cmr.19811

Sundaram, R., Sharma, D. R., & Shakya, D. A. (2020). Power of digital marketing in building brands: A review of social media advertisement. *International Journal of Management, 11*(4).

Sun, J., Peng, Z. Y., Liangkun, F., Jerry, Y. H., & Hong, G. S. (2015a). 3D food printing—An innovative way of mass customization in food fabrication. *International Journal of Bioprinting, 1*(1), 27–38. doi:10.18063/IJB.2015.01.006

Sun, J., Zhou, W., Huang, D., Fuh, J. Y. H., & Hong, G. S. (2015b). An Overview of 3D Printing Technologies for Food Fabrication. *Food and Bioprocess Technology, 8*(8), 1605–1615. doi:10.1007/s11947-015-1528-6

Sun, X., Feng, X., & Gauri, D. K. (2014). The cruise industry in China: Efforts, progress and challenges. *International Journal of Hospitality Management, 42*, 71–84. doi:10.1016/j.ijhm.2014.05.009

Suresh Babu, C. V. Rubajini, R. P., & Devi, K. (2013) An Integrated smart system for accident - avoidance in four wheelers by using GSM and GPS Module. *Fifth International Conference On Advanced Computing (Icoac).* IEEE.

Suresh Babu, C. V., Akshayah, N. S., Maclin Vinola, P., & Janapriyan, R. (2023). IoT-Based Smart Accident Detection and Alert System. In P. Swarnalatha & S. Prabu (Eds.), *Handbook of Research on Deep Learning Techniques for Cloud-Based Industrial IoT* (pp. 322–337). IGI Global., doi:10.4018/978-1-6684-8098-4.ch019

Suresh Babu, C. V., Monika, R., Dhanusha, T., Vishnuvaradhanan, K., & Harish, A. (2023). Smart Street Lighting System for Smart Cities Using IoT (LoRa). In R. Kumar, A. Abdul Hamid, & N. Binti Ya'akub (Eds.), *Effective AI, Blockchain, and E-Governance Applications for Knowledge Discovery and Management* (pp. 78–96). IGI Global. doi:10.4018/978-1-6684-9151-5.ch006

Surucu-Balci, E., & Balci, G. (2023). Building social capital in cruise travel via social network sites. *Current Issues in Tourism, 26*(7), 1096–1111. doi:10.1080/13683500.2022.2047904

Talukder, M. B. & Kumar, S. (2023). *The Effect of Food Service Quality on Customer Satisfaction in the Hotel Industry: A Conceptual Paper.* ResearchGate. https://www.researchgate.net/publication/371503829_The_Effect_of_Food_Service_Quality_on_Customer_Satisfaction_in_the_Hotel_Industry_A_Conceptual_Paper

Talukder, M., Shakhawat Hossain, M., & Kumar, S. (2022). Blue Ocean Strategies in Hotel Industry in Bangladesh: A Review of Present Literatures' Gap and Suggestions for Further Study. SSRN *Electronic Journal.* doi:10.2139/ssrn.4160709

Talukder, M. B. (2020b). The Future of Culinary Tourism: An Emerging Dimension for the Tourism Industry of Bangladesh. I-Manager's. *Journal of Management, 15*(1), 27. doi:10.26634/jmgt.15.1.17181

Talukder, M. B. (2021). An assessment of the roles of the social network in the development of the Tourism Industry in Bangladesh. *International Journal of Business, Law, and Education, 2*(3), 85–93. doi:10.56442/ijble.v2i3.21

Talukder, M. B., & Hossain, M. M. (2021). Prospects of Future Tourism in Bangladesh: An Evaluative Study. I-Manager's. *Journal of Management*, *15*(4), 1–8. doi:10.26634/jmgt.15.4.17495

Talukder, M. B., Kumar, S., Sood, K., & Grima, S. (2023). Information Technology, Food Service Quality and Restaurant Revisit Intention. *International Journal of Sustainable Development and Planning*, *18*(1), 295–303. doi:10.18280/ijsdp.180131

Tao, M., Nawaz, M. Z., Nawaz, S., Butt, A. H., & Ahmad, H. (2018). Users' acceptance of innovative mobile hotel booking trends: UK vs. PRC. *Information Technology & Tourism*, *20*(1–4), 9–36. doi:10.1007/s40558-018-0123-x

Tassikas, A. (2021). Data Processing and Legal Protection in Contracts in the Technologically Innovative Tourism Sector. *European Journal of Tourism. Hospitality and Recreation*, *11*(1), 77–90. doi:10.2478/ejthr-2021-0008

Tavakoli, R., & Mura, P. (2018). Netnography in Tourism – Beyond Web 2.0. *Annals of Tourism Research*, *73*, 190–192. doi:10.1016/j.annals.2018.06.002

Templier, M., & Paré, G. (2015). A Framework for Guiding and Evaluating Literature Reviews. *Communications of the Association for Information Systems*, *37*(August), 2–28. doi:10.17705/1CAIS.03706

Tham, A., Mair, J., & Croy, G. (2020). Social media influence on tourists' destination choice: Importance of context. *Tourism Recreation Research*, *45*(2), 161–175. doi:10.1080/02508281.2019.1700655

Thiermann, U. B., & Sheate, W. R. (2022). How Does Mindfulness Affect Pro-environmental Behaviors? A Qualitative Analysis of the Mechanisms of Change in a Sample of Active Practitioners. *Mindfulness*, *13*(12), 2997–3016. doi:10.1007/s12671-022-02004-4

Thimm, T., Bild, C., & Kalff, M. (2019). Climate change in low mountain ranges: Opportunities in sustainable Black Forest tourism. *European Journal of Tourism Research*, *23*, 63–70. doi:10.54055/ejtr.v23i.389

Thongpapanl, N., & Ashraf, A. R. (2011). Enhancing online performance through website content and personalization. *Journal of Computer Information Systems*, *52*(1), 3–13.

Thullah, A., & Jalloh, S. (2021). A Review of the Economic, Social, and Environmental Impacts of Tourism Development. *American Journal of Theoretical and Applied Business*, *7*(2), 39–46. doi:10.11648/j.ajtab.20210702.12

Tiago, F., Couto, J., Faria, S., & Borges-Tiago, T. (2018). Cruise tourism: Social media content and network structures. *Tourism Review*, *73*(4), 433–447. doi:10.1108/TR-10-2017-0155

Tian, H., Presa-Reyes, M., Tao, Y., Wang, T., Pouyanfar, S., Miguel, A., Luis, S., Shyu, M., Chen, S., & Iyengar, S. (2021). Data Analytics for Air Travel Data: A Survey and New Perspectives. *ACM Computing Surveys*, *54*(8), 1–35. doi:10.1145/3469028

Tiberius, V. (2019). Scenarios in the strategy process: A framework of affordances and constraints. *European Journal of Futures Research, 7*(1), 1–14. doi:10.1186/s40309-019-0160-5

Tiberius, V., Siglow, C., & Sendra-García, J. (2020). Scenarios in business and management: The current stock and research opportunities. *Journal of Business Research, 121*, 235–242. doi:10.1016/j.jbusres.2020.08.037 PMID:32895583

Tien, N. H. (2019). Customization and Standardization of the Business Strategy of Foreign Enterprises in Vietnam: The McDonald's case and the fast-food sector. *International Journal of Research in Marketing Management and Sales, 1*(2), 44–50. doi:10.33545/26633329.2019.v1.i2a.16

Tohmo, T. (2018). The economic impact of tourism in Central Finland: A regional input–output study. *Tourism Review, 73*(4), 521–547. doi:10.1108/TR-04-2017-0080

Toirxonovna, A., Obloqulovich, U., & Tuychiev, I. (2020). Institutional Framework for the Development of the Tourism Market. *Tourism Management, 8*. doi:10.21070/ijler.2020.V8.687

Tolkach, D., & Pratt, S. (2019). Globalisation and cultural change in Pacific Island countries: The role of tourism. *Tourism Geographies, 23*(3), 371–396. doi:10.1080/14616688.2019.1625071

Tran, J. L. (2018). 3D-Printed Foods. *Minnesota Journal of Law, Science & Technology, 17*(2), 856–880.

Tsai, F. M., & Bui, T.-D. (2021). Impact of word of mouth via social media on consumer intention to purchase cruise travel products. *Maritime Policy & Management, 48*(2), 167–183. doi:10.1080/03088839.2020.1735655

Tuorila, H., & Hartmann, C. (2020). Consumer responses to novel and unfamiliar foods. *Current Opinion in Food Science, 33*, 1–8. doi:10.1016/j.cofs.2019.09.004

Tussyadiah, I. P., & Park, S. (2018). Consumer evaluation of hotel service robots. In Information and Communication Technologies in Tourism 2018, 135-148.

Tussyadiah, I. P., Jung, T. H., & tom Dieck, M. C. (2018). Embodiment of wearable augmented reality technology in tourism experiences. *Journal of Travel Research, 57*(5), 597–611. doi:10.1177/0047287517709090

Tussyadiah, I., & Miller, G. (2019). Perceived impacts of artificial intelligence and responses to positive behavior change intervention. In *Information and communication technologies in tourism 2019* (pp. 359–370). Springer. https://www.researchgate.net/publication/329685744_Perceived_Impacts_of_Artificial_Intelligence_and_Responses_to_Positive_Behaviour_Change_Intervention doi:10.1007/978-3-030-05940-8_28

United Nations Conference on Trade and Development (UNCTAD) (2013, January). *Sustainable tourism: Contribution to economic growth and sustainable development.* UN. https://unctad.org/meetings/en/sessionaldocuments/ciem5d2_en.pdf

United Nations DESA. (2023). *The Sustainable Development Goals Report 2023: Special Edition - July 2023*. UN DESA. https://unstats.un.org/sdgs/report/2023/

United Nations Development Program. (2016). From the MDGs to Sustainable Development for All: Lessons from 15 Years of Practice. https://www.undp.org/content/dam/undp/library/SDGs/English/From%20the%20MDGs%20to%20SD4All.pdf

United Nations Development Program. (2022). Human Development Report 2021-2022: Uncertain Times, Unsettled Lives: Shaping Our Future in a Transforming World. https://hdr.undp.org/content/human-development-report-2021-22

United Nations Economic Commission for Europe, & United Nations Environment Program. (2022). *Europe's Environment: The Seventh Pan-European Environmental Assessment*. UN. https://wedocs.unep.org/20.500.11822/40733

United Nations Economic Commission for Europe. (2022). *Applying principles of circular economy to sustainable tourism*. UN. https://unece.org/sites/default/files/2022-05/CEP-SS_Sustainable_Tourism.IP_.03.e.pdf

United Nations Economist Network. (2023). *New Economics for Sustainable Development: Circular Economy*. UN. https://www.un.org/en/desa/unen/policy-briefs

United Nations Environment Program. (2013). *PROVIA Guidance on Assessing Vulnerability, Impacts and Adaptation to Climate Change. Consultation document*. UN. https://www.adaptation-undp.org/sites/default/files/downloads/provia-guidance-nov2013.pdf

United Nations World Tourism Organization. (2017). *UNWTO Annual Report 2016*. UNWTO, Madrid. http://media.unwto.org/publication/unwto-annual-report-2016

United Nations World Tourism Organization. (2018). Tourism and the Sustainable Development Goals. Journey to 2030. https://www.e-unwto.org/doi/pdf/10.18111/9789284419401

United Nations. (2007a). *Percentage of total population living in coastal areas*. UN. https://www.un.org/esa/sustdev/natlinfo/indicators/methodology_sheets/oceans_seas_coasts/pop_coastal_areas.pdf

United Nations. (2020b). *Report of the UN Economist Network for the UN 75th Anniversary: Shaping the Trends of Our Time*. UN. https://digitallibrary.un.org/record/3884187?ln=es

United Nations. (2020c). *Executive Summary Report of the UN Economist Network for the UN 75th Anniversary: Shaping the Trends of Our Time*. UN. https://www.un.org/development/desa/publications/wp-content/uploads/sites/10/2020/10/20-124-UNEN-75Report-ExecSumm-EN-REVISED.pdf

Ural, M. (2016). Risk management for sustainable tourism. European Journal of Tourism. *Hospitality and Recreation*, *7*(1), 63–71. doi:10.1515/ejthr-2016-0007

Uriely, N. (2005). The tourist experience: Conceptual developments. *Annals of Tourism Research*, *32*(1), 199–216. doi:10.1016/j.annals.2004.07.008

van Eck, N. J., & Waltman, L. (2014). Visualizing Bibliometric Networks. In Y. Ding, R. Rousseau, & D. Wolfram (Eds.), *Measuring Scholarly Impact: Methods and Practice* (pp. 285–320). Springer International Publishing., doi:10.1007/978-3-319-10377-8_13

Vancia, A., Băltescu, C., Brătucu, G., Tecău, A., Chițu, I., & Duguleană, L. (2023). Examining the Disruptive Potential of Generation Z Tourists on the Travel Industry in the Digital Age. *Sustainability (Basel)*, *15*(11), 8756. doi:10.3390/su15118756

Varkey, P. S., Walker, T. R., & Saunders, S. J. (2021). Identifying barriers to reducing single-use plastic use in a coastal metropolitan city in Canada. *Ocean and Coastal Management*, *210*, 105663. doi:10.1016/j.ocecoaman.2021.105663

Veiga, C., Santos, M. C., Águas, P., & Santos, J. A. C. (2017). Are millennials transforming global tourism? Challenges for destinations and companies. *Worldwide Hospitality and Tourism Themes*, *9*(6), 603–616. doi:10.1108/WHATT-09-2017-0047

Vogt, S. (2017). *3D Food printing: What options the new technology offers*. DLG.

Voon, S. L., An, J., Wong, G., Zhang, Y., & Chua, C. K. (2019). 3D food printing: A categorised review of inks and their development. *Virtual and Physical Prototyping*, *14*(3), 203–218. doi:10.1080/17452759.2019.1603508

Vu, H. Q., Li, G., Law, R., & Zhang, Y. (2019). Exploring tourist dining preferences based on restaurant reviews. *Journal of Travel Research*, *58*(1), 149–167. doi:10.1177/0047287517744672

Walker, T., Lee, T. J., & Li, X. (2021). Sustainable development for small island tourism: Developing slow tourism in the Caribbean. *Journal of Travel & Tourism Marketing*, *38*(1), 115. doi:10.1080/10548408.2020.1842289

Wang, D., Xiang, Z., & Fesenmaier, D. R. (2014). Adapting to the mobile world: A model of smartphone use. *Annals of Tourism Research*, *48*, 11–26. doi:10.1016/j.annals.2014.04.008

Wang, D., Xiang, Z., & Fesenmaier, D. R. (2016). Smartphone Use in Everyday Life and Travel. *Journal of Travel Research*, *55*(1), 52–63. doi:10.1177/0047287514535847

Wang, D., & Xie, C. (2017). The roles of IT in the hospitality industry: A review of the literature. *Journal of Hospitality and Tourism Technology*, *8*(1), 6–33.

Wang, Q. C., Xie, K. X., Liu, X., Shen, G. Q. P., Wei, H. H., & Liu, T. Y. (2021). Psychological drivers of hotel guests' energy-saving behaviors—Empirical research based on the extended theory of planned behaviour. *Buildings*, *11*(9), 401. doi:10.3390/buildings11090401

Wang, Y., & Feng, H. (2012). Customer relationship management capabilities: Measurement, antecedents and consequences. *Management Decision*, *50*(1), 115–129. doi:10.1108/00251741211194903

Wattal, S., Telang, R., & Mukhopadhyay, T. (2009). Information personalization in a two-dimensional product differentiation model. *Journal of Management Information Systems*, *26*(2), 69–95. doi:10.2753/MIS0742-1222260204

Webb, T., Cho, S. R., & Legg, M. (2022). Customer Lifetime Value: A Data Science Approach for Hospitality Applications. *International Journal of Gaming, Hospitality and Tourism, 2*(1).

Webster, C., & Ivanov, S. (2019). Robotics, artificial intelligence, and the evolving nature of work. In B. George & J. Paul (Eds.), *Business Transformation in Data Driven Societies*. Palgrave-MacMillan.

Webster, C., & Ivanov, S. (2020). Demographic change as a driver for tourism automation. *Journal of Tourism Futures*, *6*(3), 263–270. doi:10.1108/JTF-10-2019-0109

Webster, C., & Ivanov, S. (2020). *Robots in Travel, Tourism and Hospitality: Key Findings from a global study*. Zangador.

Wernick, D. A., & von Glinow, M. A. (2012). Reflections on the Evolving Terrorist Threat to Luxury Hotels: A Case Study on Marriott International. *Thunderbird International Business Review*, *54*(5), 729–746. doi:10.1002/tie.21496

Wirtz, J., & Lovelock, C. (2022). *Services Marketing*. World scientific.

Wise, N., & Heidari, H. (2019). Developing Smart Tourism Destinations with The Internet of Things. *Big Data and Innovation in Tourism, Travel, and Hospitality, 3*(IF: 3)

Wongsansukcharoen, J., Trimetsoontorn, J., & Fongsuwan, W. (2015). Social CRM, RMO and business strategies affecting banking performance effectiveness in B2B context. *Journal of Business and Industrial Marketing*, *30*(6), 742–760. doi:10.1108/JBIM-02-2013-0039

World Meteorological Organization. (2023). United in Science 2023. *Sustainable development edition: A multi-organization high-level compilation of the latest weather-, climate and water-related sciences and services for sustainable development*. WMO. https://library.wmo.int/records/item/68235-united-in-science-2023

World Travel & Tourism Council. (2022). *Travel & Tourism Economic Impact 2022*. WTTC. https://wttc.org/Portals/0/Documents/Reports/2022/EIR2022-Global%20Trends.pdf

World Travel and Tourism Council. (2022, November 14). *Travel & Tourism Economic Impact 2022*. WTTC. https://wttc.org/Portals/0/Documents/Reports/2022/EIR2022-Global%20Trends.pdf

Wu, D. C., Cao, Z., Wen, L., & Song, H. (2021). Scenario Forecasting for Global Tourism. *Journal of Hospitality & Tourism Research (Washington, D.C.)*, *45*(1), 28–51. doi:10.1177/1096348020919990

Wu, S.-I., & Lu, C.-L. (2012). The relationship between CRM, RM, and business performance: A study of the hotel industry in Taiwan. *International Journal of Hospitality Management*, *31*(1), 276–285. doi:10.1016/j.ijhm.2011.06.012

Xiang, Z., Du, Q., Ma, Y., & Fan, W. (2015). A comparative analysis of major online review platforms: Implications for social media analytics in hospitality and tourism. *Tourism Management*, *58*, 51–65. doi:10.1016/j.tourman.2016.10.001

Xiang, Z., & Gretzel, U. (2010). Role of social media in online travel information search. *Tourism Management*, *31*(2), 179–188. doi:10.1016/j.tourman.2009.02.016

Xiang, Z., Magnini, V. P., & Fesenmaier, D. R. (2015). Information technology and consumer behavior in travel and tourism: Insights from travel planning using the internet. *Journal of Retailing and Consumer Services*, *22*, 244–249. doi:10.1016/j.jretconser.2014.08.005

Xu, D. J. (2006). The influence of personalization in affecting consumer attitudes toward mobile advertising in China. *Journal of Computer Information Systems*, *47*(2), 9–19.

Xu, H., Lovett, J., Cheung, L. T. O., Duan, X., Pei, Q., & Liang, D. (2021). Adapting to social media: The influence of online reviews on tourist behaviour at a world heritage site in China. *Asia Pacific Journal of Tourism Research*, *26*(10), 1125–1138. doi:10.1080/10941665.2021.1952460

Xu, H., Luo, X. R., Carroll, J. M., & Rosson, M. B. (2011). The personalization privacy paradox: An exploratory study of decision making process for location-aware marketing. *Decision Support Systems*, *51*(1), 42–52. doi:10.1016/j.dss.2010.11.017

Xu, X., Chen, X., Jia, F., Brown, S., Gong, Y., & Xu, Y. (2018). Supply chain finance: A systematic literature review and bibliometric analysis. *International Journal of Production Economics*, *204*, 160–173. doi:10.1016/j.ijpe.2018.08.003

Yallop, A., & Seraphin, H. (2020). Big data and analytics in tourism and hospitality: Opportunities and risks. *Journal of Tourism Futures*, *6*(3), 257–262. doi:10.1108/JTF-10-2019-0108

Yang, E. C. L., Yang, M. J. H., & Khoo-Lattimore, C. (2019). The meanings of solo travel for Asian women. *Tourism Review*, *74*(5), 1047-1047–1057. doi:10.1108/TR-10-2018-0150

Yang, E. C. L. (2021). What motivates and hinders people from traveling alone? A study of solo and non-solo travelers. *Current Issues in Tourism*, *24*(17), 2458–2471. doi:10.1080/13683500.2020.1839025

Yasmin, A., Tasneem, S., & Fatema, K. (2015). Effectiveness of digital marketing in the challenging age: An empirical study. *International Journal of Management Science and Business Administration*, *1*(5), 69–80. doi:10.18775/ijmsba.1849-5664-5419.2014.15.1006

Yildirim, H., & Yildirim, Y. (2022). Digital Gastronomy and the Tables of Future. *Van Yüzüncü Yıl Üniversitesi İktisadi ve İdari Bilimler Fakültesi Dergisi*, *8*(15), 1–14.

Yuan, Y., Chan, C-S., Eichelberger, S., Ma, H., Pikkemaat, B. (2022) The effect of social media on travel planning process by Chinese tourists: the way forward to tourism futures. *Journal of Tourism Futures*. doi:10.1108/JTF-04-2021-0094

Zanker, M., Rook, L., & Jannach, D. (2019). Measuring the impact of online personalisation: Past, present and future. *International Journal of Human-Computer Studies*, *131*, 160–168. doi:10.1016/j.ijhcs.2019.06.006

Zarezadeh, Z. Z., Rastegar, H. R., & Gretzel, U. (2018). Reviewing the Past to Inform the Future: A Literature Review of SMin Tourism. *Czech Journal of Tourism*, *7*(2), 115–131. doi:10.1515/cjot-2018-0006

Zeng, B., & Gerritsen, R. (2014). What Do We Know about Social Media in Tourism? A Review. *Tourism Management Perspectives*, *10*, 27–36. doi:10.1016/j.tmp.2014.01.001

Zhang, K., Hou, Y., & Li, G. (2020). Threat of infectious disease during an outbreak: Influence on tourists' emotional responses to disadvantaged price inequality. *Annals of Tourism Research*, *84*, 102993. doi:10.1016/j.annals.2020.102993 PMID:32834227

Zhang, T. (Catherine), Agarwal, R., & Lucas Jr, H. C. (2011). The value of IT-enabled retailer learning: Personalized product recommendations and customer store loyalty in electronic markets. *Management Information Systems Quarterly*, 859–881.

Zhang, X., Edwards, J., & Harding, J. (2007). Personalised online sales using web usage data mining. *Computers in Industry*, *58*(8–9), 772–782. doi:10.1016/j.compind.2007.02.004

Zheng, T., Farrish, J., & Kitterlin, M. (2016). Performance Trends of Hotels and Casino Hotels Through the Recession: An ARIMA With Intervention Analysis of Stock Indices. *Journal of Hospitality Marketing & Management*, *25*(1), 49–68. doi:10.1080/19368623.2015.970725

Zhuang, X., Yao, Y., & Li, J. J. (2019). Sociocultural impacts of tourism on residents of world cultural heritage sites in China. *Sustainability (Basel)*, *11*(3), 840. doi:10.3390/su11030840

Zhu, S., Ribberink, M., Wit, M., Schutyser, M., & Stieger, M. (2020). Modifying sensory perception of chocolate coated rice waffles through bite-to-bite contrast: An application case study using 3D inkjet printing. *Food & Function*, *11*(12), 10580–10587. doi:10.1039/D0FO01787F PMID:33188381

Zoran, A. (2019). Cooking With Computers: The Vision of Digital Gastronomy [Point of View]. *Proceedings of the IEEE*, *107*(8), 1467–1473. doi:10.1109/JPROC.2019.2925262

Zupic, I., & Čater, T. (2015). Bibliometric Methods in Management and Organization. *Organizational Research Methods*, *18*(3), 429–472. doi:10.1177/1094428114562629

Zvirbule, A., Auzina, A., & Griberta-Zalite, G. (2023). Gastronomic tourism and smart solutions used for its development: The case of a region of Latvia. *Worldwide Hospitality and Tourism Themes*, *15*(5), 570–580. doi:10.1108/WHATT-06-2023-0076

About the Contributors

Célia M. Q. Ramos graduated in Computer Engineering from the University of Coimbra, obtained her Master in Electrical and Computers Engineering from the Higher Technical Institute, Lisbon University, and the PhD in Econometrics in the University of the Algarve (UALG), Faculty of Economics, Portugal. She is Adjunct Professor at School for Management, Hospitality and Tourism, also in the UALG, where she lectures computer science. Areas of research and special interest include conception and development of information systems, tourism information systems, big data, etourism, econometric modeling and panel-data models. Célia Ramos has published in the fields of information systems and tourism, namely, she has authored a book, six book chapters, conference papers and journal articles. At the level of applied research, she has participated in several funded projects.

Teresa Costa holds a PhD in Management and developed her Post PhD in Entrepreneurship and Social Capital in Tourism at the University of São Paulo. She is a coordinator professor in the Department of Economics and Management at the Business School at the Polytechnic Institute of Setúbal. She is a researcher at CiTUR - Center for Applied Research in Tourism, member of the scientific board of CITUR-Estoril, editor-in-chief of EJTHR (European Journal of Tourism, Hospitality and Recreation) during 2018-2021. She is an invited professor at several national and international universities where she collaborates in several masters and doctoral

Filipe Segurado Severino holds a PhD in Tourism since 2022, having completed his thesis in the field of events. He earned his master's degree in Hotel Management in 2017, focused on event tourism, and his bachelor's degree in Leisure Management and Tourism Entertainment in 2011. He is a Post-Doctoral Scientific Research Fellow in the SHIFT Project (Sustainability-oriented, Highly interactive, and Innovation-based Framework for Tourism Marketing) at the Estoril Higher Institute for Tourism and Hotel Studies (ESHTE). In addition to his primary occupation, he is an Invited Adjunct Professor of tourism and leisure area, at ESHTE.

Maria de Lurdes Calisto holds a PhD in Management, awarded in 2014 by the University of Évora. Currently she holds a position as assistant professor at Estoril Higher Institute for Tourism and Hotel Studies. She is a researcher (integrated) at CiTUR - Center for Applied Research in Tourism (centre accredited by FCT, the Portuguese National Funding Agency for Science, Research and Technology) and a researcher (collaborator) at CEFAGE - Center for Studies and Advanced Training in Management and Economics of the University of Évora (centre accredited by FCT). She has experience as a principal investigator, co-PI, and member of research teams in several competitive research projects. She supervises doctoral thesis and several master's dissertations. She develops research in the area of Business and Management. Her research interests are business strategy, strategic marketing, innovation in services, entrepreneurship, intrapreneurial behaviour and corporate entrepreneurship, particularly in the context of service companies. She has several publications with global book editors and indexed journals and is frequently invited as a reviewer for Q1 journals and as an invited lecturer with Portuguese and foreign universities.

***

Maha K. Al Balushi is the Head of the Marketing department in the college of Economics and Political Science at Sultan Qaboos University (SQU). She is also the Director of the Master of Business Administration Program in the collage. Dr Maha is the faculty fellow at the Centre of Excellence in Teaching and Learning (CETL) in SQU. She teaches both undergraduate and graduate courses. She has published papers in reputed journals. Her research interests include consumer behavior, branding, tourism marketing, and fashions studies. Dr. Maha has successfully supervised and examined Master and PhD theses.

Anna Alvado is a PhD Candidate and holds an Official Master's Degree in Information and Knowledge Society (Open University of Catalonia). Postgraduate in Corporate Communication and Service Quality from Blanquerna Faculty of Communication Sciences (Ramon Llull University). Degree in Communication Sciences from Blanquerna Faculty of Communication Sciences (Ramon Llull University). Head of Studies and Head of the Department of Marketing and Communication at Formatic Barcelona University School (University of Girona).

Rashed Isam Ashqar has a Ph.D. in Finance from the University of Porto in Portugal. He completed his master's degree in Finance in 2018 at the University of Minho in Portugal and his bachelor's degree in Accounting in 2016 from An-Najah National University in Palestine. He is an Assistant Professor in Finance at the Al Zaytona University of Science & Technology (ZUST). Also, he is a Collaborator

Researcher at the Centre for Tourism, Sustainability, and Well-being (CinTurs) and he is a Researcher at the Center for Economics and Finance at the University of Porto. Moreover, he was a financial analyst for some companies. He was an Invited Professor at the Faculty of Economics at the University of Algarve. He was a Post Doctoral Researcher at the School for Management, Hospitality, and Tourism at the University of Algarve. His main research interests are Behavioral Finance, Household Finance, Tourism, and Hospitality.

Cláudia Marcos Azevedo is a Lecturer at Estoril Higher Institute for Tourism and Hotel Studies. Specialist in Food Sciences, has a degree in Veterinary Medicine, a master's degree in Human Molecular Biology and a postgraduate course in Metabolic Diseases and Eating Behavior. She's interested in food production as a response to health, social reintegration and sustainability.

C.V. Suresh Babu is a pioneer in content development. A true entrepreneur, he founded Anniyappa Publications, a company that is highly active in publishing books related to Computer Science and Management. Dr. C.V. Suresh Babu has also ventured into SB Institute, a center for knowledge transfer. He holds a Ph.D. in Engineering Education from the National Institute of Technical Teachers Training & Research in Chennai, along with seven master's degrees in various disciplines such as Engineering, Computer Applications, Management, Commerce, Economics, Psychology, Law, and Education. Additionally, he has UGC-NET/SET qualifications in the fields of Computer Science, Management, Commerce, and Education. Currently, Dr. C.V. Suresh Babu is a Professor in the Department of Information Technology at the School of Computing Science, Hindustan Institute of Technology and Science (Hindustan University) in Padur, Chennai, Tamil Nadu, India. For more information, you can visit his personal blog at .

Miguel Belo has a PhD in Tourism, Miguel Belo is an invited associate professor at the Estoril Superior School of Hospitality and Tourism (ESHTE). He is an integrated member of CiTUR - Center for Research, Development and Innovation in Tourism and co-coordinates the Degree in Tourism Management at ESHTE. Develops research with an emphasis on Management and Business Sciences. His research interests are dark tourism, strategic management of tourist destinations and strategic management of tourism products. Participated in several competitive and national research projects. He has published several articles and book chapters and has several oral communications at international scientific congresses.

Josep Boyra is a Doctor in Geography with Mention European Doctor. Doctoral Thesis: Tourism and Environment in the Attica region. A spatial analysis at different scales by the University of Barcelona in 2005 and Master in Cartographic Production and Geographic Information Systems by the University of Barcelona in 2008. Deputy Director and Head of Research at the Formatic University School Barcelona center attached to the University of Girona. Head of the Research Group of the Barcelona Formatic University School called Research Group for the Analysis and Planning of Tourism (GREPAT) and officially recognized as a research group attached to the University of Girona since February 2013. Associate Professor of the Ramon Llull University and the University of Barcelona. Doctor accredited by ANECA.

Iva Rani Das is a dynamic individual, currently pursuing her MPhil in the Marketing Department of Dhaka University. Alongside her academic pursuits, she holds key positions as an Assistant Director at the Daffodil Institute of InformationTechnology and serves as Guest Faculty in the Business Faculty at the Asian Institute of Business and Technology. Her scholarly achievements extend beyond the classroom, with publications in esteemed national and international journals. Iva's dedication to education and research makes her a driving force in the fields of business and marketing.

João Ferreira do Rosário is a Ph.D. in Management and is an Adjunct Professor of Marketing at the Escola Superior de Comunicação Social (ESCS), Instituto Politécnico de Lisboa, Portugal. Coordinator of the Advertising and Marketing Department, Coordinator of a Research Line at ESCS "Communication, Strategies and Creativity". Member of the Technical-Scientific Council and Pedagogical Council of ESCS. Professor in the degree and master's degree in Advertising and Marketing and in the master's degree in Strategic Management of Public Relations. Researcher-Collaborator at CiTUR - Center for Applied Research in Tourism. With published scientific articles, communications, and book chapters in the areas of research in Marketing, Tourism and Information and Communication Technologies. Editor and reviewer of scientific journals and reviewer of scientific conferences and books. Portuguese coordinator of trans-European academic projects Businet HedCom, Businet International Trade Mission, REVE-IP and IP ISTAR-DOT-Erasmus. Coordinator of Research Projects at IPL-IDICA and member of the research team of the "SHIFT" project (FCT R&D Projects in All Scientific Domains).

Jordi Garcia is a PhD Candidate and holds an Official Degree in Political Science and Administration from the University of Barcelona. Graduated in Law from the Antonio de Nebrija University. Diploma of Advanced Studies (DEA) of the Doctorate in Political Science and Management of University Institutions by the University Abat Oliva. Director of the Escola Universitària Formatic Barcelona attached to the University of Girona. Member of the Research Group of the Barcelona

Formatic University School called Research Group for the Analysis and Planning of Tourism (GREPAT).

Joaquin Garcia-Lavernia is a professional consultant, researcher and university teacher in the field of Communication (advertising, journalism, PR, propaganda and image consultancy for natural and legal persons) is one of the members of the European Council of Doctorates and Doctores Honoris Causa.

Rowan Kennedy is an assistant professor at Marketing Department, College of Economics and Political Science, Sultan Qaboos University, Oman. She got her PhD, Monash University, Australia, 2006. She has published a number of papers in reputed journals. Her areas of interest include direct selling, leadership, recognition, turnover, multi-tasking/multi-communicating in the classroom.

Shad Ahmad Khan is serving as Assistant Professor in College of Business, University of Buraimi in Sultanate of Oman. He is an active researcher who has a professional strength in the area of Business Management and Marketing. He has a vast experience of organizing international events like conferences and seminars. His area of interest is Data Sciences, green practices, entrepreneurship, administration sciences and marketing.

Sanjeev Kumar is an accomplished expert in Food and Beverage. He currently holds the positions of Professor at the Lovely Professional University, Punjab, India. With over a decade of experience in the field, food Service Industry, his research focuses on Alcoholic beverages, Event management and Sustainable Management Practices, Metaverse and Artificial Intelligence. He has published more than 35 research papers, articles and chapters in Scopus Indexed, UGC Approved and peer reviewed Journals and books. Dr. Sanjeev Kumar participated and acted as resource person in various National and International conferences, seminars, research workshops and industry talks and his work has been widely cited.

Ana Teresa Machado has a Ph.D. in Management since 2011 from the Higher Institute of Economics and Management of the University of Lisbon. She has a Master of Science in Electronic Information Management since 1996 from the Information School- at the University of Sheffield, having completed a degree in Economics in 1983 at the Faculty of Economic and Business Sciences of the Catholic University of Portugal, where in 1994 she successfully completed his postgraduate MBA with a specialization in Marketing. She began her teaching career in 1993 and since 2021 has been Coordinating Professor at the Higher School of Social Communication of the Polytechnic Institute of Lisbon, currently coordinating the master's degree in Advertising and Marketing, a position she has held since 2018. In scientific-pedagogical terms, its fields of action are Digital Marketing, Social Media Marketing, and Marketing Analytics. As a researcher, she has been a collaborating member at the Center for Applied Research in Tourism (Citur-Estoril), since 2020. She is currently participating in the research project, funded by the FCT (PTDC/EGE-OGE/2146/2021)-SHIFT - Sustainability-oriented, Highly interactive, and In- novation-based Framework for Tourism marketing.

Ana Teresa Machado has a Ph.D. in Management since 2011 from the Higher Institute of Economics and Management of the University of Lisbon. She has a Master of Science in Electronic Information Management since 1996 from the Information School- at the University of Sheffield, having completed a degree in Economics in 1983 at the Faculty of Economic and Business Sciences of the Catholic University of Portugal, where in 1994 she successfully completed his postgraduate MBA with a specialization in Marketing. She began her teaching career in 1993 and since 2021 has been Coordinating Professor at the Higher School of Social Communication of the Polytechnic Institute of Lisbon, currently coordinating the master's degree in Advertising and Marketing, a position she has held since 2018. In scientific-pedagogical terms, its fields of action are Digital Marketing, Social Media Marketing, and Marketing Analytics. As a researcher, she has been a collaborating member at the Center for Applied Research in Tourism (Citur-Estoril), since 2020. She is currently participating in the research project, funded by the FCT (PTDC/EGE-OGE/2146/2021)-SHIFT - Sustainability-oriented, Highly interactive, and In- novation-based Framework for Tourism marketing.

Maria Mendes Guerra is a professor at Estoril Higher Institute for Tourism and Hotel Studies (ESHTE) since 2008; Member of CITUR (Center for Research, Development and Innovation in Tourism), Polo Estoril; Participation in funded research projects and development of research activities in Innovation, Quality, and Food Safety, including gastronomy. Author/co-author of articles and book chapters published in journals and books with international and national circulation and several Proceeding books of conferences in the areas of specialization: Food science and technology (includes food safety and innovation, antimicrobial resistance, and connection of food sciences with food tourism).

Zélia Raposo Santos holds a PhD in Information Management from Information Management School (Nova IMS), Universidade Nova de Lisboa (UNL), specialising in Market Research with an emphasis on Marketing. She has a Master in Statistics and Information Management from Instituto Superior de Estatística e Gestão de Informação (UNL), is an undergraduate in Applied Mathematics by Universidade

Lusíada de Lisboa and has a DEA in Social Comunicación from Universidad Complutense de Madrid. She is an Adjunct Professor at the School of Communication and Media Studies (ESCS), Instituto Politécnico de Lisboa (IPL), Sub-coordinator of the master course in Advertising and Marketing at ESCS, collaborates with the ESCS Bureau of Quality Support, and is an Invited Associate Professor at Nova IMS, UNL. Her research is mainly focused on social media marketing and consumer behaviour. She has published several articles in top-rank journals, has participated in research projects in Marketing, Tourism and Journalism, and collaborates as a reviewer in several scientific journals.

Jucinara Schena is a professional at the nexus of project management and the theme parks and attractions industry, bringing a unique blend of journalism and a Ph.D. in Communication from Universitat Pompeu Fabra to the role as Head of Project Management and Producer.

Nidhi Sharma is currently working as a research scholar at Chandigarh University, Mohali, India. Her research interest includes social media, destination marketing, travel and ecotourism. She has published several papers and book chapters in reputed journals and books.

Mohammad Soliman is currently the Head of the Research and Consultation Department at the University of Technology and Applied Sciences, Salalah, Oman. He is also a Full Professor at the Faculty of Tourism & Hotels, Fayoum University, Egypt. He has published multiple papers in reputed journals indexed in WoS and Scopus (e.g., Current Issues in Tourism, Journal of Destination Management & Marketing, Tourism Review, Tourism Management Perspectives, Journal of Service Theory & Practice, International Journal of Human-Computer Interaction, Mindfulness, Current Psychology; Geoheritage, Journal of Tourism Futures, Tourism & Hospitality Research, Journal of Medical Systems, Journal of Consumer Behaviour, etc.). Additionally, he sits on the editorial board of different academic journals (e.g., Journal of Hospitality and Tourism Education; Tourism & Management Studies, Journal of Responsible Tourism Management, Journal of Global Hospitality and Tourism, Journal of Tourism & Hospitality; and others), and serves as a reviewer for several top-tier journals. He has successfully supervised and examined several Master and PhD theses. His research interests include tourism management and marketing, tourism behavior, HR in tourism, PLS-SEM, bibliometrics and systematic reviews.

Joan Sorribes is a PhD in Economics in the discipline of Applied Economics by the University of Girona. Member of the INSETUR Research group. Member of the GREPAT research group at the Formatic Barcelona University School. Member of the competitive consolidated research group SGR „TRIP" at University of Girona. Head of Quality and Head of the Department of Economic and Legal Sciences at the Formatic Barcelona University School. Associate Professor at Applied Economics Department of the Faculty of Economic and Business Sciences at the University of Girona. Associate Professor at the School of Social and Business Sciences (Pompeu Fabra University). Scientific interests: Economic crisis, Corporate Social Responsibility, Human Resource Management, Sustainable Tourism and E-learning.

Mohammad Badruddoza Talukder is an Associate Professor, College of Tourism and Hospitality Management, International University of Business Agriculture and Technology, Dhaka, Bangladesh. He has been teaching various courses in the Department of Tourism and Hospitality at various universities in Bangladesh since 2009. His research areas include tourism management, hotel management, hospitality management, food & beverage management, and accommodation management, where he has published research papers in well-known journals in Bangladesh and abroad. Mr. Talukder is one of the executive members of the Tourism Educators Association of Bangladesh. He has led training and counseling for a wide range of hospitality organizations in Bangladesh. As an administrator, Mr. Talukder served as a debate advisor at the University, coordinator for courses and exams in the Department of Tourism and Hotel Management. He has experience as a manager in various business class hotels in Bangladesh. He is one of the certified trainers for the food and beverage service department of the SIEP project from Bangladesh. He just become an honorary facilator at Bangladesh Tourism Board's Bangabandhu international tourism and hospitality training institute.

Index